I0126411

Colonial Families
of the
Eastern Shore of Maryland

Volume 18

Vernon L. Skinner, Jr.
and
F. Edward Wright

HERITAGE BOOKS
2019

HERITAGE BOOKS

AN IMPRINT OF HERITAGE BOOKS, INC.

Books, CDs, and more—Worldwide

For our listing of thousands of titles see our website
at
www.HeritageBooks.com

Published 2019 by
HERITAGE BOOKS, INC.
Publishing Division
5810 Ruatan Street
Berwyn Heights, Md. 20740

Copyright © 2004 Colonial Roots

All rights reserved. No part of this book may be reproduced or
transmitted in any form or by any means, electronic or mechanical,
including photocopying, recording or by any information storage
and retrieval system without written permission from the author,
except for the inclusion of brief quotations in a review.

International Standard Book Number
Paperbound: 978-1-68034-748-7

CONTENTS

iv

INTRODUCTION

THE COUNTIES

Kent County is first mentioned in the records in 1642. At that time the Governor and Council appointed Commissioners for the Isle and County of Kent.[1] On 16 May 1631 King Charles I granted a license to William Clayborne to trade along the shores of the Chesapeake, and the same year Clayborne established a trading post on Kent Island. The Marylanders who came in 1634 claimed authority over Kent Island, and after many legal disputes with Clayborne, Lord Baltimore appealed to the Committee of Trade and Plantations, and in 1638 they issued a report in favor of Lord Baltimore.[2] As early as 1638 Kent Isle had sent two delegates to the General Assembly: Nicholas Brown and Christopher Thomas.[3] Baltimore County was carved out of Kent County in 1659.[4]

Cecil County, extending from the mouth of the Susquehanna and down the eastern side of the Bay to Swan Point and from there to Hell Point, and so up Chester River, to its head, was established on 6 June 1674. The area included not only a portion of Baltimore County but nearly all of what is now Kent County. In fact it contained Yarmouth town, where at times the Kent County Court had been held. This apparent error by the Governor was rectified by a supplemental proclamation on 19 June 1674, "... upon further consideration hereof it is thought most necessary that so much of the Easterne side as was formerly added to Kent County doe still remaine and belong to the said County as afore notwithstanding ..." The final description of the boundary between Cecil and Kent counties was settled with the act passed by the General Assembly of 1706 which stated, "From and after the 1st of May 1707, Kent county shall begin at the south point of Eastern neck, and from thence up Chesapeake bay to Sassafras river, and up said river to the south end of the long Horse bridge lying over the head of the said river, and from thence with a line drawn east by south, to the exterior bounds of this province." The eastern boundary and northern boundary were contested by the Calverts and Penns until resolved by Mason and Dixon.[5]

Talbot County was erected around 1661. The boundaries at that time were vague. It would appear that the northwestern boundary passed along the eastern shore of the Front Wye River northward to the head of Harris Mill Branch and thence down Tanyard Branch and possibly up Langford's Bay toward Wharton Creek on the Bay shore. To the west of this line was Kent County; on the east was Talbot County. What became the first and second districts of Kent County may possibly have been an unsettled portion of Talbot in 1667, but it seems more probable that Talbot County did not exercise jurisdiction on the north side of the Chester River. On the 4th of June, 1671, it was ordered that for the future the northeast side of Chester, as far as the bounds of Talbot County were formerly on that side, shall now be added to Kent County.

An Act of 19 April 1706 stated that after 1 May 1706, Kent County would be bounded by a line drawn from the south point of Eastern Neck, up the Bay to Sassafras river, up the said river to the south end of Long Horse Bridge, thence by a line drawn by east and by south to the exterior bounds of the Province and with the exterior bounds [south?] to the line of Queen Anne's County, and with said County down Chester River to Eastern Neck.[6] This same Act provided for the erection of Queen Anne's County.[7]

Somerset County, Maryland, was created in 1666 with the Atlantic Ocean and Chesapeake Bay as its eastern and western boundaries and its northern boundary which today lies well inside Sussex County ... the Nanticoke River. Dispute over the location of Delaware's southern boundary began in 1680 when William Penn received his charter. It continued until 1732 when both parties signed an agreement that the line would lie at 39 degrees, 43 minutes, 19 seconds and be surveyed to continue to the midpoint of the peninsula, then turn north to a point 15 miles south of Philadelphia. Unfortunately for Lord Baltimore, his decision to agree to this compromise was based on an inaccurate map which showed 39 degrees, 43 minutes, 19 seconds as lying at Cape Henlopen. In fact, Cape Henlopen lay 25 miles further north, and Lord Baltimore had inadvertently signed away present day Little Creek Hundred and parts of Broad Creek, Dagsborough and Baltimore Hundreds that had never been claimed by Penn. Realizing his mistake too late, Lord Baltimore fought the agreement in the courts for the next twenty years. When Worcester County was formed in 1742 from the eastern and southern sections of Somerset, he set the northern boundary of Worcester at Broad Creek Bridge, at the site of present-day Laurel, Delaware. From 1763 through 1768 Charles Mason and Jeremiah Dixon conducted the final survey of the so-called Mason-Dixon Line and finally, in January 1769, the new line was officially accepted.

The first evidence of the formation of Dorchester County was the writ issued on 16 Feb 1669, ordering elections to be held in the counties. The bounds of the county on the north and west extended up and along the Choptank River to the territory of New Sweden (later Pennsylvania, and still later Delaware). The eastern line was to run with the Delaware Bay, and River back to the fortieth degree, thus containing a large portion of Delaware called Sussex County. With the new line surveyed by Mason and Dixon, Dorchester County lost Northwest Fork Hundred to Sussex County. Thus families such as the Cannons were originally situated in Dorchester County and when the boundary was finally settled, found their members almost entirely in Sussex County Delaware.

Caroline County was formed in 1773 from portions of Dorchester east of the Choptank and Queen Anne's County west of the Choptank.

THE RECORDS

Many sources were used in the creation of this series. They are described below.

Land Records were combed looking for statements that provided clues to marriages, descents of property, and places of origin. Sometimes rather complicated family relationships are unraveled on the pages of land records. Sales of land of significant acreage for a small amount of money (usually 5 shillings) suggest that the land was a gift.

There is a large array of land records to consider. Primary genealogical interest in the land records centers on the land patents, certificates of survey, deeds, mortgages, leases, rent rolls, and debt books. In the early years of the settlement of the province of Maryland, land was granted to persons who transported themselves and others into the colony, including members of their own family, either from Europe or from other colonies such as Virginia. This headright system was terminated in 1780 and thereafter land patents were purchased.

Aided by the practice of naming each tract one is able to trace ownership even when the tract was expanded, divided or combined with other parcels - and sometimes even renamed. One of the problems which can be solved by following land ownership is the identification and separation of two or more individuals of the same name. For a description of the records and the process of using them for genealogical purposes, see Donna Valley Russell's article, "By Their Deeds Ye Shall Know Them," *Maryland Genealogical Society Bulletin*, Vol. 31, No. 1:38.

We tend to overlook the fact that land not mentioned in a will descended to the oldest son during the colonial period in Maryland. In Delaware ownership of land was considered to be made up of equal shares with the oldest son destined to receive 2 shares when there was no will or the will failed to specify disposition of the land. At some later time a reference may be found in the deed books to the manner by which the land had been disposed through inheritance.

We have limited our use of land records, citing only a few transactions needed to show relationships, or other genealogical evidence. The researcher interested in a thorough picture of the buying and selling of an ancestor must refer to the complete coverage given in published abstracts or examine the originals (a good idea in any case).

Criminal Proceedings were found to be full of information. Even so-called respectable families sometimes found themselves facing charges of assault, bastardy, trespass, theft, and other violations of the law.

Probate Records, including wills, inventories, administration accounts, and balances of final distributions of estates, are one of the staple resources of genealogical research. The death of an individual prompted the probate of a will if one existed. The estate might be inventoried if it were determined that it was of significant value. A very high percentage of wills were written by males leaving the widow as the executrix (or the administratrix if he died intestate). In the subsequent inventory or administration account, the fact that she has remarried is often revealed along with the name of her new husband. The names of children not identified in the will may also appear in the administration accounts and balance books.

Depositions, sworn testimony by witnesses, called deponents, are found in a variety of places. Land records, land commissions, ejectment papers are just a few of the sources for these items, which usually give the name of the deponent and his or her age, and often contain references to other family members. Ejectment Papers referred to cases involving landlords and tenants and owner-ship of land. The documents in these cases often contain much helpful family history.

Bonds and Indentures were other types of records, frequently over-looked, that were checked. A bond is a promise, backed by a financial consider-ation to perform a certain action. Trustees would post a bond that they would pay the minor children of a decedent their fair share of their father's estate when the child reached majority. Grantors would post a bond that they would convey certain property. Executors and administrators posted bond they would well and truly perform their duties in settling an estate.

Indentures are written agreements and may apply to conveyances of land, but may also be a form of contract between two persons involving matters other than real estate.

With the exception of Somerset County, few tax records have survived for the colonial period. Somerset County had an extraordinary run of tax lists from 1722 through 1759. Lists have survived for 30 of the 38 years, although some are in poor condition. Nowhere else in Maryland have such a string of yearly lists survived during the Colonial period. All males and black females, aged 16 or older were taxable, except for certain persons such as the infirm. Those disabled by illness or injury or old age could be exempt at the discretion of the county justices. The first name appearing in an entry was the head of household, for whom the tax would be levied. Much can be derived from these lists. Here are some of the clues that may be revealed:

1. The simultaneous listing of persons living in the locale allows the researcher to discern persons with the same given name.

2. The appearance of the name of a white female, first in the household, followed by names of persons who were in earlier lists associated with a male, suggest that the male had died and his widow now is responsible for the taxables.

3. The appearance of the names of white males in the household of a person with a difference surname offers the possibility that the head of household had married the widowed mother and now had her sons as his taxables.

4. The initial appearance of a male suggests that he turned age 16 sometime during the previous twelve months.

5. Persons listed nearby are likely to be relatives or in-laws.

Chattel Records are documents concerning the transfer of movable property, such as cattle, slaves, furniture or farming implements from one person to another. They contained many examples of parents conveying such movable property to their children or grandchildren.

THE EARLY SETTLERS

The early settlement of the Eastern Shore was chiefly by British subjects. Land records and depositions often provided a clue to the origins of the settlers. However a variety of other ethnic groups were found among the early settlers. A few examples - The Ricaud family in Kent County had ties to England, but may have been of French descent; John Hendrickson and Cornelius Comegys were from the Netherlands; Hans Hanson was of Swedish descent, while John Peter Zenger and Francis Ludolph Bodien were from Germany.

Among the Dutch settlers of the area that became Cecil County was Augustine Herman, one of the most influential men of Maryland, a native of Utrecht, in New Amsterdam. In consideration of the map of the province of Maryland he prepared for the Calverts, he was granted *Bohemia Manor* in 1662, a tract of about 4,000 acres; and *Little Bohemia* or *Bohemia Middle Neck*. Other Hollander settlers of Cecil County included Isaac and Matthias Van Bibber, sons of Jacob Isaacs Van Bibber.

A significant number of Swedes migrated from New Sweden on the Delaware River, into Cecil County. Note, for example, the family of John Carr whose wife Petronella was a daughter of Olof Thorsson; Jonas Auren who married Keady Justice (Gustafsson); the Numbers (Numberson) family; Evertson family; Sefferson (Severson) family; and many others.

For the most part the founders and early settlers of Old Somerset County were people from the Eastern Shore of Virginia, the present counties of

Accomack and Northampton. They were encouraged by Lord Baltimore who desired to settle these lands, in hopes of legitimizing the land as a part of the Maryland charter. Many of the immigrants from Virginia were Quakers, desiring to get away from the ill treatment by the Virginia government. Many other Virginians came north to obtain available land at reasonable quit rents. By May 1662, the settlements at Manokin and Annemessex numbered fifty tithable persons. In August 1662, the county of Somerset was founded.

FAMILY RELATIONSHIPS
Familial terms such as cousin, son-in-law, etc. often had other meanings in the colonial period. Cousin was used to indicate a niece, nephew or cousin as defined today. Son-in-law or daughter-in-law usually meant a step-child but not always. The phrase, "Next of kin," appearing in the inventory of an estate had a very broad meaning, which included in-laws. These were persons who had some relationship to the family who were available to sign off on the inventory. Sometimes it is impossible to determine the relationship.

A surprising number of children were given their mother's maiden name as their first name. This can be especially helpful when the mother's maiden name is otherwise unknown.

THE SERIES
This is the eighteenth in a series of volumes of family histories pertaining to the colonial families of the Eastern Shore of Maryland. Members of nearly all the families described in this volume lived in Old Somerset, now the counties of Somerset, Wicomico and Worcester.

Any additional material concerning the families in this volume will be published in subsequent volumes. Comments and suggestions are welcome.

F. Edward Wright
Lewes, Delaware
2004

End Notes

1.   *Maryland Manual: A Guide to Maryland State Government, 1994-1995.* Ed.by Diane P. Frese. Annapolis: Maryland State Archives. 1994.
2.   Edward B. Mathews, "The Counties of Maryland: Their Origin, Boundaries, and Election Districts," in *Maryland Geological Survey: Volume VI* (Baltimore: The Johns Hopkins Press, 1906), p. 511.
3.   *Biographical Directory of the Maryland Legislature.* Ed. by Edward C.

Papenfuse, et al. (New York: The Johns Hopkins University Press, 2 Vols., 1975-1985), I, 16.

4.   Mathews, *op. cit.*, p. 512.
5.   Mathews, *op. cit.*, p. 512.
6.   Mathews, *op. cit.*, p. 514, cites Acts of Maryland 1706: Ch. 3.
7.   Mathews, *op. cit.*, p. 534.

SOURCES AND ABBREVIATIONS

Source of entry is followed by volume and page number. Other sources are indicated with the entry itself.

1693 Swedes: *The 1693 Census of the Swedes on the Delaware.* By Peter Stebbins Craig, Winter Park, FL: SAG Publications, 1993.

AACR: *Anne Arundel County Church Records of the 17th and 18th Centuries.* By F. Edward Wright. Westminster: Family Line Publications, 1989.

AALR: Anne Arundel County Land Records.

ACTL: Accomac County, Virginia, Tax Lists.

ACW: *Wills and Administrations of Accomack County, Virginia 1663-1800,* compiled and edited by Stratton Nottingham.

ARMD: *Archives of Maryland* (published series).

ACCO: *Accomack County, Virginia Court Order Abstracts,* compiled by JoAnn Riley McKey, published by Heritage Books.

ASOS: *A Somerset Sampler, 1700-1776* (edited by Pauline Manning Batchelder. Published by Lower Delmarva Genealogical Society, 1994).

BALR: Baltimore County Land Records.

Baltimore Co. Families: *Baltimore County Families, 1659-1759* by Robert W. Barnes. Baltimore: Genealogical Publishing Company, 1988.

BDML: *Biographical Dictionary of the Maryland Legislature.* By Edward C. Papenfuse et al. 2 vols. Baltimore: The Johns Hopkins University Press, 1979, 1985.

BFD: Balances of Final Distributions (abstracted by Moxey and Skinner).

Bio of Eastern Shore: *Portrait and Biographical Record of the Eastern Shore of Maryland.* Chapman Publishing Company, New York, Chicago (1898).

Bio Record: *Biographical Records of Harford and Cecil Counties Maryland.* Originally published by Chapman Publishing Co., 1897. Reprinted by Family Line Publications, with new index by Harford County Genealogical Society, 1989.

BMGS: *Maryland Genealogical Society Bulletin.*

British Roots: *British Roots of Maryland Families.* By Robert W. Barnes. Baltimore: Genealogical Publishing Co.

Brumbaugh II: *Maryland Records: Colonial, Revolutionary, County and Church, from Original Sources.* 2 volumes. Compiled by Gaius M. Brumbaugh. Reprinted by Genealogical Publishing Co., Baltimore, 1967, 1975, 1993.

CALR: *Caroline County Land Records* as abstracted by R. Bernice Leonard. Self published, series begins in 1999.

CANH: Northwest Fork Quakers (Hicksite). Most of the records of the group prior to the split in 1827 remained with this group.

CANW: Northwest Fork Quakers (Orthodox). This group split with the Northwest Fork Monthly Meeting members who became identified as Hicksite and joined with the Quakers of Motherkiln Monthly Meeting of Delaware under Wilmington Yearly Meeting of Orthodox Quakers.

CANI: Nicholite Records. The Nicholites were followers of Joseph Nichols whose three meeting houses were all located in Caroline Co. and drew members from Caroline, Dorchester, Kent and Sussex counties. Their doctrine was very similar to that of the Quakers.

CAVL: *Cavaliers and Pioneers. Abstracts of Virginia Land Patents and Grants.* Volumes, 1-3, abstracted by Nell Marion Nugent. Volumes 4-7, edited by Dennis Ray Hudgins. (1934-1999).

CAW: Caroline County Wills.

CDSS: *Colonial Delaware Soldiers and Sailors, 1638-1776*, compiled by Henry C. Peden, Jr. Westminster: Family Line Publications, 1995.

CECH: *Early Anglican Church Records of Cecil County.* By Henry C. Peden, Jr. Westminster: Family Line Publications, 1990.

CELC: Cecil County Land Commissions.

CELR: Cecil County Land Records.

CEMM: Cecil Monthly Meeting (Quakers); Register 1678-1820; Marriages 1698-1784; Special Collections MSA M908.

CESM: Records of St. Mary Anne's Parish (North Elk).

CESS: Records of St. Stephen's Parish (North Sassafras).

CHPALR: *Abstracts of Chester County, Pennsylvania Land Records* (abstracted by Carol Bryant).

Clements/Wright: *Maryland Militia in the Revolutionary War* by S. Eugene Clements and F. Edward Wright.

COES: *Citizens of the Eastern Shore of Maryland* (by Wright).

Craig: An article in *The Pennsylvania Genealogical Magazine*, Vol. XL:4 (1998), "1671 Census of the Delaware," by Dr. Peter Stebbins Craig.

DE Bible Rcds: *Delaware Bible Records.* 6 vols. Compiled by Donald O. Virdin and Lu Verne V. Hall. Bowie, MD: Heritage Books, Inc., 1998.

Dill: *Souls in Heaven, Names in Stone Kent County, Delaware Cemetery Records*, compiled by Raymond Walter Dill, William Martin Dill and Elizabeth Ann Bostick Dill, self published, 1989.

DODO: Dorchester Parish Records (Dorchester County)

DOGC: Great Choptank Parish Records (Dorchester County)

DOLR: *Land Records of Dorchester County Maryland* (abstracted by McAllister).

ESVR: *Maryland Eastern Shore Vital Records.* Comp. by F. Edward Wright. 5 vols. Westminster: Family Line Publications, 1982-1986.

FDT: Federal Direct Tax List of 1798 for Somerset County.

Heirs and Legatees: *Heirs and Legatees of Caroline County Maryland*, compiled
            by Irma Harper. Westminster: Family Line Publications, 1989.

Historic Graves: *Historical Graves of Maryland and The District of Columbia*.
            By Helen W. Ridgely. Originally published in 1908, reprinted by
            Family Line Publications, Westminster, MD, 1992.

IKL: Somerset County Land Records, Liber IKL.

Immanuel Regtr.: The register of the Emanuel (or Immanuel) Protestant
            Episcopal Church of New Castle, established in 1704 and published in
            Early Church Records of New Castle County, Delaware, Volume 1,
            Family Line Publications, Westminster, MD, 1994. Earlier published in
            *Early Ecclesiastical Affairs in New Castle, Del. and History of
            Immanuel Church*, by Thomas Holcomb, 1890.

INAC: *Abstracts of the Inventories and Administration Accounts of the
            Prerogative Court of Maryland* (abstracted by Vernon L. Skinner, Jr.
            Westminster, MD: Family Line Publications. Originals are held by the
            MSA.

Inhabitants of CE Co.: *Inhabitants of Cecil County, Maryland, 1649-1774*.
            Compiled by Henry C. Peden, Jr. Westminster, MD: Family Line
            Publications, 1993.

Johnston: *History of Cecil County, Maryland*. By George Johnston. Originally
            published Elkton, MD, 1881. Reprinted by Clearfield Company, Inc.,
            Baltimore, 1998.

Jones: *New Revised History of Dorchester County Maryland* by Elias Jones
            (1966). Originally published in 1902. Corrections made in 1966 by
            author's daughter, Mary Ruth Jones.

KEAD: Kent County Administration Accounts.

KECH: Kent County Chancery Records.

KECP: Kent County Court Proceedings.

KECR: Kent County Criminal Records.

KECT: Kent Co. Chattel Records.

KEDELR: Kent County, Delaware, Land Records.

KELR: Kent County, Maryland, Land Records.

KESH: Shrewsbury Parish Register, Kent County.

KESP: St. Paul's Parish Register, Kent County.

KEWB: Kent County Will Books.

LCPC: Lewes and Coolspring Presbyterian Church records. (near Lewes, DE).

Lankford: *They Lived in Somerset County* by Wilmer O. Lankford.

LODB: Land Office Debt Books.

Marshall's Tombstone Records: Nellie M. Marshall, *Tombstone Records of
            Dorchester County, Maryland, 1678-1964*, published by DO County
            Historical Society, 1993}

Maryland Deponents: *Maryland Deponents, 1634-1799*. Compiled by Henry C. Peden, Jr. Westminster, MD: Family Line Publications, 1991.

MCHR: Maryland Chancery Court Records.

MacKenzie: George Norbury Mackenzie, ed., *Colonial Families of the United States* (7 volumes, 1907-1920). *Use this source with caution as a many of the statements of this work are undocumented.*

MCW: *Maryland Calendar of Wills* (from Prerogative Court) by Jane Baldwin Cotton (Volumes 1-8 and F. Edward Wright, Volumes 9-16).

MD DAR Directory, 1892: Maryland DAR Directory, 1892-1965 (Published by the Maryland Society, Daughters of the American Revolution in 1966), cited by Henry C. Peden, Jr., in his *Revolutionary Patriots of Cecil County, Maryland*. Westminster, MD: Family Line Publications, 1991.

MD DAR Directory, 1965: Maryland DAR Directory, 1965-1980 (Published by the Maryland Society, Daughters of the American Revolution in 1985), cited by Henry C. Peden, Jr., in his *Revolutionary Patriots of Cecil County, Maryland*. Westminster, MD: Family Line Publications, 1991.

MD Genealogies: *Maryland Genealogies* (2 vols.). Baltimore: Genealogical Publishing Co., 1980. Taken from the *Maryland Historical Magazine*.

MD Marriages: *Maryland Marriages, 1634-1777*. Compiled by Robert Barnes. Baltimore: Genealogical Publishing Co., 1975.

MDAD: *Abstracts of the Administration Accounts of the Prerogative Court of Maryland*. Westminster, MD: Family Line Publications. Originals are held by the MSA.

MD Militia, War of 1812: *Maryland Militia, War of 1812*, compiled by F. Edward Wright.

MDTP: Maryland Testamentary Proceedings; originals are at MSA.

MHM: *Maryland Historical Magazine.*

MHS: Maryland Historical Society, Baltimore.

Miller: *Abstracts of Commissions & Affidavits Judicial Records 1717-1767* by Rebecca F. Miller. Self published, 1991.

MINV: *Abstracts of the Inventories of the Prerogative Court of Maryland* (abstracted by Vernon L. Skinner, Jr.).Westminster, MD: Family Line Publications. Originals are held by the MSA.

MMDP: *More Maryland Deponents, 1719-1799* (by Henry C. Peden, Jr.).

Mowbray: Calvin W. Mowbray, *First Dorchester Families*

MPL: Maryland Land Patents. (As published in *The Early Settlers of Maryland*, edited by Gust Skordas, Assistant Archivist State of Maryland, and *A Supplement to The Early Settlers of Maryland*, compiled and introduced by Carson Gibb, Ph.D.

MSA: Maryland State Archives, Annapolis.

MWB: Maryland Will Book.

NCDELR: New Castle County, Delaware, Land Records.

Nelms: *Store Accounts of John Nelms of Salisbury, 1758-1787* by John E. Jacob, Jr. Published by Family Line Publications (1990), Westminster, MD.

Nottingham: *Wills and Administrations Accomack County, Virginia 1663-1800* by Stratton Nottingham.

NOTL: Northampton County, Virginia, Tax Lists.

OSES: *Old Somerset on the Eastern Shore* (by Clayton Torrence).

PA Genealogies: *Genealogies of Pennsylvania Families.* Baltimore: Genealogical Publishing Co., 1983. Taken from *The Pennsylvania Magazine of History and Biography.*

PCLR: Provincial Court Land Records of Maryland; originals are at MSA.

Polk Family and Kinsmen: *Polk Family and Kinsmen*, compiled by William Harrison Polk. Includes discussion by several early researchers.

QAEJ: Queen Anne's County Ejectment Papers.

QAJR: Queen Anne's County Judgement Records.

QALR: *Queen Anne's County Maryland Land Records* (compiled by Bernice Leonard).

QALU: St. Luke's Parish Records of Queen Anne's Co.

Records of Jesuit Mission at Cordova. These were published in *Vital Records of the Jesuit Missions of the Eastern Shore 1760-1800.* Based on compilations of Reverend Edward B. Carley. Published by Family Line Publications, 1986.

Ridgely: *Historic Graves of Maryland and the District of Columbia* by Helen W. Ridgely (1908).

RPCA: *Revolutionary Patriots of Caroline County Maryland 1775-1783*, compiled by Henry C. Peden, Jr.

RPCE: *Revolutionary Patriots of Cecil County Maryland*, compiled by Henry C. Peden, Jr.

RPDO: *Revolutionary Patriots of Dorchester County 1775-1783*, compiled by Henry C. Peden, Jr.

RPKQ: *Revolutionary Patriots of Kent and Queen Anne's Counties, Maryland*, compiled by Henry C. Peden, Jr.

RPWS: *Revolutionary Patriots of Worcester and Somerset Counties*, compiled by Henry C. Peden, Jr.

RPTA: *Revolutionary Patriots of Talbot County Maryland 1775-1783*, compiled by Henry C. Peden, Jr.

RUSSO: *Tax Lists of Somerset County 1730-1740.* Compiled by J. Elliott Russo.

Scharf: *History of Delaware, 1609-1888*, by J. Thomas Scharf, A.M., LL.D

SOAC: Administration Accounts of Somerset County.

SOMR: Somerset County Marriage Records (licenses).

SCOC: *Abstracts of the Proceedings of Sussex County Orphans' Court, Delaware*, Libers 1, 2, 3, 4, A (1708-1709 and 1728-1777). Compiled by Vernon L. Skinner, Jr., published by Willow Bend Books, Westminster, MD. (2000).

SOOP: *Somerset County, Maryland Orphans Court Proceedings* series by David V. Heise.

SJ&SG: *St. John's and St. George's Parish Registers, 1696-1851*. Compiled by Henry C. Peden, Jr. Westminster, MD: Family Line Publications, 1987.

SOA: Somerset County Accounts.

SOCO: Records of Coventry Parish, Somerset County.

SOD: Deeds of Somerset County

SOI: *Somerset County Inventories*, compiled by Rebecca Furniss Miller.

SOJR: *Somerset Judicial Records*, compiled by Rebecca Furniss Miller.

SOJUD: *Somerset Judicial Records* Vols. 1-4 Frank V. Walczyk, Peters Row, NY.1998

SOLR: *Land Records of Somerset County, Maryland* (compiled by Ruth T. Dryden).

SOSP: Records of Stepney Parish, Somerset County.

SOPS: Records of Somerset Parish, Somerset County.

SORR: Somerset County Rent Rolls

SOTL: Somerset County Tax Lists

SOW: Somerset County Wills

SOWS: *Somerset County Will Books* (abstracted by Vernon L. Skinner, Jr.).

SOWD: *Somerset County Will Books* (abstracted by Ruth Dryden).

Sussex Court Records: *Records of the Courts of Sussex County, Delaware 1677-1710*, Craig W. Horle. University of Pennsylvania Press, 1991. SXPR: Sussex County, Delaware Probate Records (abstracted by deValinger).

SUDELR: Sussex County, Delaware, Land Records.

SUTL: Tax lists of Sussex County, Delaware.

TAEJ: Talbot County Ejectment Papers.

TAGU: Talbot County Guardianships.

TAJU: Talbot County Judgments.

TALC: Talbot County Land Commissions.

TALR: *Talbot County Maryland Land Records* (abstracted by Bernice Leonard).

TAMI: St. Michael's Parish Records, Talbot County.

TAPE: St. Peter's Parish Records (Anglican), Talbot County.

TATH: Third Haven Monthly Meeting..

TP: Prerogative Court, Testamentary Proceedings.

WCOC: *Worcester County Orphans Court Proceedings*. Compiled by David V. Heise.

WCMN: Wyand, Jeffrey A., and Florence L. Wyand. *Colonial Maryland Naturalizations*.

WED: Worcester County Estate Docket.

Whitelaw: Ralph T. Whitelaw, *Virginia's Eastern Shore. A History of Northampton and Accomack Counties.*

WI Co. Graveyards: John E. Jacob, Jr., *Wicomico County Graveyards.*

WID: Deeds of Wicomico County

WILR: *Land Records of Wicomico County, Maryland 1666-1810* (compiled by Ruth T. Dryden).

Wilson: *Thirty Four Families of Somerset*, by Woodrow T. Wilson. Baltimore: Gateway Press, 1974.

Wise: *The Littleton Heritage* by Matthew M. Wise. 1997.

WOD: Deeds of Worcester County.

WOLR: *Land Records of Worcester County, Maryland 1666-1810* (compiled by Ruth T. Dryden).

WOOC: Worcester County Orphans Court Records

WOSM: St. Martin's Episcopal Church Register.

WOW: Worcester County Wills

WOWD: Worcester County Will Books (abstracted by Dryden).

WOWH: Worcester County Will Books (abstracted by Heise).

WOWJ: Worcester County Will Books (abstracted by Jones).

WOWS: Worcester County Will Book MH3 (abstracted by Skinner).

OTHER ABBREVIATIONS

a.	acre(s)	e.	east
AA Co.	Anne Arundel County	exec(s).	executor(s)
adj.	adjoining	extx(s).	executrix (executrices)
admin.	administrator or	FR Co.	Frederick County
	administered	inv.	inventoried
admx(s).	administratrix	KE Co.	Kent County
	(administratices)	KI	Kent Island
afsd.	aforesaid	m.	married
b.	born	n.	north
BA Co.	Baltimore County	(N)	Name unknown
bapt.	baptized	nunc.	nuncupative
battn.	battalion	plant.	plantation
BC	Baltimore City	prob.	probable
bro(s).	brother(s)	QA Co.	Queen Anne's County
bttn.	battalion	s.	south or shilling(s)
bur.	buried	sd.	said
c.	circa (about)	SM Co.	St. Mary's County
CA Co.	Caroline County	SU Co.	Sussex County, Delaware
CALR	Caroline County land	s.p.	died without issue
	records	TA Co.	Talbot County
CE Co.	Cecil County	T.P.	Testamentary
cont.	containing		Proceedings
conv.	conveyed	Test:	Testes (meaning
CV Co.	Calvert County		witnesses)
dau(s).	daughter(s)	tob.	tobacco
dec'd.	deceased	v.p.	during father's lifetime
dep.	deposed	w.	west
dist.	distributed	wit.	witness
DO Co.	Dorchester County		

Standard Postal Service State Abbreviations.

xxii

CORRECTIONS, ADDITIONS, AND COMMENTS TO PREVIOUS VOLUMES

CORRECTIONS AND ADDITIONS

Vol. 7 p. 129.
Show Seth Foster m. Elizabeth Hawkins, widow of Thomas Hawkins.

THE SETH FOSTER FAMILY of Westmoreland County, Virginia and Talbot County, Maryland

1. SETH FOSTER, m. Elizabeth Hawkins, widow of Thomas Hawkins.
Add the following:
    On 18 Jan 1664 Seth and Elizabeth Foster conveyed unto (18 Jan 1664) John Walker of Westmoreland Co., VA, planter, 500a. upon the head of Nomony River (Westmoreland Co.) being part of a patent formerly granted unto Thomas Hawkins, dec'd., and by him alienated to Seth Foster...upon record in Kent Co., MD.. out of patent of 2500a. {Westmoreland Co., VA, Deeds, Wills, Patents, 1653-71:249-50}
    On 20 Sep 1665 Seth Foster of Talbot Co., MD, and Elizabeth Hawkins alias Foster the wife of Seth Foster and Thomas Hawkins the lawful son and heir of Thomas Hawkins formerly of Nomony, dec'd., conveyed to Nicholas Spencer of Nomony, Gent., for a valuable sum of tobacco, 2000 a. on Nomony, part of a patent of 2500a. formerly sold to Seth Foster by Thomas Hawkins, and 500a. of that formerly sold to John Walker of Yeocomco, WE Co., the 2500 a. on s. side of Potomack River, and abutting land of Major George Read, Mr. Thomas Davis. 500a. formerly patented to Mr. Edward Kemp, assigned to Mr. Thomas Gerrard, assigned to Hawkins. 1000 a. patented to Mr. Thomas Gerrard, assigned to Hawkins, 1000a., due for the transportation of 20 persons. {DWP, 1653-71:274-6}
    On 4 March 1667 Seth Foster and wife Elizabeth of Choptank Island, conveyed to Master Alexander Dhingelsea, the tract *Poplers Island*, opposite Isle of Kent. {TALR 1:104}
    Seth Foster was Justice of Talbot Co., MD, by 25 April 1668. {DOLR 7 Old 2}
    On 28 Aug 1669 Seth Foster signed an indenture to Ralph Nickson of Norwich, county of Chester, smith: indenture of Ralph Nickson to Foster until the arrival of the ship *Charles of London* - for a term of 4 years - Foster to pay his passage and allow meat, drink and apparel and lodging and other. Elizabeth, wife of Seth Foster, signed. The ship arrived on 26 Nov 1669. {TALR 1:188}
    At March Court 1671/2 Charles Cousson, servant to Seth Foster, was adjudged to serve 17 years. {ARMD LIV 524, Liber BB No. 2:-}

On 11 Sep 1673 Seth Foster conveyed to John Hawkins, his son in law, part of a tract in Chester River, 1000 a. called *Tully's Delight.* {TALR 1:281}

Seth Foster of Great Choptank Island, TA Co., d. leaving a will dated 2 Dec 1674, proved 12 March 1674/5. To wife Elizabeth, extx., 1/3 of estate. To son in law John Hawkins, 1000 a. tract *Tully's Delight* on Chester River. To youngest dau. Sarah — 1000 a. tract *Standish Woods* on Chester River and tract *Green's Pasture* on Kent Island. To eldest dau. Elizabeth Lowe, tract *Great Choptank Island.* To 2 daus. afsd., residue of estate. Overseers were William Hamilton, Talbot Co., and son in law Vincent Lowe. {MCW 1:107}

On 25 July 1677 Coll. Nicho. Spencer, WE Co., Esqr. To (25 July 1677) Mr. Tho: Tanner, Yeocomoco, merchant, 500a...att Robt. Edwards his tree ... bounds ... land sold unto Thomas Dawson now in possession of Mr. Thomas Hobson...into land of Capt. Tho: Yowell...land lately in possession of Peter Jenkins...land formerly belonging to Henry Roach, now Mr. John Hawkins, ...land of Thomas Attwell and Walter English, includes lands formerly sold by me to Wallter English and Teag Olongall now in possession of Danniell Okenny, unto land formerly sold by me unto Mr. Tho: Dawson... part of 3250 a. by me purchased of Thomas Hawkins Junior son of Tho: Hawkins Senior and of Seith Foster, who m. Elizabeth Hawkins, relict of Tho. Hawkins to whom the land by will divided. {Westmoreland Co., VA, Deeds, Wills, Patents, 1665-77:318a-319a}
Correct the following:

Seth was father of ELIZABETH, m. Vincent Lowe; SARAH and stepfather of Thomas and John Hawkins.

2. ELIZABETH FOSTER, dau. of Seth (1) Foster, m. Vincent Lowe.

Vincent Lowe of Great Choptanke Island, Talbot Co., d. leaving a will dated 14 Dec 1691, proved 20 Oct 1692. To wife Elizabeth, tract Great Choptanke Island, "land left said wife by her father Seth Foster as his eldest dau., requesting her if she die without heirs to bequeath sd. island to Foster Turbutt." To bro. Nicholas Lowe, land in parish of Denly, England, left testator by his mother Anne Lowe. {MCW 2:56-57}

Elizabeth (Foster) Lowe apparently d.s.p.

Vol. 8

p. 49: *Correct the following:*

Robert (1) Collier, SO Co. m. 1st (N)^2 m. Elizabeth Dashiell, daughter of James Dashiell (d. 1698).
Add the following:

James Dashiell d. leaving a will dated 27 April1696 (OS), proved 31 Oct 1697 (OS). To wife Ann, plantation where she lives during her lifetime or widowhood. Mentions sons James Dashiell, Thomas Dashiell and Robert Dashiell; dau. Jane. {SOW EB5:110}

The admin. account was submitted by James Dashiell on 10 Aug 1698. Distribution to widow (unnamed), George Dashiell, Robert Dashiell, William Jones, Robert Collier, Thomas Dashiell, John Smith, accountant. {INAC 16:229}

p. 50.
In second paragraph listing the children of Robert, add after SARAH; JANE, m. Richard Phillips. {See The Roger Phillips Family, vol. 18 of this series.}

p. 52.
In the 5th paragraph show JANE, m. 1st Roger Nicholson, son of Roger Nicholson and m. 2nd Thomas Dashiell; MARGARET m. Mitchell Dashiell, son of Thomas Dashiell. {See also The Nicholson Family, vol. 18 of this series.}

p. 152.
        In the third paragraph show,
Stephen was father of the following children: JOHN; STEPHEN; KATHERINE; MARY; ANNE, m. John Stevens; SARAH, m. 1st (N) Wheatley, m. 2nd Michael Roach, and pre-deceased her mother; ELIZABETH (Betty), m. Burr Outerbridge; ABIGAIL. {See The Stevens Family, vol. 18 of this series.}

p. 167:
Add a paragraph showing information on the parents of George (1) Layfield, based on Robert W. Barnes, British Roots, Vol. II:
1. GEORGE LAYFIELD, son of Thomas and Margaret Layfield.
        Thomas Layfield, Sutton Coldfield, Warwick, England, d. c1658. Thomas, prob. of London, m. Margaret (N) who m. 2nd by 1709 (N) Nottle. Thomas and Margaret were parents of GEORGE; THOMAS, b. c1641; SAMUEL, b. c1646. {British Roots II:134}

p. 228.
Add an entry following 2. JOHN ROBINSON:
2A. WILLIAM ROBERTSON (Robinson), b. 13 Feb 1684, d. by 1767, son of William (1) and Elizabeth Robertson (Robinson), m. Rachel (N).
        On 7 Nov 1755 Thomas Willett sold 100 a. of the tract Parremores Double Purchase to William Robinson. On 3 Dec 1762 William Robertson and wife Rachel sold 100 a. to Zachariah Harris. {WOLR:453}
        William Robertson, SO Co., d. by 30 June 1767 when the inventory of his estate was filed by Rachel Robertson. Signed as next of kin: Rachel Newman, Esther Robertson. {MINV 91:271}
        The admin. account was submitted by Rachel Robertson, widow, on 4 May 1768. Distribution to accountant (1/3) with residue in equal amounts to wife

of Isaac Newman, wife of Thomas Newman and three others [all unnamed].
{MDAD 59:265}
On 4 May 1768 distribution of his estate was made by Rachel
Robertson, admx., to widow (unnamed, 1/3). {BFD 5:90}

p. 231:
Show the following:
5. WILLIAM ROBINSON, son of William (1) Robinson, m. Hannah (N) <u>who</u>
<u>later m. John Heales. Hannah d. by 6 June 1759.</u>
Add the following:
William Robertson, WO Co., d. by 20 Dec 1759 when the inventory of
his estate was filed by Hannah Heales, John Heales. {MINV 69:205}
On 6 June 1759 the admin. account of his estate was submitted by
Michael Robinson. Distribution to widow, now dead with residue to children
(unnamed minors). {MDAD 43:206}

p. 232:
Add a new entry:
7A. JOSEPH ROBERTSON, son of William (1) Robinson.
Joseph Robertson/Robinson, WO Co., d. by 14 March 1774 when the
inventory of his estate was filed by Betty Robinson, John Robinson. Signed as
next of kin: Joshua Robertson, Ester Robertson. {MINV 117:206}

p. 233:
Add a paragraph after the first paragraph:
On 6 March 1758 the admin. account of Thomas Robinson was
submitted by Thomas Robinson. Payments were made in equal amounts to son
William, dau. Molley, son Peter Robinson, dau. (unnamed wife of John Coffan),
son Thomas Robinson, accountant. Legatees: son William received negro
Moses; dau. Molley, wife of James Gray, received negro Ester; wife (unnamed)
of John Coffan; Cornelius and John received Negro Cubbers. Distribution to
widow (1/3) with residue to children: Cornelius and John.
Change current 2nd paragraph to read:
Thomas was father of the following children: THOMAS; WILLIAM;
Comfort m. <u>John</u> Coffin; JOSEPH; PETER; MOLLY, <u>m. James Gray;</u>
CORNELIUS; JOHN.

Change to read:
9. JOSHUA ROBINSON, son of William (1) Robinson, m. Priscilla Downes,
dau. of George and Margaret Downs, and widow of <u>Samuel</u> Derickson. {See The
Andreas Derrickson Family, vol. 12 of this series.}

The tax lists of SO Co. show Joshua Robinson living in the household of Mary Robinson, 1730-1731 and as head of household in Baltimore Hundred, 1733-1740. Living in the household were Littleton Tingle (1733); William Derickson (1738-1740; William Moore (1740); slave Bess (1731-1740).

Add a new section:

THE JOHN ROBERSON FAMILY

1. JOHN ROBERSON m. Mary (N).
   John Roberson, SO Co., d. leaving a will dated 5 Nov 1748, proved 19 June 1753. To son James Roberson, 150 a., at the south end of a tract called *Ireland's Eve*. To son John Roberson, 100 a. on south side of Plum Creek, called *Long Delay*. To son Jacob Roberson, 150 a. To dau. Ann Roberson, £20. If son John, die without issue, his part to dau. Ann Roberson. If son Jacob, die without issue, his part to son William. Wife Mary, extx. {MWB 28:505}
   On 18 July 1753 the inventory of his estate was filed by Mary Robinson. Signed as next of kin: James Robinson, John Roberson. {MINV 54:280}
   Mary Robinson (d. 1777), farmer, probably widow of John, left a will in which she named dau. Ann Marine; son John; Sophia Armstrong (no relationship stated) who received a furniture, "the same she lay on when with me," and Thomas Connaly. {ASOS:226, citing SOW EB1:47}
   John was father of JAMES; JOHN; JACOB; ANN, m. (N) Marine; WILLIAM.

2. JAMES ROBERTSON, prob. son of John (1) and Mary Roberson, m. Mary (N).
   James Robertson, SO Co., d. by 18 April 1768 when the inventory of his estate was filed by John Robertson. Signed as next of kin: William Robertson, John Robertson. {MINV 99:64}
   On 4 April 1769 the admin. account was submitted by John Robertson. Legatees: John Robertson (accountant), widow. Payments to Mary Robertson, widow (1/3), Mary Robertson (1/4), Ann Robertson (1/4), John Robertson (1/4, accountant). {MDAD 60:310}
   James was father of MARY; JOHN; JAMES; ANN, m. (N) Badley; (N). {ASOS:226}

3. WILLIAM ROBERTSON, probable son of John (1) and Mary Robertson, m. Ann (N), prob. Ann Wilson, dau. of John Wilson.
   John Wilson, SO Co., d. leaving a will dated 19 May 1752, proved 22 March 1758. Children: James, David, Thomas Wilson and Ann Robertson. Cousin: Mary Wilson Taylor. Friends: Benjamin Venables. Water Course:

Bunon Creek. Tract: *Duby Beginning, Wilson's Loot* and *Rattband*. Tract: *Anything* to discretion of exec David Wilson, exec {MWB 30:482}

William Robertson, SO Co., d. leaving a will dated 5 April 1771, proved 1 Aug 1771. To wife Ann. Children: Mary, Betty, Priscilla, Ann, Nelly, Sarah, Margaret Conley. Mentions plantation where my mother Mary Robertson now liveth. {MWB 38:334}

On 14 Aug 1771 an inventory of the estate of William Robertson, SO Co., was filed by William Badley. Signed as next of kin: Mary Roberson, John Roberson. {MINV 107:283}

On 23 Sep 1771 distribution of his estate was made by William Badley, admin., to Sarah Robertson. {BFD 6:189}

On 4 March 1772 another inventory of his estate was filed by William Badly. {MINV 111:11}

William was father of MARY; BETTY; PRISCILLA; ANN; NELLY; SARAH; MARGARET, m. (N) Conley.

DELETE NEXT TO LAST PARAGRAPH ON PAGE 236.

Add a new section:

THE REV. JAMES ROBERTSON FAMILY

1. Rev. JAMES ROBERTSON
The tax lists of SO Co. show Rev. James Roberson (Robinson) as head of household in Manokin Hundred, 1730-1740. Living in the household were John Roberson/Robinson (1730-1740); John Hall (1731); Will Welch (1740); slaves: Jack (1730-1740), Tobe (1730-1740), Nero (1730-1740), Prew (1730-1739), Ceasar (1733-1740), Dinah (1733-1740), Phillis (1733-1740), Sciss (1734-1740), Pesek/Perik (1740).

James Robertson, Rector of Coventry Parish, SO Co., d. leaving a will dated 28 June 1748, proved 2 Jan 1748-9. To son Alexander, tract *Arcum*. To son Thomas, my land down the river of Monocon, at the old plantation. To son James, land where I now live. Remainder to be divided between the above 3 sons and Mary Robertson. {MWB 25:521}

The inventory of the estate of Rev. James Robertson, SO Co., was filed on 6 March 1748 when the inventory of his estate was filed by Mary Robertson (alias Mary Bell). Signed as next of kin: Thomas Williams, John Williams. {MINV 40:397}

James was father of ?JOHN; ALEXANDER; THOMAS; JAMES; ?MARY.

2. JAMES ROBERTSON, prob. son of James (1) Robertson, m. Jane, dau. of

Anna Dashiell.

Anna Dashiell, Stepney Parish, SO Co., d. leaving a will dated 21 March 1773, proved 15 April 1773. To youngest son Mathias, Negro wench Thamer and land I bought of George Hobbs with all appurtenances, except 25 a. of which to my son Arthur provided he makes over as much timber land to his brother or his garden. To son Arthur, Negro Paul. To son William, Negro boy Joshua. If son Arthur refuses to make over above land to son Matthias he shall forfeit all right to my estate both real and personal and his part to go to son Matthias, if he dies before 21 years of age land left to him to his brother William. To children Jane, Milcah, Arthur, William and Matthias, residue of estate. To dau. Jane saddle and slip and cloak. To dau. Milcah, wearing apparel. To 2 youngest sons (unnamed) They and their estates to be in care of James Robertson, exec {MWB 39:520}

Ann Dashiell, SO Co., d. by 22 March 1774 when the inventory of her estate was filed by James Robertson. {MINV 114:361}

James Robertson, SO Co., d. by 7 Dec 1775 when the inventory of his estate was filed by Jane Robertson. Signed as next of kin: Hamilton Bell, Alexander Robertson. {MINV 122:326}

James Robertson, SO Co., d. by 7 Dec 1775 when the distribution of his estate was made by Mrs. Jane Robertson, admin., to widow (unnamed, 1/3), residue to Jane Robertson. {BFD 7:54}

Add Under Unplaced
Add to entry for DAVID ROBINSON:
The tax lists of SO Co. show David Roberson as head of household, Nanticoke Hundred, 1730-1734.

Add entry for JAMES ROBERTON:
JAMES ROBERTSON m. Mary (N).
James Robertson, SO Co., d. leaving a will dated 5 Dec 1767, proved 1 April 1768. Wife: Mary. Children: two daus. and two sons mentioned, but named only: Mary, John and James. {MWB 36:291}

James Robertson, SO Co., d. by 4 April 1769 when the distribution of his estate was made by John Robertson, admin., residue to James (son). {BFD 5:346}

James was father of MARY; JOHN; JAMES.

Add entry for JACOB ROBERTSON:
JACOB ROBERTSON
Jacob Robertson, SO Co., d. by 24 Oct 1764 when the inventory of his estate was filed by William Roberts. Signed as next of kin: James Robberson, John Robberson. {MINV 86:227}

The admin. account was submitted by William Robertson on 11 Oct 1765. Distribution to (in equal parts) to wife (unnamed) of Charles Merine, Mary Robertson, James Robertson, John Robertson, accountant. {MDAD 53:269}

Jacob was father of WILLIAM; (N), m. Charles Merine; MARY; JAMES; JOHN.

p. 236:
Delete entire entry for JAMES ROBINSON

Add entry for JOHN ROBERTSON
JOHN ROBERTSON m. Priscilla (N).

John Robertson, SO Co., d. by 28 June 1769 when the inventory of his estate was filed by Stephen Garland. Signed as next of kin: Prissila Robinson, Mary Sirmon. {MINV 103:45}

The admin. account was submitted by Stephen Garland on 18 June 1771. Payments included (among others) Priscilla Robertson, widow. {MDAW 63:408}

p. 238:
As last entry under the William Robinson who m. Eleanor (N) ...
Add:

On 5 June 1767 the admin. account of the estate of William Robinson was submitted by widow Eleanor, now wife of Peleg Walter. Distribution was made to accountant (1/3) with residue to dau. Mary (infant). {MDAD 58:67; 65:146}

William was father of MARY.

Vol. 10:
p. 48
16. SOLOMON CROPPER.
Add

On 2 Jan 1786 George Mitchell, Esqr., Sussex Co., DE, purchased from John Nicholson, Sussex Co., taylor, and Sipporah Crapper now wife of William Hall of said co. land that George Dirickson of DE was seized by virtue of a Maryland patent dated 26 Aug 1760 called *Georges Good Luck* formerly lying in WO Co. but now Sussex, 45 a., which on 27 Aug 1768 he conveyed to Solomon Crapper. When Solomon Crapper d. the land fell to his three daus., vizt., John Nickelson by his marriage to Puella became seized of her portion and Sipporah by her bond dated 10 Nov 1781 did bind herself. Now 28 a. is conveyed. Land begins on s. side of small branch called Herring Branch on n. side of county road leading from Cedar Neck to head of Indian River. Includes dwelling house wherein John Nicholson now lives. Acknowledged by Pauline Nicholson, wife of John Nicholson.

Solomon was father of PUELLA (Pauline), m. John Nicholson; SIPPORAH, m. William Hall; ONE OTHER DAUGHTER.

p. 139: *At the end of the entry for 10. WILLIAM JARMAN, show*
NANNY, m. James Stevenson, son of James. {See The Stevenson Family, vol. 18 of this series.}

p. 230: 5th line. Show Lydda, b. 8 March 1761, m. Jonathan Stevenson, son of Jonathan Stevenson. {See The Stevenson Family, vol. 18 of this series.}

Vol. 12:
p. 101.
Change entry to read,
2. SAMUEL DERRICKSON, son of Andreas (1) m. Priscilla Downes, dau. of George and Margaret Downs. Priscilla m. 2nd Joshua Robinson (Roberson). {See The William Robinson (2) Family of Pocomoke, Vol. 8 of this series.}
Add the folowing paragraphs:
  On 12 Dec 1726 Samuel Derrickson and wife Priscilla sold 200 a. of the tract *Vines Neck* to George Howard. {WOLR :658}
  The tax lists of SO Co. show Samuel Derexson as head of household in Baltimore Hundred, 1723-1725. Living in the same household are the following persons: Joseph Derexson (1723-1725); Benjamin Derrixson (1725). Living in the household of Joshua Robinson (1738-1740) is William Derickson.
  Samuel may be the father of JOSEPH, b. before 1707; BENJAMIN, b. c1709; WILLIAM, b. c1722.

Show the following:
3. JOSEPH DERRICKSON, possible son of Andreas (1) Derrickson or son of Samuel (2) Derickson, m. 27 Oct 173-, Mary Waples. {St. Martins Church, WO Co.}

Volume 16:
p. 188:
Show the following:
6. THOMAS STANFORD (STANDFORD), DO Co., prob. son of John (1) Stanford, m. Rachel Price, widow of Chrispian Price. {See The Alexander Price Family, vol. 18 of this series.}

Shift paragraph which begins with "Rachel Stanford, DO Co., a legatee..." to page 186 under the entry for 4. WILLIAM STANFORD. {Entry was associated with the wrong Rachel Stanford.}

p. 234:

7. Maj. Henry Trippe m. 1st Elizabeth, dau of Alex. Fisher Jr. (d. 1717) and m. 2nd Elizabeth Emerson?

There is no direct evidence establishing that Major Henry Trippe m. Elizabeth Fisher. This conclusion is reached by following the possession of the tract *Elson*.

Elson was patented on 8 Nov 1680 in DO Co. by Alexander Fisher for 50 a. *{MPL 24:279; 28:495}*

Alexander Fisher (Sr.), DO, d. leaving a will dated 28 Jan 1698, proved 4 March 1698. Legatees: 5 children of son-in-law Philip Pitt; dau. Ann Pitt, 50 a.; dau. Elisabeth, *Barron Point*; wife Elisabeth, life interest in all real estate. {MCW:6:308}

Note: Any real estate not cited in the will passes to the eldest son, Alexander (Jr.).]

Alexander Fisher (Jr.), DO, d. leaving a will dated 19 January 1716/7, proved on 25 March 1717. Legatees: To son Thomas, *Tarcell's Neck*. To son Alexander, *Ellson*. To dau. Elisabeth, *Anchor and Hope*. To unborn child, land between *Ellson* and *Tarcell's Neck*. To brother Mark, 50 a.. Mentions wife Mary, mother Mrs. Elisabeth Rawlings, and sister Sarah wife of Mark Marriott. {MCW:14:249}

It appears that the tract *Elson* passes to the remaining children since both sons, Thomas and Alexander die without issue. Thomas Fisher is apparently a minor, and disappears from the records after 1717; and Alexander Fisher (III), d. c1737, when Rosanna Fisher filed an administration bond on his estate. There are no other probate records for his estate. And neither he nor Rosanna appear anywhere else in the records.

The debts books next reveal Henry Trippe paying taxes on the tract *Elson* in 1737and 1745. There is no record that he had bought the tract which leads to the conclusion that he or his wife had acquired the tract by other means.

The debt book of 1755 reveals that Elizabeth Trippe making payment on *Elson*. Her involvement becomes clear later on. We must assume that this Elizabeth was the step-mother of Henry Trippe, Jr. and not his mother, in that the land did not descend to Henry, Jr. as will be shown below. Secondly she was probably the dau. of Alexander Fisher Jr., inheriting the land from her brother Alexander Fisher, III.

On 12 Nov 1770 James Lecompte, son of James, of DO Co., conveyed to Jonathan Patridge of the same co., ½ of a tract called *Ellson* on the e. side of Blackwater River adj. *Fishers Chance*. It was stated that the tract was originally granted to Alexander Fisher for 50 a.; the said land had by inheritance become the property of the said Lecompte and one Henry Turner, and the said Jonathan Patridge has heretofore purchased the other half from the said Turner. {DOLR 24:263}

Thus the land had descended to two men, James Lecompte and Henry Turner whose relationship to Elizabeth Trippe could only be explained by their marriage to daus. of Elizabeth Trippe. Did Elizabeth have any sons? Possibly - but if there were any male heirs they too died without heirs.

Vol. 17:
p. 177:
Show the following:
11. SOLOMON TULL, son of Richard (3) and Elizabeth (Turpin) Tull, b. 1697 (Wilson:272}, m. 1st Elizabeth Stevens, dau. of Edward Stevens.
Add the following:
On 19 Jan 1720 Solomon Tull and his wife Elizabeth, conveyed 50 a. to Thomas Benston, planter. Whereas Robert Cole of Accomack Co., VA, conveyed on 3 Nov 1714 to Edward Stevens, dec'd., 150 a. of land on the Pocomoke River called *Wooten Underedge* ... now this indenture further witnesseth that the said Edward Stevens, dec'd., by his will bequeathed to his dau. Elizabeth now wife of Solomon Tull the above 150 a.. Now Solomon Tull and wife sell to Benston 50 a. out of the said 150 a. {SOD 1722-1725:193}

1

THE BOARDMAN FAMILY

1. HUGH BOARDMAN, bur. 9 Aug 1694, m. 1st Mary (N) (bur. Nov 1657 and m. 2nd Elizabeth (N) (bur. 10 July 1658.). {British Roots II:22}

Hugh was prob. father of SAMUEL, bapt. 9 May 1641; JOHN, bur. 31 July 1650; HUGH, bur. 1 Sep 1651; JOHN, bapt. 30 May 1652; THOMAS, bapt. 23 Jan 1654/5; ELIZABETH (twin), bapt. 14 June 1659; MARY (twin), bapt. 14 June 1659. {British Roots II:22}

Second Generation

2. SAMUEL BOARDMAN, son of Hugh (1) Boardman of Groton, bapt. 9 May 1641, bur. 31 Dec 1697.

Samuel was father of MARY, bapt. 6 June 1667; (N), bapt. 25 June 1669; SAMUEL, bapt. 14 March 1694; JENNA, b. 1673; FRANCIS, b. 1675; ELIZABETH, b. 1677. {British Roots II:22}

Third Generation

3. FRANCIS BOARDMAN, b. 1675 in Gorton, Lancashire, son of Samuel (2) Boardman, m. Sarah (N).

The tax lists of SO Co. show Frank Boardman as head of household in Wicomico Hundred in 1723; living in the household was William Boarman. Sarah Bordman (Borman) was head of household in Wicomico Hundred in 1730 and 1733. Living in the household in 1730 was Graves Boardman and in 1733 Samuel Borman was living in the household. {SOTL}

Francis Bordman, SO Co., d. by 30 Aug 1727, when an inventory was filed by Sarah Boardman. Cited as next of kin: Giles Bashaw, Thomas Bashaw. {MINV:13:338} Accounts were filed on 22 Dec 1728 by Sarah Boardman. {MDAD:9:306}

Mary Garrett, SO Co., d. leaving a will dated 13 March 1727/8, proved 18 May 1728. To Groves Bordman, plantation; Winneford Watts, Bridget Gilles, Sarah Bordman, Sr., Elennor Bordman, personalty; children of brother John Gilles. {MWB:19:450}

Andrew Bashaw, SO Co., d. by 8 May 1730, when an inventory was filed by Mary Bashaw. Cited as next of kin: Sarah Boardman, Graves Boardman. {MINV:15:649}

On 14 Sep 1748 Sarah Jackson, age 84, swears that she is acquainted with Francis Boardman and his wife Sarah and was a neighbor to them for over 30 years and during that time Francis and Sarah were man and wife and had the following children by Sarah: William, Eleanor, Graves, Elizabeth, Samuel and Sarah, and that William and Samuel died without issue. She swears that she was present at the births of Graves, Elizabeth and Samuel who were all born of Sarah. She also swore that often she heard Francis Boardman say he was an

Englishman born and that his father's name was Samuel Boardman and that he was a weaver by trade. She also states that Francis went home to England to see his relations and friends and was gone upwards of 12 months. She further swears that on Francis Boardman's return that he brought with him sundry goods and after his death his son married Susanna Realph and had by her three or four children and died. She further states that Elizabeth Boardman, dau. of Francis and Sarah, married John Williams and had five daus.: Sophia, Sarah, Eunice, Eleanor, and Priscilla and that some time afterward died. The deponent also states that she saw Francis Boardman's dau. marry Thomas Goslee. {SOD D:229}

On 18 Sep 1768 Christopher Daudle, age 70, schoolmaster, swore that he saw Francis Boardman and his wife Sarah, that he lived a mile from them for nearly 5 years. He heard Francis Boardman state that he had named a child after his father, Samuel Boardman in England. Daudle also swore that he taught all the children of Boardman and that Boardman left Maryland for the space of 12 months [for England] about 40 years ago. {SOD D:230}

Francis and Sarah were parents of WILLIAM, b.p. 1707, d.s.p.; ELEANOR, m. Thomas Goslee; GRAVES; ELIZABETH, m. John Williams ; SAMUEL, b. c1716, d.s.p.; SARAH, b. 6 Oct 1725, m. Thomas Beard.

Fourth Generation
4. WILLIAM BOARDMAN, b.p. 1707, d.s.p. son of Francis (3) and Sarah Boardman.

The tax lists of SO Co. show William Boardman in the household of Francis Boardman in 1723 and 1724. He disappears from subsequent tax lists.

5. ELEANOR BOARDMAN, dau. of Francis (3) and Sarah Boardman, m. Thomas Goslee.

Mary Garrett, SO Co., d. leaving a will dated 13 March 1727/8, proved 18 May 1728. To Groves Bordman, plantation; Winneford Watts, Bridget Gilles, Sarah Bordman, Sr., Elennor Bordman, personalty; children of brother John Gilles. {MWB:19:450}

Giles Bashaw, SO Co., d. leaving a will dated 16 March 1738, proved 23 March 1744. To: Jarrett Bashaw, pt. *Hoggs Down*; his sisters Ann Bashaw & Elener Bashaw; Graves Bordman, pt. *Hoggs Down*; Samuel Bordman, land; my cousin Sarah Bordman; Priscilla Goslin daughter of Elizabeth Goslin; Frances Goslin. Balance: Eleanor Goslin, Elizabeth Harron, Sarah Bordman, Wine Cornish, Sarah Bashaw, Andrew Bashaw, Thomas Bashaw, Sarah Hardy. {MWB:24:99}

Thomas Goslee, SO Co., d. leaving a will dated 2 Feb 1748/9, proved 13 Feb 1748. He was a member of the Church of England. To son Samuel, the plantation I now live on, which I desire Graves Boardman to take unto his care my 2 daus. Frances and Eleanor. Exec. Graves Boardman. Witnessed by Daniel

Dulany and Joseph Venables. {MWB 25:527} The inventory was filed on 20 Nov 1745 by Mary Goslee. signed as next of kin: Graves Boardman, Israel Fouler. {MINV 31:337} The admin. account was submitted on 28 March 1753 by Joseph Vennables (surviving security for Graves Boardman (exec. of dec'd.) Payments to (in equal amounts): Francis Gosle, Elleoner Gosle. Legatees: Samuel Boardman Goslin paid to his guardian Sarah Hardy. Mentions children: Francis, Elleoner, Samuel Boardman. Some payments made by Sarah Hardy. {MDAD 34:81}

Eleanor and Thomas were parents of SAMUEL GOSLEE; FRANCES GOSLEE; ELEANOR GOSLEE.

6. GRAVES BOARDMAN, son of Francis (3) and Sarah Boardman, m. Susanna Ralph, dau. of Thomas Ralph, by Rev. Alexander Adams, rector of Stepney Parish. {See The Ralph Family, this vol.} Susanna m. 2nd (N) Shirman by whom she had a son Charles Shirman.

Graves Jarrett, joyner, SO Co., d. leaving a will proved 23 April 1722. To wife Mary, entire estate; at her decease dwelling plantation to Graves, son of Francis Boardman. {MWB 17:279}

Mary Garrett, SO Co., d. leaving a will dated 13 March 1727/8, proved 18 May 1728. To Groves Bordman, plantation; Winneford Watts, Bridget Gilles, Sarah Bordman, Sr., Elennor Bordman, personalty; children of brother John Gilles. {MWB:19:450}

The 1727 and 1730 tax lists of SO Co., Wicomico Hundred, show Graves Boardman living in the household of his widowed mother Sarah. He is no doubt the Graves Bashaw [various alternative spellings] living in 1733 in the household of George Dashiell in Wicomico Hundred, and from 1734 to 1740 as head of household in Wicomico Hundred. The 1753 tax lists show Susana Bordman as head of household in Nanticoke Hundred, owning 1 slave. {SOTL}

Andrew Bashaw, SO Co., d. by 8 May 1730, when an inventory was filed by Mary Bashaw. Cited as next of kin: Sarah Boardman, Graves Boardman. {MINV:15:649}

Giles Bashaw, SO Co., d. leaving a will dated 16 March 1738, proved 23 March 1744. To: Jarrett Bashaw, pt. *Hoggs Down*; his sisters Ann Bashaw and Elener Bashaw; Graves Bordman, pt. *Hoggs Down*; Samuel Bordman, land; my cousin Sarah Bordman; Priscilla Goslin daughter of Elizabeth Goslin; Frances Goslin. Balance: Eleanor Goslin, Elizabeth Harron, Sarah Bordman, Wine Cornish, Sarah Bashaw, Andrew Bashaw, Thomas Bashaw, Sarah Hardy. {MWB:24:99}

Graves Boardman, SO Co., d. by 19 June 1749 when the inventory of his estate was filed by Susanna Boarman, admx./extx. Signed as next of kin: Sarah Bordman, Sarah Hardy. {MINV 39:141}

The admin. account was submitted by Susanna Boardman on 4 June

1751. Distribution to widow with residue to children: Ralph, Sarah, Elizabeth, Graves Boardman. {MDAD 30:171}

Susannah Shirman, SO Co., d. leaving a will made on 27 April 1787, proved on 30 July 1787. To son Charles Shirman, land; daughters Sarah Beard, Elizabeth Goslee. {SOW:EB#1:271}

Graves and Susanna were parents of RALPH, went to sea in 1765 and never returned; SARAH, m. 14 Nov 1762, Thomas Beard; ELIZABETH, m. (N) Goslee; GRAVES, d. at age 2 or 3.

7. ELIZABETH BOARDMAN, dau. of Francis (3) and Sarah Boardman, m. John Williams.

Elizabeth and John were parents of SOPHIA WILLIAMS; SARAH WILLIAMS; EUNICE WILLIAMS; ELEANOR WILLIAMS; PRISCILLA WILLIAMS.

8. SAMUEL BOARDMAN, b. c1715, never married, d.s.p., son of Francis (3) and Sarah Boardman.

The tax lists of SO Co. show Samuel living in the household of his mother in Wicomico Hundred in 1733. In 1734-1737 he was living in the household of Robert Hardy. He was head of household in Wicomico Hundred in 1738 living near Thomas Gosley. He disappears from subsequent tax lists. {SOTL}

Giles Bashaw, SO Co., d. leaving a will dated 16 March 1738, proved 23 March 1744. To: Jarrett Bashaw, pt. *Hoggs Down*; his sisters Ann Bashaw & Elener Bashaw; Graves Bordman, pt. *Hoggs Down*; Samuel Bordman, land; my cousin Sarah Bordman; Priscilla Goslin daughter of Elizabeth Goslin; Frances Goslin. Balance: Eleanor Goslin, Elizabeth Harron, Sarah Bordman, Wine Cornish, Sarah Bashaw, Andrew Bashaw, Thomas Bashaw, Sarah Hardy. {MWB:24:99}

Fifth Generation

9. SARAH BOARDMAN, dau. of Graves (6) and Susannah Boardman, b. 6 Oct 1725, m. 14 Nov 1762, Thomas Beard. {SOSP}

Thomas and Sarah Beard were the parents of: MARY BEARD, b. 5 January 1763 {SOSP}; another child (unnamed).

THE JOHN NELSON (1) FAMILY of Wicomico Hundred

1. JOHN NELSON, d. c1671, m. Kathernie Bosman, dau. of William and Bridget Bosman. Katherine m. 2nd John Lawes. {See The William Bozman Family, vol. 12 of this series.}

Nelsons Choice was patented on 22 March 1662/3 by John Nelson for 300 a. in now West Princess Anne Election District 1. On 20 Dec 1668 John Nelson and wife Katherine alienated the land to Christopher Nutter. {SOLR:307}

John Nelson of Monokin River immigrated prior to 10 Feb 1665. {MPL 9:25}

On 11 Dec 1665 John Bossman, aged 15, son of William Bossman, dec'd., chose John Nellson to be his guardian. {ARMD LIV:611}

On 4 Sep 1666 John Nellson recorded in cattle mark in SO Co. {ARMD LIV:749}

John Nellson, son of John and Katherine Nellson, b. at Manokin 24 Oct 1666. {IKL}

In 1671 Bridgett Nelson, dau. of John Nelson, recorded her cattle mark in SO Co. {COES:35}

On 7 October 1671, Katherine Nelson was granted administration on estate of John Nelson. {TP:5:94}

On 22 March 1671/2, John Lawes filed the inventory for the estate of John Nelson. {TP:5:286}

On 6 April 1672 Bridgett Nelson, dau. of John Nelson, dec'd., recorded a cattle mark. {ARMD LIV: 759}

On 8 February 1674, John Laws who married Katherine filed administration accounts on the estate of John Nelson. {TP:6:348}

John was father of JOHN, b. 24 Oct 1666; BRIDGETT.

Second Generation

2. JOHN NELSON, son of John (1) Nelson, m. Ann who m. 2nd (N) Pitts.

John Nelson and William Nelson were among the signatories on a paper entitled "Address of the Inhabitants of the County of Somersett Nover. th 28th 1689," in which they pledge confidence in the monarch and pledge their defense of the Protestant Religion and "against the French and other Papists..." {OSES:349, 350}

On 13 July 1702, John Nelson was an appraiser of estate of Edward Low. {SOI:EB#14:286}

On 20 Feb 1714, John Nelson was an approver of the inventory of John Shiles. {SOI:EB#14:440; INAC:36B:222}

In 1717, John Nelson received payment from the estate of John Shiles. {INAC:39C:1}

The tax lists of SO Co., Wicomico Hundred, show John Nelson (Neilson) as head of household, 1724, 1730-1734.

John Nelson, SO Co., d. by 3 May 1737 when the inventory of his estate was filed by Ann Nelson. Signed as next of kin: John Shiles, Alice Shiles. {MINV 22:336}

On 6 Oct 1744 the admin. account of the estate of John Nelson of SO Co. was submitted by Ann Nelson (alias Ann Pitts), admx. Mentions: Children:

Sarah, Elizabeth, Alice Nelson. Payments included widow (unnamed, 1/3). {MDAD 21:77}
    John was father of SARAH; ELIZABETH; ALICE.

THE JOHN NELSON (2) FAMILY of Wicomico Hundred

1. JOHN NELSON, m. Dinah Mezick, dau. of Jacob Mezick.
    The tax lists of SO Co., Wicomico Hundred, show William Nelson (Nielson, Nilson) as head of household, 1723, 1730-1740. Living in the same household were (William Pritchett (1735); Charles Stewart (1736); John Nelson (Neilson) (1723 and 1738-1740).
    John Nelson was serving in Capt. Day Scott's militia company, SO Co., in 1748. {COES;79}
    Jacob Mezick, planter, SO Co., d. leaving a will dated 22 Dec 1755, proved 9 Feb 1761. To wife Elizabeth Mezick, the 1/3 pt. of moveable estate and dwelling plantation, during life. To son Jacob Mezick, my hand mill and etc. and land, except 17 a., *James Lott*, which I gave grand-son James Mezick, eldest son of Elihu Mezick; if Jacob Mezick die without issue, same to Aron Mezick. To my 7 children: Elihu, Joshua, Aron, Covington and Jacob Mezick, Dinah Nelson and Rachell Ellingsworth, moveable estate. Wife Elizabeth and son Jacob, execs. {MWB 12:45}
    On 5 Dec 1758 George Day Scott, son of Day Scott sold to John Nelson 150 a. of *Monmouth*. The 1783 tax list shows that James Nelson owned 100 a. In 1784 John Nelson willed part to son James Nelson and balance to son John Nelson. In 1787 John Nelson patented *Nelsons Addition to Monmouth* for 94 3/4 a. and in 1788 he patented another 204 a. On 23 Sep 1796 Samuel Wilson and wife Leah Littleton Wilson sold for 5 shillings to Eleanor Nelson, wife of John Nelson, *Chelsea* and *Monmouth*. On 23 Sep 1796 George Gale of Cecil Co. and Levin Gale with wife Leah sold to Eleanor Nelson and John Nelson for 5 shillings all rights to *Monmouth*. On 22 Sep 1800 John Nelson and wife Eleanor gave part to son Francis Nelson. On 13 Jan 1804 James Nelson and wife Esther sold to Augustus Cannon all except 63 3/4 a. and part of *Addition*, 9 3/4 a. On 9 Nov 1804 John Nelson sold to Augustus Cannon, *Monmouth*, *Addition to Monmouth* and *Gales Discovery*. {WILR:279}
    John Nelson, SO Co., d. leaving a will dated 3 June 1784, proved 13 Dec 1784. To wife Dinah all the field on the s. side of the road leading from my mill towards James Moore's; Negro girl Rose, Negro boy Spencer. To daus. Elizabeth Nelson and Martha Nelson, Negroes left to widow after her decease. To son James Nelson part of the tract purchased from George Scott called *Monmouth*. To son John Nelson a tract of land purchased from Solomon Harris called *Harris's Lott*, to be divided between John and James equally; part of a

parcel of land purchased from Henry Gale containing 30 a.; part of a tract purchased from Benjamin Gillis called *Stevenson's* whereon I now live; all lands purchased from Richard Tully including both the saw mill and grist mill; remainder of part of the tract *Monmouth*; part of a tract taken up by John Leatherbury but not conveyed to him: Negroes Ba... and Ishmael. To son in law Thomas English right to tract purchased from English called *King's Luck*. To grandson John Taylor Nelson, £10. To son Benjamin Nelson, £10. To daus. Susanna Mezick, Rebecca English and Sarah Beard, remainder of estate to be divided among them and Elizabeth, Martha, James and John. Witnessed by John Hopkins, James Moor, William Stone. {SOW EB1:218}

In 1768 Solomon Harris sold 52 ½ a. of *Harris Small Lott* to John Nelson. John Nelson willed it to sons James Nelson and John Nelson in 1784. On 21 Sep 1803 James Nelson and wife Esther sold to Augustus Cannon 43 ½ a. {WILR:194}

John was father of ELIZABETH; MARTHA; JAMES, m. Esther (N); JOHN, BENJAMIN; SUSANNA, m. (N) Mezick; REBECCA, m. Thomas English; SARAH, m. James Beard.

Second Generation

2. JOHN NELSON, poss. son of John (1) Nelson, m. Eleanor (N).

The 1783 tax list shows John Nelson owned 28 1/2 a. of *Chelsey*. On 23 1796 Samuel Wilson and wife Leah Littleton Wilson sold to Eleanor Nelson wife of John Nelson for 5 shillings all rights to *Chelsey*. On 22 Sep 1800 John Nelson and wife Eleanor gave to son Samuel Nelson part of lot # 3, 2 3/4 a. 12 poles and on 4 Nov 1800 John Nelson and wife Eleanor gave to son Cyrus Nelson, 1 a. On 22 Sep 1800 John Nelson and wife Eleanor gave to son Francis balance of estate *Chelsey* balance with part of *Monmouth*. On the same day John Nelson and wife Eleanor gave to dau. Betty Nelson 1 a. and 23 poles. {WILR:68}

John and Eleanor were parents of SAMUEL; CYRUS; FRANCIS; BETTY.

3. BENJAMIN NELSON, son of John (1) Nelson.

On 9 May 1778 Lazarus Huffington sold to Benjamin Nelson 50 a. of *Huffingtons Adventure*. The 1783 tax list shows that Benjamin Nelson owned 100 a. and John Nelson owned 60 a. In 1784 John Nelson willed to son John Nelson part bought of Henry Gale, unnamed. On 28 Dec 1793 John Leatherbury Esq. Sherriff sold to John Nelson, 50 a. as Benjamin Nelson a petitioner in jail, sold by debts. {WILR:214}

4. SARAH NELSON, dau. of John (1) Nelson m. James Beard.

Sarah and James Beard were parents of JAMES BEARD, b. 14 March 1752; THOMAS BEARD, b. 6 Nov 1755. {SOSP}

THE WILLIAM NELSON FAMILY of Wicomico Hundred

1. WILLIAM NELSON, b. c1698, m. Ann (N).

The tax lists of SO Co., Wicomico Hundred, show William Nelson (Nielson, Nilson) as head of household, 1723, 1730-1740. Living in the same household were (William Pritchett (1735); Charles Stewart (1736); John Nelson (Neilson) (1723 and 1738-1740).

On 18 March 1745/6, William Nelson, aged 47, made a deposition. {SOJR:1743/1747:200}

The tax lists of SO Co., Wicomico Hundred, show William Nelson as head of household, 1744, 1748, 1750, 1753 (as Wilson Nelson), 1754, 1757, 1759.

Levi Hopkins, SO Co., d. by 30 June 1752 when the inventory of his estate was filed by David Hopkins and his wife Sarah Hopkins. Signed as next of kin: John Hopkins, Isaac Hopkins, Isaac Handy Secundus, William Nelson. {MINV 49:7}

William Nelson, SO Co., d. leaving a will dated 4 April 1762, proved 31 Aug 1762. To grand-son William Atkerson, 70 a. whereon I now live, being pt. of tract called *Noble Quarter*, which I bought of John Evans, dec'd. 25 a. more which I bought of Edward Willen, called *Edward's Lott*; 5 a. more which I bought of Edward Willen, called *Edward's Lott*; 5 a.. which I bought of John Evans, Jr., it being pt. of the afsd. tract called *Noble Quarter*; 25 a. more of which I took up, lying between John Evans and Robert Willins; 25 a. of marsh, which I bought of Thomas Dashiell; a slave and etc.; grand-son to inherit when he is 18; legacies at the decease of my wife. To son-in-law Isaac Atkerson, use of my land at *Muddy Hole*, where he now lives, to him and his wife during their lives; at their decease, land and marsh to grand-son Wm. Atkerson. To grand-son Joshua Atkerson, 5 pounds. To dau. Betty Atkerson, some money. To grand-dau. (unnamed), money to buy a gold ring. Wife Ann Nelson. Codicil: Shd. grand-son Wm. Atkerson, die before age 18, then his pt. to be divided between my dau. Bettye's children, and the rest of estate at their grandmother's (my wife's), and dau. Betty Atkerson's death. 24 May 1762. {MWB 12:146-7}

On 7 April 1767 the inventory of his estate was filed by Isaac Atkinson. Signed as next of kin: John Nelson, Ann Nelson. {MINV 91:156}

On 9 April 1767 distribution of his estate was made by Isaac Atkison, extx. Legatees: William Atkison (grandson), Joshua Atkison, Betty Atkison. Residue to widow (unnamed) during life. {BFD 5:30}

William was father of BETTY.

Second Generation

2. BETTY NELSON, dau. of William (1) and Ann Nelson, m. Isaac Atkinson.

They were parents of WILLIAM ATKINSON (eldest son), b. 23 Feb

1758; JOSHUA ATKINSON, b. June 1759; NANCY ATKINSON, b. 28 Sep 1760; BETTY ATKINSON, b. 2 July 1763; ISAAC ATKINSON; JAMES ATKINSON; GEORGE D. ATKINSON, b. 2 Oct 1776; JOHN ATKINSON. {ASOS:9; see also The JamEs Atkinson Family, vol. 9 of this series.}

THE WILLIAM NELSON FAMILY of Mattapony/Pocomoke Hundred

1. WILLIAM NELSON.

On 28 July 1680 Joshua Light and wife Martha sold to William Nelson 125 a. of *Castle Hill*. In 1728 William Nelson Sr. and wife Elizabeth gave to son William Nelson 125 a. of *Castle Hill* and 50 a. adj., *Castle Low*. On 6 Nov 1745 William Nelson, son of William, with wife Mary sold 33 a. to William Johnson. On 9 Nov 1759 Samuel Nelson sold to Phillip Guthrey 125 a. WOLR:98}

In 1688 William Nelson recorded his cattle mark in SO Co. {COES:38}

Elizabeth Bishop, SO Co., made her will on 21 May 1721, proved on 27 March 1722. Legatees: brother Hugh Nelson; sons William, James, John Bratten; husband George Bishop; father William Nelson; daughter Hannah; children Hannah, Samuel, William, James, John. {WOW:MH#3:216}

William was the father of: WILLIAM; HUGH; ELIZABETH.

Second Generation

2. WILLIAM NELSON, son of William (1) Nelson, m. Elizabeth (N).

On 28 July 1680 Joshua Light and wife Martha sold to William Nelson 125 a. of *Castle Hill*. In 1728 William Nelson Sr. and wife Elizabeth gave to son William Nelson 125 a. of *Castle Hill* and 50 a. adj., *Castle Low*. On 6 Nov 1745 William Nelson, son of William, with wife Mary sold 33 a. to William Johnson. On 9 Nov 1759 Samuel Nelson sold to Phillip Guthrey 125 a. {WOLR:98}

In 1701 William Nelson recorded his cattle mark in SO Co. {COES:41}

On the 1724 Tax List, William Nelson is cited as head of household in Mattapony Hundred, with William Nelson, Jr. {SOTL}

William Lilson (Nelson) was head of household in Mattapany Hundred, 1730-1740). Living in the same household were James Nealson (1731-1740); Robert Nealson (Nelson) (1737-1740); John Nealson (1738); John Bratton (1738); Thomas Newton (1738); Robert Scott (1739); Daniell Patrick (1740); Samll. Nealson (1740).

William was the father of WILLIAM who m. Mary (N).

William was prob. father of JAMES, b. c1715; ROBERT, b. c1721; SAMUEL, b. c1724.

3. HUGH NELSON, son of William (1) Nelson, b. c1680, m. 1st Elizabeth (N), m. 2nd Jane (N).

Hugh Stevenson, SO Co., d. by _____ 1717 when the inventory of his estate was filed by Elizabeth Stevenson. Signed as next of kin: Hugh Nelson, Samuel Bratton. {INAC 38A:143}

Nelsons Security was patented in 1728 by Hugh Nelson, a resurvey from *Partners Choice*, for 250 a. in now Coulburns District. On 20 July 1734 Hugh Nelson gave 93 a. to dau. Mary Gray and after her death to her son William Gray. On 16 Aug 1742 John Nelson, son of Hugh, sold to Abraham Outten 200 a., part now called *Outtens Security*. On 13 March 1746 Abraham Nelson and wife Rhoda sold 93 a. to Robert King the younger of part of *Outtens Security*, now called *Kings Addition.* On 3 March 1756 William Gray sold 91 a. to Peter Chaille. {WOLR:426}

On 8 Feb 1723 Hugh Nelson and wife Jane sold to Christopher Glass ½ of lots that John Murray conveyed to him. {WOLR:599}

The tax lists of SO Co. show Hugh Nelson as head of household, Pocomoke Hundred, 1730-1735. Living in the same household were Allen Grey (1730), Isaac Dieton (Diton) (1730-1731); slave Joe (1730-1734).

On 2 March 1719 there was a division of land (*Snow Hill Tract*) by John Murray, Elizabeth Murray, Elizabeth Henderson, Hugh Nelson and wife Elizabeth, Elizabeth Henderson formerly called Elizabeth Bishop widow of Henry Bishop. {WOLR:600}

Elizabeth Bishop, SO Co., made her will on 21 May 1721, proved on 27 March 1722. Legatees: brother Hugh Nelson; sons William, James, John Bratten; husband George Bishop; father William Nelson; daughter Hannah; children Hannah, Samuel, William, James, John. {WOW:MH#3:216}

John Broton, SO Co., d. by 19 June 1723 when the admin. account of his estate was submitted by Hugh Nelson (exec. of Elizabeth Bishop (extx. of deceased.)). MDAD 4:319}

On 19 June 1723 the admin. account of the estate of Elizabeth Bishop was submitted by Hugh Nelson, exec {MDAD 4:320}

On 1724 Tax List, Hugh Nelson is cited as head of household in Mattapony Hundred. {SOTL}

Hugh Nelson, age 50 on 9 Feb 1731/2 deposed regarding the bounds of *Conveniency* and *Exon*. {Miller:28}

Hugh Nelson, SO Co., made his will on 6 May 1735, proved on 18 June 1735. Legatees: William Porter received *Poplar Hill*; son John received plantation; daughter Mary Gray; James Martain; brother William; mother; children John, Margaret, Jane. Executor: brother William. {WOW:MH#3:329}

On 20 June 1735 the inventory of his estate was filed by William Nilson. Signed as next of kin: Allen Gray, Marget Wilson. {MINV 21:178}

On 8 May 1736 the admin. account of the estate of Hugh Nilson was submitted by William Nilson. Legatees: Mary Gray (daughter), Elizabeth Nilson, John Nilson (son), paid by his guardian James Martin. James Martin, accountant.

{MDAD 15:12}

On 5 April 1738 the admin. account of his estate was submitted by William Nilson (also William Nelson), exec {MDAD 16:120}

Hugh was father of MARY, m. Allen Gray, son of John Gray; ELIZABETH; JOHN; MARGARET; JANE. {See also Miles Gray Family, vol. 9 of this series.}

4. ELIZABETH NELSON, daughter of William (1) Nelson, m. 1st John Bratten, m. 2nd George Bishop.

John Broton, SO Co., d. by 19 June 1723 when the admin. account of his estate was submitted by Hugh Nelson (exec. of Elizabeth Bishop (extx. of deceased.). MDAD 4:319}

Elizabeth Bishop, SO Co., made her will on 21 May 1721, proved on 27 March 1722. Legatees: brother Hugh Nelson; sons William, James, John Bratten; husband George Bishop; father William Nelson; daughter Hannah; children Hannah, Samuel, William, James, John. {WOW:MH#3:216}

On 19 June 1723 the admin. account of her estate was submitted by Hugh Nelson, exec {MDAD 4:320}

Third Generation

5. WILLIAM NELSON, son of William (2) Nelson, m. Mary (N).

On 11 Jan 1736 Christopher Glass and wife Elizabeth and William Nelson and wife Mary sold 250 a. of *Exon* to John Murray. {WOLR:213}

The Hammer was patented on 6 Aug 1763 by William Nelson for 213 a., a resurvey of *Conveniency*. In 1794 *Addition to Hammer* was patented to Hugh Nelson for 236 a. On 25 Oct 1799 Hugh Nelson sold to William Nelson of Moses Nelson 61 ½ a. of *Addition*. On 2 Sep 1803 Hugh Nelson sold to Levi Sturgis, son of Richard Sturgis, 7 ½ a. On 15 June 1805 Hugh Nelson sold 14 a. to Moses Nelson. In 1806 Hugh Nelson willed land to sisters Elizabeth Nelson and Jane L. Sturgis. {WOLR:279}

William Nilson, WO Co., d. by 13 March 1765 when the inventory of his estate was filed by Hugh Nilson. {MINV 88:44} On 4 April 1767 a second inventory of his estate was filed by Hugh Nilson. {MINV 93:209}

On 30 Nov 1764 another inventory of the estate was filed by Hugh Nilson. Signed as next of kin: Moses Nilson, Jesse Nilson. {MINV 86:215}

The first admin. account was submitted on 22 June 1765 by Hugh Nilson. A second admin. account was submitted by Hugh Nilson on 17 April 1767. Distribution was made to (in equal amounts) to Moses Nilson, Jesse Nilson, Jonathon Nilson, Lesse Nilson (dau.), accountant, James (infant), Sarah (infant), Mary (infant). {MDAD 52:309, 58:49}

William was father of MOSES; JESSE; JONATHON; LESSE; HUGH; JAMES; SARAH, m. (N) Mills; MARY, m. (N) Hargis.

6. ROBERT NELSON, prob. son of William (2) Nelson, m. 29 Feb 1746 (OS), Elizabeth Milburn. {St. Martins Church, WO Co.}

On 7 March 1744 Patrick Guthrey and wife Angelica sold 100 a. of *Conveniency* to Robert Nelson. On 2 Aug 1749 Samuel Stevenson and Robert Nelson with wife Elizabeth Nelson settled lines of 14 a. On 27 March 1752 Robert Nelson and wife Elizabeth sold 100 a. to Samuel Stevenson. On 8 Aug 1766 Hugh Nelson, son of William Nelson sold to Hugh Nelson, son of Samuel Nelson, 100 a. {WOLR:137}

Hardship was patented n 5 March 1757 by Robert Nelson for 30 a. On 27 Sep 1783 Michael Needham, heir of Joseph Needham, sold to Caleb Wyatt, *Hardship*, patented to Robert Nelson for 30 a. On 2 Jan 1795 Levi Nelson sold to James Conner 8 1/4 a. {WOLR:286}

Wilderness Addition to Desart was patented in 1760 by Robert Nelson for 187 a. in what is now St. Martins District. On 11 April 1763 Robert Nelson and wife Elizabeth sold to Jacob Adams 57 1/2 a. with the tract *Desart*. On 12 Aug 1764 Robert Nelson and wife Elizabeth sold 61 a. to Joseph Needham. On 9 Aug 64 Robert Nelson sold 30 a. to Nathaniel Whaley. {WOLR:672}

Robert and Elizabeth were parents of ZEXURIAH, b. 29 May 17–; WILLIAM, b. 26 April 1752; THOMAS, b. 20 March 1754. {St. Martins Church, WO Co.}

7. SAMUEL NELSON, prob. son of William (2) Nelson.

Samuel Nilson, private; Robert Nilson, sergeant, and William Nilson, lieutenant, were serving in Capt. Adam Spence's militia company of WO Co. in 1748.

Brothers Help was patented in 1748 by Samuel Nelson for 75 a. The 1783 tax list shows Mary Nelson as owner of 75 a., Mattapany Hundred. {WOLR:78}

Samuel Nelson, SO Co., d. by 14 Feb 1755 when the admin. account of his estate was submitted by Henry Graham, exec. Representative: John Passomore. {MDAD 1:128}

Samuel was father of HUGH. {WOLR:137}

8. MARY NELSON, dau. of Hugh (3) Nelson, m. Allen Gray. {See The Miles Gray Family, vol. 9 of this series.}

They were parents of WILLIAM GRAY.

Fourth Generation

9. MOSES NILSON, son of William (5) Nelson, m. Mary (N).

On 8 Jan 1773 Littleton Dennis sold to Moses Nelson 40 a. of *Conveniency*. On 20 April 1787 Moses Nelson and wife Mary sold 16 a. to Joshua Guthrey. On 8 July 1795 Moses Nelson sold to James Stevenson 6 3/8 a.

On 28 Feb 1806 Josiah Nelson and wife Mary sold to Moses Nelson 48 a. of *Conveniency*. In 1811 Moses Nelson willed part of the tract to son William Nelson. {WOLR:138}

Samuel Stevenson, WO Co., d. by 29 Sep 1770 when the inventory of his estate was filed by James Stevenson. Signed as next of kin: Moses Nilson, Hugh Stevenson. {MINV 108:245}

On 3 Aug 1796 George Ross sold Lot 67 of Snow Hill Town to Josiah Nelson, son of Moses Nelson, and William Harper. On 3 Aug 1796 Josiah Nelson and wife Margaret Nelson sold to James Duer, merchant. {WOLR:595}

Moses was father of JOSIAH, m. Margaret (N); WILLIAM.

10. JESSE NILSON, son of William (5) Nelson.

Jesse Nilson, WO Co., made his will on 4 Jan 1785, proved on 25 April 1788. Legatees: nephew Levi Nilson; niece Margaret Nilson; brother Hugh Nilson; sister Sarah Mills; brother Jessee Nilson, sister Mary Hargis. {WOW:JW#13:191}

Unplaced

(N) NELSON m. Comfort Peale, dau. of Thomas and Ansle Peale, and had a daughter Usar Nelson.

Thomas Peale, WO Co., d. leaving a will dated 13 Feb 1742, 7 June 1744. To grandson Robertson Andras, 200 a. *Coventree*. To son Thomas, dwelling plantation and residue of real estate. To dau. Rachel Ryle, and grandson Thomas Holland, personalty. To daus. Rebecca Andras, Sarah Marshall, Mary Henderson, Tabitha Franklin, Bridget Holland, Rhoda Outten, Rachel Ryle, Abilah Newton, and Comfort Nelson, 1 s. To wife Ansle and son Thomas, execs., residue of estate, wife to have life int. in entire estate. {MWB 25:536}

Philip Quinton, WO Co., d. leaving a will dated 23 Feb 1750, proved 21 March 1750. To wife Ansle, plantation I now live on, and the 200 a. called *Carter's Lodge*, and slaves. To wife's grand-dau. Usar Nelson, 1 slave. To son Dixon Quinton, plantation I now live on, and all land that I own at decease of wife; certain slaves. To dau. Mary, slaves. To dau. Sarah Adams, slaves. To dau. Abigail Hall, slaves. Came Ansley Quinton, widow of Philip Quinton and relinquished all legacies to her made by the dec'd., and in lieu thereof, to have her 1/3 pt. of sd. estate. {MWB 27:536}

(N) was father of USAR.

(N) NELSON m. Mary Milbourne, dau. of Thomas Milbourne.

Thomas Milbourne, WO Co., d. leaving a will dated 10 March 1774, proved 9 June 1776. To son John Milbourne, brandy still, hand iron, pot rack

14

and a 15 pound bond he gave my daughter Grace Milbourne. To grandson Thomas Milbourne, stock. To children: the rest of moveable estate divided between Tabitha Deal, Saloma Milbourne, Mary Nelson and Elijah Milbourne. To wife Deborah Milbourne during widowhood all of aforesaid mentioned moveable estate and then to be divided as aforesaid. {MWB 41:79}

ELIZABETH NELSON.
Elizabeth Nelson signed as next of kin the inventories of Jane Elzey (1719) and Thomas Shiles (1721) as next-of-kin. {MINV 5:33; 7:14}

JAMES NELSON
The tax list of SO Co., 1735, shows James Nelson as head of household, Pocomoke Hundred.

JOHN NELSON
The tax lists of SO Co. show John Nelson living in the household of James Backer in 1735 and in the household of Capt. James Martin in 1740; both residences were in Pocomoke Hundred. {SOTL}

MATTHEWE NELSON deposed on 14 June 1679 that Wm. Cheeseman had given to William Prentice his cattle mark. {ARMD LIV:756}

WILLIAM NELSON of Yorktown, VA.
On 15 July 1755 John Dennis and wife Anne Maria Dennis sold (mortgage) to the Hon. William Nelson of York Town, VA, 50 a. of *Security*. On 6 Oct 1779 Thomas Nelson of VA, heir of William Nelson, sold to Susanna Dennis, widow of Littleton Dennis (mortgage). {WOLR:553}

WILLIAM NELSON m. Elizabeth (Betsey) King (b. c1762, d. 1810/1819, dau. of James King. {Wise:278}
William and Betsy were parents of WILLIAM, b. c1786; named in the will of his grandmother King, 1791; JESSE; b, c1788; named in the will of his grandmother King, 1791; MARY K[ING], b. c1790, d. 1836, m. 1st (lic. SO Co. 24 Oct 1812) Ephraim Nelson (d. c1820), m. 2nd Henry Crawford; SARAH, b. c1792; PRISCILLA, b. c1794, m. 12 Jan 1815, her first cousins, Henry R. K. Costin. {WISE:278}

THE JAMES NICHOLSON FAMILY (1)

1. JAMES NICHOLSON m. 1663, Mary Price. {IKL} Mary m. 2nd 4 Sep 1677 George Carter by Mr. Charles Ballard, J.P. A marriage bann was issued for

Thomas Davis, planter of Manokin and Mary Nicholson in 1676. {SOD O:7}
     James Nicollson of SO Co. established his head rights by 1675. {MPL FF:293, SR 8206}
     James Nicholson was in the Manokin section in 1663. {OSES:453}
     James Nicollson recorded his cattle mark in SO Co. on 9 July 1666.{ARMD LIV:748}
     On 7 Jan 1679 George Carter recorded the cattle mark of a heiffer which he gave to James Nicollson. {ARMD LIV:773}
     James Nicholson, SO Co., d. and was bur. at Manokin 13 Jan 1675. {IKL}
     The inventory of his estate was filed on 27 July 1677. {INAC 4:550}
     James was father of RICHARD, b. at Manokin 4 Dec 1664; JAMES, b. at Manokin 23 Jan 1665 [sic], CHARLES, b. 25 April 1667, ROGER, 12 May 1668 at Manokin; ELIZABETH, b. 25 April 1669 at Manokin; SARAH, b. 1 Oct 1671 at Manokin; RACHEL, b. 10 Oct 1672 at Manokin; SAMUEL, b. 28 June 1674 at Manokin. {IKL}

Second Generation
2. RICHARD NICHOLSON, son of James (1) Nicholson, m. 1st (N) and m. 2nd Isabella (N)[1].
     Charrety Nicholson m. 5 April 1719 William Weatherly {SOSP}
     The tax lists of SO Co. show Richard Nicholson as head of household in Wicomico Hundred in 1723 (as Richard Nicols, Sr.), 1724 (as Richard Nickols), 1727, 1730-1740 (except for 1739 when he was living in the household of Robert Meares). Living in the same household was Joseph Nicholson (1724, 1727, 1730-1731); Abel Samuels (1723, 1724, 1727, 1730-1731); William Weatherly (1735). {Miller; Russo}
     Richard Nicholson (Nighlison), planter, SO Co., d. leaving a will dated 31 Dec 1735, proved 21 Jan 1735. To son Joseph, lower part of two tracts, viz.: *Vulcan's Vineyard*, and *Nicholson's Lott*; should sd. son not sell sd. land and die without issue to pass to son James. To son James, exec, the middle part of afsd. tracts. To grandson Richard, the upper part of afsd. tracts, he dying without issue to pass to sons James and Joseph. To wife Isabella, personalty and 1/3 personal estate. To children of son Richard, 1 s. each. To five children, viz.: James, Joseph, Rachel Young, Charity Weatherly and Sarah residue of personalty. {MWB 7:180}
     Nicholsons Lott was patented on 23 March 1687 by Richard Nicholson for 100 a. that was part of *Vulcan Vinyard*. In 1735 Richard Nicholson willed

---

1. Isabella may be the widow of Richard Samuels(d. 1710) who mentions in his will wife Isabella and son Abell (d. 1710)), and the mother of Abel Samuels (cited on the tax lists).

part to son Joseph Nicholson and part to sons James Nicholson and grandson Richard Nicholson. {WILR:298}

On 16 Feb 1735 the inventory of his estate was filed by James Nicholson. Signed as next of kin: Charity Weatherle, Joseph Nicholson. {MINV 21:367} On 4 June 1736 accounts of his estate was filed by James Nicholson. Legatees: Isabell Nicholson (widow). {MDAD:15:21}

On 17 Oct 1736 Isabell Nicholson gave to Charity Weatherly, her dau. in law, furniture, a mare, household goods and other items; also her third part of the plantation which her husband Richard Nicholson, dec'd., left to her. {SOD EI:104}

Richard was father of RICHARD, predeceased his father; JOSEPH; JAMES; RACHEL, m. (N) Young; CHARITY, m. 5 April 1719 William Weatherly; SARAH.

3. JAMES NICHOLSON, son of James (1) Nicholson. {See The James Nicholson Family (2), below.{

Roger Nicholson, SO Co., d. leaving a will dated 9 June 1729, proved 24 Aug 1732. To son John, exec, dau. Jean Hopkins, dau. Sarah Passons, children of son Nehemiah, children of dau. Margrit White and children of son Roger, personalty, some of which descends as having belonged to John Bacon. Mentions: brother James. To 3 children, viz. son John and daus. Jean Hopkins and Sarah Passons, residue of estate equally. {MWB 6:245}

4. CHARLES NICHOLSON, son of James (1) Nicholson, m. 1st Sarah Kellam, probably m. 2nd Elizabeth Hammond, widow of John Hammond.

In 1707, Charles Nicholson patented *Greenland* for 280 a. {SORR:247}

In 1718, Charles Nicholson patented *Poplar Ridge* for 160 a. {SORR:319}

John Kellam, Sr., SO Co., d. leaving a will dated 30 Sep 1719, proved 15 March 1719-20. To son John, 600 a. dwelling plantation _____. bought of Joseph and James Gray. To grandson John (son of son William), 150 a., part of *Kellams Choice* (the e. part of sd. tract), provided sd. grandson, shall not possess any of afsd. tract of 500 a. bought of Joseph and James Gray. To dau. Mary, personalty. To 5 daus. Sarah Nicholson, Charity Johnson, Anne Coard, Eliza: Marron, Catherine Taylor, 5 s. each. To son John, exec, res. of estate, including 300 a., remaining part of *Kellams Choice*. Shd. son John die without issue, sd. land to grandson Joshua. {MWB 4:225} On 5 May 1720 the inventory of his estate was filed by John Kellam. Signed as next of kin: Sarah Nicholson, Elizabeth Murray, Mary Kellam. {MINV 4:68}

Charles Nicholson made a deposition in 1720 in which he mentioned his father Killum. {Maryland Deponents 2, citing SO Co. Land Commissions 1:81}

The 1725 tax list of SO Co, Pocomoke Hundred shows Charles

Nickelson as head of household, owning 1 Negro, age 16 or older.

Charles Nicholson, SO Co., d. leaving a will dated 13 Nov 1726, proved 16 Aug 1727. To son James, 100 a. surveyed by Southy Whittington, adj. *Wolf Pit Swamp*. To wife Elizabeth, dwelling. plantation during life, to revert to son Mathias; he dying without issue, to heir at law. To sons John and Joseph, *Popular Ridge*: should either die without issue, portion of dec'd. to survivor. Sons Mathias and Joseph to care of wife until 18 yrs. of age. To daus. Sarah (of age at 16) and Mary, personalty. Wife and son John, execs. Note: 16 Aug 1727. Elizabeth Nicholson assigns rights of administration to John Nicholson. {MWB 6:36} On 24 Nov 1727 the inventory of his estate was filed by John Nicholson. Signed as next of kin: James Nichols, Joseph Nicholson. {MINV 12:508}

Charles Nicholson prob. m. Elizabeth Hammond, widow of John Hammond. John Hammond m. Elizabeth (N) and had issue: Edward, John. Elizabeth m. 1ˢᵗ Woney McClemmy (d. 1721), also (N) Purnell and last (N) Nicholson. {ASOS}

Elizabeth Nicholson, SO Co., d. leaving a will dated 12 Sep 1730, proved 20 March 1732-3. To son Owney Maclamy, son Mathew Purnal, dau. Ellener Jones, grand-dau. Sarah Jones at day of marriage, and son Edward Hammon, personalty some of which described as being at George Jones. To son John Hammond and dau. Mary Roberson, personalty. To 3 daus. Martha, Elener and Margaritt, personalty, they to give what they think fit to son John's wife. Shd. son Owney die without issue, personalty bequeathed to him to grand-dau. Betty Maclamy. Son William Maclamy, exec {MWB 7:4} On 16 Aug 1733 the inventory of her estate was filed by Woney Maccleme. Signed as next of kin: William McClemmy, William Hasick, Sr. {MINV 17:519} On 5 March 1734 the admin. account of her estate was submitted by Woney McClemy. Mentions: children: William McClemey, Marcy McClemey, Martha McClemey, Ellenor McClemey, Woney McClemey. {MDAD 12:767}

Charles was father of JAMES; MATHIAS; JOHN; JOSEPH; SARAH; MARY; poss. SAMUEL.

5. ROGER NICHOLSON, son of James (1) Nicholson, m. Elizabeth Covington, daughter of Nehemiah Covington.

Julin Mezick, planter, SO Co., d. leaving a will dated 6 Jan 1715-6, proved 28 June 1718. To eldest son Nehemiah, personalty. To 3 sons, John, Jacob and Joshua, 1 s. each. To 6 children of wife, viz.: Joseph, Isaac, Benjamin, Julin, Sarah and Mary Mezick, residue of personalty. Wife Priscilla extx. Should she desire to dispose of any of her children, son Isaac to be placed with brother Roger Nicholson. Boys, viz.: Joseph, Isaac, Benj. and Julin, to remain with wife until 21 yrs. of age if she remain a widow; to be of age at 18, otherwise. {MWB 14:618}

In 1718, Roger Nicholson and James Nicholson made a deposition.

18

{SOJR:1717-1718:119}

The 1724 tax list of Nanticoke Hundred shows Roger Nicholson Sr., Roger Nicholson Jr., Nehemiah Loadar, James Green. {SOTL}

The tax lists of SO Co. show Roger Nicholson as head of household in Nanticoke Hundred, 1725, 1730-1731. Living in the same household were James Green (1725), William Gurlling (N) (1725).

Roger Nicholson, SO Co., d. leaving a will dated 9 June 1729, proved 24 Aug 1732. To son John, exec, dau. Jean Hopkins, dau. Sarah Passons, children of son Nehemiah, children of dau. Margrit White and children of son Roger, personalty, some of which descends as having belonged to John Bacon. Mentions: bro. James. To 3 children, viz. Son John and daus. Jean Hopkins and Sarah Passons, residue of estate equally. {MWB 6:245} On 28 Aug 1732 the inventory of his estate was filed by Elizabeth Nicholson. Signed as next of kin: Francis Persons, John Hopkins. {MINV 20:181}

Roger was father of JOHN; JEAN, m. John Hopkins; SARAH, m. Francis Persons; NEHEMIAH; MARGRIT, m. (N) White; ROGER predeceased his father.

6. SAMUEL NICHOLSON, b. 28 June 1674, son of James (1) Nicholson. There is no evidence that Samuel lived to adulthood.

Third Generation

7. RICHARD NICHOLSON, son of Richard (2) Nicholson, m. Elizabeth (N).

The tax lists for SO Co. cite Richard Nicols, Jr. as head of household in Wicomico Hundred in 1723, 1724 (as Richard Nicols, Jr.). Also in his household is James Nicols (1723).

Richard Nicholson (Nickallson), Jr. d. leaving a will dated 10 June 1726, proved 7 Nov 1726. To son Richard, daus. Mary Filles and Bette, personalty. To wife (unnamed), personalty. To children afsd., residue of estate equally. {MWB 6:8} On 12 November 1726, an inventory of his estate was filed by Eliza. Nicholson. {MINV:11:761} On 21 Jan 1726 when the admin. account of the estate of Richard Nickeldson, SO Co., was submitted by Elizabeth Nickeldson, extx. {MDAD 8:165}

Richard was father of RICHARD; MARY FILLES; BETTE.

8. JOSEPH NICHOLSON, son of Richard (2) Nicholson, prob. d. before 1748 in that James mentions "where bro. Joseph did live."

In the tax lists of Wicomico Hundred, SO Co., Joseph Nicholson is shown living in the household of Richard Nicholson in 1724, 1730 and 1731 and head of his own household, 1733-1740. {Miller; Russo}

In 1745, Joseph Nicholson paid tax on *Vulcan's Vineyard* and *Nicholson's Lott*. {Provincial Land Office, Debt Books, SO Co.}

9. JAMES NICHOLSON, son of Richard (2) Nicholson, m. 1 st Phillis Hardy on 10 Jan 1723 in Stepney Parish, m. 2nd Mary, widow of George Lank/Langeake/ Lanquake (d. c1740). {ESVR}

The tax lists for SO Co. cite Richard Nicols, Jr. as head of household in Wicomico Hundred in 1723. Also in his household was James Nicols. {SOTL}

The tax lists of SO Co. show James Nicholson as head of household 1730-1740, 1744, and 1748 in Wicomico Hundred. Living in the household of James Nicholson in 1744 was Joshua Nicholson. Living in the household of James Nicholson in 1748 was James Nicholson, Jr. {SOTL}

In 1731, he is cited as a creditor. {MINV:16:277}

In 1733, Charles Nicholson [sic] is paying tax on *Nicholson's Lott.* {Provincial Land Office, Debt Books, SO Co.}

In 1735, James and Joseph Nicholson signed as next of kin to in the inventory of Thomas Humphries. {MINV:20:494}

James Nicholson was serving in the militia under Capt. Day Scott, 1748. {COES:80}

Jeams Nicholson, SO Co., d. leaving a will dated 19 Feb 1748-9, proved 22 March 1748. To wife Mary Nicholson, my estate, and at her decease, to son Joshua Nicholson, my plantation whereon I live and 110 a. To son Charles Nicholson, the plantation whereon my bro. Joseph did live, and if Charles should die without hrs., then John Nicholson shall be his heir. To young son Joseph Nicholson, my store house, and 50 a., and that tract belonging to Charles Handy, and part of land to be divided between John Nicholson and Jeams Nicholson. After decease of wife, I give to son-in-law, George Lank, cattle. To son-in-law Francis Lank, cattle. Remainder of estate to be equally divided between Isable Heatch, James Nicholson, John Nicholson, Mary Nicholson, Rachel Nicholson and Phillis Nicholson. Wife Mary, extx. Signed: Nehemiah King, Deputy Com. of Somerset Co. {MWB 10:1}

James and Phillis were the parents of: ISBELL, b. 22 Oct 1724, m. (N) Heatch; JOSHUA, b. 3 Aug 1726; JAMES, b. 15 Apr 1728; JOHN, b. 22 Jul 1731; CHARLES, b. 26 Jan 1732; RACHEL, b. 25 Jul 1736; MARY, b. 15 Feb 1738. The records of Stepney Parish show the births of these children as children of James and Phillis <u>Nichols</u> and the marriage of James <u>Nichols</u> to Phillis Hardy. Nevertheless the pattern of names and dates clearly indicates that this is the family of James <u>Nicholson.</u>

James was the father of: PHILLIS; JOSEPH.

10. CHARRETY NICHOLSON, dau. of Richard (2) Nicholson, m. 5 April 1719, William Weatherly (d. 1735), son of James Weatherly. {See The Weatherly Family, vol. 8 of this series.}

They were parents of RICHARD WEATHERLY, b. 20 March 1720; JOSEPH WEATHERLY, b. 4 Jan 1722/21; CHARRETY WEATHERLY, b. 8

July 1724; PATIENCE WEATHERLY, b. 12 Aug 1726; MARY
WEATHERLY, b. 12 Aug 1726; ELIJAH WEATHERLY, b. 23 Feb 1731/2;
WILLIAM WEATHERLY, b. 31 Aug 1734.

11. JAMES NICHOLSON, son of Charles (4) Nicholson, m. Susanna Truitt,
dau. of George and Eleanor (Meredith) Truitt.
    On 10 Jan 1721, James Nicholson patented *Kingsdale* for 100 a. On 8
March 1748, James Nicholson and his wife Susanna sold 50 a. to Joshua
Atkinson. On 2 June 1752, William Adkins and his wife Mary sold 50 a. to
Joshua White. {WOLR:347}
    In 1733, 1734, and 1735, James Nicholson paid tax on *Kingsdale*.
{Provincial Land Office, Debt Books, Somerset Co.}
    Charles Nicholson, SO Co., d. leaving a will dated 13 Nov 1726,
proved 16 Aug 1727. To son James, 100 a. surveyed by Southy Whittington, adj.
Wolf Pit Swamp. To wife Elizabeth, dwelling. plantation during life, to revert to
son Mathias; he dying without issue, to heir at law. To sons John and Joseph,
Popular Ridge: should either die without issue, portion of dec'd. to survivor.
Sons Mathias and Joseph to care of wife until 18 yrs. of age. To daus. Sarah (of
age at 16) and Mary, personalty. Wife and son John, execs. Note: 16 Aug 1727.
Elizabeth Nicholson assigned rights of administration to John Nicholson. {MWB
6:36}
    The tax lists of SO Co. show him as head of household in Pocomoke
Hundred in 1730, in 1731 as James Nichols, in 1733 as James Nichols (with
slave Hannah), in 1734 as James Nicholds (with slave Hannah), and in 1735 as
James Nickols (with slave Hannah), in 1736 as James Nichols (with slave
Hannah), in 1738 as James Nicholls (with slave Hannah), in 1739 as James
Nichols (with slave Hannah), and in 1740 as James Nicholas (with slave
Hannah).
    Eleanor Truett relict of George Truitt, SO Co., d. leaving a will dated
20 April 1732, proved 21 June 1732. To sons George and Samuel, dau. Susanna
Nicholson. Grand-dau. Sarah Nicholson (dau. of Susanna afsd.), dau. Sarah
Mumford and dau. Tabitha Parker, personalty. Sons George and Samuel, execs.
{MWB 6:226} On 20 Aug 1734 the admin. account of the estate of Ellinor Truitt,
SO Co., was submitted by George Truitt, Samuel Truitt (resigned to his brother),
admins. Mentions: (children): George Truitt, Samuel Truitt, Mary Shohannis,
Tabitha Parker, Sarah Mumford, Elizabeth Davis, Susanna Nicholson. {MDAD
12:376. See also The George Truitt Family, vol. 10 of this series.}
    James Nicholas [Nicholson], planter, WO Co., d. leaving a will dated
12 Jan 1752, proved 28 Feb 1752. To dau. Mary Atkins, dwelling house and
plantation whereon I live, 50 a., slaves. To grand-dau. Dennis Nicholas, after
decease of wife, 1 slave. Son-in-law William Atkins, exec. March 27, 1752,
came Susannah Nicholson, widow of James Nicholson, and quits claim her Right

of Dower on thirds, and chose to stand to the deceased's will. {MWB 10:245} On 24 Dec _____ (1754?) the inventory of his estate was filed by William Atkins. Signed as next of kin: Mathias Nicholas, Sarah White. {MINV 60:89} The admin. account was submitted on 14 Nov 1755 by William Atkinson (also Atkins). Legatees: dau. Mary who received Negro Jeany, wife of accountant. Distribution of residue to Dennis (granddau. age 9 who received Negro Hannah. {MDAD 38:277}

James was father of MARY, m. William Atkinson [Atkins], son of Joshua and Elizabeth (Scott) Atkinson {ASOS:8}; SARAH {mentioned in the will of her grandmother}.

12. MATHIAS NICHOLSON, son of Charles (4) Nicholson.

The tax lists of SO Co. show him in the household of Mathew Hopkins in Mattapany Hundred in 1730 as Matthias Nickals, in 1733 as Marthias Nickorles, and in 1734 as Mathias Nickols. The tax lists of SO Co. show him as head of household in Pocomoke Hundred in 1735 as Mathias Nickols, in 1736 as Mathias Nichols, in 1738 as Mathias Nicholls, in 1739 as Mathias Nichols, and in 1740 as Mathias Nicholas.

In 1735, Mathias Nicholson paid tax on *Greenland.* {Provincial Land Office, Debt Books, SO Co.}

Mathias Nicholson served as private in the Worcester Militia, Capt. John Martin's Company, 1780/1781. {RPWS:214}

On 4 February 1741, Mathias Nicholson sold to David Murray pt. of *Greenland* 141 a. {SORR:247}

David Murray, WO Co., died leaving a will dated 15 Sep 1745, and proved on 25 June 1746. Mentions: land he bought of Matthias Nicholson in Indian Town is to be sold. {MCW:24:409}

On 2 Sep 1752, Mathias Nicholson received payment from estate of Capt. Abraham Outten. {MDAD:33:120}

On 7 Nov 1754, Mathias Nicholson made payment to estate of Thomas Fletcher. {MDAD:36:512}

In 1756, Mathias Nicholson, WO Co., was a surety for the estate of John Townsend. {WED}

In 1762, Mathias Nicholson, WO Co., was a surety for the estate of James Castillo. {WED}

In 1756, 1757, 1759, 1760, 1762, 1771, Mathias Nicholson paid tax on *Greenland.* {Provincial Land Office, Debt Books, WO Co.}

13. JOSEPH NICHOLSON, son of Charles (4) Nicholson, m. Mary Cottingham, dau. of Jonathan Cottingham. Mary later m. Josiah Robins.

In 1726 Charles Nicholson willed to sons John Nicholson and Joseph Nicholson, 160 a. of the tract *Poplar Ridge.*

22

The tax lists of SO Co. show him in the household of John Nicholson in Pocomoke Hundred in 1730 as Joseph Nicholson, in 1731 in household of John Nichols as Joseph Nichols. The tax lists of SO Co. show him as head of household in Pocomoke Hundred in 1733 as Joseph Nichols, in 1734 as Joseph Nicholds, in 1735 as Joseph Nickols, in 1736 as Joseph Nichols, in 1738 as Joseph Nicholls (with Mathias Taylor), in 1739 as Joseph Nichols, and in 1740 as Joseph Nicholas.

In 1734 and 1735, as Joseph Nichols, he paid tax on *Poplar Ridge*. {Provincial Land Office: Debt Books: Somerset Co.}

In 1756, 1757, 1759, 1760, 1762, 1768, 1769, 1771, 1773, and 1774, he paid tax on *Poplar Ridge*. {Provincial Land Office: Debt Books: Worcester Co.} [He is cited in the index, for some of the entries, as Joseph Nicholson, Sr.]

In 1743, Joseph Nicholson is a surety on estate of Absolom Beseck. {WED}

Jonathan Cottingham, planter, WO Co., d. leaving a will dated 12 March 1662, proved 4 June 1762. To son William Cottingham, Mannor plantation whereon I now live and all land adjoining thereto on the north side of the Cool Spring Branch; desire wife Margaret remain on the same during widowhood; at her decease; to son William; if he shd. die without issue, then to son Thomas; cattle. To son Daniel, all land whereof he is now possessed in the southernmost side of the Cool Spring Branch, and the branch to be divided between the land of son William and son Daniel, which sd. land I give to son Daniel; cattle. To son Charles, the plantation in Kent Co., on Delaware, whereon son Jonathan now lives, together with my moveable that he had from me. To son Jonathan, all moveable he is now possessed of in Kent on Delaware, as his full share of estate. To dau. Mary Nicholson, 1 s. sterl. To wife Margaret, use of all personal estate; at decease of wife, 1/6 part to dau. Sarah Laws; remaining part to be equally divided between sons Elisha and Thomas Cottingham. Wife Margaret and son Wm. Exs. 12 March 1762: Codicil: He willed son Wm. and his wife Margarett, his stock of hoggs, which he failed to dispose of in his former will. {MWB 12:153}

Joseph Nickelson (also Joseph Nicholson), WO Co., d. by 28 Jan 1771 when an admin bond was filed on his estate by Mary Nicholson. Sureties: Thomas Cottingham, William Cottingham. {WED} [Another place cites the sureties as: William Cottingham and John Nicholson.] On 9 Feb 1771 the inventory of his estate was filed by Mary Nicholson. Signed as next of kin: Thomas Cottingham, William Cottingham. {MINV 108:155} On 10 July 1772 the admin. account was submitted by Mary Nicholson. {MDAD 67:350} On 10 July 1772 distribution of his estate was made by Mrs. Nicholson administrator, to representatives unknown to this office. {BFD 6:156} A second inventory was filed on 5 Dec 1774 by Mary, wife of Josiah Robins. Mentions: Linsey Joshua Townsend, John Nicholson, John Snead, Jr., Samuel Linsey. {MINV 117:314}

[Additional admin accounts were filed in 178x; however, the Worcester Co. Libers for this time period are no longer extant.]

Joseph is the father of: JOHN; BETTY, m. William Dickerson; JOSEPH; ISAAC; SAMUEL; MATHIAS; POLLY, m. John Green; EBBY, m. Joshua Townsend; poss. BETTY, m. William Caudrey.

14. JOHN NICHOLSON, son of Charles (4) Nicholson, m. Tabitha Paker, dau. of John Parker.

In 1726 Charles Nicholson willed to sons John Nicholson and Joseph Nicholson, 160 a. of the tract *Poplar Ridge*. On 14 Feb 1734 John Nicholson and wife Tabitha sold 80 a. to Joseph Davis. {WOLR:489}

The tax lists of SO Co. show him as head of household in Pocomoke Hundred in 1730 (with Joseph Nicholson), in 1731 as John Nichols (with Joseph Nichols), in 1733 as John Nichols, in 1734 as John Nicholds, and in 1735 as John Nickols.

On 1 June 1756 John Campbell conveyed to Parker Rogers, planter, land that John Parker by his last will left to his dau. Tabitha Nicholson, 175 a., being part of two tracts on the seaboard side on the head of the sound in or near *Rumley Marsh*; one called *Dumfries* and one called *Brotherhood* adj. John Nicholson and his wife Tabitha sold to William Smith all their right to said land. Now John Campbell sells to Rogers. {WOD D:52}

John and Tabitha are probably the parents of: JOHN; CHARLES; SAMUEL.

15. SAMUEL NICHOLSON, poss. son of Charles (4) Nicholson.

The tax lists of SO Co. show him living in the household of Charles Nicholson in Pocomoke Hundred in 1723 and 1724. [He does not appear in the records after 1724.]

16. JOHN NICHOLSON, son of Roger (5) Nicholson, m. Elizabeth Collier, daughter of Robert Collier (d. 1757). She, as Elizabeth Nichols widow, m. 2 nd John Hopkins on 20 August 1736. {ESVR}

John Nicholson recorded his cattle mark in SO Co. on 28 Oct 1719. {ARMD LIV:787}

Roger Nicholson, SO Co., d. by 14 Jan 1726 when the inventory of his estate was filed by Robert Collier. Signed as next of kin: John Hopkins, John Nicholson. {MINV 11:860}

The tax lists of SO Co. show John Nicholson as head of household in Nanticoke Hundred, 1724, 1730-1731. Living in the household was William Sherdan (Churrodon), 1724-1725; slaves Cook and Vinus (1731).

The tax lists of SO Co. show Betty or Elizabeth Nicholson as head of household, 1733-1736, in Nanticoke Hundred. Living in the household were

Robert Walter (1736) and a slave named Cook (1733-1734). {Russo}

John Nicholson, SO Co., d. by 24 Nov 1734 when the inventory of his estate was filed by Elizabeth Nicholson. Signed as next of kin: John Hopkins, Francis Persons. {MINV 20:184} On 3 Dec 1734 an additional inventory of his estate was filed by Elizabeth Nicholson. Signed as next of kin: John Hopkins, Frances Parsons. {MINV 18:75} The admin. account of John Nicholson, SO Co., was submitted on 23 July 1737 by Elizabeth Hopkins (alias Elizabeth Nicholson), admx. Payments included widow (unnamed, 1/3). {MDAD 14:344}

17. NEHEMIAH NICHOLSON, son of Roger (5) Nicholson, m. Mary Betts, widow of James Collier and dau. of George Betts. Mary m. 3rd Thomas Benson. {See The Robert Collier Family, vol. 8 of this series.}

On 5 July 1711, Nehemiah Nicholson received payment from the estate of William Winright. {INAC:32B:269}

The tax lists of SO Co. show Nehemiah Nicholson as head of household in Nanticoke Hundred in 1724. Living in the household were Betts Collier (1724), James McPherson (1724). Nehemiah was living in Nanticoke Hundred in 1727.

John Irving (also John Erwing), SO Co., d. by 5 May 1720 when the inventory of his estate was filed by Francis Erwing. Signed as next of kin: Nehemiah Nicholson, Marry Nicholson. {MINV 4:73}

George Betts (Beetts) Collier, joyner, SO Co., d. leaving a will dated 18 Feb 1733/4, proved 15 Nov 1735. To brother John Nicholson, *Good Success* at Nanticoke Point. To sisters Priscilla and Bridget and brothers Levin, John Crockett and Joseph Nicholson, personalty. Thomas Benson, exec {MWB 7:154}

On 19 Aug 1761 Mary Benston, spinster, for the docking and taking of all entail and remainder in tail and for the settling and for the sum of 5 shillings sells to George Dashiell, son of James Dashiell a parcel of land being part of a tract called *West's Neck* (?) on s. side of Nanticoke River and s. side of Quantico Creek which was conveyed by Dorothy Span (?) to John Baker, father of the grantor and containing 300 a. and that George should become a tenant of the freehold and stand sezied until a good recover with Double — made over and that George Dashiell should stand before the Provincial court and suffer the said William Hayward to go forth and prosecute against Dashiell. In case of recovery between Benston, Dashiell and Hayward, Benston to have the land for her natural life and then to Nancy Nichols, dau. of John Nicholson and Mary Nicholson, dau. of Joseph Nicholson; the land to be divided agreeable to a division made between John and Joseph Nicholson. {SOD C:97}

Mary Benson, SO Co. d. leaving a will dated 7 Dec 1761, proved 4 Oct 1764. To granddau. Nancy Nicholson, part of land where son John Nicholson formerly did live, as far as there was a division to her, the sd. Nancy. To granddau. Mary Nicholson, land live upon, being the south side of land called

Worlow Neck, and left to granddau. Mary, to be in care and possession of sons-in-law Douty and Robert Colliers, until sd. granddau. Mary is of age 14. To dau. Prescilla Collier, one slave. To dau.-in-law Mary Nicholson, one slave; at her death, sd. slave to be divided between grandchildren: Nancy, Mary and Priscilla Nicholson. To granddau. Mary Nicholson, dau. of Joseph Nicholson, one slave. To granddau. Peggy Nicholson, one slave. To granddau. Mary Bournes, one slave. Grandchildren Milla and Mary Jackson. Granddau. Alice Jackson's hrs., Anne Crockett, Levin Crockett, Elizabeth Crockett, John Crockett and Bridgett Crockett, one slave. To granddau. Bridgett Collier, one slave boy. To granddau. Elizabeth Collier, one slave. To loving grandson Betts Collier, and granddau. Luenar (or Luesar) Collier, one slave. Leah Collier and Dousty Collier, Jr. To grandson Nehemiah Crockett, and granddau. Mary Nicholson, dau of John Nicholson, one slave. To granddau. Priscilla Nicholson, dau. of John Nicholson, one slave. To granddau. Bridgett Crockett, one slave. To granddau. Nancy Nicholson. {MWB 13:49} The admin. account of the estate of Mary Benson was submitted by Robert Collier on 23 Sep 1767. Payments were made to Dowty Collier (1/4 - his portion), Leah Collier (her portion), Nancy Nicholson (her portion), Bridget Crocket (her portion). Payments to (their portions in equal amounts): John Crockett, Levin Crockett, Elizabeth Crockett, Ann Crockett. Legatees: Priscilla Collier, wife of Dowty Collier; Nehemiah Crockett; Mary Bounds (received Negro Rosse and Negro David), wife of William Bounds. {MDAD 57:83}

Nehemiah and Mary were parents of LEVIN; JOHN; JOSEPH; MARY, m. John Crocket (d. 1748); PRISCILLA, m. Doubty Collier; BRIDGET, m. Robert Collier.

18. ROGER NICHOLSON, son of Roger (5) Nicholson, m. Jane Collier, daughter of Robert Collier (d. 1756). She married second Thomas Dashiell. {Dashiell Book, p. 303}

Julin Mezick, planter, SO Co., d. leaving a will dated 6 Jan 1715-6, proved 28 June 1718. To eldest son Nehemiah, personalty. To 3 sons, John, Jacob and Joshua, 1 s. each. To 6 children of wife, viz.: Joseph, Isaac, Benjamin, Julin, Sarah and Mary Mezick, residue of personalty. Wife Priscilla extx. Should she desire to dispose of any of her children, son Isaac to be placed with brother Roger Nicholson. Boys, viz.: Joseph, Isaac, Benj. and Julin, to remain with wife until 21 yrs. of age if she remain a widow; to be of age at 18, otherwise. {MWB 14:618}

Roger Nicholson Junr. was fined for 3 oaths as recorded in the SO Co. levy list of 1724. {COES:60}

On 6 Oct 1726, Richard Ellingsworth, Jr. & his wife Elizabeth sold to Roger Nicholson pt. *Ellingsworth's Hope* for 100 a. {WILR:127}

On 11 Jan 1726, Robert Collier posted an administration bond on the estate of Roger Nicholson. {TP:27:379} On 14 Jan 1726 Robert Collier filed the inventory of his estate. Signed as next of kin: John Hopkins, John Nicholson. {MINV 11:860} On 18 June 1729 the admin. account of his estate was submitted Robert Collier. {MDAD 9:397}

In 1733, Roger Nicholson paid tax on *Ilingsworth Hope*. {Provincial Land Office, Debt Books, SO Co.}

In 1734, 1735, and 1745, Jane Nicholson paid tax on *Ilingsworth Hope*. {Provincial Land Office, Debt Books, SO Co.}

Jeane Dashiell, SO Co., d. leaving a will dated 24 Dec 1765, proved 8 Aug 1766. Legatees: granddau Jean Collier daughter of Nicholas Evans Collier; grandson Roger Nicholas son of Roger; brother Doubty Collier; grandchildren Betty, Henry, John, Thomas, and Isaac children of my son Roger Nichols; grandchildren George, Nicholas, and Priscilla children of Nicholas Evans Collier. Executor: Nicholas Evans Collier. {MWB:34:234}

Roger and Jane were the parents of: ROGER.

Fourth Generation

19. RICHARD NICHOLSON, son of Richard (7) Nicholson.

Nicholsons Lott was patented on 23 March 1687 by Richard Nicholson for 100 a. that was part of *Vulcans Vineyard*. In 1735 Richard Nicholson willed to the upper part to grandson Richard. On 19 Nov 1747 Richard Nicholson sold 150 a. to James Nicholson. On 10 March 1752 Richard Nicholson of WO Co., grandson of Richard sold to George Parris of SO Co. 100 a. of *Nicholsons Lott & Vulcans Vineyard*. {WILR:298}

The tax lists for SO Co. cite him as head of household in Wicomico Hundred in 1744 and 1750 (as Richard Nicholls).

In 1733, 1735, and 1745, he paid tax on *Nicholson's Lott* and *Vulcan's Vineyard*. {Provincial Land Office: Debt Books: SO Co.}

20. JOSHUA NICHOLSON, b. 3 Aug 1726, son of James (9) Nicholson.

The tax lists for SO Co. show Joshua Nicholson living in the household of James Nicholson in Wicomico Hundred in 1744.

21. JAMES NICHOLSON, b. 15 Apr 1728, son of James (9) Nicholson.

The tax lists for SO Co. show James Nicholson, Jr. living in the household of James Nicholson in Wicomico Hundred in 1744. In 1750, James Nicholson is shown as head of household, with Thomas Lank living in same household. In 1754, James Nicholson is shown as head of household, with William Maddox and Daniel Maddox living in the same household. In 1759, James Nichlos is shown as head of household.

22. CHARLES NICHOLSON, b. 26 Jan 1732, son of James (9) Nicholson.

In 1748, 1764, 1768, 1769, and 1774, Charles Nicholson paid tax on *Nicholson's Lott.* {Provincial Land Office, Debt Books, SO Co.}

The tax lists for SO Co. cite him as head of household in Wicomico Hundred in 1753 and 1759. In his household is John Nicholls (1753), and Edward Ellis (1759).

23. JOHN NICHOLSON, son of James (9) Nicholson.

The tax lists for SO Co. cite him in Wicomico Hundred in the household of John Hitch, Jr. (1750), in household of Charles Nicholls (1753), in household of Stephen Lank (1757, as John Nicholas).

24. JOHN NICHOLSON, son of Joseph (13) Nicholson.

On the 1783 Assessment List for WO Co., John Nicholson paid tax on pt. *Poplar Ridge* 80 a., pt. *Peter's Chance* 20 a., land bought of Mr. Johnson 55 a. in Acquango Hundred.

On 1786, Levi Outten and Barkley White sold to John Nicholson pt. *Poplar Ridge* 10 a. for 5 shillings. On same day, Levi Outten and John Nicholson sold to Barkley White pt. *Poplar Ridge* 10 a. On 14 March 1794, Isaac Nicholson, Joshua Townsend son of Barkley Townsend and his wife Ebby Townsend, William Caudrey and his wife Betty Caudrey sold to Joseph Nicholson, their rights from John Nicholson. On 5 Oct 1795, John Green sold to Joseph Nicholson part that John Nicholson had. On 4 Aug 1802 Polly Green and John Green (SU) sold to Levi Outten 1/8th part of rights from John Nicholson. {WOLR:490}

On 25 Oct 1788 Samuel Nicholson, William Dickerson and wife Betty Dickerson, WO Co., conveyed to Joseph Nicholson of SO Co., for 5 shillings, all the lands that Samuel Nicholson, William Dickerson and wife Betty have a right to that formerly belonged to our bro. John Nicholson, dec'd. land adj. Levi. Outten's land in the Indian Town, 180 a. {WOW M:525}

25. BETTY NICHOLSON, dau. of Joseph (13) Nicholson, m. William Dickerson, son of John and (N) (Riggin) Dickerson. {ASOS:96. See also The Edward Dickerson Family, vol. 9 of this series.}

On 25 Oct 1788 Samuel Nicholson, William Dickerson and wife Betty Dickerson, WO Co., conveyed to Joseph Nicholson of SO Co., for 5 shillings, all the lands that Samuel Nicholson, William Dickerson and wife Betty have a right to that formerly belonged to our bro. John Nicholson, dec'd. Land adj. Levi. Outten's land in the Indian Town, 180 a. {WOW M:525}

Samuel Nicholson d. leaving a will dated 27 Dec 1800, proved 16 Jan 1801. Mentioned niece Nancy Nicholson, dau. of bro. Isaac; children of bro. in law William Dickerson, namely, John, Betsy, Peter, Elisha, James. Friend Joseph Houston Sr. to be guardian to niece Nancy Nicholson, dau. of bro. Isaac until she

28

is of age. Exec. Capt. William Quinton, William Selby. Witnessed by William Selby, William Quinton. {WOW JBR1:189}

Betty and William Dickerson are the parents of: JOHN DICKERSON; BETSY DICKERSON; PETER DICKERSON; ELISHA DICKERSON; JAMES DICKERSON.

26. JOSEPH NICHOLSON, son of Joseph (13) Nicholson, m. Betty (N).

Joseph Nicholson served as private in the Worcester Militia, Capt. John Martin's Company, 1780/1781. {RPWS:214}

On 1786, Levi Outten and Barkley White sold to John Nicholson pt. *Poplar Ridge* 10 a. for 5 shillings. On same day, Levi Outten and John Nicholson sold to Barkley White pt. *Poplar Ridge* 10 a. On 14 March 1794, Isaac Nicholson, Joshua Townsend son of Barkley Townsend and his wife Ebby Townsend, William Caudrey and his wife Betty Caudrey sold to Joseph Nicholson, their rights from John Nicholson. On 5 Oct 1795, John Green sold to Joseph Nicholson part that John Nicholson had. On 4 Aug 1802 Polly Green and John Green (SU) sold to Levi Outten 1/8th part of rights from John Nicholson. {WOLR:490}

On 25 Oct 1788 Samuel Nicholson, William Dickerson and wife Betty Dickerson, WO Co., conveyed to Joseph Nicholson of SO Co., for 5 shillings, all the lands that Samuel Nicholson, William Dickerson and wife Betty have a right to that formerly belonged to our bro. John Nicholson, dec'd. Land adj. Levi. Outten's land in the Indian Town, 180 a. {WOW M:525}

On 14 Nov 1788, Joseph Nicholson filed an admin bond on estate of John Nicholson. Cited as next of kin: Isaac Nicholson. {Worcester Co. Bonds: JW#12}

Joseph Nicholson d. leaving a will dated 19 Dec 1797, proved 12 Jan 1798. To son Joseph dwelling plantation. To eldest son John Nicholson the above if son Joseph dies without issue. To wife Betty Nicholson bed and furniture, cow and calf. To dau. Mary Nicholson, furniture. To dau. Phillis, furniture. Exec. Bro. Isaac Nicholson, he to be guardian of son Joseph. Witnessed by John Neill, John Taylor, Joshua Atkinson. {WOW JW18 Part II:326}

On 12 Dec 1798, Isaac Nicholson filed an admin bond on estate of Joseph Nicholson. {WED}

On 27 Dec 1799 Samuel Nicholson, as administrator de bonis non, filed an admin bond on estate of Joseph Nicholson. {WED}

On 11 Feb 1800, Joseph Nicholson selected as his guardian Samuel Nicholson. {WOOC:JBR:170} On the same day, Joseph Nicholson (son of Joseph, Samuel Nicholson as guardian) was bound out to Josiah Nelson. {WOOC:JBR:228}

On 14 Feb 1809, William Quinton administrator de bonis non of Isaac Nicholson executor of Joseph Nicholson petitioned to retain a portion of the estate, as guardian to Thomas Nicholson (son of Joseph). {WOOC:MH#7:464}

Joseph was father of JOHN; JOSEPH; MARY; PHILLIS; THOMAS.

27. ISAAC NICHOLSON, b.c. 1762, son of Joseph (13) Nicholson, m. (N).

Isaac Nicholson served as private, Worcester Militia, Wicomico Battn., Capt. Benjamin Dennis' Company, 15 July 1780. {RPWS:214}

At Dec Court 1782, Isaac Nichols (son of Joseph), age 20, was bound out to James LeCount. {WOOC:JW#19:34}

On 14 Nov 1788, Joseph Nicholson filed an admin bond on estate of John Nicholson. Cited as next of kin: Isaac Nicholson. {Worcester Co. Bonds: JW#12}

At June Court 1789, Joshua Atkinson (son of Angelo Atkinson), over age 14, selected Isaac Nicholson as his guardian. {WOOC:JW#21:15}

On 12 Dec 1798, Isaac Nicholson filed an admin bond on estate of Joseph Nicholson. {WED}

On 9 Sept 1799, an arbitration was established in suit of Isaac Nicholson vs. Comfort Nicholson. {WOOC:JBR:127}

Isaac Nicholson, WO Co., d. p. 27 Dec 1799 when Samuel Nicholson filed an admin bond on his estate. {WED}

Isaac Nicholson, WO Co., d. p. 27 Dec 1799 when Samuel Nicholson filed an admin bond on his estate. {WED}

On 27 Dec 1799 Samuel Nicholson, as administrator de bonis non, filed an admin bond on estate of Joseph Nicholson. {WED}

Samuel Nicholson d. leaving a will dated 27 Dec 1800, proved 16 Jan 1801. Mentioned niece Nancy Nicholson, dau. of bro. Isaac; children of bro. in law William Dickerson, namely, John, Betsy, Peter, Elisha, James. Friend Joseph Houston Sr. to be guardian to niece Nancy Nicholson, dau. of bro. Isaac until she is of age. Exec. Capt. William Quinton, William Selby. Witnessed by William Selby, William Quinton. {WOW JBR1:189}

On 11 Sept 1801, William Selby and William Quinton, as administrators de bonis non, filed an admin bond on estate of Isaac Nicholson. {WED}

Isaac was father of NANCY.

28. SAMUEL NICHOLSON, son of Joseph (13) Nicholson.

On 25 Oct 1788 Samuel Nicholson, William Dickerson and wife Betty Dickerson, WO Co., conveyed to Joseph Nicholson of SO Co., for 5 shillings, all the lands that Samuel Nicholson, William Dickerson and wife Betty have a right to that formerly belonged to our bro. John Nicholson, dec'd. Land adj. Levi. Outten's land in the Indian Town, 180 a. {WOW M:525}

Isaac Nicholson, WO Co., d. p. 27 Dec 1799 when Samuel Nicholson filed an admin bond on his estate. {WED}

On 27 Dec 1799 Samuel Nicholson, as administrator de bonis non, filed an admin bond on estate of Joseph Nicholson. {WED}

Samuel Nicholson d. leaving a will dated 27 Dec 1800, proved 16 Jan 1801. Mentioned niece Nancy Nicholson, dau. of bro. Isaac; children of bro. in

30

law William Dickerson, namely, John, Betsy, Peter, Elisha, James. Friend Joseph Houston Sr. to be guardian to niece Nancy Nicholson, dau. of bro. Isaac until she is of age. Exec. Capt. William Quinton, William Selby. Witnessed by William Selby, William Quinton. {WOW JBR1:189}

On 16 Jan 1801, William Selby and William Quinton filed an admin bond on estate of Samuel Nicholson. {WED}

29. MATHIAS NICHOLSON, b. p. 1769, son of Joseph (13) Nicholson.

At Dec Court 1783, Mathias Nicholson (son of Joseph), over age 14, chose Samuel Nicholson as his guardian. {WOOC:JW-19:86, 103}

On 29 April 1791 Matthias Nicholson sold to James Ducator Negro woman Marear and Negro boy Jacob - already at present in South Carolina. {WOD O:90}

On 7 June 1792 Matthias Nicholson and John Townsend were bound to the state of Maryland for £40 to keep WO Co. From any costs and charges that may arise by reason of Scarborough Bennett bearing a bastard child, she the said Bennett swearing that the said Matthias Nicholson was the father. {WOD O:522}

30. JOHN NICHOLSON, prob. son of John (14) Nicholson.

On 8 Nov 1780, John Nicolson (SU) conveyed to Jacob Rogers (SU) pt. of *Dumfrieze* and pt. of *Brotherhood*. {SUDELR:M:358}

31. CHARLES NICHOLSON, prob. son of John (14) Nicholson, m. Mary Dulaney, dau. of John Patrick Dulaney. Mary later m. (N) Handy.

Woodcrafts Purchase was patented in 1737 to William Woodcraft for 150 a. In 1738 he sold the tract to John Patrick Dulaney. On 26 Oct 1762 Nathaniel Wyatt and wife Sarah, Elizabeth Dulaney and Comfort Dulaney sold 114 a. to Charles Nicholson, that John Patrick Dulaney d. with and descended to five daus., Elizabeth Dulaney, Sarah Dulaney (now Sarah Wyatt), Comfort Dulaney, Mary Dulaney and Diligence Dulaney. On 8 Sep 1767 Charles Nicholson resurveyed it to 147 a. On 22 Oct 1774 Mary Handy sold 58 ½ a. to Parker Nicholson. On 31 Oct 1785 John Nicholson, son of Charles, of Sussex Co., DE, sold to Dr. John Hayward and Tabitha Bayley Hayward of WO Co., 50 a. {WOLR:681}

In 1768, 1769, 1771, 1773, 1774, Charles Nicholson paid tax on *Hopewell* and/or *Woodcroft's Purchase*. {Provincial Land Office, Debt Books, WO Co.}

Charles Nicholson, WO Co., d. leaving a will dated 6 May 1774, proved 6 June 1774. To wife Mary, extx., land *Woodcraft's Purchase*, 40 a. of *Hopewell*: wife mill during widowhood. Son Parker Nicholson, to pay my 2 sons John and Charles Nicholson, 10 pounds each, when he takes possession of my lands. Mary Nicholson, widow of Charles Nicholson, quits claim and elects her third of estate according to law. {MWB 16:32} On 15 June 1774 the inventory of the estate of Charles Nicholson was filed by Mary Nicholson. Signed as next of kin: John Parker, George Parker. {MINV 118:73}

Parker Nicholson served as private in Capt. David Hall's Company, Continental; he enlisted 17 Jan 1776; mustered in barracks at Lewistown on 11 April 1776. {RPD:202}

Charles was father of PARKER; JOHN; CHARLES.

32. SAMUEL NICHOLSON, prob. son of John (14) Nicholson, m. Tabitha (N).

Samuel Nicholson, WO Co., d. by 25 May 1771 when the inventory of his estate was filed by Tabitha Nicholson. Signed as next of kin: Charles Nicholson, Jacob Rogers. {MINV 111:22} On 13 Aug 1773 the admin. account was submitted by Tabitha Nicholson. {MDAD 68:132}

33. JOSEPH NICHOLSON, son of Nehemiah (17) and Mary Nicholson, m. Sarah, dau. of George Dashiel. Sarah m. 2nd Levin Walter. {MDAD:63:161}

The tax lists of SO Co. show Joseph Nicholson living in the household of Mary Benston, Nanticoke Hundred, 1744, 1748, and 1750. Joseph Nickelson is cited as head of household in Nanticoke in 1753, 1754, 1757, and 1759.

Levin Nicholson, SO Co., d. by 30 May 1745 when the inventory of his estate was filed by Elizabeth Nicholson. Signed as next of kin: John Nicholson, Joseph Nicholson. {MINV 31:224}

Joseph Nicholson, SO Co., d. by Feb 1762 when the inventory of his estate was filed by Sarah Nicholson. Signed as next of kin: Dowty Collier, Priscilla Collier. {MINV 77:298} On 14 Sep 1763 the admin. account was submitted by Sarah Nicholson. Distribution to accountant (1/3) and Mary Nicholson and Peggy Nicholson. {MDAD 49:565} On 14 Sep 1763 distribution of his estate was made by Sarah Nicholson administrator, to (equally): Mary Nicholson, Peggy Nicholson. {BFD 4:66}

George Dashiel, Senr., SO Co., d. leaving a will dated 3 Feb 1768, proved 18 March 1768. Wife: Rebecca. Children: Sarah Walter. Mentioned: Rebecca and Nancy Mackmurray; Jesse and George Dashiel; Isaac Hopkins. Granddaus.: Mary and Peggy Nicholson, children of Joseph Nicholson. Mentioned: Land deeded to me by Matthew Cannon. Tracts: *Smitty's Invention*, *George's Meadow*, *Bedford*, on rivers Wiccomoco and Nanticoke. Rebecca Dashiel, extx. {MWB 14:29}

Joseph was father of MARY; PEGGY.

34. JOHN NICHOLSON, son of Nehemiah (17) and Mary Nicholson, prob. m. Mary Dashiell, dau. of Christopher Dashiell. {Dashiell Book}

The tax lists of SO Co. show John Nicholson living in the household of Mary Benston, Nanticoke Hundred, 1740. In 1744, 1748, 1753, 1754, and 1757, John Nicholson is cited as head of household in Nanticoke Hundred, with 3 slaves. In 1759, Mary Nicholson is cited as head of household in Nanticoke Hundred.

In 1733, 1745, 1748, 1755, 1761, 1764, 1768, 1769, and 1774, John Nicholson paid tax on *Dudley, Collier's Good Success*, and *Betty's Priviledge*. {Provincial Land Office, Debt Books, SO Co.}

Levin Nicholson, SO Co., d. by 30 May 1745 when the inventory of his estate was filed by Elizabeth Nicholson. Signed as next of kin: John Nicholson, Joseph Nicholson. {MINV 31:224}

On 15 Aug 1748 John Nicholson and wife Mary of SO Co. and William Owens and wife Elizabeth of WO Co. sold to Joseph Bounds 137 a. that became by will of James Dashiell the right of Christopher Dashiell who d. before he conveyed to Mary Dashiell and Elizabeth Dashiell his heirs (adj. John Bonds' plantation in Quantico).

John Nicholson, SO Co., d. by 14 Nov 1759 when the inventory of his estate was filed. {MINV 68:265} On 20 Aug 1760 the inventory of his estate was filed by Mary Nicholson. Signed as next of kin: Winder Dashiell, George Dashill. {MINV 70:278}

John and Mary were the parents of: ANN, m. William Graham; PRISCILLA, m. Phillip Covington; MARY, m. Phillip Jones.

35. LEVIN NICHOLSON, son of Nehemiah (17) and Mary Nicholson, m. Elizabeth (N).

The tax lists of SO Co. show Levin Nicholson living in the household of George Irvin in 1737 and in the household of Mary Benston, Nanticoke Hundred, 1739-1740. John Nickelson was living in the same household in 1740.

In 1745, Levin Nicholson paid tax on *Down's Choice* and *Bett's Priviledge*. {Provincial Land Office, Debt Books, SO Co.}

Levin Nicholson, SO Co., d. by 30 May 1745 when the inventory of his estate was filed by Elizabeth Nicholson. Signed as next of kin: John Nicholson, Joseph Nicholson. {MINV 31:224}

36. ROGER NICHOLSON, son of Roger (18) Nicholson, m. Mary Dashiell, dau. of Henry and Jeane Dashiell. Mary later m. Aaron Mezick.

The tax lists of SO Co. show Roger Nicholson living in the household of Jane Nicholson in 1744. The tax lists of SO Co. show Roger Nicholson as head of household in Nanticoke Hundred in 1748, 1750, 1753, 1754, 1757, and 1759.

In 1748, 1758, 1759, 1761, 1764, 1768, 1769, and 1774, Roger Nicholson paid tax on *Ilingsworth Hope*. {Provincial Land Office, Debt Books, SO Co.} [The entries for 1764, 1768, 1769, and 1774 are most probably for the heirs of Roger Nicholson. He is also paying tax on *Cooper's Choice* and *Benjamin's Good Success*; however, it is unclear how he acquired this land.]

Thomas Dashiel, SO Co., d. leaving a will dated 1756, proved 17 Feb 1756. Children: Henry, Thomas, Levin, Betty West, Irene Gillis, Ann Handy, Sarah Irving, Charles. Grandchildren: Thomas, son of Henry, Thomas, son of George, Ann Colburn, Priscilla Willen, Mary Handy, dau. of John Handy, Josiah Dashiel, son of Thomas, Betty Handy, wife of Isaac Handy, Betty Smith, Mary Nicholson, Sarah Henry, dau. of Isaac Handy, Priscilla Jones, dau. of Levin, Sarah Dashiel, dau. of Charles, Ann Irving, dau. of George Irving. To son Levin part of lot sold to Samuel Worthington, purchased of Peter Bodey, 100 a., Creek Tipqueen and Teashin River; Lot in Whitehaven Town on Wiccomoco; tracts: *Becknam*, 150 a., *Shilles Folley*, 350 a., *Somerset*, whereon Munny Church now stands. Levin Dashiel, exec {MWB 11:120-1}

Henry Dashiell, SO Co., d. leaving a will dated 7 Sep 1755, proved 20 Jan 1756. Wife: Jane/Jean. Children: Thomas, Henry, Mary, Elinor, Arthur, Leah. Exec: Thomas Dashiell. On 26 Feb 1756 the inventory of his estate was filed by Thomas Dashiell. Signed as next of kin: Henry Dashiell, Mary Nicholson. {MINV 60:635} On 29 Oct 1757, admin accounts were filed on his estate by Thomas Dashiell. Legatees: accountant, Jane Dashiell (widow), Henry Dashiell, Mary Dashiell wife of Roger Nicholson, Eleanor Dashiell wife of John Lagdell, Leah Dashiell paid to her guardian John Lagdell, Arthur Dashiell retained by accountant. {MDAD:41:265}

Roger Nicholson, SO Co., d. by 10 March 1763 when the inventory of his estate was filed by Mary Nicholson. Signed as next of kin: Douty Collier, George Collier. {MINV 81:69} On 27 Nov 1767 an admin. account was submitted by the widow Mary, now wife of Aaron Mezick. {MDAD 58:14} On 7 Nov 1765 [sic] distribution of his estate was made by Mary Messick, widow of Aaron Messick, to widow (unnamed, 1/3). Residue to children (unknown, equally). {BFD 6:137}

Jeane Dashiell, SO Co., d. leaving a will dated 24 Dec 1765, proved 8 Aug 1766. Legatees: granddau Jean Collier daughter of Nicholas Evans Collier; grandson Roger Nicholas son of Roger; brother Doubty Collier; grandchildren Betty, Henry, John, Thomas, and Isaac children of my son Roger Nichols; grandchildren George, Nicholas, and Priscilla children of Nicholas Evans Collier. Executor: Nicholas Evans Collier. {MWB:34:234}

On 1783 Assessment for SO Co., Mary Messick paid tax on pt. *Ellensworth's Hope.*

Roger and Mary are the parents of: ROGER; BETTY; HENRY; JOHN; THOMAS; ISAAC.

Fifth Generation

37. HENRY NICHOLSON, prob. son of Roger (36) Nicholson, m. Elizabeth (N).

On 2 July 1775 William Ellingsworth sold to Henry Nicholson

34

Cooper's Choice 21 a. on s. side of Nanticoke River, e. side of Wetpquin Creek. On 2 July 1796 Henry Nicholson and wife Elizabeth sold to Levin Willis 20 a. {WILR:85}

On the 1783 Assessment for SO Co., Henry Nichols paid tax on *Benjamin's Good Success, Cooper's Choice, Ellensworth's Hope,* and (unnamed).

38. ISAAC NICHOLSON, prob. son of Roger (36) Nicholson, m. Peggy Dashiell (b. 18 Oct 1763 in Stepney Parish), dau. of Mitchell and Margaret[2] Dashiell.

Mitchell Dashiell Sr. d. leaving a will dated 3 Feb 1789, proved 1789. Mentioned sons Thomas Dashiell, grandson Nicholson Collier, dau. Peggy Nicholson, wife of Isaac Nicholson to whom he left all lands that were left to Thomas provided that part over the branch and the branch to be a division to the gate and from the gate out to a plant bed I had last year and thence till it intersects *Mount Epharim*; dau. Ann Collier, wife of Evans Collier, dau. Priscilla Dashiell, dau. Betty Collier, granddau. Amelia Dashiell, and others. {SOW EB17:65}

Jane Collier d. leaving a will dated 10 July 1795, proved 30 Nov 1795. Mentioned mother Betty Collier; Amelia Moor; Mary Nicholson, dau. of Isaac Nicholson to whom she left Negro boy Joseph after mother's decease; Peggy Nicholson, dau. of Isaac; Henry Nicholson, son of Isaac Nicholson; Cheney Collier, son of Nancy Collier. {SOW EB17:40}

Isaac was father of MARY; PEGGY; HENRY.

THE JAMES NICHOLSON FAMILY (2)

1. JAMES NICHOLSON[3], m. 1st (N), m. 2nd Susanna Hoffington/Huffington. Susanna was the widow of James Tulley (d. 1744). She m. 3rd James Hardy.

On 29 July 1715, James Nicholls received payment from the estate of Col. George Gale. {INAC:36B:237}

In 1718, Roger Nicholson and James Nicholson took a deposition. {SOJR:1717-1718:119}

---

2. Margaret was the dau. of Robert Collier.

3. James Nicholson is probably the son of James Nicholson (son of James (1)) above. So far, no data has been found to confirm or deny this. James may also be the son of Elizabeth the second wife of Robert Twilley (d. 1721). Elizabeth Twilley is cited on the 1724 Tax List as head of household in Nanticoke Hundred with Robert Twilley. She also is cited as head of household on 1730 and 1731. Also in her household is Robert Twilley (1730) and George Twilley (1730, 1731).

The tax lists of SO Co. show James Nicholson as head of household, 1723, 1727, and 1730-1740, in Nanticoke Hundred. In 1724, he was living in the household of Thomas Dashiell, Jr.; also in the household is Richard Nicholson and Philip Currey. In 1725 he was living in the household of Elizabeth Twilley. Robert Twilly appears in household of Elizabeth Twilley at the same time and in the household of James Nicholson in 1723 and 1736. Richard Nicholson also appears in the household of Elizabeth Twilley in 1730. Living in the household of James Nicholson in 1740 was slave Tom.

John Hoffington, Sr., Stepney Parish, SO Co., d. leaving a will dated 17 Feb 1748-9, proved 22 March 1742. To dau.-in-law Patience Records, my slaves, during her life, and after her decease, to her son William Ponson (or Wm. Ponson Records). To son-in-law Leavin Ponson, 1 slave. To grand-son James Hofington, 1 slave. To Ann and Mary Cooper, slaves. To dau.-in-law Luraina Ponson, 1 slave; I leave her as her grandmother brought to me with a silk rug, and etc. To son John Hofington, my now dwelling plantation with lands belonging thereto; if sd. John Hofington pays to my grand-son James Hoffington and Littleton Hoffington, 50 pounds to each of them, when they are of age 21; if the sd. John Hoffington don't pay the sd. sum, the division between James and Littleton is this beginning at a marked walnut tree standing at the plat landing with a line drawn north 23 degrees westerly 90 poles, thence north 50 degrees, and etc. To friend David Cordery, 100 a., part of tract called *lll Neighborhood*. To dau. Elizabeth Acworth, 1 slave. To dau. Susannah Nicholson, 1 slave. To grand-daus. Mary and Ann Hoffington, 1 slave. To son John Hoffington, 1 slave. To grand-son Duke (or Luke) Hoffington, 1 slave. To son John Hoffington, my clothing, to be divided in 4 pts., 1 to son Jonathan Hoffington's children, and his children and their estates in care of son John Hoffington, until they are of age. Son John, exec To friend Robert Brown, my right to 200 a. land called *Which You Please*. {MWB 10:2}

The tract *Late at Night* was patented in 1734 by James Nicholson for 50 a. On 15 Aug 1775 Roger Nicholson sold 50 a. to Arthur Dashiell. {WILR:241}

In 1734, 1735, and 1745, James Nicholson paid tax on *Late at Night*. {Provincial Land Office, Debt Books, SO Co.}

In 1745, 1748, 1755, 1759, and 1761, (heirs of) James Nicholson paid tax on *Late at Night*. {Provincial Land Office, Debt Books, SO Co.}

James Nickelson, SO Co., d. by 17 June 1749 when the inventory of his estate was filed by Susannah Nickelson (alias Susannah Hardy). Signed as next of kin: Richard Nickelson. {MINV 41:410} On 6 Aug 1751 the admin. account of his estate was submitted by Susanna Hardy, wife of James Hardy. Residue to (orphans): Mary Nicholson, Roger Nicholson, Esther Nicholson, Jonathon Nicholson, Houfington Nicholson. {MDAD 30:250}

Susanna Hardy, SO Co., d. by 7 April 1762 when the inventory of her estate was filed by William Tulley and Joshua Moor. Signed as kin: James Hitch,

36

Thomas Magee. {MINV:77:303} On 16 March 1764, admin accounts on her estate were filed by William Tully and Joshua Moor. Payments to representatives (their portions, in equal amounts): Stephen Stevens, Thomas Magee, Josiah Ricards, James Hitch, John Langford, each of the accountants, Huffing. Nicholson. {MDAD:51:45}

James was father of MARY, m. George Wilson; ROGER; ESTHER; JONATHAN.

James and Susanna were the parents of: HOUFINGTON.

2. RICHARD NICHOLSON, prob. brother of James (1) Nicholson.

The tax lists of SO Co. show Richard Nicholson in the household of James Nicholson in 1723 (with Robert Twilley). In 1724, he is cited in the household of Thomas Dashiell, Jr. He is cited as head of household, Nanticoke Hundred, 1727, 1730-1740. Living in the household were: Joseph Nicholson (1727, 1730, 1731), Abel Samuels (1727, 1730, 1731), George Twilley (1733-1734); slave Biner (1739), slave Sevina (1740).

In 1745, 1748, and 1755, he paid tax on *Acworth's Folly* (115 a.), *Snakey Island* (26 a.), *The Addition* (128 a.), and *Agnew & Largee* (200 a.).[4] {Provincial Land Office: Debt Books: SO Co.}

James Nickelson, SO Co., d. by 17 June 1749 when the inventory of his estate was filed by Susannah Nickelson (alias Susannah Hardy). Signed as next of kin: Richard Nickelson. {MINV 41:410}

The inventory of the estate of Richard Nicholson, SO Co., was filed on 9 June 1752 by Robert Twilley, Joseph Weatherly. Signed as next of kin: George Twilley, Marion Twilley. {MINV 49:1} On 22 Nov 1753 the admin. account of his estate was submitted by Robert Twilley and Joseph Weatherly, admins. Payments to: William Tulley, Patience wife of Joseph Weatherly, Joseph Weatherly for Thomas Acworth & Elijah Weatherly. Distribution to: Eunice Nicholls. {MDAD:36:43, 304}

Second Generation

3. ROGER NICHOLSON, son of James (1) Nicholson.

Roger Nicholson, age 36, deposed on 6 Oct 1761 regarding the bounds of the tract *Beckman*. {Miller:28}

In 1764, 1768, 1769, and 1774, Roger Nicholson paid tax on *Late at Night* and *Chance*. {Provincial Land Office, Debt Books, SO Co.}

On 29 Oct 1762 Matthew Parremore sold 100 a. of *Chance* to Roger

---

4. There is no indication as to how he acquired this land. Per 1744 Rent Rolls, *Acworth's Folly* and *Snakey Island* were owned by members of the Weatherly family. Also per 1744 Rent Rolls, *Agnew and Largee* were owned by Richard Nicholson and William Giles, Jr., as heirs of Capt. John Gale.

Nicholson of SO Co. The 1783 tax list shows Roger Nicholson owning 100 a. of *Chance*. In 1790 Roger Nicholson willed to dau. Sarah Nicholson 100 a. On 12 April 1802 James H. West and wife Sarah, John Harris Sr., William Harris and wife Alse of Solomon Harris sold to George Twilley that Roger Nicholson gave to dau. Sarah Nicholson who m. James H. West, 100 a. {WILR:61}

Roger Nicholson served as private in the Somerset Militia, Salisbury Battn., Capt. William Turpin's Rewastico Company, 1778/1781. {RPWS:214}

Roger Nicholson, SO Co., d. leaving a will dated 22 Sep 1790, proved 18 Oct 1790. To dau. Sarah Nicholson, part of a tract called *Chance*, 100 a., remainder of estate. Plantation to be rented yearly and stock to be sold and the money arising from this to be given her when she comes of age. To sister Mary Wilson the care and management of Sarah until she comes of age. To bro. Huffington Nicholson care of Sarah should Mary die. Bro. in law George Wilson, exec. Witnessed by Arthur Dashiell, Sr., Henry Dashiell, Levin Dashiell. {SOW EB17:119}

Roger was father of SARAH, m. James H. West.

4. HUFFINGTON NICHOLSON, son of James (1) Nicholson.

Huffington Nicholson is shown on the 1785 tax list of Little Creek Hundred, Sussex Co., DE. {Scharf:1318}

THE WILLIAM NICHOLSON FAMILY

1. WILLIAM NICHOLSON m. Arcadia (N).

In 1757 William Ewell and his wife Leah sold a parcel of land in Accomack Co., VA, to William Nicholson. He d. intestate leaving a widow Arcadia, and 24 years later, William Ewell confirmed the title to John Nicholson, son of William. John and his wife Elizabeth sold it to George Layfield in 1791. {Whitelaw:1248}

William Nicholson d. by 7 Oct 1760 when admin. of his estate was granted to Arcadia Nicholson. Covington Corbin, security. {ACW:171}

William was father of JOHN.

Second Generation

2. JOHN NICHOLSON, son of William (1) Nicholson, m. Elizabeth Whittington, dau. of Southy Whittington.

Southy Whittington, Accomack Co.,VA, d. leaving a will dated 3 Aug 1789, proved 27 Feb 1790. Mentioned dau. Elizabeth Nicholson to whom he left a Negro Moll with reversion to her two eldest daus. Ann and Arcadia Nicholson. {ACW:387}

On 20 March 1790 John Nicholson conveyed to John Watson all that part of a tract called *Woods Beaver Dam Enlarged*, 50 a. Elizabeth Nicholson, wife of John, relinquished her dower right. {WOD N:181}

On 14 March 1791 John Laws of SO Co. sold to John Nicholson of Accomac Co., VA, a part in WO Co. called *Woods Bever Dam Enlarged* which is the land purchased by Laws from George Whittington and John Nicholson containing 147 a. {WOD O:82}

John and Elizabeth were parents of ARCADIA; ANN.

(N) NICHOLSON FAMILY

1. (N) NICHOLSON[5] m. (N) Dashiell, dau. of George Dashiell and had children: GEORGE, WILLIAM; MARGARET.

George Dashiell, SO Co., d. leaving a will dated 24 Sep 1733, proved 10 Jan 1733-4. To wife Priscilla, 1/3 of plantation and personal estate. To Mitchel, son of Thomas Dashiell, deceased, part of *Recovery* and plantation, *Improvement* on Quantico Creek where Joseph Dashiell now lives. To son Robert, residue of *Recovery* and plantation, *Improvement*, sd. son dying without issue, *Improvement* and the sd. part of *Recovery* to be right of Mitchell Dashiell, and that part of *Recovery* formerly laid out for son Benjamin where Isaac Cadrew now lives, to be right of son William; and personalty. To 2 sons Mitchell and William, Priscilla, lying at Roastica, Mitchell to have lower and William the upper part, to be divided at discretion of kinsman James and George Dashiell; and personalty. Marsh called *Venture Privilege* and Nanticoke River in common amongst sons and grandson Mitchell, not to be sold or divided. To dau. Peggie, granddau. Priscilla, 3 grandchildren, George, William and Margaret Nicholson, personalty. Son Robert, exec, and with dau. Peggie residuary legatee. Overseers: James and George Dashiell. {MWB 7:65} On 17 Jan 1733, admin accounts were filed on his estate. Legatees: wife of George Dashiell, Jr., Margaret Nicholson paid to her guardian George Dashiell, Jr., William Dashiell, Priscilla Dashiell (widow), Mitchell Dashiell, George Dashiell paid to his guardian Mitchell Dashiell, Robert Dashiell (accountant), William Nicholson paid to his guardian Robert Dashiell. {MDAD:15:272}

Second Generation

2. GEORGE NICHOLSON, son of (N) (1) Nicholson.

The tax lists of SO Co. cite him in Nanticoke Hundred in the household

---

5. He is most probably a brother of James Nicholson (d. 1749) and Richard Nicholson (d. 1752) of Nanticoke Hundred, of the James Nicholson (2) Family. This Nicholson would have died prior to 1723 Tax List.

of Mitchell Dashiell in 1736, 1737 (as George Nickolds), and 1738. He is cited in Nanticoke Hundred in the household of John McCuddy in 1739 (as George Nickolds) and 1740 (as George Nickolds).

In 1735, George Nichols paid tax on *Choice* 200 a. {Provincial Land Office, Debt Books, SO Co.}

George Nicholson disappears from the records after 1740.

3. WILLIAM NICHOLSON, son of (N) (1) Nicholson.

William Nicholson is cited in the admin accounts of George Dashiell in 1733. He disappears from the records after that.

Unplaced

(N) NICHOLSON m. Violet Blades, dau. of Benjamin Henderson Blades.

Benjamin Henderson Blades d. leaving a will dated 27 April 1778, proved 5 May 1778. Mentioned wife Comfort, sons Benston, Jesse and Jehu Blades; daus. Bridget Carter, Barsheba White, Violet Nicholson, Grace Houston Blades. {SOW EB1:69} See also will of Comfort Blades. {SOW EB1:130}

(N) NICHOLSON m. Elizabeth Wellet, dau. of Ambrose Wellet. Elizabeth prob. m. 2nd James Linzey.

Ambrose Wellet, WO Co., d. leaving a will dated 1 Feb 1758, proved 1 March 1758. Children: Thomas, William, John, Elizabeth Nicholson, Ann Holland, Jane Bradshaw, Ruth Wettel and Mary Wettel (may be Willet or Wellet). Mentioned: Tobias Rogers. Tract: *Paramour's Double Purchase.* Thomas Wellet, exec {MWB 30:458}

Ambrous Nicholson, WO Co., d. by 2 July 1773 when an admin bond on his estate was filed by James & Betty Linzey. {WED} On 10 Aug 1773 the inventory of his estate was filed by James Linzey. Signed as next of kin: Thomas Willett, Ruth Slovium. {MINV 117:429} On 31 March 1775 the admin. account was submitted by James Linzey. {MDAD 72:104}

LEAH NICHOLSON m. 13 March 1773 William Cottingham, son of John of WO Co. by Rev. John Rosse. {SOCO}

40

40

PARTHENA NICHOLSON[6]

John Hopkins, Sr., SO Co., d. leaving a will dated 5 Feb 1752, proved 17 July 1752. To son Isaac Hopkins, plantation or part of *Cannon's Shot*, where I live, according to the directions I made between son John Hopkins and son Isaac Hopkins. To sd. sons, land at Cagoes Island. To grand-son John Hopkins, son of my son Levy Hopkins, tract which belonged to Juda Cannon, according to the division that was formerly made; if sd. grand-son die without issue, then son Isaac Hopkins, shall inherit sd. land. I desire Jessey Dashiell and Isaac Hopkins should have the plantation in care. To grandson, son of Levi Hopkins, 5 pounds. To grand-dau. Parthena Nicholson, 1 shilling. To grand-dau. Mary Laremore, 1 shilling. To grand-dau. Mary Cooper, 1 shilling. To grand-dau. Eunice Cooper, 1 shilling. To grand-daus,: Sarah and Ann Ellingworth, 1 shilling each. To grand-son Thos. Cooper, 1 shilling. To dau. Mary Roberts, 1 shilling. To sons John and Isaac Hopkins, and grand-son John Samuells, balance. Sons John ad Isaac, execs. {MWB 10:227-8}

RICHARD NICHOLSON

Rachel Hitch, SO Co., d. by 27 Feb 1773 when the inventory of her estate was filed by Benjamin Hitch. Signed as next of kin: Leah Hitch, Richard Nicholson. {MINV 113:333}

THE HENRY PHILLIPS FAMILY

1. HENRY PHILLIPS, m. 1st Ann (N), m. 2nd Bridget (N).

Henry Philips signed a petition in 1689 along with other inhabitants of SO Co. in which they were resolved "to continue ... in the Profession and defence of the Protestant Religion and your Majesty's Title and interest against the French and other Papists that oppose and trouble us ..." {COES:49}

On 20 Jan 1687 Capt. Henry Smith and wife Ann sold to Henry Phillips the tract *Smiths Hope*. Henry Phillips d. intestate and this parcel of land descended to son Charles Phillips. {SOLR:371} On 1 Aug 1713 Charles Phillips sold *Smiths Hope* to William Owens. {SORR:56}

On 8 March 1691/2 Edward Sadbury, planter of Manokin, was indicted for stealing and killing a hogg of Henry Phillips. One of the witnesses was Anne Phillips. {SOJR:33}

Henry Phillips, SO Co., d. by 28 June 1708 when Bridgett Phillips filed

---

6. Parthenia may be the daughter of John Nicholson (d. 1734) and his wife Elizabeth of Nanticoke Hundred. Elizabeth married second John Hopkins, Jr. John Hopkins, Sr. may be calling her his granddaughter, when she is actually his step-granddaughter.

an administration bond on his estate. Her surety: William Gullett. {TP:21:63} On 27 July 1708 the inventory of his estate was filed. {INAC 28:317; TP:21:63}

Henry and Anne were parents of MARY, b. 19 July 1683; CHARLES, b. 3 Oct 1686; EDWARD, b. 25 Jan 1688; HENRY, b. 17 Sep 1692. {IKL}

Second Generation

2. CHARLES PHILLIPS, b. 3 Oct 1686, son of Henry (1) Phillips.

On 20 Jan 1687 Capt. Henry Smith and wife Ann sold to Henry Phillips the tract *Smiths Hope*. Henry Phillips d. intestate and this parcel of land descended to son Charles Phillips. {SOLR:371} On 1 Aug 1713 Charles Phillips sold *Smiths Hope* to William Owens. {SORR:56}

Charles Phillips, SO Co., d. by 22 August 1719 when an administration bond was filed on his estate by Henry Phillips, with sureties: William Denson, Samuel Marchment. {TP:24:46} In March 1721, Henry Phillips was cited by the Prerogative Court for not filing an inventory for the estate. {TP:24:366} On 22 Oct 1723 when the inventory of his estate was filed. {MINV 9:141} On 23 Oct 1723 when the admin. account of his estate was submitted by Henry Phillips, admin. {MDAD 5:249}

3. HENRY PHILLIPS, b. 17 Sep 1692, son of Henry (1) Phillips.

Charles Phillips, SO Co., d. by 22 August 1719 when an administration bond was filed on his estate by Henry Phillips, with sureties: William Denson, Samuel Marchment. {TP:24:46} In March 1721, Henry Phillips was cited by the Prerogative Court for not filing an inventory for the estate. {TP:24:366} On 22 Oct 1723 when the inventory of his estate was filed. {MINV 9:141} On 23 Oct 1723 when the admin. account of his estate was submitted by Henry Phillips, admin. {MDAD 5:249}

On the 1723 tax list for Pocomoke Hundred, Henry Philips is scratched through for Pocomoke Hundred. Thereafter the name of Henry Phillips disappears from the records. {SOTL}

THE ROGER PHILLIPS FAMILY

1. ROGER PHILLIPS m. 22 Oct 1672, Dorothy Clark, by Robert Maddox, clerk.

Roger Phillips of SO Co. immigrated by 1672. {MPL 18:35}

Roger Phillips patented the following tracts in SO Co.: *Phillips Addition* (25 a.) on 9 Oct 1695 and *Roxborough* (210 a.) on 10 June 1695. {MPL 37:124, 223}

On 8 Sep 1677 Phillip Ascue and wife Lydia sold to Roger Phillips the tract *Horseys Bailywick*, now called *Better Than It Promises*. On 4 Dec 1695

Richard Phillips sold to Phillips Ascue 50 a. called *Hogsdown*. On 26 April 1730 Thomas Phillips sold to Roger Kellett 107 a. and 12 ½ a. of *Phillips Addition* adj. land left Sarah Phillips by will adj. land Roger Kellett bought of Richard Phillips, unnamed. On 1 Feb 1739 Richard Phillips, son of Richard, sold to Roger Kellett and wife Eunice Kellett his wife's part of *Horseys Baliwick, Little Belean, Phillips Addition*, total 132 ½ a., 12 ½ a. being *Phillips Additon*. On 26 April 1730 Thomas Phillips sold to Roger Kellettt with wife Eunice, Kellett's part. On 11 Feb 1739 Richard Phillips sold to Henry Lowe 80 a. with *Little Belean* now called *Lowes Enlarged*. {WILR:213}

On 8 July 1682 Randal Revell patented *Smithfield* and assigned it to James Ingram for 100 a. On 12 June 1698 James Ingram of Wicomico and wife Mary sold 100 a. to Roger Phillips. In 1698 Roger Phillips willed the tract to dau. Phoebe Phillips. In 1745 Thomas Pollitt willed it to wife Sarah Pollitt. {SOLR:170}

Roger Phillips recorded his cattle mark in SO Co. on 11 7br 1673 and again in 1688/9. {ARMD LIV:764}

Abergaveny was patented on 10 May 1675 for 100 a. by Roger Phillips in Nanticoke Hundred on s. side of Quantico Creek. On 8 Jan 1677 Roger Phillips and wife Dorothy sold 100 a. to Samuel Jackson. {WILR:1}

Roger Phillips was one of the signatories of the paper entitled "Address of the Inhabitants of the County of Somersett Nover. the 28th 1689," expressing confidence in the monarchy and "interest against the French and other papists that oppose and trouble us ..." {OSES:349}

Phillips Addition was patented on 17 April 1695 by Roger Phillips for 25 a., taken out of *Horseys Baliwick*. The rent rolls, 1666-1723, show it possessed by Richard Phillips, son of Roger. On 4 Dec 1695 Roger Phillips sold to Phillip Ascue. On 1 Feb 1739 Richard Phillips, son of Richard, sold to Roger Kellett and wife Eunice, 12 ½ a. On 26 April 1746 Thomas Phillips sold to Roger Kellett and wife Eunice 107 a. and 12 ½ a. of marsh adj., being land left Sarah Phillips by Roger Phillips. {WILR:323}

Roger Phillips, Stepney Parish, SO. C., d. leaving a will dated 14 Oct 1698, proved 31 Dec 1699. To wife Dorothy, personalty and life interest in dwelling plantation. To son Richard and young. dau. Sarah jointly, 100 a. (unnamed) purchased from Simon Perkins, and 25 a. additional thereto. To eldest son Thomas and dau. Dorothy jointly, *Oxbury*. To dau. Phoebe, *Smithfield* To dau. Eliza: Crouch and granddau. Eliza: Crouch, personalty. Wife and son Richard afsd., joint execs. Residue of estate among wife and 3 daus., Phoebe, Dorothy and Sarah. {MWB 2:188} Codicil, dated 31 Dec 169x: to eldest dau. Elizabeth Crouch, *Haphazard*. {SOW:EB#5:191}

Thomas Phillips, son of Roger and Dorothy Phillips b. at Wikocomoco 12 March 1672. {IKL}

Roger Phillips, son of Roger and Dorothy Phillips b. 12 March 1674.

{IKL}
      Elizabeth Phillips, dau. of Roger and Dorothy Phillips b. at
Wickocomoco 1 June 1679. {IKL}
      Henry Phillips, son of Roger and Dorothy Phillips b. 15 April 1687.
{IKL}
      Pheby Phillips, dau. of Roger and Dorithy Phillips b. 18 April 1684.
{IKL}
      Dorothy Phillips, dau. of Roger and Doroty Phillips b. 29 Feb 1688.
{IKL}
      Roger was father of THOMAS, b. at Wicomico 12 March 1672;
ROGER, b. 12 March 1674; ELIZABETH, b. at Wickocomoco 1 June 1679, m.
Robert Crouch; RICHARD, b. 8 Feb 1681; HENRY, b. 15 April 1687; SARAH;
PHOEBE, b. 18 April 1684; DOROTHY, b. 29 Feb 1688.

Second Generation

2. THOMAS PHILLIPS, b. 12 March 1672, son of Roger (1) Phillips, m. Mary
(N).
      Roger Phillips, Stepney Parish, SO. C., d. leaving a will dated 14 Oct
1698, proved 31 Dec 1699. To wife Dorothy, personalty and life interest in
dwelling plantation. To son Richard and young. dau. Sarah jointly, 100 a.
(unnamed) purchased from Simon Perkins, and 25 a. additional thereto. To
eldest son Thomas and dau. Dorothy jointly, *Oxbury*. To dau. Phoebe, *Smithfield*
To dau. Eliza: Crouch and granddau. Eliza: Crouch, personalty. Wife and son
Richard afsd., joint execs. Residue of estate among wife and 3 daus., Phoebe,
Dorothy and Sarah. {MWB 2:188}
      In 1712, Thomas Phillips & his wife Mary sold to Alexander Vance,
Roxborough 210 a. Signed: Thomas Phillips, Mary "T" Phillips, John Barth,
Sarah Barth. {SOD:CD:817}
      Thomas Phillips, SO Co., d. by 23 Aug 1717, when an administration
bond was filed on his estate by Mary Phillips, with sureties: William Hayman,
Nicholas Todvine. {TP:23:169} On 17 Feb 1720 the admin. account of his estate
was submitted by Mary Phillips, admin. {MDAD 3:322}
      Thomas and Mary are the parents of: ROGER; RICHARD, m. Alice
Holbrook; THOMAS; JOHN; WILLIAM.

3. ELIZABETH PHILLIPS, b. 1 June 1679, dau. of Roger (1) Phillips, m.
Robert Crouch.
      Roger Phillips, Stepney Parish, SO. C., d. leaving a will dated 14 Oct
1698, proved 31 Dec 1699. To wife Dorothy, personalty and life interest in
dwelling plantation. To son Richard and young. dau. Sarah jointly, 100 a.
(unnamed) purchased from Simon Perkins, and 25 a. additional thereto. To
eldest son Thomas and dau. Dorothy jointly, *Oxbury*. To dau. Phoebe, *Smithfield*

To dau. Eliza: Crouch and granddau. Eliza: Crouch, personalty. Wife and son Richard afsd., joint execs. Residue of estate among wife and 3 daus., Phoebe, Dorothy and Sarah. {MWB 2:188} Codicil, dated 31 Dec 169x: to eldest dau. Elizabeth Crouch, *Haphazard*. {SOW:EB#5:191}

Robert Crouch, SO Co., d. by 27 April 1727 when legacies were paid by Elizabeth Crouch to John Reddish (his wife's part) and John Taylor (his wife's part); incomplete distribution. {SOWD EB14:165}

The 1735 tax lists shows Widow Crouch as head of household in Nanticoke Hundred; living in the household was William Phillips. {SOTL} [William Phillips would be the son of her bro. Thomas.]

On 27 March 1740, Robert Crouch sold to William Taylor, *Haphazard* 125 a. {SOLR:196}

Robert and Elizabeth Crouch were the parents of: ELIZABETH; ROBERT.

4. RICHARD PHILLIPS, b. 8 Feb 1681, son of Roger (1) Phillips, m. Jane Collier, dau. of Robert (1) Collier. {See The Robert Collier Family, vol. 8 of this series.}

Richard Phillips patented *Addition* (50 a.) in SO Co. in 1707. {MPL DD5:248}

Richard Phillips, SO Co., d. leaving a will dated 10 Feb 1724, proved 2 June 1725. Legatees: wife Jane, extx,; son Richard (under 21); son George; son James; 5 daus. {SOW:EB#9:102}

On 30 July 1725 the inventory of his estate was filed by Jean Phillips. Signed as next of kin: Thomas Collier, George Collier. {MINV 11:124}

The 1723 tax lists shows Richard Phillips as head of household in Wicomico Hundred. Living in the household was Negro Grace and Stephen Hall.

The 1725 tax lists shows Jane Phillips as head of household in Wicomico Hundred. Living in the household was Negro Grace.

On 15 Aug 1727 the admin. account of his estate was submitted by John Jones (exec. of Jane Phillips (extx. of dec'd.)). Legatees: Jean Phillips, George Phillips, James Phillips, Ann Phillips & Sarah Phillips & Elizabeth Phillips & Dorothy Phillips. {MDAD 8:333}

Jane Phillips, SO Co., d. leaving a will dated 15 June 1726, proved 15 September 1726. To 2 youngest children, Dorothy and James, personalty left by dec'd. husband, Richard Phillips; to pay for schooling. To son Richard and 3 eldest daus., Ann, Sarah and Betty, personalty. To 8 children _____ thirds equally. Children to be kept together until 2 youngest sons are educated and bound to a trade. {MWB 6:9}

On 19 Jan 1726 the inventory of her estate was filed by John Jones. Signed as next of kin: Thomas Collier, Robert Collier. {MINV 12:149} On 29 March 1728 the admin. account of her estate was submitted by John Jones, exec. Legatees: Dorothy Phillips, Anne Phillips, Richard Phillips. {MDAD 9:142}

Richard and Jane were parents of RICHARD, b. c1708; ANN; SARAH; BETTY (Elizabeth); DOROTHY; JAMES; GEORGE; JEAN (Jane).

5. SARAH PHILLIPS, dau. of Roger (1) Phillips, m. William Serman (Surnam, Sherman), son of Thomas Serman.

Thomas Serman, SO Co., d. leaving a will dated 21 Feb 1704/5, proved 8 April 1706. Mentioned wife Margaret and sons Thomas, Edward, Peter and William. To sons Peter and William he left 300 a. called *White Chappell* on w. side of Barren Creek. {MWB 12:52}

On 20 Dec 1721, William Serman & his wife Sarah sold to Roger Phillips, 100 a. plus pt. *Phillips' Addition* 12½ a. {SOD:IK:216}

William Surman d. by 28 Jan 1748 when the admin. account was submitted by Isaac Surman. Payments in equal amounts to wife (unnamed) of William Right, wife (unnamed) of John Anderson, accountant, Esther (under age), Joseph (under age), Richard Surman (under age). Admin. Isaac Surman. {MDAD 25:267}

Betty Write d. leaving a will dated 16 Feb 1754, proved 5 March 1754. To her sister Easter Righte, my third of my dec'd., husband's estate. Remainder of estate to sons Zebulon and Steven Right. Witnessed by N. Dashiell, Thos. Philip, Isaac Parremore. {MWB 29:141} Distribution of the estate of William Wright, SO Co., was made on 7 June 1755 by Isaac Sirnam, admin. Representatives were Zebulon Wright, aged c12 and Stephen Wright, aged c10. {BFD 1:133. See also The William Wright Family (2), vol. 8 of this series.}

William was father of ISAAC SURMAN; JOSEPH SURMAN; SARAH SURMAN, m. 22 Sep 1749, John Anderson and had issue: John Anderson, b. 14 Feb 1752; James Anderson, b. 15 April 1751; Isaac, b. 2 April 1756; Joseph, b. 15 Oct 1758, John, Joshua; BETTY SURMAN, m. William Wright; ESTHER SURMAN; JOSEPH SURMAN; RICHARD SURMAN. {See also ASOS:252}

6. DOROTHY PHILLIPS, b. 29 Feb 1688, dau. of Roger (1) Phillips, may have married a Barth.

In 1712, Thomas Phillips & his wife Mary sold to Alexander Vance, *Roxborough* 210 a. Signed: Thomas Phillips, Mary "T" Phillips, John Barth, Sarah Barth. {SOD:CD:817}

Third Generation

7. ROGER PHILLIPS, son of Thomas (2) Phillips.

On 20 Dec 1721, William Serman & his wife Sarah sold to Roger Phillips, 100 a. plus pt. *Phillips' Addition* 12½ a. {SOD:IK:216}

The 1724 tax lists shows Roger Phillips as head of household in Wicomico Hundred. The 1727 tax lists shows Roger Phillips as head of household in Nanticoke Hundred. Living in the household was Thomas Phillips.

Rodger Phillips (also Roger Phillips), SO Co., d. by 1 April 1725 when the inventory of his estate was filed by George Dashiell. {MINV 11:244} On 26 Aug 1726 the admin. account of his estate was submitted by George Dashiell, admin. {MDAD 8:37}

8. RICHARD PHILLIPS, b.c. 1700, son of Thomas (2) Phillips, m. Alce Holbrook, dau. of Thomas Holbrook.

The rent rolls, 1666-1723, show 200 a. of *Little Belean* possessed by Richard Phillips. On 1 Feb 1739 Richard Phillips, son of Richard, sold to Roger Kellett and wife Eunice 132 ½ a. that Roger Phillips left to son Richard who since d. intestate, part of three tracts: *Horseys Baliwick, Little Belean* and 12 ½ a. of *Phillips Addition*, except 80 a. sold to David Hurt. On 11 Feb 1739 Richard Phillips sold to Henry Lowe 80 a. out of *Horseys Baliwick* and *Little Belean* now called *Lowes.* On 26 April 1746 Thomas Phillips sold to Roger Kellett and wife Eunice 107 a. and 12 ½ a. of marsh adj. land left Sarah Phillips by Roger Phillips, bought of Richard Phillips. {WILR:247}

Richard Phillips was head of household in Wicomico Hundred, SO Co., 1730. Richard Phillips was head of household in Nanticoke Hundred, SO Co., 1731-1736, 1738-1740, 1744, 1748, 1750, 1753, 1754. In 1730, he is cited as Richard Phillips, Jr. [This has to be in error, since it does not agree with any of the other information.] In 1740 he was head of household in Nanticoke Hundred, living at Rewastico. Living in the same household was Thomas Phillips (in 1730), John Phillips (1730, 1731, 1733), William Phillips (1733, 1738), Richard Tully (1753), Arthur Tully (1753).

Alice Phillips was head of household in Nanticoke Hundred, SO Co., 1757. Living in the same household was John Phillips and James Phillips.

Richard Phillips was serving in the militia under Capt. Thomas Gillis, SO Co., in 1732. {COES:77}

On 1 Feb 1739 John Mezick sold 150 a. of *Rotterdam* to Richard Phillips. On 31 May 1773 John Phillips, son of Richard, sold to Sarah McClester, Rachel McClester, daus. of George McClester that father gave bond to George McClester of 150 a. {WILR:352}

John Phillips d. by 20 Nov 1745 when the inventory of his estate was filed by Susanna Phillips. Signed as next of kin: Richard Phillips, Thomas Phillips. {MINV 31:331}

Thomas Holdbrook (Holbrook), SO Co., d. by 31 March 1748 when the inventory of his estate was filed by Sarah Holbrook, Thomas Holbrook. Signed as next of kin: Mary Holbrook, Alce Phillips. {MINV 33:160} On 3 May 1749 the admin. account of his estate was submitted by Sarah Holbrook, Thomas Holbrook. Mentions: children: Ann Ricards (1/7), Mary Pullett (1/7), Martha Holbrook (1/7), Alce Phillips (1/7), Elizabeth Holbrook (dead, 1/7, paid to her sons Thomas and Samuell Covington). Payments included widow (unnamed, 1/3). {MDAD 26:43}

Richard Phillips, age 53, deposed on 17 Oct 1752 regarding the bounds of *Covingtons Folly* and *Covingtons Vineyard*. {SOJR:1752-1754:185}

Richard Phillips was head of household in Nanticoke Hundred as indicated in the 1754 tax list of SO Co. {Lankford}

Richard Phillips, planter, SO Co., d. leaving a will dated 20 Oct 1754, proved 31 Dec 1754. To son John Phillips, one horse. To son James Phillips, slaves. Wife Alce Phillips, extx., desire that Thomas Holdbrook and William Pullett may be her assistants. {MWB 11:71} On 18 Jan 1754 the inventory of his estate was filed by Ellianer Phillips. Signed as next of kin: Richard Phillips, Thomas Phillips. {MINV 60:296} The admin. account was submitted by Alce Phillips on 29 June 1761. Legatees: James Phillips, John Phillips. {MDAD 46:413}

Richard was father of JOHN; JAMES, b. 1740, d. 1785.

9. THOMAS PHILLIPS, b.c. 1702, son of Thomas (2) Phillips.

In 1727, Thomas Phillips is cited in Nanticoke Hundred in the household of Roger Phillips. In 1730, he is cited in Wicomico Hundred in the household of Richard Phillips, Jr. In 1731, he is cited as head of household in Wicomico Hundred. In 1734-1736, 1738-1740, 1744, 1748, 1750, 1753, 1754, 1757, and 1759, he is cited as head of household in Nanticoke Hundred. He is cited as Thomas Phillips, Sr. in 1759. Living in his household is: William Phillips (1734), Thomas Phillips, Jr. (1759).

John Phillips d. by 20 Nov 1745 when the inventory of his estate was filed by Susanna Phillips. Signed as next of kin: Richard Phillips, Thomas Phillips. {MINV 31:331}

Thomas Phillips, age 63, deposed on 30 March 1765 regarding the bounds of *Sarahs Security*. {SOJR:1763-1765:236}

Thomas was probably the father of: THOMAS, Jr., b.c. 1743.

10. JOHN PHILLIPS, son of Thomas (2) Phillips, m. Susanna Tulley, dau. of Stephen Tulley, Sr.

In 1730, John Phillips is cited in Wicomico Hundred in the household of Richard Phillips, Jr. He is cited in Nanticoke Hundred in the household of Richard Phillips in 1731, 1733. He is cited as head of household in Nanticoke Hundred in 1734-1736, 1738-1740, 1744. Living in his household in 1736 is William Phillips.

Stephen Tully, SO Co., d. leaving a will dated 20 March 1737, proved 10 March 1745. To wife Jane, extx. To children: Stephen, Jane, Benjamin, Mary, Susanna, Sarah, Elizabeth, Joshua. {SOW:EB#9:258} On 8 June 1745, admin accounts were filed on his estate (as Stephen Tulley, Sr.) by Edward Bennett & George Bennett (sureties for Benjamin Tulley administrator). Distribution to:

48

Jane (dau), Elizabeth (dau), Susanna Phillips (dau), Elizabeth Tulley (widow of Benjamin Tulley), Edward Bennett who married the widow. {MDAD:21:412}

Stephen Tulley, Jr., SO Co., d. by 1744 when the inventory of his estate was filed by Richard Tulley. Signed as next of kin: Edward Bennet, John Phillips. {MINV 29:372} On 8 June 1745, admin accounts were filed on his estate by Richard Tulley. Sureties: William Phillips, George Bennett. Distribution to: Catherine (widow), children: accountant, Stephen, Betty, Jane, Arthur, Dorothy. {MDAD:21:411}

John Phillips, SO Co., d. by 20 Nov 1745 when the inventory of his estate was filed by Susanna Phillips. Signed as next of kin: Richard Phillips, Thomas Phillips. {MINV 31:331} On 4 June 1748 the admin. account of his estate was submitted by Susanna Phillips, admx. {MDAD 25:112}

Benjamin Tulley, SO Co., d.p. 8 Feb 1745, when admin accounts were filed by Elizabeth Tulley. Sureties: John Phillips, Richard Tulley. {MDAD:22:79}

11. WILLIAM PHILLIPS, son of Thomas (2) Phillips, m. 1st (N), m. 2nd, Margaret (Peggy) Low, dau. of Ralph Low.

William Phillips is cited in Nanticoke Hundred in the household of Richard Phillips in 1733, in the household of Thomas Phillips in 1734, in the household of the widow Crouch in 1735, in the household of John Phillips in 1736, in the household of Richard Phillips in 1738, as head of household in 1739, 1740, 1744, 1748, 1750, 1753, 1754, 1757, 1759. In 1740, he is cited as William Phillips of Rewastico. Also living in his household is Roger Phillips (1757, 1759).

Stephen Tulley, Jr., SO Co., d. by 1744 when the inventory of his estate was filed by Richard Tulley. Signed as next of kin: Edward Bennet, John Phillips. {MINV 29:372} On 8 June 1745, admin accounts were filed on his estate by Richard Tulley. Sureties: William Phillips, George Bennett. Distribution to: Catherine (widow), children: accountant, Stephen, Betty, Jane, Arthur, Dorothy. {MDAD:21:411}

Ralph Low, Stepney Parish, SO Co., d. leaving a will dated 25 Feb 1750-1, proved 17 March 1756. Wife: Rachel. Children: John, George, Hudson, Ralph, Robert, Sarah Henry, Margaret Phillips, Liddia, Rachel. George and Ralph Low, execs. {MWB 11:124}

William Phillips d. leaving a will dated 12 Sep 1793, proved 3 Feb 1794. To son Elisha Phillips lands and plantation whereon I now live. All lands and plantation whereon he now lives agreeable to the division between he, William and Isaac. To son William Phillips all lands and plantation he lives on for his natural life. To grandson, son of William, lands left to William at his decease. To grandson Whitty Phillips, son of Elijah, lands where his father now lives after his father's decease. To grandson Roger Phillips, a young mare his father Isaac has in his possession. To dau. Rachel Phillips, furniture, livestock.

To dau. Mary Phillips, furniture, tableware. To wife Peggy Phillips, furniture, livestock. To dau. Betty Trader, remainder of estate, to be divided among children except son Roger Phillips. Witnessed by Benjamin Wailes, Epharim Wilson, John Wilson. Execs. wife and son Elisha. {SOW EB17:294}

Patta Phillips, dau. of Elijah and Alla Phillips, b. 26 Dec 1792. {SOSP} William was the father of: ROGER, b.c. 1741.

William and Margaret were parents of ISAAC, b. 13 Feb 1751; ELIZABETH/Betty, b. 26 Dec 1753; RACHEL, b. 10 Oct 1756; WILLIAM, b. 10 Jan 1758; ELIJAH (Elisha), b. 21 May 1760; MARY, b. 25 Nov 1762. {SOSP}

12. RICHARD PHILLIPS, b. c1708, son of Richard (4) Phillips, m. 4 Jan 1733/4, Ann Bennett, dau. of Edward Bennett. {See The Edward Bennett Family, vol. 8 of this series.}

Edward Bennett, SO Co., d. by 1 Feb 1734 when the admin. account of his estate was submitted by Elizabeth Bennett. Mentions: Children: Edward Bennett, George Bennett, Elizabeth Bennett, Ann Bennett (alias Ann Phillips), John Bennett, William Bennett. {MDAD 12:766}

George Phillips, son of Richard Phillips Junr. and his Ann his wife, b. 15 July 1738. {SOSP}

Mary Phillips, dau. of Richard Phillips and his wife Ann, b. 16 Oct 1740. {SOSP}

Richard Phillips, age 37, deposed on 10 June 1746 regarding the bounds of *Horseys Balewick* {SOJR:1743-1747:124}, and at age 42 on 5 Feb 1750 on the bounds of *Hold Holland*. {SOJR:1752-1754:20}

Joshua Phillips, son of Richard and Anne Phillips, b. 2 Dec 1751. {SOSP}

Richard Phillips was head of household in Wicomico Hundred, SO Co., 1727, 1730-1739. Richard Phillips was head of household in Monie Hundred, SO Co., 1748, 1750-1752. He was head of household in Nanticoke Hundred, SO Co., 1753, 1754, 1757, 1759. In 1730, he is cited as Richard Phillips, Sr. [This has to be in error, since it does not agree with any of the other information.] In 1753, he is cited as Richard Phillips, Jr. In 1740 he was head of household in Nanticoke Hundred, living at Nanticoke. Living in the same household was: George Phillips in 1737; slave Grace, 1730-1731; James Covington (1750-1752); Daniel Phillips (1753, 1754), George Phillips (1757).

In 1748, James Covington chose Richard Phillips as his guardian. {SOJR:1747-1749:187}

In 1752, James Covington petitioned the court that his guardian Richard Phillips wasted his estate and he is married to a daughter of Daniel Jones, and desires Daniel Jones as his guardian. {SOJR:1751-1752:140}

Richard was father of DANIEL, b. 27 Oct 1734; BETTY, b. 22 July

1736; GEORGE, b. 15 July 1738; MARY, b. 16 Oct 1740; SARAH, b. 29 June 1742/3; PRISCILLA, b. 11 March 1744/5; RICHARD, b. 16 Feb 1746/7; JOSHUA, b. 2 Dec 1751. {SOSP}

13. SARAH PHILLIPS, prob. dau. of Richard (5) and Jane Phillips, m. 11 Feb 1731, Daniel Hurt.

The rent rolls, 1666-1723, show 200 a. of *Little Belean* possessed by Richard Phillips. On 1 Feb 1739 Richard Phillips, son of Richard, sold to Roger Kellett and wife Eunice 132 ½ a. that Roger Phillips left to son Richard who since d. intestate, part of three tracts: *Horseys Baliwick, Little Belean* and 12 ½ a. of *Phillips Addition*, except 80 a. sold to David Hurt. On 11 Feb 1739 Richard Phillips sold to Henry Lowe 80 a. out of *Horseys Baliwick* and *Little Belean* now called *Lowes*. On 26 April 1746 Thomas Phillips sold to Roger Kellett and wife Eunice 107 a. and 12 ½ a. of marsh adj. land left Sarah Phillips by Roger Phillips, bought of Richard Phillips. {WILR:247}

They were parents of NELLY(?) HURT, b. 10 Oct 1731; JOHN HURT, b. 19 March 1733; JANE HURT, b. 6 Aug 1735.

14. GEORGE PHILLIPS, son of Richard (4) Phillips.

Stephen Hall, Stepney Parish, shipwright, SO Co., d. leaving a will dated 21 Oct 1722, proved 13 April 1724. To George Phillips, one year's schooling, personalty. To John Johns, personalty. To Richard Phillips, exec, residue of estate. {MWB 5:164}

George Phillips was living in Wicomico Hundred in the household of Thomas Collier in 1731 and in the household of George Lancake (Lank) in 1733-1736. In 1737 George was living in the household of his brother Richard. {SOTL}

George Phillips disappears from the records after 1737.

15. JAMES PHILLIPS, son of Richard (4) Phillips. There is no evidence that he survived to adulthood.

Fourth Generation

16. JOHN PHILLIPS, son of Richard (8) and Alice Phillips.

John Phillips is cited in the household of Alice Phillips in Nanticoke Hundred in 1757. He is cited as a head of household in Nanticoke Hundred in 1759.

17. JAMES PHILLIPS, son of Richard (8) and Alice Phillips, m. 18 March 1762, Mary Acworth, dau. of Henry and Mary (Givans) Acworth. {See The Ackworth Family, vol. 8 of this series.}

James Phillips is cited in the household of Alice Phillips in Nanticoke

Hundred in 1757. He is cited in the household of Joshua Whittington in Nanticoke Hundred in 1759.

Mary Acworth, SO Co., d. leaving a will dated 26 Sep 1765, proved 1 April 1772. Children: Henry, Mary Phillips and her son Henry and her dau. Nelly Phillips. Son Henry Acworth, exec {MWB 38:549}

James Phillips d. 12 Sep 1785. {RPWS:226}

James Phillips served as ensign, Somerset Militia, Salisbury Battn., Capt. William Turpin's Rewastico Company, 1778 to 22 Aug 1781 or later. {RPWS:226}

James Phillips d. leaving a will dated 7 June 1784, proved 12 Sep 1785. To wife Mary all estate. To friend William Harris 60 a. being part of the land purchased from Dr. George Gale. To son Henry Phillips remainder of land from Dr. George Gale with exception of timber - for the benefit of the plantation whereon I now live until the three youngest children come of age 21. To dau. Nelly Phillips furniture and her spinning wheel. To dau. Ann Phillips, furniture, mare and a cow and calf. To Henry Acworth rights to tract of land purchased from him and 50 a. of land purchased from John Killum and 17 ½ a. of *Collier's Mistake*. To sons Day Givans, Whitty and Isaac Phillips, remainder of estate at wife's decease. Witnessed by John Phillips, Cornelius Rudy, Ann Dorman. {SOW EB1:230}

James and Mary were parents of HENRY, b. 4 Dec 1762; NELLY, b. 25 Dec 1764; ANN, b. 27 Oct 1769; ROBERT GIVANS, b. 21 Dec 1772; DAY GIVANS; WHITTY; ISAAC. {Stepney Parish Records}

18. ROGER PHILLIPS, son of William (11) Phillips.

In 1757 and 1759, Roger Phillips is cited in Nanticoke Hundred in the household of William Phillips.

19. DANIEL PHILLIPS, b. 27 Oct 1734, son of Richard (12) and Anne Phillips, m. Ann (N) 2 Nov 1756. {SOSP}

The 1753 tax list shows Daniel Phillips living in Nanticoke Hundred in the household of Richard Phillips, Jr. In 1754, he was living in the household of Richard Phillips. In 1757 and 1759, he is cited as head of household.

They were parents of AMELIA, b. 22 May 1758; MARY, b. 20 April 1760; RICHARD, b. 3 June 1762; DANIEL, b. 24 June 1764; JOHN, b. 7 April 1767; NANCY, b. 3 May 1769; JAMES, b. 22 Jan 1774; JOSHUA, b. 16 Nov 1775; THOMAS, b. 29 Nov 1777. {SOSP}

20. GEORGE PHILLIPS, b. 15 July 1738, son of Richard (12) and Anne Phillips, m. 11 Jan 1758, Betty Twilly (widow). {SOSP} She is the widow of Robert Twilley (d.c. 1752).

In 1757 tax list, George Phillips was living in Nanticoke Hundred in the

52

household of Richard Phillips. In 1759, he is cited as head of household.

Late at Night was patented in 1760 by George Phillips for 50 a. in SO Co. On 17 April 1767 George Phillips and wife Elizabeth sold it to Arthur Dashiell at Barren Creek adj. *Woodstock.* {WILR:241}

George Phillips served as private in the Somerset Militia, Salisbury Battn., Capt. William Turpin's Rewastico Company, 1778/1780. {RPWS:226}

They were parents of ANN, b. 16 Oct 1758; GEORGE, b. 23 June 1763.

21. MARY PHILLIPS, prob. dau. Richard (12) and Anne Phillips, m. 6 April 1759, James Twilley.

They were parents of BETTY TWILLEY, b. 21 Feb 1760; ANNE TWILLEY, b. 4 June 1762. {SOSP}

Fifth Generation

22. NELLY PHILLIPS, b. 25 Dec 1764, dau. of James (17) and Mary Phillips, m. Isaac Giles (b. 30 July 1762 in Stepney Parish, d. by 5 March 1811. {RPWS:108}

Isaac Giles served as private, Somerset Militia, Salisbury Battn., Capt. Levin Irving's Black Water Company, 1778/1780. {RPWS:108}

Nelly and Isaac were parents of WILLIAM GILES, b. 1795, d. 1872; JOHN PHILLIPS GILES, b. 1799. {RPWS:108}

THE JOHN PHILLIPS FAMILY

1. JOHN PHILLIPS (c1740-95) and Sarah Brothers (c1744-98) of Sussex Co., DE, were parents of Ruth. {ASOS:267}

John and Sarah were parents of RUTH.

2. RUTH PHILLIPS, dau. of John Phillips, m. Charles Tindall, son of Charles and Sarah (Hearne) Tindall. {ASOS:267}

Ruth and Charles were parents of SARAH TINDALL, b. c1783; JOHN A. TINDALL, b. 1 Jan 1785; LOVEY TINDAL, b. 1787. {ASOS:267}

Unplaced

(N) PHILLIPS m. Elizabeth Tilghman, dau. of Joseph Tilghman.

Elizabeth Phillips d. leaving a will dated 27 Dec 1786, proved 30 Jan 1787. To sister Margaret Hayman, saddle and bridle. To sister Sary Hayman a mare and remainder of estate to be divided with Margaret. To bro. William Tilghman, Negro wench Rachel and negro girl Sary. To bro. Joseph Tilghman, livestock. To bro. Isaiah Tilghman livestock. To Edmond Smulling a cow and yearling. To Jenney ...ling a loom, chest and 5 chairs. To John Riggin a small pot. Witnessed by John Puzey, John MackDaniel. {SOW EB1:255}

(N) PHILLIPS m. Sarah Wright, dau. of Solomon Wright.
Solomon Wright, SO Co., d. leaving a will dated 12 Feb 1772, proved 5 March 1772. Children: Jacob, Levin, Sarah Phillips, Patience Jackson, Priscilla Robertson, Charity Twiford. Grandson: William Wright. Levin Wright, exec {MWB 14:203} On 11 March 1772, an inventory was filed on his estate by Levin Wright. Cited as kin: James Wright, Sarah Philips. {MINV:108:370} On 29 Oct 1772, admin accounts were filed by Levin Wright. {MDAD:67:261} On 25 Aug 1773, additional admin accounts were filed by Levin Wright. Distribution to: Jacob Wright, accountant, Sarah Philips, Patience Jackson, Priscilla Robertson, Charity Twyford. {MDAD:68:234}

(N) PHILLIPS m. Ruth, dau. of Ann Davis.
Ann Davis, WO Co., d. leaving a will dated 12 Feb 1788, proved 29 Feb 1788. Mentioned daus. Tamer Major, Sally, Ruth Phillips, Naomy, Nixon, Elizabeth and William, Mathias; grandson Josiah Davis. {WOW JW13:161}

CHARLES PHILLIPS served as private in the Somerset Militia, Salisbury Battn., Capt. William Turpin's Rewastico Company, 1778/1780. {RPWS:226}

GEORGE PHILLIPS
On 6 Nov 1681 Henry Smith sold to George Phillips 330 a. of *Davis's Choice*, now called *Georges Delight*. {SOLR:119} [This land is probably later owned by John Fisher.]

ISAAC PHILLIPS
Batchellors Lott was patented on 29 Sep 1762 by Isaac Phillips for 50 a. in WO Co. {MPL BC17:547; BC19:43}
On 17 Oct 1772 John Winright sold to Isaac Phillips 64 a. of *Baileys Chance*. On 5 Jan 1775 Ezekiel Jones of DO Co. sold to Joshua Philllips of SO Co., 50 a. On 2 May 1776 land warrants of *Baileys Chance* were recorded in Sussex Co., DE, patented in SO Co. by Joshua Phillips (son of Isaac Phillips). {WILR:23}
Isaac Phillips served as private in the Worcester Militia, Snow Hill Battn., Capt. Ebenezer Handy's Company, 9 April 1776 and as private, Worcester Militia, Wicomico Battn., Capt. James Perdue's Company, 15 July 1780. {RPWS:226}
The 1783 tax lists shows Isaac Phillips owned 100 a. of *Florida* & 150 a. of *Goshen*. On 6 Sep 1803 Thomas Phillips, Joshua Phillips, William

Philllips, Kendal Phillips, Isaac Phillips, heirs of Isaac Phillips, sold to Spencer Davis of George Davis, 230 a. {WOLR:228}

Isaac Phillips, WO Co., d.p. 13 Feb 1801, when an admin bond was filed on his estate by Joshua Phillips. {WED}

Isaac was father of JOSHUA; THOMAS; WILLIAM; KENDAL; ISAAC.

JACOB PHILLIPS

Jacob Phillips was living in the household of John Ellis in Pocomoke Hundred in 1723 and in the household of John Colbern in 1725; and head of his own household in Wicomico Hundred, 1730-1740. Living in the same household was Hill Cocks (1733).

Jacob Phillips patented the following tracts in WO Co.: *Gordy's Disappointment* (50 a.) on 10 Aug 1753; *Phillips' Desire* (50 a.- assigned to Isaac Phillips) on 6 May 1760; *Gordy's Disappointment* (100 a.) on 29 Sep 1763. {MPL BY4:693; BC1:79; BC14:216; BC16:192; BC24:481; BC25:186}

On 2 May 1771, Jacob Phillips sold to David Melson, *Phillips' Desire* 50 a. {WILR:323}

Jacob Phillips took the Oath of Allegiance in WO Co. 25 Feb 1778. {RPWS:226}

Jacob Phillips is cited on the 1783 Assessment List in Pocomoke Hundred, WO Co., paying tax on *Gordy's Disappointment* 100 a.

On 30 May 1785, Jacob Phillips sold to Benjamin Hearn, *Gordy's Disappointment* 100 a. {WILR:178}

JACOB PHILLIPS, Jr.

Jacob Phillips, Jr. is cited on the 1783 Assessment List in Pocomoke Hundred, WO Co., with no land.

JAMES PHILLIPS

The tax lists of SO Co. show James Phillips living in the household of Andrew Thomson in Manokin in 1730. There was also a James Phillips living in the household of Charles Banster in Annamessex Hundred in 1740.

JAMES PHILLIPS

On 17 June 1783 George Gale sold to James Phillips part of *Largee* and *Akalow*, 148 ½ a. In 1783 Rachel Phillips willed to daus. Ann Mills, Jane Lloyd, Patty Mills and her son William Washington Mills, 180 ½ a. of *Largey* and *Kellums Lott*. {WILR:237}

JAMES PHILLIPS m. Sarah (N).

James Phillips, SO Co., .d leaving a will dated 14 Dec 1770, proved 5 March 1772. Exec: wife Sarah. Grandsons: Johnson Wheatly, James Phillips Wheatly, William Wheatly. Granddaus.: Esther Joyns, Elizabeth Wheatly, Ann Wheatly. {MWB 14:203} On 31 March 1772 the inventory of his estate was filed by Sarah Phillips. Appraisers: John Phillips, Joseph Venables. Signed as next of kin: Elizabeth Wheatley, William Wheatley. {MINV 108:378}

James was father of ELIZABETH, m. WILLIAM Wheatly.

JAMES PHILLIPS, son of James Phillips, m. 2 Jan 1746, Leah Henderson. {SOCO}

On 4 March 1747 Joseph Feddeman and wife Urlando of Accomack Co., VA, sold to James Phillips of WO Co., 200 a. of *Truebridge*. On 28 July 1787 James Phillips, son of James Phillips, and wife Leah Phillips sold 15 a. to Aaron Hudson. On 1 Sep 1807 James Phillips and wife Leah sold 15 a. to Aaron Hudson. {WOLR:646}

James Phillips was serving in the company of Capt. William Lane, SO Co., c1749. {COES:78}

James Phillips served as private in the Worcester Militia, Wicomico Battn., Capt. James Patterson's Company, 15 July 1780. Recommended for promotion to ensign in Quantico Company on 17 April 1781. {RPWS:227}

James Philips (also James Phillips), WO Co., d. by 6 July 1775 when the inventory of his estate was filed by Leah Philips. Signed as next of kin: Benjamin Henderson, Lemuel Henderson. {MINV 124:353}

They were parents of BETTEY, b. 11 April 1747; MOLLEY, b. 22 Aug 1749; JANE, b. 10 July 1752; JAMES, b. 12 Oct 1756. {SOCO}

JESSE PHILLIPS served as private, Somerset Militia, Salisbury Battn., Capt. John Span conway's Nanticoke Point Company, 1778/1780. {RPWS:227}

JOHN PHILLIPS recorded a cattle mark in SO Co. for his dau. Elizabeth Phillips in 1704. {COES:42}

JOHN PHILLIPS m. Rhody Hoffington, dau. of John Hoffington.

In 1771 John Phillips patented 50 a. called *Friendship*. On 5 Dec 1772 John Phillips and wife Rhoda sold to John Sterling ½ part of undivided right of inheritance, 50 a. on s. side of Barren Creek.

John Hoffington, SO Co., d. leaving a will dated 18 May 1773, proved 17 Jan 1774. To wife Betty Huffington, Negro man Peter, mare, saddle and 1/3 of moveable estate, ½ of my plantation whereon I now live. To son Jonathan Huffington, my plantation whereon I now live and if he dies without issue then to go to my grandson John Huffington son of William Huffington. To dau. Betty

Malalley, 80 acres which formerly belonged to Samuel Melson on which she now lives, Negro wench Merron during her lifetime and after her death the lands to go to grandson John Malolley and after decease of my dau. Betty Malalley I leave Negro wench Merron to two of my grandchildren Betty Malolly and William Malloly. To dau. Betty Mallelley, 20 pounds. To dau. Rhody Phillips, Negro woman called Hannah. To grandson Samuel Phillips, Negro child Ephraim. To dau. Mary Williams, Negro boy Somerset. To my four grandchildren: John Acworth, Thomas Acworth, Louder Acworth and Betty Acworth, Negro girl Big Sall, when they arrive of age. To grandson John Huffington, son of Gilbert, Negro child, Isaac. All other lands and marsh to my two sons, Joshua Huffington and Jonathan Huffington. That my son Gilbert Huffington shall have privilege of living in my house as long as he remains single. All other estate to Gilbert Huffington, Joshua Huffington, William Huffington, Jonathan Huffington, Rhody Phillips, Mary Williams and my four grandchildren which Richard Acworth had by my dau. Priscilla. Jonathan Huffington, exec {MWB 15:176}

Gilbert Huffington, SO Co., d. leaving a will dated 15 July 1775, proved 26 Sep 1775. To son John Huffington, silver teaspoons marked PD. To dau. Mary Huffington, Negro Jesse, furniture, silver spoons marked GH, gold ring, bob, buttons; she to be in care of her grandmother Mrs. White, 10 pounds to be applied toward her education and clothes, she to also get all my wife's clothes. To Thomas White, to bring up my son Isaac and teach them both the art of Shipwright and 10 pounds to my son for education. To John Phillips, exec., tract, *Batchelors Choice*. To my two children, remainder of personal estate equally if they die without issue to Edward Phillips son of John Phillips and Thomas Melaley son of Patrick Melaley. {MWB 16:74}

John was father of EDWARD; SAMUEL.

JOHN PHILLIPS served as Captain, Somerset Militia, 1st Battn., 13 May 1776. {RPWS:227}

JOHN PHILLIPS served as 2nd lieutenant, Somerset Militia, Salisbury Battn., Capt. William Turpin's Company, 22 Sep 1777 and 1st lieutenant 7 Jan 1778 to 31 July 1778 or later. {RPWS:227}

JOHN PHILLIPS served as private, Somerset Militia, Salisbury Battn., Capt. John Span Conway's Nanticoke Point Company, 1778/1780. On 30 July 1781 he was drafted from SO Co. to serve in the Continental Army. {RPWS:227}

JOHN PHILLIPS, m. Elizabeth Furniss, dau. of James Furniss (b. at Manokin 22 Dec 1701). {ASOS:117}

In 1708, William Gullett was an appraiser of the estate of Henry

57

Phillips. {INAC:28:317}

William Gyllot, SO Co., d. leaving a will dated 21 Jan 1716, proved 20 March 1716. To eldest son William, all lands and plantation, including *Buchaneer Green*. Two sons, William and John, till age of 18, to care of bro.-in-law Abraham Tripe. Son Abraham to Richard Chambers till 18 years of age. To dau. Mary, personalty; she to be in care of Olife Chambers. To son George, personalty. Bro. John Phillips, exec, to have debt that is in hand of Wm. Willson, to pay for nursing of son George. Remainder of personal estate divided among children. afsd. {MWB 4:83} On 18 August 1721, admin accounts were filed on his estate by John Philips. {MDAD:4:3}

The tax lists of SO Co. show John Phillips as head of household in Pocomoke Hundred, 1733-1740, 1744, 1748, 1750, 1753, 1754, 1757, 1759. Living in the same household was: George Gullett (1733-1734); Ezekiel Phillips (1738-1740, 1744, 1748); John Phillips, Jr. (1757, 1759).

On 4 Dec 1729 Richard Kellum of Sussex Co., DE, weaver, and wife Jane, sold to John Phillips, schoolmaster, 200 a. now called *Cambridge* (previously named Good *Neighbourhood*). In 1762 John Phillips willed land to son John. Absalom Phillips sold to Obed Outten, a little below Deep Creek and it was surveyed in Sussex Co., DE, 30 March 1776 and patented to Solomon Turpin. {WILR:176}

John Phillips patented the following tracts in SO Co.: *Privilege* (50 a.) on 10 Aug 1753; *Phillips' Conclusion* (439 a.) on 7 Oct 1775. {MPL GS2:322; BC4:51; BC51:188; BC52:55}

John Phillips, SO Co., d. leaving a will dated 13 Aug 1762, proved 25 Oct 1762. To grand-son Nathaniel Smulling , 50 a., called *The Wolf Pit Ridge*. To son John Phillips, all the rest of land; if he die without issue, land to be divided between daus. Elizabeth and Grace Phillips, Elizabeth to have her first choice; also to John, plow, etc. To dau. Elizabeth, mare etc. To dau. Grace, stock. To son-in-law William Layfield, one s. sterl. Wife Elizabeth Phillips. Daus. Elizabeth and Grace, shall have free liberty in my dwelling house. Son John, exec {MWB 12:54-5} The inventory of his estate was filed by John Philips. Signed as next of kin: Elizabeth Philips, Bridget Silivan. {MINV 81:60} The admin. account was submitted by John Phillips on 5 Feb 1767. Distribution to widow Elizabeth Phillips with residue to (in equal amounts): wife (unnamed) of Nathaniel Smullen, Elizabeth Philips, Grace Philips, wife (unnamed) of William Silliven, accountant. Legatees: Elizabeth Philips, Grace Philips, accountant, William Lafield. {MDAD 56:223}

Priviledge was patented in 1750 by John Phillips for 50 a. in now East Princess Anne Election District; 30 a. adj. was patented in 1758. In 1762 John Phillips willed to daus. Elizabeth Phillips and Grace Phillips; no land was mentioned. On 22 March 1786 John McDaniel and wife Elizabeth sold to Jonathan Stanford and wife Grace 30 a. and 5 ½ a. On 3 Jan 1789 Jonathan

Stanford and wife Grace of WO Co. sold to John Handy 5 ½ a. On 17 March 1792 Jonathan Stanford and wife Grace sold 30 a. to Phillip Riggin. On 5 Jan Elizabeth McDaniel, co-heir of John Phillips, sold 35 a. to Caleb Bevans McDaniel. {SOLR:145}

John was father of EZEKIEL; JOHN; ELIZABETH, m. John McDaniel; GRACE, m. Jonathan Stanford; (N), m. Nathaniel Smullen; (N), m. William Silliven.

JOHN PHILLIPS

John Phillips is cited as head of household in Nanticoke Hundred in 1723, 1724. Living in his household in 1724 is John Smith.

Charlton Smith, SO Co., d by 10 June 1724 when the inventory of his estate was filed by John Phillips. Mentions: John Hofington. {MINV 11:3} Charlton Smith, SO Co., d. by 1 Sep 1726 when the admin. account of his estate was submitted by John Philips, admin. {MDAD 8:40} [John Huffington & Richard Jefferson are creditors to this estate.]

JOHN PHILLIPS

John Philips, WO Co., d. leaving a will dated 27 May 1765, proved 25 June 1765. Children: Benjamin, Elizabeth and John Philips. (No relationship regarding the following): Rachel and Ann Winsor, Ann Middleton. To Benjamin, ½ of sawmill. To Ann Winsor, other ½ of sawmill. Benjamin Philips, exec {MWB 13:78}

John Phillips, WO Co., d. by 2 July 1765 when the inventory of his estate was filed by Benjamin Phillips. Signed as next of kin: Joan Phillips, Ann Winser. {MINV 90:125} The admin. accuont was submitted by Benjamin Phillips on 17 July 1767. {MDAD 58:58}

John was father of BENJAMIN; ELIZABETH; JOHN.

JOHN PHILLIPS patented the following tracts in SO Co.: *Security* (51 a.) in SO Co. on 2 May 1750; *Privilege* (30 a.) on 24 May 1758; *Friend's Assistance* (485 a.) on 20 May 1774. {MPL BY2:615; BY5:164; BC10:243; BC11:201; BC45:415; BC46:398}

JOHN PHILLIPS patented the following tracts in WO Co.: *Mill Lot* (26 a.) on 4 July 1754; *Phillips' Choice* (68 a.) on 25 June 1759; *Good Fortune* (6 a.) on 26 Aug 1762. {MPL GS2:233; BC4:181; BC11:118; BC13:13; BC24:532; BC28:220}

JONAH PHILLIPS served as private, Somerset Militia, Salisbury Battn., Capt. John Span Conway's Nanticoke Point Company, 1778/1780. {RPWS:227}

JOSIAH PHILLIPS m. 23 Nov 1761, Elizabeth Bennet. {SOSP} Elizabeth was dau. of George Bennet.

Josiah Phillips is cited on the tax lists in Nanticoke Hundred in 1757, 1759, in the household of Richard Tulley. Also living in that household is Arthur Tulley.

George Bennet, SO Co., d. leaving a will dated 1 Oct 1782, proved 26 Nov 1782. Mentioned wife Betty; sons Edward and George Bennet; daus. Jean Shaw, Charity Gunby and Elizabeth Phillips; grandson Richard Bennet; granddau. Joanne Bennet. {SOW EB1:174}

Josiah Phillips is cited on the 1783 Assessment List, with no land, 4 males & 2 females in his household.

Bennett Phillips, served as private in the North Carolina Line. He applied for a pension on 20 May 1834 in Rutherford Co., TN, stating he was b. SO Co., MD, 27 Dec 1763, m. Miss Isabella Moore in Spring 1784 in Granville Co., NC, moved to TN in 1797. Isabella Phillips applied for a pension on 20 Nov 1843, stating she was b. 9 Feb 1765, had a son Samuel and that her husband Bennett d. 20 Sep 1842. {RPWS:226}

Josiah and Elizabeth were parents of PRISCILLA BENNET, b. 25 Oct 1762; prob. BENNETT, b. 27 Dec 1763, d. 20 Sep 1842, m. 1784, Isabella Moore (b. 9 Feb 1765).

JOSHUA PHILLIPS m. Mary (N).

Joshua and Mary were parents of BETTY, b. 21 March 1799. {SOSP}

PATRICK PHILLIPS served as private, SO Co., Capt. John Gunby's 2nd Independent Maryland Company, sick at Princess Anne on 12 March 1776; mustered on 21 Aug 1776. {RPWS:227}

SAMUEL PHILLIPS m. Betsy Robert, dau. of John Roberts.

On 24 Nov 1797 Samuel Phillips and wife Betsy of DO Co., sold to Whittington White as Joseph Wallace conveyed to John Roberts by mortgage. He died and left unpaid and left only dau. Betsy Roberts, wife of Samuel Phillips and encumbered with mortgage and dower rights now held by Job Parks and wife Mary Parks, 200 a. between Manokin and Wicomico River. {SOLR:145}

SARAH PHILLIPS. Rachel Caldwell, SO Co., d. by 5 Feb 1761 when the inventory of her estate was filed by Christopher Piper. Signed as next of kin: Ann Hardy, Sarah Philips. {MINV 73:134}

STEPHEN PHILLIPS patented *Stephen's Security* (150 a.) in WO Co. on 29 Sep 1761. {MPL BC14:326; BC16:47}

RICHARD PHILLIPS. In 1734 he was head of household in Pocomoke Hundred.

WILLIAM PHILLIPS patented the following tracts in SO Co.: *Dispute* (100 a.), on 3 July 1741; *First Choice* (50 a.) on 5 July 1741; *Second Choice* (150 a.) on 3 July 1741; *Partnership* (100 a.) on 6 May 1759). {MPL EI5:555, 558, 559; EI6:357; LGB:334, 392; BC18:143; BC21:90}

WILLIAM PHILLIPS There is a second Wm. Phillips in Nanticoke Hundred in 1739.

WILLIAM PHILLIPS m. Ann
    Henry Mariner, WO Co., d. by 28 July 1755 when the inventory of his estate was filed by An Phillips, wife of William Phillips. Signed as next of kin: Jacob Mariner, Boman Mariner. {MINV 59:95} On 28 July 1755, admin accounts were filed on his estate by Ann wife of William Philips. Distribution to (children): accountant, Peter, Robinson, John, Mary, Wrixham. {MDAD:38:108}

THE PITT FAMILY of Talbot County

JOHN PITT m. 1st Frances (N), m. 2nd Sarah Thomas, and m. 3rd Rebecca Hosier, widow of Henry Hosier and dau. of Stephen Keddy. {See The Hosier Family, vol. 1 of this series.}
    On 26 Feb 1671 John Clement of TA Co., merchant, received from John Pitt and Frances his wife *Hockeday*, 600 a. in DO Co. on the western most side of Blackwater. {TALR 1:203}
    On 10 Feb 1673 John Pitt and his wife Frances conveyed to Thomas Booker, 200 a., *Dutch Creeke*. {TALR 1:309}
    On 10 Sep 1675 John Pitt, merchant, and his wife Frances, conveyed to Edward Man, merchant, land in Tred Haven Creek at or near the head of the middle branch, all tenanted by John Pitt and his wife or assigned under tenants: *Exchange, Westmoreland, Pitt's Chance* and *Pitt's Range*, containing as by patent in the whole 1400 a. {TALR 2:345}
    John Pitt, TA Co., planter, and Sarah Thomas, Kent Co., m. 25th da., 6th mo., 1680, at the house of William Berry. {TATH}
    On 21st day, 8th mo., 1687 the meeting expressed concern for the orphans of Thomas Taylor. On 2nd day, 9th mo., 1688 Thomas Taylor was advised to go home with his uncle John Pitt and Aunt until he is otherwise disposed of and that he keep meetings with his uncle. {TATH}
    On 17 Jan 1687 John Pitt, planter, and his wife Sarah conveyed to Edward Turner, planter, 400 a. called *John's Hill* in a branch of King's Creek,

Great Choptank River adj. Henry Parker's land called *Parker's Freshes*. {TALR 5:159}

On 24th day, 12th mo., 1697 John Pitt expressed an inclination to remove with his wife to Pennsylvania. {TATH}

On 30th day, 10th mo., 1702 John Pitt complains that Robert Register owes him and takes no care to pay his debt. {TATH}

On 22 Nov 1699 John Pitt of TA Co., merchant, and his wife Sarah, the late wife of John Woolcott of Kent Island, dec'd., conveyed to John Copedge, planter, 40 a. on the Isle of Kent near the head of Bever Neck Creek adj. the land of William Hemsley and also one other tract called *Bever Neck* lying betwixt Beaver Neck Creek and the Chesapeake Bay. {TALR 8:003}

Sarah Pitt, wife of John Pitt, d. 15th da., 2nd mo., 1704. She was keeper of the books and papers of the women's meeting. {TATH}

On 26th day, 2nd mo., 1705 John Pitt and Daniel Powell who are relations of James Berry's orphans are appointed to enquire into the father in law of sd. orphans and how things stand in relation to their estate. {TATH}

John Pitt, TA Co., merchant, and Elizabeth Baynard, TA Co., m. 6th da., 9th mo., 1706 at Tuckaho meeting house. {TATH}

Sarah Pitt, of John and Elizabeth Pitt, b. 7th day., 3rd mo., 1709. {TATH}

Elizabeth Pitt d. 3rd day, 5th mo., 1709.

On 13th day, 11th mo., 1711 John Pitt and Rebecka Hosier declared their intentions to marry at Cecil Monthly Meeting. {CEMM}

John Pitt d. 27 Oct 1717. {TAPE}

John Pitt, merchant, TA Co., d. leaving a will dated 21 Oct 1717, proved 14 Nov 1717. To dau. Elizabeth Sherwood, personalty, she and her husband, John Sherwood, to be content therewith, in consideration of the estate settled on grandson James Berry. To dau. Susannah, wife of Daniell Powell, personalty; to have no further interest in estate, in consideration of the estate already given to sd. Daniell Powell. To grandson Howell Powell, personalty. To grandson John Powell, 500 a. of a tract of 1500 a. called *Colerain* on Tuckahoe Creek, and personalty. To grandson James Berry, dwelling plantation after decease of testator's wife. He to live with her if he chooses, and may build on the uncultivated part of sd. plantation; also residuary legatee of estate, and in event of wife's death, exec. of estate. To wife Rebecca, extx., dwelling plantation for life unless she marry, when dwelling plantation shall pass in 6 mos. to grandson James Berry, and water mill for life. Also to her that part of Henry Hosier's estate which belonged to her when she was his widow, and personalty. To the monthly meeting of Quakers of TA Co., £5. Should any differences arise between extx. and legatees, testator directs that the Monthly Meeting appoint 2, 4, or 6 of its male members, who shall have absolute authority to settle such differences; any beneficiary not abiding by their decisions to forfeit all benefits from testator's estate. Witnessed by Robt. Walker, William Harrell, William

Dobson, Thomas Anderson, James Townsend. {MWB 14:377}

On 29 Nov 1720 the admin. account of the estate of John Pitt, TA Co., was submitted by Rebecca Pitt. Legatees: Quaker Monthly Meeting, paid to Samuel Dickenson; James Berry; wife (unnamed) of Daniel Powell and 2 of their children (unnamed); Elizabeth Sherwood then m. to John Sherwood, paid to James Berry. {MDAD 3:164}

On 7 Nov 1722 Rebeckah Pitt released James Berry of all his debts for all time.{TALR 13:55}

John was father of ELIZABETH, m. 1st on 11 Dec 1691, James Berry, son of William and Margaret Berry and m. 2nd 28 Jan 1702, John Sherwood; SUSANNAH, d. 9th da., 8th mo., 1745, m. 20th da., 7th mo., 1694, Daniell Powell (b. c1670, d. 16th da., 4th mo., 1731); SARAH, b. 7th day, 3rd mo., 1709. {See The Berry Family and The Howell Powell Family, vol. 3 of this series.}

THE PITT FAMILY of Dorchester County

1. PHILLIP PITT m. Ann Fisher, dau. of Alexander Fisher.

On 27 July 1687, Phillip Pitt patented *Strawberry Garden Addition,* 50 a. {MPL 25:408, 32:700}

In Aug 1688 Edward Pindar of DO Co., Gent., conveyed to Phillip Pitt *Strawberry Garden* on n.w. branch of Transquakin River on w. side of the river adj. Michaell Mason's land and containing 150 a. {DOLR 4 Old 228}

On 4 Dec 1694 Anthony Squires of DO Co. and his wife Mary conveyed to Philip Pitt of the same co., ½ of 300 a. called *The Plaines* on Hunting Creek. {DOLR 5 Old 56}

Alexander Fisher, DO Co., d. leaving a will dated 28 Jan 1698, proved 4 March 1698. To the 5 children (unnamed) of son in law Philip Pitt, personalty. To dau. Ann Pitt (widow), 50 a. on branch of Blackwater River. To dau. Eliza: 40 a., *Barron Point*. To wife Eliza:, extx., personalty and life interest in all real estate. Witnessed by Wm. Hagan, Avid Melville, And. Parker.[7] {MWB 6:308}

Philip Pitt, DO Co., d. leaving a will dated 9 Aug 1698, proved 2 Oct 1698. To son John, dwelling plantation; to pass to son Charles in event of death of son John without issue. To son Philip, land at Hunting Creek purchased of Anthony Squires. Wife Ann, extx., all personal estate and interest in dwelling

---

7. Alexander Fisher (Sr.) had 3 tracts of land on the Blackwater River: *Ellson* (50 a.), *Barren Point* (40 a.), and *Littleworth* (10 a.). The Dorchester Co. Rent Rolls cite that Barren Point is in the possession of Phillip Pitt. {DORR:10:408} The Dorchester Co. Rent Rolls cite that *Ellson* and *Littleworth* are in the possession of Alexander Fisher. {DORR:10:407, 408} Thus, his son Alexander (Jr.) ended up with *Ellson* and *Littleworth*. And that Alexander (Sr.)'s daughter Ann received *Barren Point*.

plantation afsd. during widowhood. In event of her marriage she is to possess land at Hunting Creek afsd. during minority of son Philip. Witnessed by Jno. Winsemore, Jno. Rawlings, Obediah King. {MWB 6:237} The inventory of the estate was filed in 1698. {INAC 18:247}

Ann Pitt d. by 10 March 1698 when the inventory of her estate was filed. {INAC 19:139} The admin. account was submitted c1703 by Thomas Snelson, admin. of John Snelson, admin. of the dec'd. {INAC 24:204; TP:20:18} [The entry cites the dec'd. as Phillip Pitt. The Testamentary Proceedings cite that Thomas Snelson presented admin accounts for both Philip & Ann at the same time.]

Philip was father of: THOMAS; JOHN; CHARLES; PHILIP; ELIZABETH, who married John Snelson..

Second generation
2. THOMAS PITT of DO Co., eldest son of Phillip (1) Pitt, m. Sarah (N).

In Nov 1721, Thomas Pitt and his wife Sarah sold to Mark Fisher, *Barren Point* 40 a. {DOLR:2:100}

Thomas Pitt, DO Co., d. by 16 Jan 1721 when an admin bond was filed by Sarah Pitt. Sureties: Anthony Rawlings, Sr., Anthony Rawlings, Jr. {TP:25:78} On 5 Jul 1722, the inventory of his estate was filed. Signed as next of kin: John Pitt, Mary Fisher. {MINV 7:211; TP:26:7} The admin. accounts were submitted on 25 July 1722 and 14 March 1723 by Sarah Pitt, admx. {MDAD 5:15, 132}

Thomas is prob. father of: JOHN; MARY, m. (N) Fisher.

3. JOHN PITT, son of Philip (1) Pitt, m. Mary Woolford (b. 29 Feb 1691), dau. of Roger Woollford. {See The Woolford Family, vol. 14 of this series.}

On 11 March 1728 John Pitt and his wife Mary of DO Co., Gent., conveyed to William Ennalls of said co., merchant, part of *Masons Hopyard* on n. w. side of Transquakin River adj. *Pitts Desire* and *Ennalls Lott* and containing 50 a.; also part of *Pitts Desire* containing 20 a. {DOLR 8 Old 266}

On 1 Aug 1744 Charles Dickinson of DO Co., Gent., conveyed to John Pitt of the same co., mariner, ½ of *The Plaines* on the n. side of the head of Hunting Creek, said ½ interest having been conveyed by Anthony Squires to Phillip Pitt in 1694. It having been found that no patent had issued for said land, Dickinson has obtained a patent and John Pitt has paid him ½ of the cost thereof. {DOLR 12 Old 17}

Between 6 March 1740 and 12 August 1741, Mary Pitts, wife of Capt. John Pitts, aged 50, made a deposition. {DOLR:12:122}

John Pitt, DO Co., mariner, d. leaving a will dated 31 Jan 1745, proved 12 March 1745. To son Roger Pitt, my dwelling plantation, land formerly called *Nick's Branch* and *Refuge* and *Pitts* and land belonging to *Mason's Happyyard* which I bought of Wm. Ennals. Also mentioned sons Thomas Pitt, William Pitt and Philip Pitt. Dau. Sarah Pitt and son Roger Pitts, execs. Witnessed by F. Ennals, Thos. Airy, Henry Hayward, Henry Hayward, Jr. {MWB 24:360}

On 11 June 1746 the inventory of the estate of Capt. John Pitt, DO Co., was filed by Thomas Airey. Signed as next of kin: Thomas Pitt, Sarah Pitt. A second inventory was filed c1747. Signed as next of kin: Thomas Woollford, Thomas Pitt. {MINV 32:345; 35:227}

On 4 July 1747 the first admin. account was filed by Thomas Airey, clerk. Legatees: Sarah, dau. and wife of Levin Gillis. Payments to Sarah (dau., her portion) wife of Levin Gillis; Mary (dau., her portion), wife of Ebenezar White. On 13 May 1749 a second admin. account of his estate was submitted by Rev. Thomas Airey, admin.. Payments to Daniel Dulany, Esq.; Joseph Ennalls; Eben. White who m. Mary Pitt, representative; accountant, legal representative; Thomas Woolford, guardian of Thomas Pitt and William Pitt (sons, representatives); Henry Hooper, Jr. {MDAD 23:347; 27:2}

John was father of MARY, m. Ebenezar White; ROGER; THOMAS; WILLIAM; PHILIP; SARAH, m. Levin Gillis.

4. CHARLES PITT, son of Philip (1) Pitt. He is not found in the records after 1698.

5. PHILLIP PITT, son of Philip (1) Pitt. He is not found in the records after 1698.

6. ELIZABETH PITT, dau. of Philip (1) Pitt, m. John Snelson.

Ann Pitt d. by 10 March 1698 when the inventory of her estate was filed. {INAC 19:139} The admin. account was submitted c1703 by Thomas Snelson, admin. of John Snelson, admin. of the dec'd. {INAC 24:204} [The entry cites the dec'd. as Phillip Pitt. However, an examination of the applicable records indicates that the dec'd. must be Ann Pitt.]

On 1 & 4 Nov 1698, Howell Powell & his wife Joanna (TA) sold to John Snelson (mariner of London), *East Town* 82 a., and *Weston* 300 a. {DOLR:5:122}

Capt. John Snelson, DO Co., d. by 12 April 1701 when an inventory of his estate was filed. {INAC:21:42} On 1 Oct 1703, admin accounts were filed on his estate by Thomas Snelson. {INAC:24:250}

On 21 Dec 1723, John Ogle of Chapel Charlton (Staffordshire) sold to William Ennalls, *East Town* 82 a. and *Weston* 300 a., both tracts were sold by Howell Powell & his wife Joanna to John Snelson, mariner of London, who devised the land in his last will to his wife Elizabeth Snelson for her lifetime and then to her children, or for want of issue, to his two nephews John Ogle (son of Andrew and Mary Ogle) and Thomas Snelson (son of Thomas and Elizabeth Snelson). Said Ogle being the sole surviving devisee. {DOLR:8:55}

Third Generation

7. JOHN PITTS of DO Co., poss. son of Thomas (2) Pitts, m. Anne Snelson, widow of John Snelson.

John Snelson, DO Co., d. by 25 April 1717 when an inventory of his estate was made. Signed as kin: Charles Wheeler, John Wheeler. {INAC:39B:5} On 26 May 1718, admin accounts were filed by Ann Snelson. Payments to (included): Mary Fisher admx. of Alexander Fisher[8]. {MDAD:1:110}

John Pitts, shoemaker, DO Co., d. leaving a will dated 11 Jan 1723, proved 16 Feb 1723/4. To son in law John Snellson and daus. in law Mary and Elizabeth Snellson, personalty. Wife Anne, extx., residue of estate; at her decease, to be divided among the children of Jno. Snelson, dec'd. Witnessed by Wm. Murray, Richd. Badly, Jno. Vincent. {MWB 18:232} The inventory of the estate of John Pitts, Blackwater, DO Co., was filed on 23 May 1724 by Ann Pitts. Signed as next of kin: Charles Wheeler. {MINV 9:422} On 10 March 1724 the admin. account of his estate was submitted by Ann Pitts, extx. {MDAD 6:302}

John was step-father of JOHN SNELSON; MARY SNELSON; ELIZABETH SNELSON.

8. THOMAS PITT, son of John (3) Pitt.

From 13 Nov 1759 to 10 March 1762, Capt. Thomas Pitts was a member of a commission to perpetuate the bounds of Charles Goldsborough's land *Canterbury*. {DOLR:18:78}

William Pitt, DO Co., d. making a verbal will on 4 Nov 1761 on his death bed who d. Wednesday, 4 Nov about 9 o'clock at night. The subscribers heard Thomas Pitt ask his bro. William Pitt on Sunday, 1 Nov 1761, to make his will, and he answered his bro. and said, "Let me alone for I am low enough in spirits already, for all I have shall be yours when I die." Witnessed on 5 Nov 1761 by John Travers, Wm. Cook, Jr. {MWB 31:534} A list of debts was filed on 26 Sep 1764 by Thomas Pitt, exec. {MINV 86:110} On 26 Sep 1764, admin accounts were filed by Thomas Pitt. Representatives (siblings): Thomas, Sarah, Mary wife of Ebenezar White.

9. WILLIAM PITT, son of John (3) Pitt.

William Pitt, DO Co., d. making a verbal will on 4 Nov 1761 on his death bed who d. Wednesday, 4 Nov about 9 o'clock at night. The subscribers heard Thomas Pitt ask his bro. William Pitt on Sunday, 1 Nov 1761, to make his will, and he answered his bro. and said, "Let me alone for I am low enough in spirits already, for all I have shall be yours when I die." Witnessed on 5 Nov

8. By 7 July 1718, Mary Fisher (admx. of Alexander Fisher) had married Pettigrew Salisbury. {MDAD:1:108}

1761 by John Travers, Wm. Cook, Jr. {MWB 31:534} A list of debts was filed on 26 Sep 1764 by Thomas Pitt, exec. {MINV 86:110} On 26 Sep 1764, admin accounts were filed by Thomas Pitt. Representatives (siblings): Thomas, Sarah, Mary wife of Ebenezar White.

Unplaced

JANE PITT m. Thomas Parsons 29 Sep 1748. {QALU}

JOHN PITTS of TA Co. m. Rachel Sheild, dau. of William Shield and Rhoda Blackwell.

On 16 Nov 1727, Robert Noble and Charles Stevens appraised the land of Thomas Emerson and Phillip Emerson (monors). Cites plantation where John Blackwell lives, toward the plantation where John Pitts and James Saunders live. {TALR:13:391}

John Pitts appears on the tax list of TA Co., Island Hundred, in 1733. {COES:17}

On 19 Aug 1751 John Pitts, late of TA Co. but now of SO Co., conveyed to Edward Lloyd, Esq., of TA Co., 400 a. called *Hambleton's Park* which belonged to Rachel Sheild, the wife of John Pitts and also any and all other tracts in TA Co. the said Pitts hath any claim to. {TALR 18:8}

On 3 Aug 1773 John Pitts, formerly of TA Co., planter, but now in the county of Baltimore, conveyed to John Gibson, the elder of TA Co., a moiety of 137 ½ a., part of *Hambleton's Park* on the easternmost branch of Wye River, devised by Jane Blackwell (d. 1723) of TA Co. to her granddau. Rachel Shields, mother of the said John Pitts. {TALR 20:310}

THOMAS PITT, Kent Co., age 40, made a deposition in Dec 1752. {ESVR 1}

THE PITT FAMILY of Northampton and Isle of Wight Counties, Virginia

1. ANDREW PITT m. Alee/Elizabeth (N). Alee/Elizabeth m. 2nd Thorne Wills.

The tax lists for Accomack Co. cite Andrew Pitt(s) as head of household in 1690, 1692-1694. {ACTL}

On 20 Nov 1696, Andrew Pitt sued Mr. Justinian Yeo and William Randolph. {ACCO :8:221} Suit was dismissed. {ACCO:8:229}

On 2 March 1696/7, Andrew Pitt admitted to owing Capt. George Nich. Hack. {ACCO:8:239}

On 7 Dec 1697, Mr. Robert Hutchinson sued Andrew Pitt. The sheriff could not find said Pitt. {ACCO:9:1}

On 7 Feb 1700/1, Andrew Pitt sued Mr. Justinian Yeo. {ACCO:9:113, 120}

Suit was dismissed. {ACCO:9:122}

Andrew Pitt, Northampton Co., VA, carpenter, d. leaving a will dated 13 Feb 1710, proved 10 Sep 1715. Mentioned wife Alee, son John, son Thomas, son Andrew (under age 21), son Edward, dau. Mary Pitt, dau. Ann Pitt. dau. Margaret, dau. Amy. Wife residuary legatee and extx. Witnessed by William Goulding, Richard Turner, Luke Taylor. {Marshall:206}

The tax lists for Northampton Co. cite Alice Pitts as head of household in 1720. {NOTL}

Thorne Wills, NO Co., d. by 8 June 1725, when an admin bond was filed on his estate by Elizabeth Wills his widow. {Marshall:252}

Elizabeth Wills d. leaving a will dated 11 Jan 1734, proved 8 April 1735. To cousin Bescaner Bennit. Remaining estate to my grandson Edmund Pitts but if he dies under 18 then estate to fall to William Dixon, son of Tilney. Exec. friend Dingly Gray. Witnessed by Isaac Smith, Major Pitts. {Marshall:287}

Edmund Pitts d. leaving a will dated 20 Dec 1748, proved 13 June 1749. To uncle Major Pitts the plantation whereon I now live bounded by John Cobb and Michael Ward and my plantation on the n. side of Naswadox Creek bounded by John Smith and John Johnson. Uncle Major Pitts residuary legatee and exec. Witnessed by Benjamin Dingly Gray, Southy Cobb, Sarah Cobb. John Pitts, heir, contested the will. {Marshall:325}

Andrew was father of ANDREW, b. after 1689; THOMAS, b.c. 1705; JOHN, b.c. 1707; EDWARD; MARY; ANN; MARGARET; AMY; MAJOR, b.c. 1713; JACOB, b.c. 1715.

Second Generation

2. ANDREW PITT, b. after 1689, son of Andrew (1) Pitt, m. Alice Green, widow of John Green, and sister of Thomas Bold.

John Green, Northampton Co., d. by 17 March 1717/18 when admx. of his estate was Alice Green widow of dec'd. Approvers: Major Joyne, Edward Joyne, Arthur Robins, William Nickolson. The widow Alice m. Andrew Pitt. {Marshall:217}

In his will dated 24 Dec 1721, proved 9 Jan 1721/2 Thomas Bold mentioned his sister Alee Pitts. {Marshall:239}

The tax lists for Northampton Co. cite Andrew Pitt(s) as head of household in 1720-1723, 1725-1731, 1733, 1734, 1737-1744. Living in his household is Robert Lennard (1729), Littleton Pitt (1742-1744). {NOTL}

Andrew is probably the father of: LITTLETON.

3. THOMAS PITTS, b.c. 1705, son of Andrew (1) Pitts, m. Elisha (N).

The tax lists for Northampton Co. cite Thomas Pitt(s) in the household of Thorne Wills in 1721-1724. Thomas Pitt(s) is cited as head of household in 1725-1729. Living in his household is Nat. Johnson (1728), Major Pitt (1729).

68

The tax lists for Northampton Co. cite widow Pitt(s) as head of household in 1731. {NOTL}

Thomas Pitts, Northampton Co., d. leaving a will dated 24 April 1730, proved 9 June 1730. Mentioned wife (unnamed), son William, son Edmond and his mother, bro. Jacob. Wife extx. Son Edmond to remain with his mother in law. Witnessed by George Green, Isaac Smith. Probate: The will appointed extx. is Elisha Pitts.{Marshall:267}

Thomas was father of WILLIAM, d.s.p. by 1749; EDMOND, b.c. 1728.

4. JOHN PITTS of Northampton Co., b.c. 1707, son of Andrew (1) Pitt, m. Leah (N).

The tax lists for Northampton Co. cite John Pitt(s) in the household of Francis Downame in 1723[9], at Elizabeth Johnson's in 1724. The tax lists for Northampton Co. cite John Pitt(s) as head of household in 1725-1731, 1734, 1735, 1737-1744, 1765, 1769. Living in his household is Major Pitt (1731), Jacob Pitt (1731), Hillary Pitt (1742-1744), Edmund Pitt (1744). {NOTL}

Edmund Pitts d. leaving a will dated 20 Dec 1748, proved 13 June 1749. To uncle Major Pitts the plantation whereon I now live bounded by John Cobb and Michael Ward and my plantation on the n. side of Naswadox Creek bounded by John Smith and John Johnson. Uncle Major Pitts residuary legatee and exec. Witnessed by Benjamin Dingly Gray, Southy Cobb, Sarah Cobb. John Pitts, heir, contested the will. {Marshall:325}

John Pitts, Northampton Co., VA, d. leaving a will dated 26 March 1759, proved 11 Aug 1761. To son Jacob, 112 a. bounded by Park and Turner's lands and for want of heirs to my son John. To son Jacob, Negro girl Pleasant and my smith's tools. To my son John all the remainder of my land being 113 a. bounded by Turner's and Ward's land and for want of his heirs to my son Jacob. To my son John, Negro boy Toney, my new gun, all my clothes and my boat. To wife Leah, Negro wench Nell. To dau. Ann, Negroes Israel and Jamey and horse Spark. To dau. Annmary, bed and furniture. To granddau. Anne Evans £5. To granddau. Tabitha £5. To grandson Amos Johnson £10. Residuary legatees: wife and son John and Jacob and Annmary and Bridget and dau. Anne. Wife and son John execs. Witnessed by John Milby, Lazarus Rogers, Jackson Rogers. {Marshall:390}

In 1777 Jacob Pitts, son of John Pitts, and his wife Tamar Pitts of Isle of Wight Co. sold his inherited land to Edward Turner. {Whitelaw:551}

John was father of HILLARY, b.c. 1726; JACOB; JOHN; ANNE;

---

9. There is a second entry for 1723 which cited John Pitt in the household of Thomas Cable.

ANNMARY; BRIDGET.

5. MAJOR PITTS, b.c. 1713, son of Andrew (1) Pitts, m. Jamima Gray, dau. of Dingley and Mary Gray.

The tax lists for Northampton Co. cite Major Pitt(s) in the household of Thomas Pitt(s) in 1729, in the household of John Pitt(s) in 1731. Major Pitt(s) is cited as head of household in 1737-1744. {NOTL}

Dingly Gray d. making a verbal will dated 23 Aug 1742, proved 8 Feb 1742. As I have already given sundry goods to my two daus. Johnson Violata Louise and Jemima Pitts, my other children to have a part of my estate equal to that already given my daus. My son Benjamin Dingly Gray to have my man slave Kitts provided my wife Mary approves. Witnessed by Nicholas Campbell, John Smith, Rebekkah Smith. {Marshall:311}

Mary Gray, Northampton, widow, d. leaving a will proved 11 Dec 1750. Mentioned son Benjamin Dingley Gray, dau. Jos: — Vilater Laws; dau. Mary Taylor; dau. Jemima Pitts; son Jacob Johnson Gray. Witnessed by William Glover, Ann Mary Glover, John Smith, Nicholas Bull. {Marshall:329}

Major Pitts, Northampton Co., d. leaving a will dated 5 April 1762, proved 11 May 1762. To son Hezekiah all my lands, 1/5 of my crops, Negro fellow Tucker after my wife's decease, black horse Dapple and all my clothes. To all the rest of my children £15 apiece before my dau. Margaretta Booth should have any part. Excepting legacies to Hezekiah, my wife to have entire estate during her widowhood and then to be divided by all my children, viz., Margaretta Booth, Vianna Pitts, Mary Pitts, Major Pitts, Edmund Pitts and William Pitts. Son Hezekiah shall be of age to act and do for himself from this date. Son Hezekiah and wife Jamima, execs. Witnessed by Thomas James, Nathaniel Savage. {Marshall:393}

The tax lists for Northampton Co. cite Major Pitt(s) in the household of Esau Jacobs in 1766. In 1769, Any Pitts is cited as head of household, with Hezekiah Pitts. {NOTL}

In 1774 Esau Jacob left 270 a. to his wife Vianna Grey, dau. of Major Pitts. {Whitelaw:278}

Major was father of MARGARETTA, m. (N) Booth; VIANNA GREY, m. Esau Jacob; MARY; MAJOR; EDMUND; WILLIAM; HEZEKIAH.

6. JACOB PITT, b.c. 1715, son of Andrew (1) Pitts.

The tax lists for Northampton Co. cite Jacob Pitt(s) in the household of John Pitt(s) in 1731, in household of John Dolby in 1738, in household of Thomas Preeson in 1739-1743. {NOTL}

Third Generation

7. LITTLETON PITT, b.c. 1726, son of Andrew (2) Pitt.

The tax lists for Northampton Co. cite Andrew Pitt(s) as head of household in 1720-1723, 1725-1731, 1733, 1734, 1737-1744. Living in his household is Littleton Pitt (1742-1744). [Littleton disappears from the records after 1744.] {NOTL}

8. EDMUND PITTS, b.c. 1728, d.s.p. 1749, son of Thomas (3) Pitts.

Elizabeth Wills d. leaving a will dated 11 Jan 1734, proved 8 April 1735. To cousin Bescaner Bennit. Remaining estate to my grandson Edmund Pitts but if he dies under 18 then estate to fall to William Dixon, son of Tilney. Exec. friend Dingly Gray. Witnessed by Isaac Smith, Major Pitts. {Marshall:287}

The tax lists for Northampton Co. cite John Pitt(s) as head of household in 1725-1731, 1734, 1735, 1737-1744. Living in his household is Edmund Pitt (1744). {NOTL}

Edmund Pitts d. leaving a will dated 20 Dec 1748, proved 13 June 1749. To uncle Major Pitts the plantation whereon I now live bounded by John Cobb and Michael Ward and my plantation on the n. side of Naswadox Creek bounded by John Smith and John Johnson. Uncle Major Pitts residuary legatee and exec. Witnessed by Benjamin Dingly Gray, Southy Cobb, Sarah Cobb. John Pitts, heir, contested the will. {Marshall:325}

9. HILLARY PITTS, b.c. 1726, son of John (4) Pitts, m. Tamar (N).

The tax lists for Northampton Co. cite John Pitt(s) as head of household in 1725-1731, 1734, 1735, 1737-1744. Living in his household is Hillary Pitt (1742-1744). {NOTL}

Hilary Pitts, NO Co., d. by 11 Mar 1755, when an admin bond was filed on his estate by Tamar Pitts. {Marshall:363, 381}

10. JACOB PITT, son of John (4) Pitts, m. Tamar (N).

The tax lists for Northampton Co. cite Jacob Pitt(s) in the household of John Pitt(s) in 1731, in household of John Dolby in 1738, in household of Thomas Preeson in 1739-1743. Jacob Pitts is cited as head of household in 1765, 1769. {NOTL}

Jacob Pitt, Isle of Wight Co., VA, d. leaving a will dated 4 Sep 1778, proved 3 May 1781. Mentioned wife Tamar, son Parnall when 21; and all my children. Execs.: Wife, Brewer Godwin and Henry Pitt. Witnessed by John Scarsbrook Wills, Jeremiah Godwin, Martha King. Security: George Norsworthy and Jeremiah Godwin. {*Wills and Administrations of Isle of Wight County, Virginia, 1647-1800*, compiled by Blance Adams Chapman, (1938) p. 252. Hereafter cited as Chapman.}

The account of the estate of Jacob Pitt was examined by William Waltham, Joseph Driver, Willis Corbell on 1 Dec 1800. Signed by Ishmiah Pitt,

admin. of Tamer Pitt, who was the admx. of Jacob Pitt. {Chapman:319}
Jacob was father of PARNALL; OTHER CHILDREN.

11. JOHN PITTS, son of John (4) Pitts, m. Polley (N).
John Pitts, Northampton Co., d. leaving a will dated 17 Jan 1770, proved 10 April 1770. To son Revel, Negro man Toney. To dau. Salley Pitts, young Negro girl Nanny. To son John, Negro boy Toby. To wife Polley, Negro wench Phylis. Residuary legatees wife and three children. Wife extx. Witnessed by William Christian, Josiah Heath, Maddox Turner. {Marshall:418}
John was father of REVEL; SALLEY; JOHN.

THE JOHN PITT FAMILY of Somerset County, Maryland

1. JOHN PITTS, m. Elizabeth (N).
On 26 Feb 1694, John Pitts was one of appraisers of estate of Francis Gunby. {INAC:13A:339}
John Pitts, SO Co., d. by 27 Jan 1699 when the inventory of his estate was filed. (Administrator unnamed). Appraisers: John Henderson; Henry Schoolfield. {INAC 11B:18; TP:18B:9}
At April Court 1703, Elizabeth the admx. of John Pitt (SO) was summoned to render accounts. {TP:19A:125} At July Court 1703, and then again at August Court 1703, Col. Francis Jenkins administrator of John Pitt (SO) was summoned to render accounts. {TP:19A:161, 194}
Elizabeth Pitts, SO Co., d. leaving a will dated 22 April 1715, proved 25 Aug 1716. To son George, personalty. To eldest dau. Ann, personalty, some of which is on Edward Stevens' place. To second dau. Jane, personalty. Execs.: John and Ann Tilman. Witnessed by Mary Upshur, Robert Mills. On 29 Dec 1715 John Tilman and Ann Tilman by joint consent made over admin. of the will to John Pitts. {MWB 14:292} On 18 Sep 1716, an admin bond was filed by John Pitts, administrator. Sureties: Alexander Willson, Samuel Merchment. {TP:23:109} On 16 Oct 1716 the inventory of her estate was filed. {INAC 39C:150} On 23 May 1718 the admin. account of her estate was submitted by John Pitts. {MDAD 1:155}
John and Elizabeth were parents of: JOHN; GEORGE; ANN, m. by 1715 John Tilghman {ASOS:263}; JANE.

Second Generation
2. JOHN PITTS, son of John (1) Pitt, m. Hannah Henderson, dau. of John Henderson.
John Pitts recorded a cattle mark in SO Co. in 1700. {COES:41}
On 31 Oct 1702, John Pitts was a witness to will of John

72

Upshott/Upshur. {WOW:MH#3:182} [Robert Blades is cited as brother-in-law of testator.]

On 14 March 1705, James Atkinson and his wife Patience deeded to John Pitt (carpenter) pt. *Adventure* 200 a. {SOD:L:11} This land is cited as the land of the widow Pitts, later known as *Adventure*. {SORR:70}

On 4 Sep 1707, John Pitts gave evidence in suit of Robert Pitts vs. William Timmons. {SOJR:1707-1708:192}

Henry Bishop, SO Co., d. by 22 Nov 1709, when an admin bond was filed by William Henderson who married Elizabeth Bishop extx. of said Henry. Sureties: John Pitt, Robert Blades. {TP:20:233}

On 5 Feb 1711, John Pitts (heir apparent of John Pitts) and his wife Hannah deeded to Robert Pitts (tanner), pt. *Adventure* 200 a. bought of James Atkinson. {SOD:CD:683}

Elizabeth Pitts, SO Co., d. leaving a will dated 22 April 1715, proved 25 Aug 1716. To son George, personalty. To eldest dau. Ann, personalty, some of which is on Edward Stevens' place. To second dau. Jane, personalty. Execs.: John and Ann Tilman. Witnessed by Mary Upshur, Robert Mills. On 29 Dec 1715 John Tilman and Ann Tilman by joint consent made over admin. of the will to John Pitts. {MWB 14:292} On 18 Sep 1716, an admin bond was filed by John Pitts, administrator. Sureties: Alexander Willson, Samuel Merchment. {TP:23:109} On 16 Oct 1716 the inventory of her estate was filed. {INAC 39C:150} On 23 May 1718 the admin. account of her estate was submitted by John Pitts. {MDAD 1:155}

On 18 March 1717/8, John Pitts was member of a jury. {SOJR:1717-1718:14}

On 26 Nov 1724, John Pitts was an appraiser of estate of Silas Chapman. {WOI:JW#15:132}

The name John Pitt appears on the tax lists of SO Co. in 1723, 1724, 1725 and 1730 has head of household in Pocomoke Hundred. In 1723 living in the same household are 2 Negroes age 16 or greater and Francis Brooks. In 1724 appear the names John Pitts and John Pitts, Jr. His name does not appear in 1733-40.

John Henderson, Sr., planter, WO Co., d. leaving a will dated 1 Aug 1723, proved 9 Jan 1743-4. To son Benjamin, *Haphazard* where he now dwells. To son Charles, *Ropemakers* on Potomac R. lying next to land formerly given his bro. John. To son James, part of *Mortlack* bordered by land where testator's bro. James lived. To dau.-in-law Sarah, use of residue of Mortlack at her marriage or death to pass to grandson John. To wife Elizabeth, extx., entire personal estate and dwelling plantation for life. At her death, land to pass to son James. To sons afsd. grandson Joseph, son of James, granddau. Jemima and her sis. Comfort, to dau. Comfort Newbold and her children William, Eliza and John, to dau. Hannah Pitts, grandson Barnaby son of Charles, grandson James, dau.-in-law Parthenia and granddau. Mary Small, personal estate at death of

wife. Note: Jan. 9th, widow Elizabeth elects to stand by her husband's will.
{MWB:23:309}

On 5 Sep 1793 James Bennett, Micajah Bennett with wife Nancy, coheirs of William Pitts and wife conveyed to Bayley Young 75 ½ a. of *Adventure, Kickotans Choice, Bennetts Purchase.* On 5 Sep 1793 they conveyed 80 ½ a. of same to James Bennett. {WOD P:97}

John Pitts d. leaving a will dated 3 March 1744/5, proved 24 Sep 1745. To wife Hannah, extx. To son John Pitts after the decease of his mother, land on the n. side of the Mill Branch. To son Isaac Pitts land on the s. side of the Main Mill Branch after the decease of his mother. To son Samuel Pitts the remainder of my tract of land after my said wife's decease. To son William Pitts. To dau. Jemima Pitts. To son Robert Pitts all my lands in Maryland. To dau. Mary Blades. To dau. Elizabeth Merrill. To dau. Hannah Benston. To grandau. Ann Blades. To grandau. Hannah Blades. To grandau. Levinah Benston. Sons William and Samuel and dau. Jemima residuary legatees. Witnessed by George Douglas, Robert Pitt, Joseph Feddeman, Arthur Emmerson. {ACW:145}

Hannah Pitts d. leaving a will dated 29 March 1751, proved 30 June 1752. Grandsons John and William Pitts (under 21). To sons Samuel and William Pitts. To dau. Elizabeth Merril. Dau. Hannah Benston. Grandau. Sophia Blades. Grandau. Levinah Pitts. Grandau. Hannah Pitts, dau. of John Pitts, dec'd. Daus. Elizabeth Merril and Hannah Benston residuary legatees. Witnessed by Robert Pitt, Robert Pitts. Codicil: To son William Pitts. To dau. Jemimah Morse. {ACW:176}

John was father of JOHN; ISAAC; SAMUEL; WILLIAM; JEMIMA, m. (N) Moss; ROBERT; MARY, m. John Blades; ELIZABETH, m. (John) Merrill; HANNAH, m. Ezekiel Benston.

3. GEORGE PITTS, son of John (1) Pitt.

The tax lists for Somerset Co. cite George Pitts living in the household of John Tillman in Manokin Hundred in 1724. [Portions of the 1723 tax list for Manokin Hundred are unreadable.] {SOTL}

In 1754, George Pitts took an oath as a schoolmaster in Somerset Co. {1754 Black Books IV:133}

Third Generation

4. JOHN PITT, son of John (2) Pitt m. Katherine Revill, widow of Randall Revill.

The tax lists for Somerset Co. cite John Pitt as head of household in Manokin Hundred in 1744 and 1748. Also living in his household is Randall Revell.

The tax lists for Somerset Co. cite Cath. Pitt as head of household in Manokin Hundred in 1750. Also living in her household is Randall Revell.

John Pitt is cited as paying tax on 330 a. of *Double Purchase* in right of heirs of Randall Revell. {SORR}

Randall Revill, SO Co., d. by 18 Aug 1744 when the admin. account of his estate was submitted by Katherine Pitts, wife of John Pitts. Distribution was made to widow with residue to orphans Betty Revill, Randall, Katey, Sarah, Mary and Anne Revill. {MDAD 20:380}

Randall Revill, SO Co., d. by 18 Aug 1744 when the admin. account of his estate was submitted by Katherine Pitts, wife of John Pitts. Payments included widow (unnamed, 1/3). {MDAD 20:380}

John Pitts, SO Co., d. leaving a will dated 13 Feb 1749, proved 1 Dec 1749. To wife Katharine, 1/3 personal estate and 1/3 real estate in VA. To dau. Hannah Pitts, my land which is or may be mine that came to me by my father John Pitts, lying in Accomack Co., which he purchased of Col. Levin Gale, Esq., and in case of her death without issue, then to her sister Leah. To dau. Hannah furniture and slaves. To dau. Leah, slaves. To bro. William Pitts, silver shoe buckles and knee buckles and personalty. Wife extx. Witnessed by L. Hollyday, Jacob Airs, Randall Revell. {MWB 27:146} The inventory of his estate was filed by Katharine Pitts on 9 March 1750. {MINV:45:2} The admin. account was submitted by Katherine Pitts on 27 July 1751. Distribution was made to widow (unnamed) with residue to Leah Pitts. Mentioned estate of Randall Revill appraised in estate of dec'd. Legatees: William Pitts, Hannah Pitts, Leah Pitts. {MDAD 30:248}

John was father of HANNAH, m. John Morrison; LEAH, m. Andrew Gootee. {Whitelaw:1311}

5. ROBERT PITTS, son of John (2) Pitts.

Robert Pitts was serving in the militia company of Captain William Lane, SO Co., c1749. {COES}

On 17 Nov 1768 John Waller conveyed to Robert Pitts parts of *Stepney* and *Paris [Parish]* which Thomas Waller conveyed to the grantor in a deed dated 10 Jan 1768 {SOD D:245}

Robert is the father of: JOHN; WILLIAM; LEVINAH; HANNAH.

6. ISAAC PITTS, d.s.p. 1747, son of John (2) Pitts.

Isaac Pitts d. leaving a will dated 29 June 1747, proved 25 Aug 1747. To bro. William Pitts land bequeathed me by my father John Pitts. To mother Hannah Pitts. To bro. Robert Pitts. To bro. Samuel Pitts. To bro. John Pitts. To sister Jemima Pitts. To cousin Anne Blades. Bro. William, exec. Witnessed by Robert Pitts, Samuel Feddeman, Joseph Feddeman, Christopher Banks. {ACW:148}

7. SAMUEL PITTS, d.s.p. 1766/7, son of John (2) Pitts.

In 1766 Samuel Pitt left land to his cousin (niece) Leah Pitt, dau. of his bro. John Pitt; she m. Andrew Gootee and in 1773 they sold as 280 by survey to George Holden. {Whitelaw:1311}

The admin. of his estate was granted to Andrew Gootee on 1 July 1767. Littleton Dennis was security. {ACW:209}

8. WILLIAM PITTS, d.s.p. 1751, son of John (2) Pitts.

William Pitts d. leaving a will dated 5 April 1751, proved 26 Nov 1751. To bro. Samuel Pitts the land that was my bro. Isaac's given to him by his father, John Pitts and also one man called Jack and Negroes Pleasant and Peter to Samuel Pitts to school Hannah Pitts, the dau. of Robert Pitts, and also my part of the Negro Little Harry left me by my mother to the said Samuel Pitts. To Hannah Benston Negro, reversion to her dau. Hannah Benston. To Sophia Blades, Negro Rachel and the first child of the said Rachel to be delivered to John Benstone, the son of Ezekiel Benstone. To John Merril's son William Merril. To Samuel Pitts all my part of the cattle belonging to me by my mother's death. To John Blades, Jr. To Levin Merril, son of John Merril. To Zepheniah Benston, son of John Benston. To John Pitts, son of Robert Pitts. To bro. Robert Pitts. To sister Jemimah Moss. Brothers and sisters residuary legatees. Samuel Pitts, exec. Witnessed by Anderson Patterson, Samuel Feddiman, Massey Benson. {ACW:1666}

9. HANNAH (Ann) PITTS, dau. of John (2) Pitts, m. Ezekiel Benston.

Ezekiel Benston d. leaving a will dated 24 Feb 1762, proved 27 April 1762. To eldest son John Benston (under 21) all my land that I now hold. Bro. Micajah Benston. Son William Benston. Son James Benston. Daus. Mary and Grace Benston. Wife (unnamed) and bro. execs. Witnessed by Lisney Goottee, Joseph Gootee, Hannah Benston. In order of probate: Samuel Pitts appointed guardian to John Benston, infant heir at law to the testator. Micajah Benston and Ann Benston qualified. {ACW:211}

Ezekiel and Hannah were the parents of: JOHN BENSTON; WILLIAM BENSTON; JAMES BENSTON; MARY BENSTON; GRACE BENSTON; LEVINAH BENSTON; HANNAH BENSTON.

10. MARY PITTS, dau. John (2) Pitts, m. John Blades.

Sophia Blades, dau. John and Mary Blades, b. 17 July 1747. {SOCO}

Mary Blades, wife of John Blades, d. 23 July 1747. {SOCO}

John Blade, WO Co., d. leaving a will dated 9 Feb 1767, proved 10 April 1767. Legatees: son John, pt. *Adventure*, pt. *Kickoton Choice*; brother Samuel Blades, pt. *Adventure*, pt. *Kickoton Choice*; daus. Ann Benston, Elizabeth Blades, Sophia Tyler; granddau. Mary Glaster; granddau. Leah Pitt Blades; dau. Mary, pt. *Kickoton Choice*. Witnesses: Thomas Tyler, William Pitts, Jemimah Tyler. {WOW JW#3:137} On 21 May 1767 the inventory of his estate was filed by Mary Pitt (late Mary Blade). Signed as next of kin: Samuel Blade, Johnna Blade. {MINV 94:83}

John and Mary were the parents of: JOHN; ANN, m. (N) Benston; ELIZABETH; SOPHIA, m. (N) Tyler; MARY, m. William Pitts.

Fourth Generataion

11. WILLIAM PITTS, prob. son of Robert (5) Pitts, m. Mary Blades, dau. of John Blades.

John Blade, WO Co., d. leaving a will dated 9 Feb 1767, proved 10 April 1767. Legatees: son John, pt. *Adventure*, pt. *Kickoton Choice*; brother Samuel Blades, pt. *Adventure*, pt. *Kickoton Choice*; daus. Ann Benston, Elizabeth Blades, Sophia Tyler; granddau. Mary Glaster; granddau. Leah Pitt Blades; dau. Mary, pt. *Kickoton Choice*. Witnesses: Thomas Tyler, William Pitts, Jemimah Tyler. {WOW:JW#3:137} On 21 May 1767 the inventory of his estate was filed by Mary Pitt (late Mary Blade). Signed as next of kin: Samuel Blade, Johnna Blade. {MINV 94:83}

William Pitts, WO Co., d. leaving a will dated 4 Feb 1773, proved 24 March 1773. To wife Mary Pitts, extx., all of estate. {MWB 39:187} On 30 Aug 1773 the inventory of the estate of William Pitts, WO Co., submitted by Mary Pitts. Signed as next of kin: John Blades, Samuel Blades. {MINV 117:38}

Unplaced

ANN PITTS

John Nelson, SO Co., d. by 3 May 1737 when the inventory of his estate was made. Signed as kin: John Shiles, Alice Shiles. Admx.: Ann Nelson. {MINV:22:336} On 6 Oct 1744 the admin. account of his estate was submitted by Anne Nelson (alias Ann Pitts). Mentioned children: Sarah, Elizabeth and Alice Nelson. {MDAD 21:77}

HENRY PITTS m. 1776, Ester Powel (b. 17 April 1757), dau. of Samuel and Rachel Powel. {St. Martin's Register}

ROBERT PITTS

On 1 Aug 1710, Robert Blades and his wife Ann Mary deeded to Robert Pitts (Pocomoke), 400 a. of land granted to Thomas Davis (now dec'd.). {SOD:CD:566}

At October Court 1708, Robert Pitts (carpenter) vs. James Lang. {SOJR:1707-1708:165}

At March Court 1708 (OS), Robert Pitts (carpenter) vs. William Timmons. {SOJR:1707-1708:191}

At October Court 1710, Robert Pitts paid the security for James Smith.

{SOJR:1709-1711:428}

At January Court 1710/11, Robert Pitts brought James Smith into court. {SOJR:1709-1711:447}

On 5 Feb 1711, John Pitts (heir apparent of John Pitts) and his wife Hannah deeded to Robert Pitts (tanner), pt. *Adventure* 200 a. bought of James Atkinson. {SOD:CD:683}

At August Court 1714, suit of Robert Pitts vs. Robert Blades. {SOJR:1713-1715:125}

At May Court 1715, suit of Robert Pitts vs. Francis Roberts. {SOJR:1713-1715:214}

Robert Pitts recorded a gift of cattle in SO Co. court for his sons John and William Pitts on 12 July 1719. {ARMD LIV:786}

The name of Robert Pitts appears on the tax lists of SO Co., in Pocomoke Hundred in 1739 and 1740. In 1740 Bevins Moriss was living in the same household. {Russo}

Robert is the father of: JOHN; WILLIAM.

THE PITT FAMILY of Isle of Wight Co. and Accomack Counties, Virginia and Somerset County, Maryland

Ref. Boddie: For more details on this family see John Bennett Boddie, *Seventeenth Century Isle of Wight County Virginia*. Bodie claims this family descends from the famous William Pitt, Earl of Chatham, Prime Minister of England.

1. ROBERT PITT m. Martha (N).

Robert Pitt of Isle of Wight Co., VA, d. leaving a will dated 6 June 1672, proved 9 Jan 1674. Mentioned dau. Martha, son John, grandson John Pitt, grandson William Pitt, grandson Robert Pitt, dau. Mary Brassieur, dau. Hester Bridget, dau. Elizabeth Norsworthy, grandson Robert Pitt son of Robert Pitt dec'd.; my house and land to be for the relief of poor women as a gift from my dec'd. wife Martha. Exec. son John. Witnessed by Richard Jones, Thomas Hill. {Chapman:13}

Robert was father of MARTHA; JOHN; ROBERT (pre-deceased his father); MARY, m. (N) Brassieur; HESTER BRIDGET; ELIZABETH, m. (N) Norsworthy.

Second Generation

2. JOHN PITT, son of Robert (1) Pitt purchased or patented the tract *Musketta Quarter* c1660s in DO Co. Perhaps this is the John Pitt who was transported to Maryland from Virginia by 1664. {MPL CC:509; SR 8201; transcript 7:469}

On 6 Feb 1665 John Pitt of Isle of Wight Co., VA, conveyed to John Alford of Little Choptank, *Musketta Quarter* on Tobacco Stick Creek, 200 a. (in Dorchester Co., MD). {DOLR 1 Old 68}

John Pitt of the City of Bristol, d. leaving a will dated 28 Nov 1702, proved in Isle of Wight Co., VA, 9 Jan 1702/3. Mentions: father Colonel Robert Pitt. To son John land at Chuckatuck, whereon he now lives, son James, son Henry, grandson Robert Pitt, dau. Sarah Norsworthy, dau. Martha Norsworthy, dau. Prudence Driver, dau. Mary Drury, dau. in law Ann Bromfield her father John Brumfield's estate. Exec. son. Witnessed by Daniel Carver, George Allen, Richard Grammell. {Chapman:43, citing original Deed and Will Book 2:454}

John was father of ROBERT, m. Sarah, dau. of Col. Arthur Smith and left a son Robert; JOHN; HENRY; JAMES; SARAH, m. Tristram Norsworthy; PRUDENCE, m. Charles Driver; MARY, m. (N) Drury; MARTHA, m. George Norsworthy. {Boddie:511}

3. ROBERT PITT, d. by 16 June 1670, son of Robert (1) Pitt, m. Elizabeth (N) who later m. John Willie.

Robert Pitt had *Chuckatuck*, 1000 a., surveyed in Old Somerset on 23 Oct 1665 on n. side of the Pocomoke River. It was possessed by Thomas Layfield, purchased by George Layfield from Robert Pitts, son of Robert and given to said Thomas Layfield. {SORR}

On 28 Oct 1665 Robert Pitt received headrights for transporting Jno. Hudson, Mary Allen, Ellis Emperor, Susanna Serle, Jno. Noble, Jno. Wells, Ellen Wells, Elizabeth Jenkins, Thos. Saywells, Wm. Johnson, Ann Morgan, Allen Moyer, John Monkey(?), John Dawes. {OSES:475}

Following the marking in 1668 of the MD/VA boundary line on the Eastern Shore there were certain grants for lands south of the Pocomoke River made by the Virginia government which were determined to be within SO Co. These included those made on 2 Oct 1663 by Robert Pitts for 3000 a. and on 12 March 1662 by Robert Pitts for 1000 a. initially assumed to be in Accomack Co. {OSES:479; Boddie:510}

The inventory (described) begun on 8 July 1670 and filed on 8 Feb 1672/3 included a ship's bell and a great gun. {ACCO 3:111}

Upon intelligence of the death of Mr. Robert Pitt, Devoras Browne produced a will formerly made by the sd. Pitt appointing him to be his exec. Browne willing to take charge of said estate for 9 mos. from this date, and if no other will appears the Court to grant admin. upon the petition of sd. Brown, he in the meantime to take an inventory of the estate in this country and Mr. Richard Hill to be present. 16 June 1670. {ACW:4}

Admin. of the estate of Robert Pitt was granted to Devorax Browne upon the petition of Tabitha Brown, wife of sd. Devorax, in accordance with an order dated 16 June 1670. {ACW:5}

In 1674 Thomas Newbold leased for 11 years *Pitts Neck*, a 3000 a. tract on s. side of Pocomoke River in Accomack Co., from John and Elizabeth Willie. Elizabeth had been the widow of Robert Pitt, mariner, who d. with underage children, Elizabeth and Robert. {ASOS:188}

Robert was father of ROBERT; ELIZABETH.

Third Generation

4. ROBERT PITT, probable son of Robert (3) Pitt, m. Elizabeth Morris, dau. of Dennis and Elizabeth Morris. {Of Purse and Person:78} She later m. Nathaniel Andrews, son of William and Comfort Andrews. {Of Purse and Person:78}

Robert Pitt patented 4000 a. on the Pocomoke River in Accomack Co., 12 March 1662/3 and 2 Oct 1663. {Of Purse and Person, citing Patent Bk. 5:219 (129), 190 (81). "The Pitts were of a family of mariners from Bristol, England, and were seated in Isle of Wight Co. and apparently carried on a brisk trade between the lower James River and the upper Chesapeake."}

On 17 May 1666 Capt. Robert Pitt entreth his action against William Duffe in the SO Co. Court. {ARMD LIV:624}

Elizabeth Morris, widow of Dennis Morris, d. leaving a will dated Nov 1703, proved 6 Feb 1703/4. To sons John, Dennis and Joseph Morris, 1 s. each. To daus. Sarah Read and Elizabeth Pitt, 1 s. each. Dau. Ann Blake. Dau. Mary Morris. Dau. Ann Blake's youngest son born this present year. Granddau. Sarah Read. Son Jacob Morris and dau. Mary Morriss residuary legatees. Robert Pitt and John Morris to make division. Son Jacob, exec. Witnessed by John Blockson, Sr., John Dimzie. {ACW:34}

Robert Pitt, Accomack Co., d. leaving a will dated 20 July 1711, proved 4 May 1714. To son John Pitt land and marsh where Dennis Morris now lives, except a piece of marsh called *Impossible Marsh*. If he should die without issue to my son Robert Pitt. To son John all my land or estate in England by right belonging to me by virtue of the last will and testament of Mary Pitt of Bristoll, dec'd. To dau. Martha Pitt, plantation containing 300 a. To son Robert (under 21) all my remaining land, including *Impossible Marsh*. Capt. John Brodhurst and James Kemp trustees and to divide personal estate between wife Elizabeth and children. Wife and son John, execs. Witnessed by John Morris, Dennis Morris, John Bradhurst. {ACW:50}

Nothing in the will of Robert Pitt was said about the land in Maryland although the Pitt family continued to own that for some time. Also, the son Robert later made reference to a bro. Jabez, who was not mentioned in the will. {Whitelaw:1296}

Nathaniel Andrews d. leaving a will dated 16 Feb 1720/21, proved 2 May 1721. Wife Elizabeth. To dau. Elizabeth (under 16), 200 a. near Pocomoke Road and should she die without issue to my bro. Isaac Andrews. To son in law Jabez Pitt. Sister Dorothy Hastings. Wife extx. Friends Capt. John Bradhurst and

80

Hancock Custis to assist her. Witnessed by Robert Dalrymple, Martha Pitt, Elizabeth Morris, James Houlston, Thomas Merrill. {ACW:67}

On 4 Sep 1722 Robert Pitts in behalf of himself and his bro. Jabes Pitts, petitioned that they and their estates be placed in the custody of their bro. in law, Nicholas Fountain. They would remain in Fountain's custody till reaching age 14, which would be "sometime in Febry. Next coming." Since their father, Robert Pitts (dec'd.) had not appointed any guardians in his will, the court agreed to their request. upon giving security Fountain asked that Mr. Hancock Custis (exec. of the will of Nathaniel Andrews, who m. Elizabeth the widow and extx. of Robt. Pitts, gent.) Be ordered to deliver the estates belonging to the orphans. The court granted this and accepted Capt. Jno. Watts, Mr. Richard Kittson and Mason Abbot as Fountain's security. {ACCO 14:115}

Robert was father of JOHN; ROBERT; MARTHA, m. Nicholas Fountain; JABEZ.

Fourth Generation

5. ROBERT PITT, son of Robert (4) Pitt, m. Ann Hack.

Robert Pitt d. leaving a will dated 16 Oct 1755, proved 30 Nov 1756. To wife Ann Pitt. To son John Pitt land where I now live containing 2180 a. To dau. Anne Pitt. To son Robert Pitt 165 a. purchased of Dennis Blake and Joseph Gootee, lying on the head of Pitts Creek and Mill Dam Branch and for want of heirs to dau. Anne Pitt, and for want of heirs to my brother's son Jabis Pitt, and for want of heirs to Robert Pitt, son of Jabis Pitt and for want of heirs to Slocomb Blake, and for want of heirs to Matilda Hack and for want of heirs to John Blake. Bro. Jabiz Pitts' 2 daus. Elizabeth and Susanne Pitts. Son Robert and dau. Anne Pitt residuary legatees. To Thomas Wilkerson. Cousin Dennis Blake and Frances, his wife. Wife and friend George Douglas, execs. Witnessed by John Cam, Dennis Blake, Tobis Blake. Codicil: To sister in law Elizabeth Rodgers. {ACW:186}

In 1756 Robert Pitt III (wife Anne Hack) left a home plantation of 2,180 a. to his son John, who later became a surgeon in the Virginia State Navy. In 1779 John Pitt left the land to his bro. Robert and sister Anne; the latter m. Robert Foreman who d. intestate without issue, and in 1791 Mrs. Foreman deeded her half interest in the neck to her bro. Robert. In 1794 Robert Pitt IV (wife Catherine) left everything to an only child Ann Hack Pitt, who m. Matthew Beard, and they had one child Ann Hack Pitt Beard, who inherited the land. {Whitelaw:1297}

Ann Pitt d. leaving a will dated 23 Oct 1761, proved 24 Nov 1772. To be buried near my last husband. To son Robert (under age), the land I bought lying at the head of Pitts Creek adj. William Drummond's mill and for want of heirs to my dau. Anne Pitt (under age). To son John Pitt (under age). To my Aunt Buncle. Balance of estate to be sold and after payment of debts to pay off the estates of my 2 children Robert and Anne that shall be coming to them of their father's estate and the balance to be divided between my 3 said children, John, Robert and Anne. George Holden, James Henry and William Drummond, execs. Witnessed by Richard Benneston, Sabra Walker, Moses Virgin. Codicil dated 23 Oct 1779 refers to children as being "almost all of the age of 21 years." {ACW:269}

Robert was father of JOHN; ANNE, m. Robert Foreman, d.s.p.; ROBERT, b. after 1751.

6. JABEZ PITT, son of Robert (4) Pitt, m. Hannah (N).

John Clifton, SO Co., d. by 28 Sep 1751, when an admin bond was filed on his estate by Hannah Clifton his extx. Sureties: Jabez Pitts, Solomon McCready. {TP:35:135}

The Debt Book shows Jabez Pitts having the tract *Millbourn's Mistake* surveyed on 10 Nov 1752, 1 1/8 a. {SO Co. Debt Book, 1734-1759}

On 3 Sep 1753 John Evans, shipwright, conveyed to Jabez Pitt, planter, 3 1/4 a. on n. side of the Pocomoke River called *Crooked Island*. {SOD 1753-1759:10}

Dr. Charles Ballard, SO Co., d. by 7 Dec 1757 when an admin bond was filed by Jabez Pitt. Sureties: Lodowick Milbourn, Ephraim Evans. {TP:37:24} On 8 April 1758 the inventory of his estate was filed by Jacobis Pitts [*sic*]. Signed as next of kin: Levin Ballard, Robert Ballard. {MINV 66:243}

On 22 Dec 1764 Jabez Pitt gave to his son Robert land purchased from William Hall (?) called *Entrance* and land purchased from Thomas Evans, 15 a.; also land purchased from John Evans running to the Pocomoke River, 1 a.; also a parcel beginning at a bounder of *Gyneath*, 1 1/8 a. called *Milbourne's Mistake*. {SOD C:251}

Jabez Pitt, Accomack Co., VA, d. leaving a will dated 1 Nov 1773, proved 25 Jan 1774. To son John Pitt and dau. Esther Pitt all my lands, Negroes and moveable estate. To my other children I give 1 s. each. Son Jabez to take their estates and maintain them well on it. Witnessed by Francis Houston, Esther Hill, Michael Robbins. In order of probate: Jabez Pitt qualified. {ACW:275}

In 1793 Jabez and Hannah Pitt sold 149 a. to a William Marshall and it continued in Marshall ownership for some time. In 1794 the Pitts sold another 149 a. to Samuel Wilson Pitt and he and his wife Mary, of DO Co., resold to William Selby. {Whitelaw:1315}

Jabez was father of JABEZ; JOHN; ESTHER; ROBERT.

Fifth Generation

7. JOHN PITT, son of Robert (5) Pitt.

John Pitt d. leaving a will dated 14 Nov 1778, proved 25 May 1779. To sister Ann Pitt and bro. Robert Pitt all my land and marshes where I live to be divided between them. To Joshua George a piece of ground cleared by Howell Gladen at the upper end of my land. Friends William Selby and George Stewart, execs. Witnessed by William Selby, Michael Robins, Joseph Waggaman. {ACW:317}

Admin. of the estate of John Pitt, unadministered by George Stewart, dec'd., was granted to Robert Pitt on 29 April 1789 - Jabez Pitt, security. {ACW:371}

8. ROBERT PITT, son of Robert (5) Pitt, m. Catherine (N) who m. 2nd Charles Beard and m. 3rd Lemuel Henderson. {Whitelaw:1297}

On 1 March 1755 James Baker mortgaged to Robert Pitt of Accomac Co., VA, for the sum of £75 the following Negroes: Titus, Sarah, Grace. {SOD 1753-1759:59}

Robert Pitt, Accomack Co., d. leaving a will dated 19 Jan 1794, proved 29 April 1794. To dau. Ann Hack Pitt during her life all the lands I am now possessed with and should she have issue to dispose of same as she shall think fit. To wife (unnamed), personalty, my black mare that I had of Thomas Custis and should my dau. die without issue my relation Samuel Wilson Pitt to have all my lands and should they offer to sell or mortgage the same Robert Pitt, the son of Jabez Pitt and his heirs to enjoy the same. My desire is that my exec. get Robert Conner Pitt and John Corbin Pitt bound in Philadelphia to a grade. To my exec. 50 pounds for his services. Friend John Burton, exec. Witnessed by William Downing, Dixon Hall. {ACW:416}

Admin. of the estate of Robert Pitt was granted to John Burton on 30 April 1794. Securities: John Custis, Thomas Custis, John Wise, Thomas Evans and Edmund Bayly. {ACW:410}

Robert was father of ANN HACK who m. Matthew Beard and they had a child Ann Hack Pitt Beard who m. Dr. Henry H. Hall. {Whitelaw:1297}

Unplaced

MAJOR S. PITTS is mentioned as nephew in the will of Charles Scarburgh who d. leaving a will dated 25 Nov 1796, proved 26 Dec 1796. {ACW:443}

THE EDWARD PRICE FAMILY of Annamessex Hundred

1. EDWARD PRICE m. 1st Katherine and m. 2nd by 1677 Jane (N).

Edward Price of SO Co. immigrated with Katherine his wife and James his son and Jenkin Price or Morris, his servant, and Mary Ratcliff from VA by 1671. {MPL 16:535; HH:248; 12:203}

Edward Price patented *Price's Hope*[10], 200 a., 13 Feb 1663, lying in Annamessex. {OSES:470; SORR}

On 17 June 1672, George Smith & his wife Martha sold to Edward Price *Penyinsula* (formerly *Smith's Island*) 150 a. {SOD:SC:47}

On 17 May 1676, Edward Price patented *Price's Hope* 200 a. {MPL:9:278, 19:267} On 30 May 1677, Edward Price and his wife Jane sold to Edward Furlong *Price's Hope* 200 a. {SOD:WW:30}

At Nov Court 1691, suit of Capt. William Coulbourne vs. Edward Prise. {SOJR:1690-1692:134}

He patented *Price's Conclusion* (500 a.) on 10 March 1696. {MPL 37:522} It adjoined *Yorkshire* at Smith's Island. It was possessed, 1666-1723, by Samuel Horsey (100 a.) and Thomas Ward (400 a.). Cornelius Ward conveyed 50 a. to John Riggen on 26 March 1737/8 (OS). {SORR}

Edward Price, SO Co., d. leaving a will dated 31 Dec 1695, proved 13 Sep 1696. To wife Jane, extx., by deed of gift, personalty; to have charge of son James during his minority. To first son of son James, residue of estate, real and personal. In event of death of son James without issue estate to pass to testator's next of kin. {MWB 7:243} On 10 Oct 1696, an inventory was filed. {INAC:15:145} On 16 Feb 1696 the admin. account of his estate was submitted by Jane Price, admx. {INAC 15:145}[11]

Jane Price, SO Co., d. by 7 Nov 1699 when an admin bond was filed on her estate by Thomas & Cornelius Ward. Surety: John Taylor. {TP:18A:11} On 12 Dec 1699 the inventory of her estate was filed. {INAC 19½A:150}

Edward was father of: JAMES, b.p. 1664.

THE JAMES PRICE FAMILY of Annamessex Hundred

1. JAMES PRICE[12], d. 1688, m. Mary (N).

James Price patented *Price's Vineyard*, 200 a., 14 Feb 1663. {OSES:470}
James Price of Annemessex d. last day of Feb 1688. {IKL}
Margarett Price, dau. of James and Mary Price, b. 10 Nov 1676. {IKL}

---

10. Per the Rent Rolls, this land can not be found.

11. There are admin accounts filed on the estate of James Price on 22 July 1699. The amount of the inventory and the amount of the accounts are identical to those of the accounts for Edward Price. The admx. is Jane Price (relict). Distribution to: grandson of husband of admx. {INAC:19½A:107; TP:18A:51}

12. It is possible that James Price is the brother of Edward Price. However, no substantial evidence can be found to support that theory.

Ann Price, dau. of James and Mary Price, b. 7 May 1679. {IKL}

James Price patented the following tracts in SO Co.: *Oxhead* (300 a.) in 1675, *Agreement* (100 a.) and *Mickle Meadow* (300 a.) - both on 15 June 1683. {MPL 19:142; 25:72; 30:217; 33:187}

On 1 August 1676, James Price sold to John King *Oxhead* 300 a. {SOD:M-4:422}

Mickle Meadow was patented by James Price for 300 a. in Asbury Election Dist. the rent rolls, 1666-1723, show it possessed by Mary Price, widow of James Price. On 26 Aug 1758 Cornelius Ward Sr. sold to Outerbridge Horsey 150 a. that came to Cornelius from his mother Ann Ward, dau. of James Price. On 7 Jan 1800 John Ward, son of Stephen Ward, now of KY, sold to John Cullen. {SOLR:286. See also SOD 1753-1759:226.}

James Price, SO Co., d. leaving a will dated 2 Nov 1688, proved 11 March 1689. Legatees: daus Margarett Price, Anne Price; cousin James Price; wife Mary. Witnesses: John Tyler, James Prise, Patrick Mitchell. Mary Prise was appointed admx., with sureties: Cornelius Ward, John Roach. On 14 April 1690, an inventory of his estate was filed. {SOJR:1690-1692:8}

Whereas James Price, dec'd., was granted on 7 Jan 1677 (OS) a parcel of land called *Price's Vineyard* near Pocomoke Bay containing 200 a. and on 1 Aug 1685 (OS) the tract *Agreement* was granted to James Price at the head of Back Creek of Little Annamessex. James Price in his last will dated 2 Nov 1688 left to his two daus. Margaret and Ann Price the afsd. tract called *Price's Vineyard* to be divided equally between them. On 18 Jan 1736 (OS) Cornelius Ward, son of Ann, dau. of James Price, and Alice his wife, sell to Jacob Ward, son of Thomas Ward, their right to *Price's Vineyard* and *The Agreement*, containing 300 a. {SOD EI:113}

In 1726, Cornelius Ward and Thomas Ward petitioned for division of lands of James Price, that he willed to his daughters Margaret and Ann. {SOD:GH:136}

James and Mary were parents of MARGARETT, b. 10 Nov 1676, m. Thomas Ward; ANN, b. 7 May 1679, m. Cornelius Ward. {See The Ward Family of Somerset County, vol. 8 of this series.}

THE THOMAS PRICE FAMILY of Annamessex Hundred

1. THOMAS PRICE, b. c1624, possibly related to Jenkin Price[13] [above], m. Katherine (N).

---

13. Torrence describes Thomas Price but does not connect him to Jenkin Price. He makes the point that although Thomas was one of the original Quaker settlers at Annemessex and Jenkin took the Quaker practice of affirming in Court, there is not evidence of any relationship.

Thomas Price was one of the founders of the Annemessex settlement. He was in Northampton Co., VA, as early as Nov 1651, when he made a deposition as aged about 27 years.

Thomas Price patented *Cheap Price*, 500 a., 4 Sep 1663. {OSES:470}

Catherine Price (spinster) patented *Cambrooke [Crambrook?]*, 300 a., 20 Oct 1663 on n. side of Pocomoke River by the land of William Smith. {OSES:472; SORR} On 22 Sep 1666, Thomas Price and his wife Catherine deeded *Crambrook* to George Day. {WOLR:150}

Thomas Price lived at *Cheap Price*, on n. side Annamessex River, and went from there to live in Slater's Neck, Sussex Co., DE, where he d. 1695. Thomas Price and Katherine, his wife, had issue: Thomas Price, b. Annemessex, November 9, 1665; went to Sussex Co., and had issue: (a) William; (b) Catherine; (c) Jean; (d) Rachel. {OSES, citing Sussex Co. Wills}

On 11 Jan 1665 Thomas Price of Annamessex on the Easterne Shore in Province of Maryland, plantor and his wife Katherinne conveyed to William Planner of Annamessix a parcel of land called *Planners Purchase* on the Annemessex River, southernmost side of said river beginning at Williamses Creek as by a patent granted to Thomas Price on 8 Feb 1663. {ARMD LIV:611; SOD:B-1:2}

Thomas Price, son of Thomas and Katherine Price, b. at Annemessex 9 Nov 1665. {IKL}

On 11 Jan 1665 Thomas Price recorded his cattle mark in SO Co. {ARMD LIV:741}

William Taylor d. at the house of Thomas Price in Annamessex last day of Oct 1666. {IKL}

On 17 June 1680 Thomas Price and Katherinne Price acknowledged a cattle marke given by Wm. Taylor dec'd. unto Joseph Taylor. {ARMD LIV:274}

On 21 Sep 1685, Thomas Price and his wife Katherine sold to William Planner *Cheap Price* 500 a. {SOD:MA:758}

Thomas Price, Sr., planter, Slaughter Neck, d. leaving a will dated 14 March 1694/5, proved 25 March 1695. Heirs: wife Catharine Price; son Thomas Price; grandson William Price; granddaus. Catharine, Jane and Rachel Price. Exec., son Thomas Price. Witnessed by Thomas Phelmon, Jeremiah Barthelmy, William Fisher. {Arch. A94:140. Reg. of Wills (Sussex Co., DE), A:19. Penna. Hist. Soc. Papers, AM. 2013:177}

Thomas and Katherine were parents of THOMAS, b. Nov 1665.

Second Generation

2. THOMAS PRICE, b. Nov 1665, son of Thomas (1) and Katherine Price, m. (N) Carpenter.

On 4 June 1713 William Airey and his wife Jane (along with Thomas and Rachel) of Thomas Price late of Sussex Co., yeoman, dec'd., sold to John Nutter of same co., yeoman, part of 750 a. in Slaughter Neck. Since the death of said Thomas Price and her marriage with said William Airey, by virtue of an order of the Orphans Court on 6 Sep 1712 the land was divided. {SUDELR I:7}

On 22 May 1747 James White, yeoman of Sussex Co., DE, and his wife Margaret, admx. of John Langen, dec'd., yeoman, late of Sussex Co., conveyed to Daniel Wilson, yeoman of the same place, 300 a. in two tracts. Land is situate in Slaughter Neck and one contains 200 a. and was purchased by Thomas Price, grandfather of John Langden, from William Clark, dec'd., late of Sussex Co. and admin. of Henry Bowman, dec'd. who first took up the land and was called part of *Bowman's Farms*; the other tract of 100 a. was also purchased by Thomas Price of William Stapleford, dec'd., who purchased the land from Henry Bowman. The 2 tracts of land descended to John Langden by his mother, Rachel, dau. of Thomas Price who d. intestate and his estate was divided amongst his 3 children, Thos., Jane and Rachel, and Rachel's part by order of the Court was to be the 2 tracts. {SUDELR H8:127}

14 Sep 1748. Daniel Willson and his wife Rachel vs. Thomas White and his wife Margaret in a petition to divide the land. It is stated that Thomas Price the elder d. intestate leaving issue a son and 2 daus., Thomas, Rachel, and Jane. Jane d. leaving issue: afsd. Rachel and Margaret. {SCOC:50}

Thomas was father of THOMAS; CATHERINE, prob. d. young; JEAN (Jane); RACHEL, m. 1st Thomas Langden and had a son John and m. 2nd Daniel Willson; WILLIAM, d. young.

Third Generation

3. THOMAS PRICE, son of Thomas (2) Price.

Thomas Price, yeoman, d. leaving a will dated 21 Feb 1744/45, proved 23 March 1744/45. Heirs: cousins John Langan, Rachel Willson, Margret White; uncles Napthali, Labon, William, James and Benjamin Carpenter; Affiance Wattson; Elizabeth Hill. Exec'r, uncle Napthali Carpenter. Wits., Henry Draper, Isaac Draper, Avery Draper. {Arch. A94:142. Reg. of Wills (Sussex Co.), A:363-364}

4. JANE (Jean) PRICE, dau. of Thomas (2) Price, m. William Airey.

Jane and (N) were parents of RACHEL AIREY, m. Daniel Willson; MARGARET AIREY, m. Thomas White.

5. RACHEL PRICE, dau. of Thomas (2) Price, m. 1st Thomas Langdon and m. 2nd Daniel Willson.

At Orphans Court on 2 Sep 1740 reference is made to Rachel Langdon, widow of Thomas Langdon and his son John. {SCOC:28}

Daniel Wilson d. leaving a will dated 10 Dec 1755, proved 23 Dec 1755. Heirs: sons William and Daniel Wilson; daus. Rachel and Mercy Wilson; William Wattson; Isaac Wattson; Joshua Wattson. Exec. son-in-law Isaac Wattson. Witnessed by Jas. White, Thomas Hinds, Mark Davis. {Arch. A108:68. Reg. of Wills

(Sussex Co.), B:112-114}

At Orphans Court on 2 Feb 1763 James White and his wife Margret, admx. of John Langdon. Additional accounts. Payments to accountants for maintenance of 3 children: Thomas, John, Prudence. Accounts are £19.11.2. {SCOC:114}

Rachel and Thomas were parents of JOHN LANGDON; THOMAS LANGDON; PRUDENCE LANGDON.

Rachel and Daniel were parents of: RACHEL WILSON.

THE DAVID PRICE FAMILY[14] of Mattapony Hundred

1. DAVID PRICE.

The tax list of Mattapany Hundred, SO Co., shows David Prise/Price as head of household in 1723, 1724, 1725, and 1730. {SOTL}

David is probably the father of: JOHN; WILLIAM; THOMAS; ANN; ELIZABETH.

2. JOHN PRICE, prob. son of David (1) Price, m. Mary (N).

In 1756, 1757, 1759, 1760, 1762, 1768, 1769, 1771, 1773, and 1774, John Price paid tax on *Bridgewater*. {Debt Books, Worcester Co.}

On 2 Jan 1748 John Lilliston of Accomack Co., VA, sold to John Price of WO Co., 50 of *Bridgewater*. On 5 Aug 1757, Eliakim Johnson & his wife Bridget sold to John Price 28 a. On 20 March 1767 Eliakim Johnson sold to William Price 200 a. On 29 March 1774 John Price and wife Mary sold 28 a. to Ezekiel Costen. The 1783 tax lists shows William Price owned 212 a.{WOLR:73}

William Price, WO Co., d. leaving a will dated 31 Jan 1768, proved 26 Sep 1783. To eldest son John Price, plantation bounded by the Great Island Branch to the head of the Gum Swamp. To youngest son Arthur Price, the privilege to cut cypress timber for his own use from the plantation; also lands northward of the Great Island Branch. To daus. Mary Price, Betty Price, Sarah Price, Martha Price, lands of sons if either son dies without issue. Witnessed by Nehemiah Holland, Eliakim Johnson, John Price. {WOW JW13:3}

On 14 Aug 1767 John Price and wife Mary conveyed to Nathan Watson part of *Price's Addition* on s.e. side of Pocomoke River, beginning on n.w. side of county road leading from Snow Hill Town to Littleton Creek and to Stevens Ferry - 44 a., part of a tract surveyed for John Price on 22 March 1768. {WOD E:128}

In 1778, John Price took the Oath of Fidelity, before Nehemiah Holland.

---

14. All these people are in the same area in Mattapony Hundred. In the second and third generations, various ones are interfacing with each other.

In 1783, John Price is cited as head of household in Mattapony Hundred, with no land. In his household are 4 males and 2 females. {1783 Assessment} John is prob. father of: WILLIAM; probably others.

3. WILLIAM PRICE, prob. son of David (1) Price, m. Rebekah (N).

On 2 Jan 1748 John Lilliston of Accomack Co., VA, sold to John Price of WO Co., 50 of *Bridgewater*. On 5 Aug 1757, Eliakim Johnson & his wife Bridget sold to John Price 28 a. On 20 March 1767 Eliakim Johnson sold to William Price 200 a. On 29 March 1774 John Price and wife Mary sold 28 a. to Ezekiel Costen. The 1783 tax lists shows William Price owned 212 a.{WOLR:73}

On 7 March 1789 Elisha Johnson and his wife Sarah and Arthur Price and John Conner and his wife Elizabeth were bound unto Nathaniel Davis for £500. The condition of the obligation being that the above will make over, at the request of Davis the right and title to *Bridge Water Supply*, part of *Discovery*, and part of *Pickpoohi* [*Pickpocket*] containing 97 a., situate on e. side of the Pocomoke River near the river swamp and a little below Mattpony Landing. This containing 97 a. as by a divisional line made by John Killam and Eliakim Johnson between the parties, being chosen by the parties for that purpose and run by James Stevenson, surveyor. {WOD M:496}

Discovery was patented on 2 Sep 1755 by William Price for 105 a. in Mattapany Hundred. On 21 March 1763 it was resurveyed by William Price for 303 a. On 26 Feb 1769 Arthur Price, Elisha Johnson and wife Sarah, Nathaniel Davis sold to John Conner 98 a., a division of land. ... {WOLR O:230}

On 4 Oct 1791 Arthur Price and wife Jemima sold to Eliakim Johnson 18 ½ a. in Mattapony Hundred being part of a tract of land on which John Connor lives. {WOLR:181; WOD O:230}

In 1757, 1760, 1762, 1768, 1769, 1771, 1773, and 1774, John Price paid tax on *Bridgewater* and *Discovery*. {Debt Books, Worcester Co.}

In 1783, William Price is cited as head of household in Mattapony Hundred, paying tax on *Bridgewater* 212 a. In his household are 4 males and 5 females. {1783 Assessment}

William Price, WO Co., d. leaving a will dated 31 Jan 1768, proved 26 Sep 1783. To eldest son John Price, plantation bounded by the Great Island Branch to the head of the Gum Swamp. To youngest son Arthur Price, the privilege to cut cypress timber for his own use from the plantation; also lands northward of the Great Island Branch. To daus. Mary Price, Betty Price, Sarah Price, Martha Price, lands of sons if either son dies without issue. Witnessed by Nehemiah Holland, Eliakim Johnson, John Price. {WOW JW13:3} On 26 Sep 1783, an admin bond was posted on his estate by Rebecca Price. Sureties: Eliakim Johnson, Nathaniel Davis. {WED}

Rebekah Price, WO Co., d. leaving a will dated 21 Oct 1786, proved 14

March 1788. To son Arthur Price, livestock, still head, still tub and worm and other items. To dau. Betty Conner, saddle, wooling wheel, and other items. To dau. Sarah Johnson, spinning wheel, petticoat, and other items. To grandson William Price Davis, furniture, etc. To grandson John Davis, furniture, etc. To Levin Price, sheep, chairs, dish. To children Arthur Price, Betty Conner, Sarah Johnson, remainder of estate. Exec. son Arthur. Witnessed by Levin Reed, Solomon Carey, Ezekiah Johnson. {WOW JW13:196}

William was father of JOHN; ARTHUR; MARY; BETTY (Elizabeth), m. John Conner; SARAH, m. Elisha Johnson; MARTHA; dau. (one of the previous), m. Nathaniel Davis.

4. THOMAS PRICE, prob. son of David (1) Price, prob. m. Tabitha Holland, dau. of Nehemiah Holland.

Nehemiah Holland, WO Co, d. leaving a will dated 2 Feb 1758, proved 4 Jan 1760. Wife: Ann. Children: Sarah Tarr, Tabitha Price, Bridget Johnson, Betty Moore, Nehemiah, Thomas, William and Benjamin. Friends: William Aydelott, John Selby, Ephraim Waggamon. Deed made to children, recorded 26 April 1746. Ann Holland, extx. 4 Jan 1760: Widow election. {MWB 30:789}

Richard Conner, WO Co., d. by 11 July 1761 when the inventory of his estate was filed by Elizabeth Conner. Signed as next of kin: Thomas Price, Ann Holland. {MINV 76:117}

In 1783, Thomas Price was living in Snow Hill, with no land. In his household are 2 males and 2 females. {1783 Assessment}

Thomas and Tabitha are probably the parents of: HOLLAND; maybe others.

5. ANN PRICE, prob. dau. of David (1) Price, m. Nehemiah Holland as his second wife.

Nehemiah Holland, WO Co, d. leaving a will dated 2 Feb 1758, proved 4 Jan 1760. Wife: Ann. Children: Sarah Tarr, Tabitha Price, Bridget Johnson, Betty Moore, Nehemiah, Thomas, William and Benjamin. Friends: William Aydelott, John Selby, Ephraim Waggamon. Deed made to children, recorded 26 April 1746. Ann Holland, extx. 4 Jan 1760: Widow election. {MWB 30:789}

Nehemiah Holland and (N) are the parents of: SARAH HOLLAND, m. (John) Tarr; TABITHA HOLLAND, m. (Thomas) Price (#4); BRIDGET HOLLAND, m. Eliakim Johnson (d. 1792); ELIZABETH HOLLAND, m. (N) Moore; NEHEMIAH; THOMAS; WILLIAM.

Nehemiah and Ann were the parents of: BENJAMIN. {BDML:446}

6. ELIZABETH PRICE, prob. dau. of David (1) Price, m. 1st Richard Conner, m. 2nd Joseph Bishop, Jr.

Richard Conner, WO Co., d. by 11 July 1761 when an admin bond was posted on his estate by Elizabeth Conner. Sureties: Thomas Davis, Isaac Pain. {WED} On the same day, the inventory of his estate was filed by Elizabeth Conner. Signed as next of kin: Thomas Price, Ann Holland. {MINV 76:117} On 15 Dec 1759, admin accounts were filed on his estate by Elizabeth (widow) now wife of Joseph Bishop. Distribution to: accountant (⅓), 2 children: Frederick, Sophia (now dec'd.). {MDAD:62:393}

Joseph Bishop, Jr., WO Co., d. leaving a will dated 6 Apr 1773, proved on 13 Aug 1773. Legatees: wife, plantation Scarborough Castle (or Durham House), then to son; son Benjamin Ennis Bishop; son Samuel. Executrix: wife. {WOW:JW#4:148} On 13 Aug 1773, an admin bond was posted on his estate by Elizabeth Bishop. Sureties: Thomas Martin, Jesse Ennis. {WED} On 11 Feb 1774, an inventory was filed for his estate, as Joseph Bishop of Joseph. Signed as next of kin: Joseph Ennis, Charles Bishop. Executrix: Elizabeth Bishop. {MINV:117:74} On 26 May 1775, admin accounts were filed on his estate. Payments to: Frederick Conner (son of Richard Conner (dec'd. married his widow), balance of said estate), et.al. Executrix: Elizabeth Bishop. {MDAD:73:171}

Richard and Elizabeth were the parents of: FREDERICK, b.c. 1759; SOPHIA, d.p. 1769.

Joseph and Elizabeth were the parents of: BENJAMIN ENNIS BISHOP; SAMUEL BISHOP, b.c. 1769.

7. WILLIAM PRICE, prob. son of John (2) Price, prob. m. Rachel Ellis, dau. of William Ellis.

William Ellis, WO Co., d. leaving a will dated 7 Feb 1779, proved 8 April 1783. Mentioned wife Joyce; sons William, Jesse, and Levi Ellis; daus. Rhoda Ellis, dau. Rebecca, dau. Rachel Price. {WOW JW4 Part II:532}

On the 1790 Census, he was living near Snow Hill, with 3 males over age 16 and 4 females in his household.

Joice Ellis, WO Co., d. leaving a will dated 5 Jan 1790, proved 4 Mar 1791. Legatees: daus. Rachel Price, Nancy Ellis, Rhoda Ellis; dau. Rebeckah Carey and her dau. Joice Carey; son William Ellis and his dau. Sarah; sons Jesse, Levi. Executrix: dau. Rebeckah Carey. {WOW:JW#18:15}

8. ARTHUR PRICE, son of William (3) Price, m. 1st Jemima Merrill (dau. of Comfort Merrill (d. 1793)) and m. 2nd Sarah (N).

On 4 Oct 1791 Arthur Price and his wife Jemima for £10 sold to Eliakim Johnson part of *Discovery* in Mattapany Hundred, being part of a tract on which John Connor lives - 19 a. {WOD O:230}

Arthur Price, WO Co., d. leaving a will dated June 1800, proved 27 June 1800. To sons John Merrill Price and Peter Price all land on the s. side where I now live To son --- Price, 50 a. of land where Michael Tarr now lives. To son William Price all remaining land. Witnessed by James Willis, Hezekiah Johnson, Elisha Johnson. Wife Sarah Price and Ezekiah Johnson, execs. {WOW I:86}

On 26 Feb 1790 Arthur Price, John Conner with wife Elizabeth, and Nathaniel Davis sold to Elisha Johnson, 33 a. On 15 Aug 1804 Littleton Robins sold to John Price, Martha Price, William Price and Arthur Price, children of Arthur Price, dec'd. {WOLR:74}

Arthur was father of JOHN MERRILL, b. prior to 1790; PETER, d. prior to 1811 {WOOC:MH#15:368}; WILLIAM; MARTHA; ARTHUR; PRISCILLA, d. c1803 {WOOC:JBR#9:268}.

9. (N) PRICE, dau. of William (3) Price, m. Nathaniel Davis.

She was the mother of: JOHN DAVIS, b.c. 1779; WILLIAM PRICE DAVIS, b.c. 1781.

10. HOLLAND PRICE, prob. son of Thomas (4) Price.

In 1778, Holland Price took the Oath of Allegiance before Hon. James Selby. {Patriots of Somerset & Worcester Cos.}

THE JENKIN PRICE FAMILY of Pocomoke Hundred

1. JINKIN PRICE, b. 1617/1622, m. Mathewe/Martha (N).

Ginkin Price witnessed the appointment of an attorney by Frances Carsley on 26 March 1647 in Northampton Co., VA. {Northampton Co. Record Book:102}

On 24 Aug 1649 Jenkin Price of the county of Northampton (alias Accomacke), planter, purchased a neck of land between the branches of "towards the head of Occahannocke of that North side neere where the Indyan bridge was ..." {Northampton Co. Record Book:192}

According to Torrence,

"Jenkin Price, in Northampton County, Virginia, 1650; trader with Eastern Shore Indians. It was Price who found and guided to safety (January, 1650) the party of Cavaliers, consisting of Henry Norwood, Francis Morrison, Francis Cary and Philip Stevens, whose vessel, the 'Virginia Merchant,' going from London to Jamestown, in Virginia, was driven by storm into Assoteague bay and there wrecked. For this service Price was rewarded by the Virginia Assembly. After living in Virginia about 17 years Jenkin Price and his wife went to England in 1656 intending to settle at Canterbury (XXII Wm. and Mary Quarterly ... p. 53; Wise, Accawamacke, pp. 111-112). Evidently Jenkin Price returned to Northampton County, Virginia, and his trade with the Indians and went to Somerset County, in Maryland, about the time of its creation in 1666. He owned lands (as shown by patents and deeds) along the Pocomoke River and finally settled on tract called 'Newtowne,' on n. side Pocomoke River, near Aquintica Swamp (now in Worcester County), not far from the present town of Snow Hill (O1, pp. 59, 71 and 96; DT, pp. 100-2). Jenkin Price's wife, Mathew [Martha?], joined in several deeds with him. In 1652 Jenkin Price was 'about 30 years of age' and in 1667 stated his age to be 'about 50 years.' He was born probably between 1617 and 1622 (Northampton Court, Order Book, 1651-4, p. 97; Somerset Court, O 1, p. 55). Jenkin and Mathew Price had issue (1) Sarah; (2) Margaret; (3) Thomas (XLIX Arcv. Md., p. 34; Somerset O 1 [reverse], pp. 1-21, list of cattle marks; see under September, 1670)." {OSES:454}

On 24 Aug 1652, William Boucher gave a calf to John Price son of Jenken Price. {Northampton Co. Orders:1651-1654:78}

On 3 Sep 1663 Jenkin Price was granted headrights for transporting into the province, himself, wife Martha and his children, John and Margaret, and servants, Edwd.. Whitty, Jeremy Bursted, Thos. Miller. {OSES, citing MPL 5:441}

Jenkin Price patented *Glyneath*, 400 a., on 23 July 1663. {OSES:469} *Glyneath* was resurveyed for Col. William Stevens, as part of The Entrance. {SORR}

Jenkin Price patented *Pungatesex*, 500 a., 3 March 1663. {OSES:469} *Pungatesex* may be cut off by MD/VA divisional line. {SORR}

Jenkin Price patented *Northfield*, 500 a., 8 Nov 1663; *The King's Neck*, 300 a., 20 Nov 1665; *Aquintica*, 300 a., on 20 Oct 1665; and *New Towne*, 450 a., 2 Oct 1665. {OSES:472}

On 4 Oct 1666 Jinkin Price and his wife Mathewe conveyed to John Renny, planter, SO Co., a parcel of land called *Newe Towne* lying on the n. side of the Pocomoke River standing by a swamp called Aquintica Swamp and by a parcel of land taken up by George Whale - 225 a. {ARMD LIV:694; SOD:B-1:96}

On 27 Nov 1666 Jinkin Prise and others were appointed surveyors for the highwayes . {ARMD LIV:648}

On 26 March 1667 Jinkin Price and his wife Mathewe conveyed to Macum Thomas, planter, a parcel of land called the *Kings Neck* lying in Pocomoke as by a patent dated 24 Feb 1665 - 300 a. {ARMD LIV:664; SOD:B-1:59}

On 28 May 1667 Jinkin Price of SO Co., gent., and his wife Mathewe, conveyed a parcel of land patented on 4 Oct 1666 called *Northfeild* on the n. side of Pocomoke River to Ambross White of Wing in county Bucks in England, mariner - 500 a. {ARMD LIV:673; SOD:B-1:71}

On 4 Oct 1670 the cattle mark of Margarett Prise, dau. of Jinken and Martha Prise, was recorded. {ARMD LIV:757}

Jinkin and Martha were parents of JOHN, b.p. 1652; MARGARETT;

SARAH; THOMAS. [The latter two were mentioned by Torrence.]

2. JOHN PRICE, prob. son of Jinkin (1) Price, m. 1st Sarah Rackliffe, m. 2nd Elizabeth (N) who m. 2nd Henry Tilchberry[15].

On 24 Aug 1652, William Boucher gave a calf to John Price son of Jenken Price. {Northampton Co. Orders:1651-1654:78}

The widow Elizabeth Rackliffe d. 1686 in Accomack Co., naming in her will daus. Sarie, wife of John Price, Elizabeth Whalee, wife of Edward Whalle of SO Co., and Bridget Tailer; son in law Nathaniel Enis; and son Nathaniel. John Price is to have no part of Elizabeth's estate. Sarah's portion is to be held by Edward Wale, for her children. {ASOS:277}

John Price of Pocomoke immigrated by 1675 with his wife Sarah. {MPL SR 7548; LL:814}

On 25 Oct 1667 Martin Moore of Annamesssick, SO Co. assigned over his cattle mark to John Price living in the same place. {ARMD LIV:752}

In 1679, John Price patented *Linneath* 300 a. {MPL:20:236} On 18 Sep 1682, John Price sold to John Cropper *Linneath*. {SOD:MA:601}

On 5 Jan 1683 John Price recorded his cattle mark in SO Co. {ARMD LIV:784}

John Price patented the tract *Refuge* (160 a.) on 18 Oct 1684. {MPL 25:361} Refuge is claimed by Gabriel Waters (VA), but the tax has not been paid. {SORR}

In 1687 John Price of SO Co. sold his cattle mark to John Rock Cooper of said co. {COES:38}

John Price, SO Co., d. leaving a will dated 12 Sep 1703, proved 19 Oct 1703. To son Nathaniel, personalty. To wife Elizabeth and 6 children born of her, viz., Elizabeth, Jr., Deanah, Jenkins, John, Sarah and Thomas, residue of estate equally. No exec. noted. {MWB 3:260} On 4 February 1703, an inventory was filed for his estate. {MWB:3:355} On 24 Feb 1707 the admin. account of his estate was submitted by Elizabeth Tilchberry (relict) now wife of Henry Tilchberry, admx. {INAC 28:106}

At Oct Court 1710, suit of John Henry & his wife Mary vs. Henry Tuchberry & his wife Elizabeth extx. of John Price. {SOJR:1709-1711:438}

John and Sarah were the parents of: NATHANIEL; ELIAS; BRIDGET, m. Elias Blake.

John and Elizabeth were the parents of: ELIZABETH; DEANAH; JENKINS; JOHN; SARAH; THOMAS.

---

15. Henry Tuchberry may be the son of John Tutchberry (Accomac Co.) who fathered a bastard child in 1679, and was cited on the tax lists in 1683.

4. NATHANIELL PRICE, son of John (2) Price.

In 1691 and 1693, Nathaniel Price is cited as head of household in Accomac Co. {Accomac Co. Tax Lists}

On 2 June 1697, the will of Mr. John Stratton was proved by oaths of Thomas Perry and Nathaniel Price. {Accomac Co. Orders, 1690-1697:250}

Richard Talbott, SO Co., d. by 13 Nov 1705 when an admin bond was filed on his estate by Nathaniel Price. Security: William Henderson, Sr. {TP:19C:56} On 25 Feb 1705 an inventory of his estate was submitted. {INAC:25:291} On 4 Jan 1706, an additional inventory was submitted. On 10 June 1708 admin. account of his estate was submitted by Nathaniell Price, admin. {INAC 28:202}

At Sep Court 1707, suit of James Stanfield vs. Nathaniel Price. {SOJR:1707-1709:63}

At Oct Court 1708, suit of Edward Poynter vs. Nathaniel Price administrator of estate of Richard Talbott. {SOJR:1707-1709:166}

At Mar Court 1708, suit of Thomas Murphey vs. Nathaniel Price administrator of estate of Richard Talbott. {SOJR:1707-1709:190}

At Apr Court 1708 and Nov Court 1709, suit of Nathaniel Price vs. Thomas Davis. {SOJR:1707-1709:97; 1709-1711:287}

Elias Price, Accomac Co., d. leaving a will undated, proved on 1 May 1709. Legatees: sister Bridget Blake; elder bro. Nathaniel Price; children of Elias Blake--Jane, Elias, William, Charles. {ACW:1692-1715:488} On 3 May 1709, Bridget Blake was granted administration on his estate. Securities: Samuel Taylor, Jonathon Owin. Appraisers: Jonathon Waggaman, Jacob Waggaman, Capt. John Watts, John Blake. {Accomac Co. Orders, 1703-1710:197} On 7 June 1709, Bridget Blake exhibited inventory of his estate. {Accomac Co. Orders, 1703-1710:202}

At Dec Court 1716, suit of John Dennis vs. Nathaniel Price of All Hallows Parish. {SOJR:1715-1717:190}

At Oct Court 1717, Nathaniel Price received payment. {SOJR:1717-1718:3} Nathaniel may be the father of ELIAS; BENJAMIN.

5. ELIAS PRICE, son of John (2) Price, d.s.p. 1709.

Elias Price, Accomac Co., d. leaving a will undated, proved on 1 May 1709. Legatees: sister Bridget Blake; elder bro. Nathaniel Price; children of Elias Blake--Jane, Elias, William, Charles. {ACW:1692-1715:488} On 3 May 1709, Bridget Blake was granted administration on his estate. Securities: Samuel Taylor, Jonathon Owin. Appraisers: Jonathon Waggaman, Jacob Waggaman, Capt. John Watts, John Blake. {Accomac Co. Orders, 1703-1710:197} On 7 June 1709, Bridget Blake exhibited inventory of his estate. {Accomac Co. Orders, 1703-1710:202}

6. BRIDGET PRICE, m. Elias Blake.

Elias Price, Accomac Co., d. leaving a will undated, proved on 1 May 1709. Legatees: sister Bridget Blake; elder bro. Nathaniel Price; children of Elias

Blake--Jane, Elias, William, Charles. {ACW:1692-1715:488} On 3 May 1709, Bridget Blake was granted administration on his estate. Securities: Samuel Taylor, Jonathon Owin. Appraisers: Jonathon Waggaman, Jacob Waggaman, Capt. John Watts, John Blake. {Accomac Co. Orders, 1703-1710:197} On 7 June 1709, Bridget Blake exhibited inventory of his estate. {Accomac Co. Orders, 1703-1710:202}

Elias and Bridget are the parents of: JANE BLAKE; ELIAS BLAKE; WILLIAM BLAKE; CHARLES BLAKE.

7. ELIAS PRICE[16], grandson of John Price, prob. son of Nathaniel Price.

The 1738 tax list of SO Co. shows Elias Price living in the household of Jacob Wagaman[17] in Mattapony Hundred. {SOTL} He is probably cited as Edward Price in 1739, as head of household in Mattapony Hundred. {SOTL}

On 13 Sep 1739, Elias Price is cited as a creditor to the estate of Jacob Waggaman. {MINV:24:241}

On 22 May 1740, Elias Price received payment from estate of Jacob Waggaman. {MDAD:17:480}

Refuge was patented on 18 Oct 1684 by John Price for 150 a. at the MD/VA line. On 24 March 1743 John Smith of Accomack Co., VA, assignee of Elias Price, heir and grandson of John Price, dec'd., sold 100 a. to Joshua Chapman. {WOD A:174}

Silas Chapman, ACC Co., d. making a nuncupative [verbal] will declared on 17 Aug 1749, proved on 16 Sep 1749, probated on 28 Nov 1749. Legatees: daus. Elizabeth, Mary; son Silas; wife Mary; wife's son Ambrose Willis. Proved by: Luke Watson, Elias Price. {ACW:1749-1752:10}

6. BENJAMIN PRICE, prob. son of Nathaniel Price.

The 1740 tax list of SO Co. shows Benja. Price living in the household of Ephram Wagaman in Mattapany Hundred. {SOTL}

THE WILLIAM PRICE FAMILY of Pocomoke Hundred, Somerset Co. and Cecil Co.

1. WILLIAM PRICE m. Margarett (N).

On 9 March 1663, William Price patented *Aracco*, 250 a., 9 March 1663 and *Price's Grove*, 400 a. {OSES:472}

---

16. He may be the same person as Ellis Price, who in 1696 is cited as a servant, age 14. {Accomac Co. Orders:1690-1697:195}

17. Jacob Waggaman is the brother of Jonathon Waggaman (d. 1724, Accomac Co.).

On 2 June 1691, William Prise (CE) and his wife Margarett sold to Ralph Milbourne *Prises' Grove*. {SOJR:1690-1692:107}

On 18 May 1694, William Price, Sr. (CE) sold to William Merrill (SO) *Arracoco* 250 a. {SOD:L:184}

William Price, Sr., CE Co., d. by 1704 when an inventory of his estate was filed. {MWB:3:532} On 11 June 1709, admin accounts were filed by William Price, Jr. {INAC:30:342}

William is the father of: WILLIAM; poss. JOHN.

2. WILLIAM PRICE, b.c. 1675, son of William (1) Price, m. Mary (N).

In June 1707, William Price, Sr. (of Cecil Co.), age 32, deposed that on 1 June 1694, he marked a certain tree, which he had marked before. John Price also swore it was the same tree. {Accomac Co. Orders, 1666-1670:207} [This is in regard to a land dispute between William Merrill and William Brittingham]

William and Mary were the parents of: WILLIAM, b. 18 Sep 1699; RICHARD, b. 10 Jan 1701; ANDREW, b. 16 Nov 1704; HYLAND, b. 13 Jan 1709; REBECCA, b. 18 Oct 1714, d. 18 March 1716/7; JOHN, b. 9 Aug 1718. {St. Stephen's Parish, Cecil Co.}

THE ALEXANDER PRICE FAMILY of Wicomico/Nanticoke Hundred

1. ALEXANDER PRICE m. 29 Jan 1680, Rebecca Thomas, dau. of Lambrook Thomas[18]. {IKL}

Alexander Price patented the following tracts in SO Co.: *Newberry* (300 a.) on 27 Nov 1688; and *Price's Purchase* (100 a.) on 10 Aug 1695. {MPL 27:119; 37:82}

Newbury was patented on 27 Nov 1688 by Alexander Price for 300 a. The rent rolls, 1666-1723, show it possessed Rebecca Price, widow and relict of Alexander Price. On 8 June 1746 Alexander Thomas Russell and wife Ann Russell sold sd. land to Obediah Reed 100 a. being part of a tract taken up by Alexander Price called *Newbury* containing 300 a., for 5 shillings. Levin Hitch and his wife Eve conveyed to Obadiah Reed 100 a. (no date) {SORR; SOD X:201}

Lambrook Thomas, SO Co., d. leaving a will proved 5 Aug 1713. To son and dau., John Cadrey, exec, and Mary, his wife, watermill and land belonging to same. To dau. Rebecca Price, granddau. Mary Cadrey (dau. of John and Mary afsd.), grandchildren Crispine, Elick, Anne and Grace Price, personalty. {MWB 13:548} An inventory was filed about 1714 for the estate of Mr. Lambrock Towers. Approvers: Crispin Price, Grace Price. {INAC:34:97} On 24 March 1714, admin

---

18. Liber IKL cites Rebecca's father as Alexander Thomas. Based on other information, she has to be the dau. of Lambrook Thomas, an error either by the clerk or the transcriber.

accounts were filed on his estate. {INAC:36B:345}

In 1733, 1745, 1748, 1755, Rebecca Price paid tax on *Price's Purchase*.
{Debt Books, Somerset Co.}

On 12 Aug 1748 Levin Hitch and wife Eve Hitch, dau. of Crispin Price,
sold 100 a. that became right of Eve by the death of her bro. Solomon Price. On
13 Oct 1778 John Reed of WO Co. sold to Henry Handy of SO Co. 100 a. (as
Crispin Price left two sons and 3 daus. Both sons d. young and dau. Rachel m.
Obediah Reed who purchased of the other two daus. Ann Price who m. Alexander
Thomas Russell and Eve Price who m. Levin Hitch. Obediah Reed d. intestate
and left son John Reed. The widow Rachel Price m. Thomas Stanford and she d.
intestate.) {WILR:293-294}

Alexander was father of: CRISPINE; ALLIXSINE/ELICK, b. 5 Nov
1689; ANNE, b. 8 Oct 1691; GRACE, prob. m. Finch Jones. {IKL}

2. CRISPIN PRICE, son of Alexander (1) Price, m. Eve Heatch, daughter of
Adam Heatch. Eve Price m. 2nd James Smith.

Edward Tully, SO Co., d. by 8 Feb 1726 when an admin bond was filed
on his estate by Crispen Price. Surety: Adam Heatch. {TP:27:379} On 24 Feb 1726
the inventory of his estate was filed by Chrispian Price. Signed as next of kin:
James Tully, Benjamin Tully. {MINV 13:272} On 20 Nov 1728 the admin. account
of his estate was submitted by Crispin Price, admin. {MDAD 9:306}

The tax lists of SO Co. show Crispen Price as head of household in
Wicomico Hundred in 1724, 1727 and Eve Price as head of household in
Wicomico Hundred in 1730. Living in the same household were slaves: Will and
Bridgett. James Smith is head of household, Wicomico Hundred, in 1731 and
living in his household is Allexander Price. There is also a Allexander Price living
in the household of Finch Jones that year [same Alexander?]. Alexander was
living in the household of Elgate Heatch in 1734, in the household of George
Lank in 1735 and 1739.

Adam Heatch, SO Co., d. leaving a will dated 22 Jan 1730, proved 15
Feb 1730. To wife Mary, 1/3 dwelling plantation during life, Negro man Toby,
1/3 personal estate and an equal interest with children in watermill during her
widowhood. To son Elgatt, plantation included between Samuel Heatches land
and the mill branch, part of *Come by Chance* and part of *High Suffolk*. To
grandson Adam Prise, 90 a. where John Price now lives, after decease of his
mother. To all children, viz. Solloman Heatch, exec, John Heatch, Elgatt Heatch,
Elizabeth Heatch, Catherine Heatch, Mary Prise and Eve Smith, personal estate
and water mill, equally; William Heatch's children having an equal part thereof.
Overseer: John Handy. {MWB 20:188} On 22 Nov 1732, admin accounts were filed
on his estate by Solomon Heatch. Payments to (equal amounts): Samuell Heatch,
Elgat Heatch, John Heatch, Rachel Heatch, Elizabeth Heatch, Catherine Heatch,
John Price for his wife's portion, James Smith, Jr. for his wife's portion.

98

{MDAD:11:551}

Crispian Price d. leaving a will proved 10 June 1730. To eldest son Alexander, dwelling plantation according to its division. To son Solomon, remainder of dwelling plantation. To daus. Rachall, Ann and Eve, moveable estate. Wife (unnamed), extx. Witnessed by Adam Heatch, Thomas Humphris, Samuell Hitch, Finch Jones. {MWB 20:64; SOW EB9:132} On 6 May 1730 the inventory of the estate of Crispin Price was filed by James Smith and his wife Eve Smith. Signed as next of kin: Finch Jones, Grace Jones. {MINV 16:176} On 18 Aug 1731 the admin. account of the estate of Chrispian Price was submitted by James Smith and his wife Eve Smith, admin. Representatives: Widow (unnamed), 5 children (unnamed). {MDAD 11:189}

Persons appointed to valuate the land of the orphan Solomon Price, now in the possession of Solomon Hitch, Sr., reported on 17 Dec 1736 (OS) that the land contained 133 apple trees, a 30 foot barn and 20 foot house, estimated at an annual value of £3. {SOD EI:145}

Crispin was father of ALEXANDER, d. young; RACHEL, m. Obadiah Reed; ANN, m. Alexander Thomas Russell; SOLOMON, d. young; EVE, m. Levin Hitch.

4. GRACE PRICE, dau. of Alexander Price, prob. m. Finch Jones. {See The Finch Jones Family, this vol.}

THE JOHN PRICE FAMILY of Wicomico Hundred

1. JOHN PRICE of Wicomico Hundred, m. Mary Heatch, dau. of Adam Heatch.

The tax lists of SO Co. show John Price as head of household in Nanticoke Hundred, 1723, 1724, in Wicomico Hundred, 1730-1740. Living in the household were Thomas Price (1735-1737); David Price (1736-1739); Francis Price (1738); James Brady (1737, 1739); Joseph Piper (1739); John Maggee (1740); slave Hannah (1731).

Adam Heatch, SO Co., d. leaving a will dated 22 Jan 1730, proved 15 Feb 1730. To wife Mary, 1/3 dwelling plantation during life, Negro man Toby, 1/3 personal estate and an equal interest with children in watermill during her widowhood. To son Elgatt, plantation included between Samuel Heatches land and the mill branch, part of *Come by Chance* and part of *High Suffolk*. To grandson Adam Prise, 90 a. where John Price now lives, after decease of his mother. To all children, viz. Solloman Heatch, exec, John Heatch, Elgatt Heatch, Elizabeth Heatch, Catherine Heatch, Mary Prise and Eve Smith, personal estate and water mill, equally; William Heatch's children having an equal part thereof. Overseer: John Handy. {MWB 20:188} On 22 Nov 1732, admin accounts were filed on his estate by Solomon Heatch. Payments to (equal amounts): Samuell Heatch, Elgat Heatch, John Heatch, Rachel Heatch, Elizabeth Heatch, Catherine Heatch,

John Price for his wife's portion, James Smith, Jr. for his wife's portion. {MDAD:11:551}

In 1734, 1735, and 1745, John Price paid tax on *High Suffolk*. {Debt Books, Somerset Co.}

John Price, SO Co., d. by 16 Nov 1745 when the inventory of his estate was filed by Joshua Caldwell. Signed as next of kin: Mary Price, John Hitch. {MINV 31:339}

On 23 May 1763 Mary Price and Adam Price, planters, were firmly bound to William Adams, merchant, for the sum of £200. The Prices put up as security part of a tract called *High Suffolk*, containing 90 a. {SOD C:180}

John may have been father of THOMAS; DAVID; FRANCIS; ADAM.

2. THOMAS PRICE, son of John (1) Price of Wicomico, m. 22 Dec 1756 Patience Kibble, dau. of John & Sarah Kibble. {Stepney Parish}

Thomas Price was living in the household of John Price, 1735-1737 and in the household of Elgatt Heatch in 1739 (Wicomico Hundred), in the household of Robert Given in 1740 (Nanticoke Hundred), and in the household of Henry Lowes in 1744. He is cited as a head of household in Nanticoke Hundred in 1754, and in Wicomico Hundred in 1757. {SOTL}

On 22 March 1764 Thomas Price and his wife Patience conveyed to William Kennerly a tract called *Wilson's Discovery* now called *Delight* on e. side of the Nanticoke River, 75 a. {SOD C:207}

On 1 Aug 1770 Benjamin Hitch and wife Mary sold 50 a. of *Mt. Pleasant* to Thomas Price. On 31 July 1802 Solomon Kibble Price and mother Patience Price sold to Jacob Morris 50 a. {WILR:287}

Thomas Price d. leaving a will dated 22 June 1788, proved 10 Oct 1801. To wife Patience 50 a. of *Mount Pleasant*. To son Solomon Kebble Price land after death of mother. To son George Price land if Solomon dies without issue. To son Souther Price land if George dies without issue. Wife extx. Witnessed by Jacob Morris, Joshua Taylor, Jacob Morris, Jr. {WOW JBR1:257}

Thomas was father of SOLOMON KEBBLE, m. Elizabeth Harris {marr. lic. dated 10 Oct 1797}; GEORGE; SOUTHER.

3. DAVID PRICE, son of John (1) Price of Wicomico.

David Price was living in the household of William Venables, 1735, in the household of John Price, 1736-1739, in the household of Thomas Cooper, 1740 (in Nanticoke Hundred), and in the household of Susannah Tulley, 1744 (in Nanticoke Hundred). {SOTL}

4. ADAM PRICE, son of John (1) Price of Wicomico.

Adam Price was living in the household of Mary Price, 1744 (in Nanticoke Hundred), as head of household in Nanticoke Hundred, 1748, 1750,

1753, 1754 (as Adam Prier). {SOTL}

In 1755, 1759, 1761, and 1764, Adam Price paid tax on *High Suffolk*. {Debt Books, Somerset Co.}

On 23 May 1763 Mary Price and Adam Price, planters, were firmly bound to William Adams, merchant, for the sum of £200. The Price's put up as security part of a tract called *High Suffolk*, containing 90 a. {SOD C:180}

Unplaced

(N) PRICE m. Ann Langford, dau. of Thomas Langford.

Thomas Langford, SO Co., d. leaving a will dated 11 March 1755, proved 29 March 1756. Children: Thomas, Mary and Ann Price. Grandson: Benjamin Langford. Thomas Langford, exec Note: As my husband Thomas Langford has made no provision for me, I claim what the law allows widows. Signed: Judea Langford (her mark). {MWB 30:90}

CHRISTIAN PRICE

Richard Nickollson (also Richard Nickolson), SO Co., d. by 12 Nov 1726 when the inventory of his estate was filed by Elizabeth Nickolson. Mentions: Christian Price, James Nickolson, Richard Nickolson, Joseph Nickolson. {MINV 11:761}

EDWARD PRICE

On 22 Oct 1706, Edward Price was an appraiser of estate of Steven Smith. {INAC:27:245}

At Dec Court 1707, suit of Edward Price vs. Able Tuder. {SOJR:1707-1709:131}

At Aug Court 1709, suit of Edward Price vs. Hugh McCallagen. {SOJR:1709-1711:268, 290}

On 19 Sep 1710, Edward Price received payment from estate of James Furniss. {INAC:32A:88}

On 8 April 1712, Edward Price received payment from estate of Peter Dent. {INAC:33A:159}

On 9 Nov 1713, Edward Price received payment from estate of Col. Francis Jenkins. {INAC:34:95}

Edward Price, SO Co., d. by 5 Aug 1714, when an admin bond was filed on his estate by Peter King and Charles Ballard. Securities: William Planner, Robert Catherwood. {TP:22:378} On 3 Nov 1714 the inventory of his estate was filed. {INAC 36B:295} On 12 Oct 1715 admin. account of the estate of Edward Price was submitted by Charles Ballard, Robert King, admins. {INAC 36C:13}

EDWARD PRICE

Edward Price was head of household in Annemessex Hundred, 1733-1739. Living in the household were Francis Price, 1733-1736; Thomas Price, 1733-1734; Johnson Price, 1735-1737. Johnson Price had moved to the household of Kirk Gunby in Annemessex Hundred in 1738. Johnson Price is cited as head of household in 1738 in Annamessex Hundred. {SOTL}

In 1733, 1745, 1748, and 1755, Edward Price paid tax on *Price's Hope*. {Debt Books, Somerset Co.}

FRANCIS PRICE

Francis was head of household in Nanticoke Hundred in 1723, 1724 and living in the household of James Tulley, 1731-1736 and in the household of Isaac Cooper, 1739-1740. {SOTL}

JANE PRICE

Jane Price, SO Co., d. by May 1702 when an admin bond was filed on her estate by Daniel O'Donelle. Securities: Robert Robertson, Bartho. Hays. {TP:19A:100} About May 1702 an inventory of her estate was filed. {INAC 21:391} On 14 April 1703, admin accounts were filed on estate of Jane Price by Daniel O'Dullovan. {INAC:23:57}

MARGARET PRICE, m. Rowland Bevend.

A marriage bann was published for Margaret Price and Rowland Bevend, both of Somerset on 27 Dec 1670. {OSES:401}

MARY PRICE was transported into the province by Arnold Elzey who received headrights on 14 June 1665. {OSES:475}

MARY PRICE of Manokin m. 1663, James Nicholson. {IJK}

RICHARD PRICE was transported into the province by John Winder who received headrights on 5 June 1666. {COES:477}

RICHARD PRICE m. Sarah Parker, dau. of George Parker.

George Parker, WO Co., d. leaving a will dated 5 Aug 1765, proved 9 March 1770. To wife Sarah. Children: John, Jacob, Sarah, now wife of Richard Price[19], and John Parker. Tract: *Mill Wright's Good Intent*. {MWB 38:18}

ROBERT PRICE m. Mary (N).

---

19. A second abstraction cites his name as Robert Price.

The tax lists of SO Co. show Robert [Robarts] Price as head of household in Nanticoke Hundred, 1739-1740, 1744. Living in the household (1739-1740) was slave Nell.

Robert Price, SO Co., d. leaving a will dated 17 Sep 1746, proved 17 June 1747. My children: Betty, William, Mary, Robert and John Price. Wife Mary Price, extx. {MWB 25:103} On 17 June 1747, an admin bond was posted on his estate. Executrix: Mary Price. Sureties: Robert Givan, George Hardy. {TP:32:114} On 13 Aug 1747 the inventory of his estate was filed by Mary Price. {MINV 35:208} On 2 July 1748 the admin. account of his estate was submitted by Mary Price, extx. Mentions: children (all underage): Betty, William, Mary, Robert, John. {MDAD 25:118}

The tax lists of SO Co. show Mary Price as head of household in Nanticoke Hundred in 1757. Living in the household are: Robert Price, Roger Patrick.

Robert was father of BETTY; WILLIAM; MARY; ROBERT; JOHN.

THOMAS PRICE
The 1723 tax list of SO Co. for Nanticoke Hundred shows Thomas Price as head of household. {SOTL}

THOMAS PRICE.
Thomas Price patented *Privilege* in SO Co., 9 Nov 1767. {MPL BC32:346; BC34:137}

In 1747, 1754, and 1774, Thomas Price paid tax on *Priviledge*. {Debt Books, Somerset Co.}

TOWNS (?) PRICE
He is cited in the household of Samuel Hitch in Nanticoke Hundred for 1744. {SOTL}

WILLIAM PRICE
On 22 Sep 1666, Thomas Price and his wife Catherine deeded *Crambrook* to George Day. {WOLR:150}

William Price, SO Co., d. by 12 March 1707 when the admin account of his estate was submitted by George Day, admin. {INAC 28:87}

WILLIAM PRICE
He was living in the household of Henry Richards in Nanticoke Hundred in 1753. He is cited as head of household in 1754 in Nanticoke Hundred. {SOTL}

THE THOMAS RALPH/RELPH/ROLPH FAMILY (1)

1. THOMAS RELPH, m. (N).

The tract *Contention* was patented on 15 Aug 1688 by Thomas Ralph for 95 a. on Wicomico Creek. On 7 April 1742 Robert Lowe and wife Jane sold to George Dashiell 95 a. patented by Thomas Ralph who d. intestate and left son Thomas Ralph who also d. intestate and left a dau. Jane now wife of Robert Lowe. {WILR:84}

Thomas was the father of THOMAS.

2. THOMAS RELPH, son of Thomas (1) Relph, m. Ann (N)[20]. She m. 2nd John Lankford.

Thomas Relph Jr. recorded his cattle mark in 1702 in SO Co. {COES:41}

Thomas Relph, SO Co., d. by 4 March 1713 when an administration bond was filed by John Lankford, with surety: Jonathon Jackson. {TP:22:331} The inventory of the estate of Thomas Ralph was submitted on 20 July 1714. Cited as kin: John Davis. {INAC:36B:213} The admin. account of the estate of Thomas Ralph was submitted on 17 Nov 1715 by John Lankford, admin. Payments included Thomas Ralph, Sr. {INAC 37A:101}

Ann Ralph m. 24 Aug 1714, John Langford. {SOSP}

The tax list for 1724 for SO Co. cites John Lankford as living in Nanticoke Hundred. {SOTL}

Thomas and Ann were the parents of: JANE.

3. JANE RELPH, daughter of Thomas (2) Relph, m. Robert Lowe.

The tract *Contention* was patented on 15 Aug 1688 by Thomas Ralph for 95 a. on Wicomico Creek. On 7 April 1742 Robert Lowe and wife Jane sold to George Dashiell 95 a. patented by Thomas Ralph who d. intestate and left son Thomas Ralph who also d. intestate and left a dau. Jane now wife of Robert Lowe. {WILR:84}

The tax list for 1744 for SO Co. cites Robert Lowe as living in Nanticoke Hundred. {SOTL}

THE THOMAS RALPH/RELPH/ROLPH FAMILY (2) of Quantico

1. THOMAS RALPH, b. c1680, m. Elizabeth (N)[21].

---

[20] She may be the dau. of John Davis.

[21] She may be the dau. of John Collins, Sr.

Truelock Grange was patented on 23 March 1672 by Phillip Ascue for 250 a. Phillip Ascue and wife Lydia sold to John Evans. On 1 Feb 1675 James Jones, atty. for John Evans, sold 250 a. to Alexander Thomas. In 1695 Alexander Thomas willed to Ganer Waller 100 a. and to daus. Elizabeth Thomas and Frances Thomas. {WILR:408}

On 30 May 1707, John Collins and his wife Ganer/Jane sold to Thomas Relph 100 a. of *Trullicke Grange*. {SOD:CD:466}

On 4 Aug 1713, Jonathon Jackson deeded to Thomas Ralph (of Quantico), pt. *Warwick*. {SOD:IKL:97}

On 11 May 1720, James Boutcher and his wife Frances deeded to Thomas Ralph (of Quantico), pt. *Turvill Grange*, patented by Philip Ascue. {SOD:IK:66}

On 1 July 1721, Thomas Ralph (of Quantico and Stepney Parish) and his wife Elizabeth deeded to William Richardson pt. *Warwick* 100 a. {SOD:IK:153}

John Collins, Sr., SO Co., d. by 12 Feb 1723 when an inventory was made of his estate. Administrators: Thomas Relph, John Collins. {MINV:10:59} On 8 July 1726 admin. accounts of his estate was submitted by Thomas Rolph, John Collins. {MDAD 7:34}

On 27 Oct 1732, Thomas Ralph and his wife Elizabeth deeded to William Richardson, pt. *Warwick*, that Jonathon Jackson deeded to said Thomas. {SOD:AZ:53}

Thomas Ralph patented the following tracts: *Ralph's Venture* (100 a.) on 1 Aug 1732.

The tax lists of SO Co., Nanticoke Hundred, show Thomas Relph as head of household, 1723, 1724, 1727, 1730, 1731, 1733-1736, 1738-1740. Living in the same household was John Relph (1723); Peter Shirman (1733-1734); slaves: Pompe (1735-1736), Sambo (1738), Harry (1739), Marreah (1740).

Thomas Ralph, age 57, on 13 Sep 1736, deposed regarding the bounds of *Wrights Choice* and *Wrights Adventure*. {Miller:31}

On 10 Oct 1738, John Gale and his wife Milcah deeded to Thomas Ralph, pt. *Gale's Purchase* 17 a. {SOD:MF:3}

Thomas Rolph, SO Co., d. leaving a will dated 16 Feb 1743/4, proved 3 March 1743. To dau. Mary Goslee *Tallege Grain* [*Tidley Grain*?] where she now lives. To dau. Susannah Borman, dwelling plantation *Good Success*, 100 a. of *The Venture*, 17 a. of *Gale's Purchase*. To Sarah Darby, Negro girl Moroor, furniture. To daus. Charity Rider, personalty. To dau. Rachel More, Negro man Sambo, furniture, personalty. Remainder of estate to be divided among three daus. Son-in-law Wilson Rider, exec. {MWB 23:405; SOW EB9:232} On 6 March 1743 the inventory of his estate was filed by Wilson Rider. Signed as next of kin: John Goslee, Thomas Goslee. {MINV 29:197} On 22 Sep 1744 the admin. account of his estate was submitted by Wilson Ryder (also Wilson Rider), exec. {MDAD 21:75}

On 14 Sep 1768 Mary Goslee, aged 63, swore that she was present when

Graves Boardman and Susanna Relph, dau. of Thomas Realph were m. by Rev. Alexander Adams, rector of Stepney Parish and that Graves and Susannah had the following children: Ralph, Sarah, Elizabeth, and Graves, and that Graves was the last born of the children and thet he lived to the age of 2 or 3 and then d. and that the other son of Graves Boardman first went to sea with a Captain Tomson in a brig belonging to John Pennell bound to Lisbon in the year 1765 in November and that neither the brig nor the son Relph Boardman had been heard from since. Also Goslee swears that Sarah Boardman, first-born dau. of Graves and Sarah m. Thomas Beard but did not see them get married yet she was at the wedding on the same day they were married and that the two had since lived together as man and wife and have two children. Goslee further stated that Elizabeth Boardman, dau. of Graves Boardman and sister of Sarah Beard, wife of Thomas is now in full life and that Elizabeth and Sarah are the only issue of Graves Boardman's first that are supposed to be living. {SOD D:230}

On 14 Sep 1768 Charity Rider, aged 54, swore that she was present when Graves Boardman and Susannah Relph married. She stated that Sarah Boardman, dau. of Graves first married Thomas Beard about 6 years ago and that they have lived together as man and wife since then. {SOD D:231}

Thomas was father of MARY, b. c1705, m. James Goslee; SUSANNAH, m. Graves Boardman; CHARITY, b. c1714, m. Wilson Rider; RACHEL, m. William More; SARAH, m. Walter Darby.

2. MARY RALPH, b. c1705, dau. of Thomas (1) Ralph, m. James Goslee.

James Goslee, SO Co., d. leaving a will dated 17 May 1745, proved 21 Aug 1745. To wife Mary Goslee, son James Goslee, son Levin Goslee, 85 a. To daus. Sarah, Susanna and Elizabeth Goslee, personal estate. Witnessed by Joshua Jackson, Wilson Ryder and James Astin. {MWB 24:202} On 20 Sep 1746 the admin. account of his estate was submitted by Mary Goslee, widow. Distribution to widow with residue to 3 daus. (unnamed).

James and Mary was parents of JAMES GOSLEE; LEVIN GOSLEE; SARAH GOSLEE; SUSANNA GOSLEE; ELIZABETH GOSLEE.

3. SUSANNAH RALPH, dau. of Thomas (1) Ralph, m. 1st Graves Boardman, by Rev. Alexander Adams, rector of Stepney Parish. Susannah m. 2 nd (N) Shurman/Sirman/Serman. {See The Boardman Family, this vol.}

Graves Boardman, SO Co., d. by 19 June 1749 when the inventory of his estate was filed by Susanna Boarman, admx./extx. Signed as next of kin: Sarah Bordman, Sarah Hardy. {MINV 39:141}

The admin. account was submitted by Susanna Boardman on 4 June 1751. Distribution to widow with residue to children: Ralph, Sarah, Elizabeth, Graves Boardman. {MDAD 30:171}

Susannah Shirman, SO Co., d. leaving a will made on 27 April 1787, proved on 30 July 1787. To son Charles, land; daughters Sarah Beard, Elizabeth Goslee. {SOW:EB#1:271}

 Graves and Susanna were parents of RALPH BOARDMAN, went to sea 1765 and never returned; SARAH BOARDMAN, m. 14 Nov 1762 Thomas Beard; ELIZABETH BOARDMAN, m. (N) Goslee; GRAVES BOARDMAN, d. at age 2 or 3.

 (N) and Susanna were the parents of CHARLES SERMAN.

4. CHARITY RALPH, b. c1714, dau. of Thomas (1) Ralph, m. Wilson Rider, son of Richard Ryder[22].

 Richard Rider, blacksmith, d. leaving a will dated 26 Aug 1734, proved 2 Jan 1734/35. To son Heathly, 200 a. called *Midfield* beginning at a chestnut at the Spring Landing ... To son Willson Rider 200 a. called *Venter* being my now dwelling plantation, smith's tools. To wife Sarah, furniture. Witnessed by Thomas Benson, Jonathan Jackson, Walter Derby. {SOW EB9:168}

 Wilson Rider maintained an account at the store of John Nelms, 24 Jan 1766 - 15 Feb 1768. {Nelms:65}

 Wilson Rider d. leaving a will dated 22 Jan 1784, proved 2 Feb 1784. To wife Charity, all Negroes for her natural life. To grandson John Moor, Negro boy Jacob, furniture. To son Charles, exec., legacy given to John Moor until John comes of age; 2 tracts of land, one containing 34 ½ a. called *Ralph's Purchase* and the other called *West---'s Adventure* containing 200 a.; still and ½ of the crosscut saw. To the children of son John Rider, son George Rider and Sarah Moor the remainder of the personal estate. Witnessed by James Haynie, Mary Fletcher, Charles Shirman. {SOW EB1:191}

 Charity Rider d. leaving a will dated 2 Nov 1789, proved 16 Sep 1794. To granddau. Charity Moor, Negro boy Bob, to be free when age 25. To granddau. Ann Moor, Negro girl Leah, to be set free at age 25. To granddau. Elizabeth Moore increase of Negro girl Leah until age 25 and then to be set free. To dau. Mary Moor, tea spoons. To grandson John Moor, various items. To granddau. Rachel Rider, loom, sleigh, saddle. To son Charles Rider, exec., silk handkerchief. To dau. Sarah wearing apparel. Witnessed by James Haynie, Edward Austen. {SOW EB17:315}

 They were parents of CHARLES RIDER; GEORGE RIDER; SARAH RIDER, m. (N) Moor.

---

22. Richard Ryder, son of Richard Ryder of St. Mary's Co., d. 1670, m. Jane (Wright) Lawson. She m. 3rd William Harris of St. Mary's Co. Their son Richard Ryder, father of Wilson Rider, moved to SO Co. where he d. in 1734. {Hester Dorsey Richardson, *Side-Lights On Maryland History*:431}

5. RACHELL RALPH, dau. of Thomas (1) Ralph, m. William More.

Rachell Ralphs m. 7 March 1732, William More, Junr. {SOSP}

William Moor Sr., SO Co., d. leaving a will dated 4 Feb 1788, proved 29 Dec 1788. To wife Rachel, plantation whereon I now live with all lands being part of two tracts called *Turkey — Hill* and *Woodyard*, for her natural life; still, cap, and worm; negroes Ned and Hannah, Phillis, Rose; 1/3 of personal estate. To grandson Thomas Moor, son of Levin, the tract called *Moors Ventur* in Leatherburys Neck provided he comply with condition of a bond passed to John Anderson. To son James Moor all that tract of land beginning at the swamp then running down a gulley which binds by the iron mine till it comes to James Moore's fence then with the fence to a ditch that separates James' land and that which testator's son William Moor held in his lifetime and then up the ditch to the back line of *Woodyard* next to Wicomico mills and lands. To grandson John Moor, son of William, all the land lying on the s. side of the gully; still, cap and worm after widow's decease or remarriage. To grandson Samuel Fletcher, mills and lands when he comes of age, in possession of James Moor until then. To granddau. Sarah Fletcher, Negro girl Patience. To dau. Elizabeth Fletcher — Simon, Sue (?). To granddau. Rachel Fletcher, Negroes after mother's decease; also negro girl Tamer. To granddau. Martha Fletcher, a share of Negro left to her mother. To grandson Thomas Rider, John Rider, James Rider, negro woman Leah and the child she nos has. Witnessed by William Moore, Jr., George Tull, Archibald Records. {SOW EB17:31}

Rachel Moor d. leaving a will dated 26 March 1794, proved 22 Jan 1795. To dau. Elizabeth my old mare, yoke of oxen, furniture, wearing apparel. To grandson John Moor, son of William, Negro man Edward and negro woman Hannah, yoke of oxen, mare, livestock, furniture. Grandson William to have all the crop either sowed or planted. Grandson John, exec. Witnessed by John Leatherbury, Lamer Records, Thomas Records. {WOW EB 17:354}

Rachell and William More were parents of LEVIN MORE, b. 1 April 1733; ELIZABETH MORE, b. 2 Jan 1734/5, m. (N) Fletcher; RALPH MORE, b. 8 Oct 1736; JAMES. {SOSP and Wills.}

6. CHARLES RIDER, son of Charity (4) and Wilson Rider, m. Mary (N).

Charles Rider served as private in the Somerset Militia, Salisbury Battn., Capt. Henry Gale's Quantico Company, 1778/1780. {RPWS249}

Charles Rider (1785) was an employee of James Hill, as an apprentice or journeyman shoemaker when he made 5 pairs of shoes in 3 1/2 weeks. {Nelms:65}

7. RALPH MORE, b. 8 Oct 1736, son of Rachell (5) and William More.

Capt. Ralph More maintained an account at Nelms' store, 1785-27 March 1788. {Nelms:54}

108

THE THOMAS RALPH/RELPH/ROLPH FAMILY (3)

1. THOMAS RELPH, m. 12 March 1680, Ann Boston. {IKL} Ann was dau. of Henry Boston, b. c1663, prob. in the Annemessex area. {The Boston Family:16}
　　Thomas Ralfe (Relfe) of SO Co. was granted a patent for service in 1679. {MPL WC2:77, 140, 142} Thomas R(e)alph of SO Co. was granted the following tracts: *Ralph's Prevention* (9 a.) on 23 May 1688; *Friend's Chance* (300 a.) on 1 Nov 1710. {MPL 25:402, 420; 32:644, 654; DD5:700; PL4:444}
　　Thomas Relfe recorded his cattle mark on 9 Aug 1681 in SO Co. {ARMD LIV:780}
　　Susanna Relph, dau. of Thomas and Ann Relph, b. 10 Dec 1686[23]. {IKL}
　　Elizabeth Relph, dau. of Thomas and Ann Relph, b. 12 Dec 1691. {IKL}
　　John Relph, son of Thomas and Ann Relph, b. 29 Jan 1693/4. {IKL}
　　In 1693, Thomas Ralfe and his wife Anne deeded to Elizabeth Holland dau. of John Holland *Ralfe's Purchase* (part of *Robertson's Lott*) 30 a. {SOD:L:262} [William Robertson assigned the land to said Thomas in 1681.]
　　On 10 Feb 1695/6, Thomas Relph and his wife Anne deeded to William Robinson, *Robinson's Lott* 325 a. {SOD:L:345}
　　On 12 Dec 1711, Thomas Ralfe deeded to George Gale, *Ralph's Prevention*. {SOD:CD:673}
　　The admin. account of the estate of Thomas Ralph was submitted 17 Nov 1715 by John Lankford. Payees included Thomas Ralph, Sr. {INAC 37A:101}
　　On 14 Nov 1721, Thomas Ralph sold *Friend's Chance* 300 a. to Affradozi Johnson. {SOD:IK:177}
　　Thomas Relph, Sr., SO Co., d. leaving a will dated 7 Oct 1723, proved 21 Oct 1723. To: son-in-law Thomas Perremore, plantation. where he lives; son John, plantation where he lives; daus. Anne Downes, Merren King; son William. Exec.: son William. {MWB:18:177} On 8 July 1725 the inventory was filed by William Relph. Signed as next of kin: Elizabeth Perremore, Marren King. {MINV 11:69} On 22 June 1726 the account of his estate was submitted by William Relph. {MDAD 7:422}
　　Thomas was father of ANNE, m. (N) Downes; SUSANNA, b. 10 Dec 1686; ELIZABETH, b. 12 Dec 1691, m. Thomas Parramore; JOHN, b. 29 Jan 1693/4; MARREN, m. (William) King; WILLIAM.

2. JOHN RELPH, b. 29 Jan 1693/4, son of Thomas (1) Relph, m. Ann (N).
　　John Relph, SO Co., d. by 17 Sep 1724 when the inventory of his estate was filed by Ann Relph. Signed as next of kin: Thomas Paremore, William Relph. {MINV 11:68} On 2 June 1726 the admin. account of his estate was submitted by

---

23. The abstract says that the father's name is John. A re-examination of the records shows that the father's name is Thomas.

Ann Relph, admin. {MDAD 7:417}

The 1730 tax list of SO Co., Nanticoke Hundred, shows Ann Relph as head of household; living in the household was Charles Buckworth. {SOTL} Ann Relph disappears from the tax lists after 1730.

3. WILLIAM RELPH, son of Thomas (1) Relph, m. Sarah (N).

The tax lists of SO Co., Nanticoke Hundred, show William Relph as head of household, 1723, 1725, and 1730-1740, 1744, 1748, 1750, 1753, 1754, 1757, and 1759. Living in the same household was Thomas Ralph (1740, 1744, 1748, 1750), Mitchel Relph (1744, 1748, 1750, 1753), John Ralph (1754, 1757), and William Ralph, Jr. (1757, 1759).

William Ralph, only son and heir of Thomas Ralph, patented *Anything* (50 a.) and *Good Luck* (150 a.) on 1 Sep 1732. {MPL PL8:695, 696; AM1:88, 101}

William Ralph paid tax on *Anything* and *Good Luck* in 1733, 1734, 1735, 1745, 1748, 1755, 1759, and 1761. {Debt Books}

In May 1720 James Boucher and wife Frances sold to Thomas Ralph of Quantico 48 a. of the tract *Good Luck*. In 1732 William Ralph re-patented it as *Good Luck at Last*. On 8 Sep 1733 William Ralph and wife Sarah sold 50 a. to Thomas Parremore. On 10 Nov 1770 Thomas Ralph, son of William Ralph, sold To William Ralph part of the tract. In 1769 William Ralph willed to Joseph Parremore 25 a., he to pay for said land, and parts to sons Mitchell Ralph and George Ralph. On 2 Jan 1775 Thomas Parremore and William Ralph sold 73 ½ a. to Joseph Parremore. On 6 April 1776 land warrants were recorded by Thomas Ralph in Sussex Co., DE. {WILR:173}

The tract *Anything* was patented in 1732 by William Ralph for 50 a. On 8 June 1734 William Ralph and wife Sarah sold 50 a. at the head of Barren Creek to Edward Collins. {WILR:17}

William Ralph paid tax on *Good Luck at Last* and *Anything* in 1733, 1734, 1735, 1745, 1748, 1755, 1759, and 1761. {Debt Books}

The account of William Ralph, Sr., in Nelms' store, 20 April 1767 - 26 Jan 1768, shows he bought a pair of trace ropes for 2 shillings, 6 pence and paid in corn in 1768. Both deliveries were made by son George. {Nelms:63}

William Relph, SO Co., d. leaving a will dated 1 Feb 1766, proved 26 April 1769. Wife: Sarah. Children: Mitchell, William, George, Thomas, Rachel, John and Sarah. Mentioned: Joseph Parremore. Tracts: *Good Luck at Last* and *Black Water*. Son William. Exec. {MWB 37:83} On 5 May 1769 the inventory of his estate was filed by William Relph. Signed as next of kin: George Relph, Rachel Relph. {MINV 101:185} A second inventory was filed by William Ralph on 14 May 1770. {MINV 104.295} The admin. account was submitted by William Relph on 29 April 1774. Legatees: George Relph, Rachal Relph, accountant, Sarah Relph, Thomas Relph, John Relph. Distribution in 4 equal amounts to George Relph, accountant, Sarah Relph, Rachael Relph.

William was father of THOMAS, b. c1724; MITCHELL, b. 1724/1728; JOHN, b. 1737; WILLIAM, b. 1738/1741; GEORGE; RACHEL; SARAH.

4. THOMAS RALPH, b. c1724, son of William (3) Ralph, m. Charity Callaway.

The tax lists of SO Co., Nanticoke Hundred, show William Relph as head of household, 1723, 1725, and 1730-1740, 1744, 1748, 1750, 1753, 1754, 1757, and 1759. Living in the same household was Thomas Ralph (1740, 1744, 1748, 1750).

Thomas Ralph m. 12 Dec 1751, Charity Callaway. {SOSP}

Thomas Ralph patented the following tracts: *Ralph's Delight* (20 a. SO) on 15 March 1748; *Ephraim's Purchase* (15 a. WO) on 4 Oct 1758; *Ralph's Venture* (12 a. WO) on 4 Oct 1758; *Realph's Property* (46 a. SO) on 18 Dec 1758.

Thomas Ralph paid tax on *Relph's Delight* and *Relph's Property* in Somerset County in 1759 and 1761. He paid tax on *Ephraim's Purchase* and *Ralph's Venture* in Worcester County in 1761, 1762, 1768, 1769, 1771, 1773, and 1774. {Debt Books}

On 8 Jan 1765, Thomas Ralph deeded to William Ralph, *Ralph's Delight* and *Ralph's Property*, total of 66 a. {SUDELR:O:518}

On 28 July 1788, Col. Joshua Mitchell (WO) sold to Jonathon Betts, *Ephraim's Purchase* 15 a. Said land was granted to Thomas Relph, who conveyed it to Robert Nelson, who conveyed it to Esme Bayly, who conveyed it to Col. Joshua Mitchell. {SUDELR:B:329}

Thomas and Charity were parents of SARAH, b. 14 Oct 1752; EPHRAIM, b. 11 Nov 1754; ESTHER, b. 13 April 1757; EUNICE, b. 6 June 1759; ELEANOR, b. 29 Oct 1761. {SOSP}

5. MITCHELL RALPH, b. 1724/1728, son of William (3) Ralph, m. Elizabeth Moor, dau. of John Moor.

The tax lists of SO Co., Nanticoke Hundred, show William Relph as head of household, 1723, 1725, and 1730-1740, 1744, 1748, 1750, 1753, 1754, 1757, and 1759. Living in the same household was Mitchel Relph (1744, 1748, 1750, 1753).

Mitchell Ralph maintained an account at Nelms' store, 13 Feb 1767 - 29 June 1776. He bought rum, cordage, trace ropes, pipes, needle and a lace for 8 shillings and paid in corn in 1768. He made similar purchases in 1775. In 1776 he paid by plank delivered by George Ralph and by credit on George's account. {Nelms:63}

John Moor, SO Co., d. leaving a will dated 19 Feb 1774, proved 17 Aug 1774. To son Thomas Moor, my dwelling plantation, and that tract called *Cockland* that I bought from Henry Low, 146 a., furniture. To son John Moor, my house and plantation on the west side of the country road from my dwelling house called *His Lot*, 110 a., furniture. To dau. Sarah Moor, furniture. Residue of estate to my 4 children: Thomas Moor, John Moor, Sarah and Elizabeth Relph. Son Thomas Moor, exec 24 Aug 1774: Alice Moor, widow of John demands her dower. {MWB 39:848}

Mitchell Ralph, Sussex Co., d. by 13 April 1782 when an admin bond was posted on his estate by Elizabeth Ralph. {SUAA:A94:182}

6. GEORGE RALPH, son of William (3) Ralph.

George Ralph, son of William Sr., maintained an account at Nelms' store, 20 April 1767 - 29 June 1776. He made deliveries for his father in 1767 and 1768. {Nelms:63}

On 30 Mar 1776, William Relph deeded to George Relph, *Good Luck at Last* 50 a., in Little Creek Hundred. {SUDELR:M:89}

In 1782, George Ralph, Little Creek Hundred, Sussex Co., was cited for an assessment of 2. {1782 Assessment, Delaware}

7. WILLIAM RALPH, son of William (3) Ralph, m. Mary (N).

The tax lists of SO Co., Nanticoke Hundred, show William Relph as head of household, 1723, 1725, and 1730-1740, 1744, 1748, 1750, 1753, 1754, 1757, and 1759. Living in the same household was William Ralph, Jr. (1757, 1759).

On 8 Jan 1765, Thomas Ralph deeded to William Ralph, *Ralph's Delight* and *Ralph's Property*, total of 66 a. {SUDELR:O:518}

On 30 Mar 1776, William Relph deeded to George Relph, *Good Luck at Last* 50 a., in Little Creek Hundred. {SUDELR:M:89}

In 1782, William Ralph, Little Creek Hundred, Sussex Co., was cited for an assessment of 4. {1782 Assessment, Delaware}

Richard Waller, Sussex Co., d. leaving a will dated 6 June 1784, proved 13 Sep 1784. Witnesses: William Low, Thomas Goslee, William Ralph. {SUW:D:62}

William Ralph, Sussex Co., d. by 6 Sep 1787, when an admin bond was posted on his estate by Mary Ralph. {SUAA:A94:184} Said estate is too little to pay the debts; therefore the court permitted Mary to sell *Ralph's Delight* and *Ralph's Property* to James English. {SUDELR:O:518} On 4 Aug 1791, said James English sold the land back to said Mary. {SUDELR:O:520}

THE SHILES (Shields, Sheals) FAMILY

1. THOMAS SHIELS m. Alce (N).

Thomas Shiels witnessed a deed on 8 Feb 1663. {SOD:B:119}

Thomas Shiall recorded his cattle mark in SO Co. on 6 Feb 1665. {ARMD

LIV:742}

Thomas Shiall was in Wicomico section (n. side the river) in Aug 1666. His plantation was just s. of the present town of Whitehaven, Wicomico Co. {OSES:458}

On 26 March 1667 the SO Co. Court ruled in favor of John Haynes, servant to Thomas Shieles who claimed freedom. The court ordered Thomas Shieles pay to Haynes his corn and clothes according to law. {ARMD LIV:660}

The early patents show Thomas Shiell of SO Co. had immigrated by 1668. {MPL 11:313}

Thomas Sheilds, son of Thomas and Alce Shields b. at Wickocomoco 12 Nov 1668. {IKL}

Elizabeth Shieles, dau. of Thomas and Alce Shiels b. at Wikocomoco 8 May 1671. {IKL}

John Shilles, son of Thomas and Alce Shiells b. at Wickocomoco 22 Aug 1673. {IKL}

Thomas Shiles patented *Hog Quarter* (50 a.) on 24 Nov 1674. In 1674 he devised to son John, two patents (unnamed). In 1714 John Shiles willed to his son John the plantation (unnamed). In 1745 John Shiles sold 50 a. to Thomas Willin. {WILR:207}

Thomas Shiels, Wickocomacco, SO Co., d. leaving a will dated 16 Feb 1674, proved 30 Nov 1675. To son Thomas, 300 a. home plantation, at 18 yrs. of age. To son John, 100 a. in 2 patents. To dau. Elizabeth Shiels, personalty. {MWB 5:108}

Alice Shiels patented *Shields His Choice* (200 a.) on 21 Sep 1676 on n. side of Quantico Creek. The rent rolls, 1666-1723, show it possessed by Christopher Nutter (110 a.) and Matthew Nutter (110 a.). {WILR:375}

On 23 Jan 1676 when the inventory of his estate was filed. {INAC 3:119}

On 20 Aug 1679 Edward Davis gave a calf to John Shiles, son of Thomas Shiles, lately dec'd. of this co. {ARMD LIV:771}

Thomas and Alce were parents of THOMAS, b. 12 Nov 1668; ELIZABETH, b. 8 May 1671, prob. m. (John) Nelson; JOHN, b. 22 Aug 1673.

Second Generation

2. THOMAS SHILES, b. 12 Nov 1668, son of Thomas (1) and Alce Shiles, m. Naomy (N) (b. before 1686).

Thomas Shiels patented *Whitty's Contrivance* (100 a.) in SO Co. on 28 May 1681. {MPL 24:325; 29:53}

Thomas Shild was one of the signers of a address of the inhabitants of SO Co. on 28 Nov 1689 expressing to the King and Queen of Great Britain their resolve to continue in the defense of the Protestant Religion against the French and other Papists. {COES:49}

Alice Shiles, dau. of Thomas and Naomi Shiles, b. 26 Oct 1689. {IKL}

Elizabeth Shiles, dau. of Thomas and Naomi Shiles b. 11 April 1692.
{IKL}

Sarah Shiles, dau. of Thomas and Naomi Shiles b. 14 Feb 1694/5. {IKL}

Thomas Shields, SO Co., d. by 9 Oct 1718 when the inventory of his estate was filed by Naomy Shiles. Signed as next of kin: Elizabeth Nelson. {MINV 5:33}

Thomas Shiles, SO Co., d. by 25 March 1721 when the admin. account of his estate was submitted by Naomy Shiles, admx. {MDAD 3:380}

The 1723 tax list of SO Co., Wicomico Hundred, shows Naomi Shils as head of household. Living in the household is Thos. Shiels. Nearby was Jno. Shiels as head of household; living in the same household was Peter D. Brasier.

Naomey Shiles, aged upwards of 60 years, on 31 Aug 1746, deposed regarding the bounds of *Rice Land*. {Miller:34}

Thomas and Naomi were parents of ALICE, b. 26 Oct 1689; ELIZABETH, b. 11 April 1692; SARAH, b. 14 Feb 1694/5.

3. JOHN SHILES, b. 22 Aug 1673, son of Thomas (1) and Alce Shiles, m. (N) Betts, dau. of George Betts.

John Shiels patented *Shiel's Meadows* (60 a.) on 4 July 1702. {MPL DSF:393; DD5:70}

A cattle mark was recorded for John Shiles on 20 Aug 1679. {ARMD liv:772}

Alice Shiels patented *Shields His Choice* (200 a.) on 21 Sep 1676 on n. side of Quantico Creek. The rent rolls, 1666-1723, show it possessed by Christopher Nutter (110 a.) and Matthew Nutter (110 a.). {WILR:375} On 20 July 1694, John Shiels sold to Christopher Nutter land on Quantico Creek. {SOD:L:227}

George Betts, SO Co., d. leaving a will dated 26 March 1709, proved 1 Dec 1711. To 2nd dau. Mary, 300 a., *Westloe Neck* on Quantico Creek, on which she now lives; if she dispose of same, to her heirs, is devised tract on Monocan River, otherwise devised to Jno. Erving and his wife. To son-in-law John Erving and eldest dau. Frances (his wife), dwelling plantation and 50 a., *Hab-nab* and 3 tracts, viz., 100 a., *Bett's Delight*, 200 a., *St. Giles*, 364 a., *George's Adventure*. To grandchildren John Shyles and Bridget Shyles, personalty. To wife Bridget, extx., life interest in dwelling plantation afsd. and residue of personalty during widowhood. {MWB 13:381}

John Shiles, SO Co., d. leaving a will dated 17 Aug 1714, proved 3 Nov 1714. To Thomas Carey, land _____, mentioned in certain bond to Jno. Collins and purchased by Thomas Carey. To Sarah Green, personalty. To Thos. Rensher and Bridgett, his wife, personalty, including John Reynolds. To godson John Shiles, personalty. To son John Shiles at majority, all lands, including dwelling plantation _____, and residue of personal estate jointly with Thomas and Bridgett Rensher afsd. brother-in-law Jno. Irvin and son-in-law Thomas Rensher, execs. {MWB 14:51} The inventory on his estate was filed on 20 Feb

114

1714. Signed as next of kin: Thomas Shiles, John Nelson. {INAC:36B:222} On 22
Feb 1717 the admin. account of his estate was submitted by Mr. John Irving,
Thomas Rencher, admins./exs. Legatees: Thomas Shiles, Sarah Green. {INAC
39C:1}
     John was father of JOHN; BRIDGET, m. Thomas Rensher/Renshaw.

Third Generation
4. ELIZABETH SHILES, b. 11 April 1692, prob. dau. of Thomas (2) and Neomi
Shiles.
     Elizabeth Shiles, SO Co., d. leaving a will dated 25 March 1765, proved
24 June 1766. Mentioned were John Crockett, God-child: Elizabeth Crockett;
Elizabeth Wainwright, wife of William Wainwright; Thomas Willin; Elizabeth
Ballard, dau. of Charles Ballard; Ann Fullin; Elizabeth McKintior, William
Venable's first dau. (name not given). Estate consists of chattles and personal
property. {MWB 34:78} On 7 July 1766 the inventory of her estate was filed by
John Crocket. Signed as next of kin: Leah Fleweling, John Shiles. {MINV 92:287}
The admin. account was submitted on 14 Dec 1767 by exec. John Crockett.
Distribution was made to Elizabeth Ballard, eldest dau. (unnamed) of William
Venables. Legatees: Thomas Willen, Elizabeth Whenwright, Ann Flewelling,
Elizabeth Mackintyor, Elizabeth Crockett, accountant. {MDAD 59:102}

5. THOMAS SHILES, prob. son of Thomas (2) Shiles.
     The tax lists of SO Co., Monie Hundred, show Thomas Shiles as head of
household, 1724.
     The tax lists of SO Co., Wicomico Hundred, show Thomas Shiles as
head of household, 1727, 1731-1735. Also in his household is John Shiles (1727,
1733), John McCoy (1734, 1735).
     The tax lists of SO Co., Nanticoke Hundred, show Thomas Shiles as
head of household, 1736-1740. Also in his household is John McCoy (1736).
Thomas Shiles disappears from the records after 1740.

6. JOHN SHILES, Jr., prob. son of Thomas (2) Shiles, m. 14 Sep 1737 Ann
Evans.
     The tax lists for SO Co., Wicomico Hundred, show John Shiles in the
household of Thomas Shiles, 1727, 1733. John Shiles is shown as head of
household in 1735, and probably 1736. He is shown as John Shiles, Jr. in 1737,
with William Alexander in his household. He is shown as John Shiles in 1738,
John Shiles, Jr. in 1739, John Shiles secundus in 1740, John Shiles, Jr. in 1744,
John Shiles in 1748, John Shiles in 1750, John Shiells in 1753, John Shiells in
1754, John Shiles (with John Shiles, Jr.) in 1757, and John Shiels (sailor, with
John Shiels) in 1759.
     John Shiles, Junr. was serving in the militia company of John Handy in

1749. {COES:77}

John Shiles Jr. m. 14 Sep 1737, Ann Evans. {SOSP}

John Shiles, SO Co., d. by 26 Aug 1774 when the inventory of his estate was filed by John Shiles. Signed as next of kin: Thomas Shiles, Sarah Shiles. {MINV 116:364}

John and Ann were parents of JOHN, b. 9 Sep 1739 {SOSP}; prob. THOMAS; prob. SARAH.

7. JOHN SHILES, b. c1711, d.s.p. 1759/1760, son of John (3) Shiles.

The tax lists of SO Co., Monie Hundred, show John Shiles as head of household in 1724, with Peter Brasher.

The tax lists of SO Co., Wicomico Hundred, show John Shiles as head of household, 1727, 1731-1740 and 1753. Living in his household in 1727 was Isaac Renalds. Living in the household were slaves: Tom (1731-1740), Hannabil (1735-1740). In 1737, he is cited as John Shiles, Sr. In 1740 he is identified as John Shiles, ferry. In 1753 he is identified as John Shiells, Sr., owner of slaves: Tom, Anibel, Sambo, Judith. He is cited as John Shiles, Sr. in 1744, John Shiles in 1748, John Shiles, Sr. in 1750, John Shiles, Sr. in 1753, 1754, 1757, and 1759. {SOTL}

John Shiles Senr. was serving in the militia company of John Handy in 1749. {COES:77}

John Shiels (Shiles) patented *Safety* (50 a.) in SO Co. on 10 April 1735 and *Finish* (58 a.) on 5 June 1752. {MPL EI2:215; EI3:403; YS7:332}}

John Shiles, age 25, son of John Shiles, dec'd., deposed on 2 Nov 1736 regarding the bounds of *Hickory Ridge*. {Miller:34}

The debt book of 1759 for SO Co. shows that John Shiles owned *Might Have Had More (400 a.), Adventure (44 a.), Noble Quarter (33 a.), Point Marsh (6 a.), Sidney (50 a.), Finish (58 a.), Part of Noble Quarter* (85 a.).

John Shiles, SO Co., d. prior 26 March 1760 when an admin bond was posted by Henry Lewes. {TP:37:380}

On 15 April 1745, Thomas Willin and his wife Mary sold to John Shiles pt. *Might Have Had More* 200 a. On 27 July 1763, Benjamin Huggins and his wife Ann sold to William Rencher land that descended to Ann Huggins on the death of John Shiles, as niece and coheir. On 4 June 1766, Bridget Chapley, SO Co., and John Span Conway, SO Co., sold to Ann Huggins and William Waller part of land from John Shiles, that descended to Ann and Bridget. {WILR:272}

8. BRIDGET SHILES, dau. of John (3) Shiles, m. Thomas Rencher. He married second (N).

On 15 April 1745, Thomas Willin and his wife Mary sold to John Shiles pt. *Might Have Had More* 200 a. On 27 July 1763, Benjamin Huggins and his wife Ann sold to William Rencher land that descended to Ann Huggins on the death of John Shiles, as niece and coheir. On 4 June 1766, Bridget Chapley, SO Co., and John Span Conway, SO Co., sold to Ann Huggins and William Waller part of land from John Shiles, that descended to Ann and Bridget. {WILR:272}

Thomas Rencher, SO Co., d. leaving a will dated 1 November 1764, proved on 28 April 1772. Legatees: son Thomas; daughter Mary wife of John Ballard; son William; son Samuel; daughter Bridget Chapley, daughter Ann Huggins; Sarah Beard; Francis Hitch. {SOW:EB#5:2}

Thomas and Bridget were the parents of: ANN RENCHER, m. Benjamin Huggins; BRIDGET RENCHER, m. (N) Chapley.

Thomas was the father of: THOMAS RENCHER; MARY RENCHER, m. John Ballard; WILLIAM RENCHER; SAMUEL RENCHER.

Fourth Generation

9. JOHN SHILES, son of John (6) Shiles.

The 1783 Assessment for SO Co., Wicomico Hundred, cites John Shiles as head of household, paying tax on *Little Belane* (163 a.) and *Allen's Disappointment* (9 a.). There are 3 males and 1 female in the household.

10. THOMAS SHILES, prob. son of John (6) Shiles.

He is cited on the 1783 Assessment for SO Co. as head of household, Wicomico Hundred, with no land, and no other inhabitants.

Unplaced

ANN SHILES

The levy list of SO Co., 1724, shows that Merrick Ellis had paid a fine for Ann Shiles who was charged with fornication, 600 lbs. of tobacco. {COES:61}

ANN SHEALS

Ann Shiel, WO Co., d. leaving a will dated 28 Jan 1755, proved 16 March 1764. To Richard Taler, gun that he has at Trangle Taylor. To son Rindal Hog Shiel, a handmill. Clothing to be divided between Sarah Taylor and Margaret Linsey. To Thomas Grimes, cattle. To son John Melton's children, stock. Balance of estate to be divided between Rindal Hog Shiel's children, Margaret Linsey's children and Sarah Taylor's children, except Richard and Amy Taylor is to have no more than is left them in legacies. James Linsey, exec {MWB 31:7} On 3 Nov 1764 the inventory of Ann Sheal's estate was filed by James Linsey. Signed as next of kin: Mary Linse, Sarah Taylor. {MINV 86:198} The admin. account was submitted by James Lindsey on 16 Jan 1767. Legatees: children (unnamed) of John Melton, Richard Taylor, Teagle Taylor, Kendal Hogshere (son), Sarah Taylor wife of Roger Taylor, Sarah Linsey wife of accountant, Thomas Grimes. Distribution to (chiefly minors): children (unnamed, excepting Richard Taylor

and Ann Taylor) of Sarah Taylor. {MDAD 56:290}
Ann was the mother of: KENDAL (Rindal) Hoggsheir; prob.
MARGARET, m. James Linsey; SARAH, m. Roger Taylor.

EDMOND SHILES m. 7 Feb 1733/4, Elinor Harris. {SOSP}
The tax lists of SO Co. show Edmund Shiles as head of household,
Nanticoke Hundred, 1738-1739. {Russo}
They were parents of ELIZABETH, b. 28 Aug 1737. {SOSP}

PATRICK SHIELDS/SHIELS
Patrick Shields was living in the household of James Hardy Sen. in 1723
in Wicomioc Hundred. {Tax lists of SO Co.}
Patrick Shiels was living in the household of Walter Jacobs, Nanticoke
Hundred, in 1730 and in the household of James Train, Nanticoke Hundred, 1 in
1731.
Patrick Shields/Shiels, SO Co., d. by 30 March 1734 when the inventory
of his estate was filed by William Weatherly. {MINV 18:62}
On 22 Feb 1734 when the admin. account of Patrick Sheills's estate was
submitted by William Weatherly, exec. {MDAD 12:766}

THOMAS SHILES served as Adjutant General in the SO Co. militia, 1775.
{RPWS:268}

WILLIAM STEVENS of *Rehoboth* on the Pocomoke River.

WILLIAM STEVENS, b. 1630, d.s.p. 1687, m. Elizabeth (N) who later m.
George Layfield.
On 28 May 1667 William Stevens and his wife Elizabeth conveyed to
Thomas Jarvis of Elizabeth City Co., VA, merchant, the tract *Suffolk*, patented on
6 April 1667, located on n. side of Pocomoke River. {ARMD LIV:672-3}
On 23 Sep 1668 William Stevens and his wife Elizabeth conveyed to
James Weedon of SO Co. 400 a. patented on 24 Feb 1665. {ARMD LIV:718}
William Stevens recorded his cattle marks in SO Co. in 1667, 1678 and
1686. {COES:34, 36, 38}
William Stevens was commissioned a justice of the peace of the lower
Eastern Shore of Maryland in Aug 1665. He was re-commissioned on 22 Aug
1666 when SO Co. was erected, continuing to serve until his death in 1687. He
was the son of John Stevens of Ledburn in the parish of Mentmore,
Buckinghamshire, England. There is some evidence that he had been in
Northampton Co., VA, before appearing on the Eastern Shore of Maryland in
1665. He was a member of the Lower House of the Maryland Assembly as the

first representative of SO Co. in 1669 and again represented the co. in 1678. He lived on his plantation, *Rehoboth* on the Pocomoke River where he d. 23 Dec 1687, and a tombstone to his memory still exists there. The death record of Richard Stevens, the bro. of William, reveals their parentage, and with some misspellings their English background. {ARMD LIV:xxxii, citing Som Co. Court Proceedings Liber IKL:241} John White who d. 1685 was a member of the lower Eastern Shore court in 1665 and prob. a bro. in law of William Stevens. {LIV xxxii}

On 29 Sep 1676 William Stevens was granted a parcel called *Snow Hill* on s. side of Pocomoke River, 500 a. On 4 Dec 1685 William Stevens and wife Elizabeth sold the land to Henry Bishop. {SOD 1722-1725:10}

Frances, dau. of John and Sarah White, b. at Pocomoke, d. and bur. at the plantation of Col. William Stevens in Pocomoke 2 March following. [c1680]. John White of Pocomoke, Gent., d. and bur. 3 June 1685 at the plantation of Col. William Stevens called *Rehoboth*. {IKL}

David Lindsay, SO Co., d. leaving a will dated 14 Jan 1680, proved 8 Oct 1681. To wife Sarah and two children (unnamed), entire estate, real and personal, including 300 a. on Pokomoke River. Col. Wm. Stevens, exec {MWB 4:75}

Coll. William Stevens, Esqr., one of his lordships lieutenants deputies for Maryland, d. and was bur. at his own plantation called *Rehobeth* 26 Dec 1687. {IKL}

On 17 July 1689 Elizabeth Stevens, widow, conveyed to George Trewett, the tract *Mulberry Grove*, situate on s. side of Pocomoke River, 600 a. {SOJR}

William Stevens, *Rehobeth*, Pocomoke, SO Co., d. leaving a will dated 29 Aug 1687, proved 26 March 1688. To Sarah White, widow, plantation during life which she now lives on. To Stevens White, son of sd. Sarah, sd. plantation at her death; also property on which testator lived, and *The Points*. To John White's children, 200 a. (unnamed) in common. To cousin William White, 500 a. (unnamed). To cousin Elizabeth White, 500 a., *Cedar Hall*. To 3 youngest daus. of sister White, viz., Tabitha, Priscilla, and Sarah, personalty. To Edmund Howard and his son, William Stevens Howard, land (for description see will). To George, 2nd son of Edmund Howard, land (for description see will). To Benjamin Keysar, 300 a., part of *Rich Ridge*, and personalty in Rehobeth Town. To wife Elizabeth, extx., dower rights, and to hold land bequeathed to Stevens White afsd. during life. {MWB 4:296} The inventory of his estate was filed in 1688. Mentions: widow (unnamed) of Col. William Stevens, dead. {INAC 10:56 & 10:162}

On 16 Jan 1725 (OS) Henry Baily, planter, Elizabeth Baily wife of Henry, Whittington Baily, planter, and his wife Elisha - all of Accomack Co., VA, conveyed to John Mills, wheelwright, *King's Land* which was granted by patent in 1679 to William Stevens, Esq., dec'd., on s. side of Pocomoke River about 4 miles from the river near the divisional line between Maryland and Virginia... laid out for 500 a. and said Stevens by his will devised to his wife Elizabeth the said tract. Afterwards Elizabeth m. George Layfield, who with his wife conveyed 200 a. out of sd. tract to Richard Baily of Accomack Co. who devised same to Henry Baily and for want of heirs to his son Whittington by which they became seized of the sd. land. {SOD 1722-1725:301}

William White, SO Co., d. leaving 29 Aug 1706, proved 10 May 1708. To son John at majority, dwelling plantation *The Entrance* and *Buckingham*, also interest in a vessel; he to be bound to Capt. James Bradly. To 2 eldest daus. Rose and Sarah, all interest in the Indian town Askiminconson at Acquongo, to be laid out by brothers Stevens White and William Powell. To youngest dau. Katharine, interest in land 500 a. given testator by uncle William Stevens. If child shall be born, sd. child to share with dau. Katharine if a dau.; and if a son, he to have *Buckingham* afsd. bequeathed son John. To wife Catherine, extx., 1/3 of personal residue of estate, balance to be divided among children afsd. of testator. {MWB 12:256}

On 6 April 1744 (OS) William Howard of Charles Co., son and heir of William Stephens Howard, dec'd., of Charles Co., conveys to Stephens White, son and heir of William White, dec'd. who was son and heir at law of Stephens White, gent., dec'd., part of the tract *The Entrance*. Whereas William Stevens, dec'd., was seized of a tract called *The Entrance* on n. side of the Pocomoke River and near the mouth thereof containing 850 a. and on 29 Aug 1687 (OS) did by his will devise to George Howard his uncle[24] who was the 2nd son of Edmund Howard, dec'd. all the land that belongs to the tract called *The Entrance* lying on the westernmost side of a branch between the plantation of Richard Lewis then lived upon and the plantation of Richard Buckland had lived upon and from the head of the branch separating the same from the land given to Stephens White, grandfather of the present grantee by a n.e. line to the savannah leaving all the land to the westward of the said branch on which Richard Buckland and William Lewis had formerly lived to the said George Howard and the said William Stevens having d. seized and the said George Howard survived him and d. in his minority without issue by means whereof the above named William Stephens Howard, as eldest bro. and heir of said George Howard was seized thereof and afterward on 8 Sep 1714 (OS) did contract for the sale of the land to Stephens White, grandfather of the present grantee and part of the purchase money was received from the said Stephens White but no conveyance being made in the lifetime of the said William Stephens Howard the same by descent is now the right of the said William Howard who being willing to fulfill the above bargain made by his ancestor, now this indenture, further witnesseth that the said William Howard sells to White. {SOD X:165}

---

24. Presumably means that William Stevens was the uncle of George Howard.

On 20 April 1744 (OS) William Howard, gent. of Charles Co., son and heir of William Stevens Howard, gent., dec'd. conveyed to William Holland a part of the tract *The Entrance*. Whereas William Stevens, dec'd., by his last will dated 9 Aug 1687 (OS) devised to Edmund Howard, grandfather of the grantor, during his natural life and after his death to his son the above named William Stevens Howard, a part of *The Entrance* lying on the n. side of the Pocomoke River. After the death of Edmond Howard the said son William Stevens Howard so seized on 30 April 1720 (OS) by his deed did convey to Thomas Bellin, and the said William Holland by several small purchases and means and conveyances from the said Thomas Bellin is now possessed and seized of the whole parcel of land afsd. And whereas the said William Stevens Howard is since departed this life leaving the above named William Howard his eldest son and heir and by the end that the right of the said heir may be granted and confirmed to the said William Holland in fee, now this indenture is made. {SOD X:136}

THE STEVENS FAMILY of (N) and FLORENCE STEVENS of Pocomoke Hundred

1. EDWARD STEVENS, m. Ruth (N).
    Edward Stevens immigrated to Somerset Co. by 1673, with his wife Ruth and Edward Stevens. {MPL:18:48}
    On 9 June 1679, Henry Smith and his wife Anne conveyed to Edward Stevens *Blake's Hope*. {SOLR:49}
    Edward Stevens, Pokomoke, SO Co., d. leaving a will dated 12 May 1684, proved 29 Sep 1685. To wife Ruth, ½ of *Blake's Hope*, and 1/3 of personalty. To Edward, William and John Stevens, children of Florence Tucker, equally, residue of estate, real and personal, absolutely. Florence Tucker, extx. {MWB 4:151} On 29 Aug 1686 the inventory of his estate was filed. {INAC 9:113} On 9 April 1688 the admin accounts of his estate was filed by Florence Tucker, admx. {INAC 9:506}

2. (N) STEVENS, prob. brother of Edward (1) Stevens, m. Florence (N) who m. 2nd (N) Tucker and m. 3rd William Melvin (Malvin). {See The Melvin Family, vol. 9 of this series.}
    Edward Stevens immigrated to Somerset Co. by 1673, with his wife Ruth and Edward Stevens. {MPL:18:48}
    On 9 June 1679 Henry Smith and wife Ann gave to Edward Stevens part of the tract *Blakes Hope*. In 1684 Edward Stevens devised 1/3 to wife Ruth. The rent rolls, 1666-1723, show it possessed by Edward Stevens (233 1/3 a.), William Stevens (233 1/3 a.) and John Stevens and his mother (223 1/3 a.). In 1695 Edward Stevens gave to John Broughton 100 a. In 1716 Edward Stevens gave to

dau. Tabitha Stevens or unborn son. On 12 Jan 1727 William Stevens and his wife Isabel, Samuel Stevens and his wife Jane, and Eleanor Stevens, widow of William dec'd., sold to Thomas Hayward 200 a. - that Edward Stevens had willed to the three sons of Florence Tucker commonly known by the name of Edward Stevens, William Stevens and John Stevens. They sold to John Broughton 100 a. William Stevens Sr. bequeathed to his youngest sons William and Samuel Stevens and wife Eleanor Stevens. On 8 Nov. 1730 John Stevens sold to Edward Cluff 1/3 of 600 a., 200 a. On 26 Jan 1737 William Stevens, son of Edward Stevens, sold to Thomas Hayward, 1 a., 9 perches. In 1758/9 William Stevens left to son John. On 13 Oct 1795 William Stevens sold to Jesse King part devised to William Stevens, father of William, by the will of Edward Stevens. {SOLR:49}

(N) was father of EDWARD; WILLIAM; JOHN.

Second Generation

3. EDWARD STEVENS, son of (N) (2) Stevens, m. Mary (N).

On 3 Nov 1714, Robert Cole deeded to Edward Stevens, *Wooten Purchase* 150 a. On 19 Nov 1720, Solomon Tull and his wife Elizabeth sold 50 a. to Thomas Benston. On 5 March 1743, William Stevens quitclaimed 50 a. to Samuel Dorman. On 1 April 1783, John Dorman sold 2 a. to Daniel Young. On 1 April 1783, John Dorman and his wife Rachel deeded to Levi Houston, 48 a. that Edward Stevens bequeathed to his daughter Catherine. {WOLR:683}

Edward Stevens, SO Co., d. leaving a will dated 11 Aug 1715, proved 18 Dec 1716. To dau. Mary Whorton, the part of dwelling plantation she lives on, and personalty. To dau. Cattran Dormond, part of tract bought of Robert Cole (being the under side Isaac Wheeler's plantation, but not to touch sd. land). To dau. Sarah Wheller, 50 a. of tract bought of Robert Cole, beginning where the 50 a. of Dormand's ends, and personalty. To dau. Elizabeth Stevens, 50 a. of afsd. tract, being the uppermost part of sd. tract, and personalty. To Tabbither Stevens, dwelling plantation, *Blackshop [Blake's Hope]*, after decease of her mother. Should unborn child be a son, he to have sd. dwelling plantation. Should the child be a dau., to have equal part of sd. plantation, Tabbither to have first choice. In event of death of either without issue, the survivor to have portion of deceased. To the public, ½ a. for use of meeting house, where it now stands. Wife, extx. and residuary legatee. {MWB 14:290} On 26 Jan 1716 the inventory of his estate was filed. Signed as next of kin: Robert Melvin, Samuel Dorman. {INAC 38A:142} On 22 May 1718 the admin. account of his estate was submitted by Mary Stevens, admx. {MDAD 1:177B}

Edward and Mary were parents of MARY, b. 19 Oct 1691, prob. m. Charles Wharton; KATHERINE, b. at Pocomoke 10 Sep 1693, m. Samuel Dormon; SARAH, m. Isaac Wheeler; ELIZABETH, m. Solomon Tull, son of Richard and Elizabeth (Turpin) Tull; TABITHA (Tabbither); WILLIAM, b. 1715/1716. {See The Thomas Tull Family, vol. 17 of this series.}

4. WILLIAM STEVENS, son of (N) (2) and Florence Stevens, m. Elinor (N).

William Stevens, SO Co., d. leaving a will dated 5 July 1708, proved 7 June 1709. To eldest son William and youngest son Samuel, plantation at decease of their mother. To wife Elinor, extx., residue of estate. Mother, Florence Malvin, to dwell on plantation during life. {MWB 2-12:168} On 29 Aug 1709 the inventory of William Stevens' estate was filed. Approvers: John Stevens and Robert Melvin. {INAC 30:88; SOI by Keddie} On 11 July 1711 the admin. account of his estate was submitted by Ellinor Stevens, admx. {INAC 32C:130}

On 15 Nov 1715 John Henry, plaintiff, complained against Elioner Stephens, defendant of Coventry Parish, spinster, to answer her indebtedness of 14 shillings, 5 pence. {SOJR 1715-1717}

The 1723, 1724, 1725 and 1736 tax lists of SO Co., Pocomoke Hundred, show Ellenor Stevens as head of household. Living in the household were Samll. Stevens (1723), William Stevens (1723 and 1724) and Edwain (Edward) Stevens (1725 and 1736). William Stevens is cited as head of household in 1725. Edward Stevens was living in the household of John Fleming in 1730 and 1733; in the household of Samuell Dorman in 1731; in the household of William Stevens in 1734; and head of his own household, 1738-1740. Samuel Stevens was living in the household of John Fleman (Pocomoke Hundred) in 1725. {SOTL}

William was father of: SAMUEL; WILLIAM; EDWARD.

5. JOHN STEVENS of Pocomoke Hundred, son of (N) (2) Stevens, m. Mary (N).

On 22 April 1718 the inventory of his estate was filed. Approvers: Thomas Jukes (or Dukes), Robert Malven. {MINV 1:187} On 26 March 1720, admin accounts were filed by Mary Stevens. Distribution to: admx. {MDAD:3:298}

Mary Stevens, Sr., SO Co., d. leaving a will dated 1 Feb 1721, proved 11 Feb 1720-21. To dau. Mary, care of dau. Sarah until 16 yrs. of age. To daus. Mary (at age of 16) and Sarah, Mary Maddux and her son Lazarus, exec, son John and dau. Alse (at age of 16), mother Florence Melvin and bro. Robert Melvin, personalty. To son John, dwelling plantation. To 4 children, personal estate. {MWB 16:300} Mary Stevens, SO Co., d. by 2 May 1721 when the inventory of her estate was filed. {MINV 7:333} On 21 Dec 1722 the admin. account of the estate of Mary Stephens was submitted by Lazarus Madux, exec {MDAD 5:40}

On the tax list for Somerset Co., Lazarus Maddox is cited as head of household in Pocomoke for 1727. Living in his household is John Stevens.

Mary was mother of MARY; SARAH; JOHN; ALSE.

Third Generation

6. MARY STEVENS, dau. of Edward (3) Stevens, prob. m. Charles Wharton.

Chas. Wharton, planter, SO Co., d. leaving a will dated 28 Sep 1716, proved 15 May 1717. To son William, 15 a. dwelling plantation and 100 a. adj.

being ½ of tract bought by testator called *William's Hope* at decease of his mother
Mary. To unborn child residue of *William's Hope*. To wife Mary, extx, real estate
during life. Witnessed by Sam. Dorman, Wm. Noble, Wm. Paine. {MWB 14:357}
On 20 March 1717, an inventory was filed on estate of Charles Warton. Signed as
next of kin: Mary Stevens, John Caldwell. {INAC:39C:149} On 17 June 1719, admin
accounts were filed on his estate, by administrator John Caldwell. {MDAD:2:185}
        Charles and Mary were parents of WILLIAM WHARTON; UNBORN
CHILD.

7. SARAH STEVENS, dau. of Edward (3) and Mary Stevens, m. Isaac Wheeler
(b. 18 Oct 1693, d. 1744/5), son of Edward Wheeler. {ASOS:281}
        Isaac Wheeler appeared in tax list for Pocomoke Hundred in 1724 and
continued in Pocomoke Hundred lists through 1740. {SOTL; ASOS:281}
        William Wheeler, WO Co., d. leaving a will dated 11 Jan 1743/4, proved
on 10 Feb 1743/4. Legatees: wife Rachel, extx., plantation. At her death, to
unborn child. {MWB:23:432} On 26 Feb 1743 the inventory of his estate was filed
by Rachel Wheeler. Signed as next of kin: William Wharton, William Stevens,
John Webb, Jr. {MINV 28:465} On 22 Feb 1744, admin accounts were filed on his
estate by Rachel Wheeler (alias Rachel Tillman). Distribution to: accountant (she
having no child). {MDAD:21:205}
        Isaac Wheeler, WO Co., d. by 6 March 1744 when an admin bond was
filed on his estate by Mary Harper. Sureties: Thomas Lambden, Edward Harper.
{WED}
        They were parents of EDWARD WHEELER, b. c1717, disappears from
records by 1735; WILLIAM WHEELER, b. c1720, d.s.p. by 26 Feb 1743, m.
Rachel (N); poss. MARY WHEELER; poss. REBECCA WHEELER. {ASOS:281}

8. KATHERINE STEVENS, dau. of Edward (3) Stevens, m. Samuel Dorman. {See
The John Dorman Family, vol. 8 of this series.}
        On 3 Nov 1714, Robert Cole deeded to Edward Stevens, *Wooten
Purchase* 150 a. On 19 Nov 1720, Solomon Tull and his wife Elizabeth sold 50 a.
to Thomas Benston. On 5 March 1743, William Stevens quitclaimed 50 a. to
Samuel Dorman. On 1 April 1783, John Dorman sold 2 a. to Daniel Young. On 1
April 1783, John Dorman and his wife Rachel deeded to Levi Houston, 48 a. that
Edward Stevens bequeathed to his daughter Catherine. {WOLR:683}
        On 5 March 1743 William Stevens quit claim to 50 a. to Samuel
Dorman, part of a tract of 150 a. on s.e. side of Pocomoke River called *Wooden
Under Ridge* according to the will of Edward Stevens to his dau. Cathron
Dorman. {WOD A:150}
        They were parents of JOHN DORMAN; SAMUEL DORMAN; SARAH
DORMAN; ELEANOR DORMAN; TABITHA DORMAN.

9. ELIZABETH STEVENS, dau. of Edward (3) Stevens, m. Solomon Tull. Solomon m. 2nd Rachel Tull, widow of his cousin Thomas Tull. {See The Tull Family, vol. 17 of this series.}

On 19 Jan 1720 Solomon Tull and his wife Elizabeth, conveyed 50 a. to Thomas Benston, planter. Whereas Robert Cole of Accomack Co., VA, conveyed on 3 Nov 1714 to Edward Stevens, dec'd., 150 a. of land on the Pocomoke River called *Wooten Underedge* ... now this indenture further witnesseth that the said Edward Stevens, dec'd., by his will bequeathed to his dau. Elizabeth now wife of Solomon Tull the above 150 a. Now Solomon Tull and wife sell to Benston 50 a. out of the said 150 a. {SOD 1722-1725:193}

Solomon was father of SOLOMON TULL; prob. RICHARD TULL. {The Tull Family, vol. 17 of this series.}

10. WILLIAM STEVENS, b. 1715/1716, son of Edward (3) Stevens, m. 19 Nov 1738, Mary Gray, dau. of John Gray.

On 30 March 1737 (OS), William Stephens, planter, son and heir of Edward Stephens, dec'd., sold to Thomas Hayward 1 a., 9 sq. perches of land out of a tract called *Blake's Hope* lying on n. side of the Pocomoke River, on left side of the road as goes to the ferry land over the Pocomoke formerly called Stephens' Ferry. {SOD 1737-1738:235}

On 3 Nov 1714, Robert Cole deeded to Edward Stevens, *Wooten Purchase* 150 a. On 19 Nov 1720, Solomon Tull and his wife Elizabeth sold 50 a. to Thomas Benston. On 5 March 1743, William Stevens quit claim to 50 a. to Samuel Dorman. On 1 April 1783, John Dorman sold 2 a. to Daniel Young. On 1 April 1783, John Dorman and his wife Rachel deeded to Levi Houston, 48 a. that Edward Stevens bequeathed to his daughter Catherine. {WOLR:683}

The tax lists of SO Co., Pocomoke Hundred, show William Stevens living in the household of Samuel Dorman in 1730 and head of household, 1733-1740. Living in the household of William Stevens, Pocomoke Hundred was Thomas Clark (1738); slave Mokey (1739); slave Harry (1740). The 1753 tax list of Wicomico Hundred shows William Stephens, James Pope, slave Ross. {SOTL}

On 30 Oct 1743 (OS) William Stevens, planter, was firmly bound to Thomas Hayward for and in the full sum of £200. The condition of the bond is such that whereas there is a certain tract of land called *Blake's Hope* containing 800 a. lying on the Pocomoke River that was left by the will of Edward Stevens, dec'd., to Edward Stevens, William Stevens and John Stevens, three bros. who were sons of Florence Tucker - and to be equally divided among them and a few months afterwards the 3 bros. did sell and dispose of 100 a., part of the said 700 a. to John Broughton, dec'd., so that there remains but 600 a. to be divided equally between them and without ever making a division of the said 600 a. by sundry means, conveyances, alienations has become the right of William Stevens, Edward Cluff and Thomas Hayward. Therefore the above bounden William

Stevens do keep to a division of the said 600 a. which was made by William Lane, gent., on 6 Feb 1734. {SOD X:118}

John Hutchinson, SO Co., d. by 23 July 1746 when the inventory of his estate was filed by William Stevens. {MINV 33:168} On 19 Aug 1747 the admin. account of his estate was submitted by William Stephens (also William Stevens), admin. Heirs: Unknown, overseas. {MDAD 24:91} A second admin. account was submitted on 12 June 1750 by William Stevens, admin. {MDAD 28:154}

On 9 March 1748, John Tilghman and his wife Rachel deeded to William Stevens (merchant), *Cowley* 100 a., adjacent Robert Melvin. {WOLR:148}

On 9 July 1757 William Stevens mortgaged to Edward Watson and William Fleming a number of slaves named Adam, Jane, Jenny, Tait, Joe and Pleasant. Now on 9 Sep 1757 for the fees and interest, Watson and Fleming convey to Mary Stephens the above named slaves. {SOD 1753-1759:182; 1759:16}

In 1759, William Stevens paid tax on: *Blake's Hope* 200 a., *Wooten Underidge* 50 a., *Cowley* 100 a., pt. *Piney Point* 150 a. {Debt Books}

William Stevens, SO Co., d. leaving a will dated 30 Oct 1758, proved 21 March 1759. Wife: Mary. Children: John, William, Ephraim, Mary and Betty. Land in WO Co. Tracts: *Cowley, Cole, Payne's Point*. Mary and John Stevens, execs. {MWB 30:658} On 4 April 1759 the inventory of his estate was filed by Mary Stevens. Signed as next of kin: John Stevens, Mary Stevens. {MINV 70:38} The admin. account was submitted on 14 May 1761 by Mary Stevens, acting extx., widow. Legacies: John Stevens, William Stevens, Ephraim Stevens, Mary Stevens, Betty Stevens. Distribution to widow with residue to above children: John Stevens, William Stevens, Ephraim Stevens, Mary Stevens, Betty Stevens. {MDAD 46:410} On 18 May 1761 distribution of his estate was made by Mary Stevens, (acting) extx., to widow (unnamed, 1/3), residue to children (equally): William, Ephraim, Mary, Betty. {BFD 3:75}

William and Mary were parents of JOHN, b. 14 Aug 1739; MARY, b. 3 May 1742; WILLIAM, b. 13 July 1744; EPHRAIM, b. 16 Jan 1747/8; BETTY, b. 11 July 1749. {SOSP}

11. SAMUEL STEVENS, son of William (4) Stevens, m. Jane (N)[25].

The 1723, 1724, 1725 and 1736 tax lists of SO Co., Pocomoke Hundred, show Ellenor Stevens as head of household. Living in the household were Samll. Stevens (1723). Samuel Stevens was living in the household of John Fleman (Pocomoke Hundred) in 1725. In 1727, Samuel Stevens was living in the household of William Davis in Boquerternorton Hundred. The tax lists of SO Co. show Samuel Stevens as head of household in Bogerternorton Hundred, 1730-1738 and head of household in Baltimore Hundred, 1739-1740. Living in the

---

25. She was probably the daughter of William Davis (d.c. 1735) of Boquerternorton Hundred.

same household was Thomas Daley (1730), Thomas Dicks (1731). {SOTL}

William Davis, WO Co., d. by 26 Feb 1743 when the inventory of his estate was filed by Margaret Davis. Signed as next of kin: Samuel Stevens, Jean Stevens. {MINV 29:47} On 25 June 1747 a second inventory of his estate was filed by Margaret Wells (widow). Signed as next of kin: Samuel Stevens, Jane Stevens. {MINV 35:292}

Samuel is probably the father of: WILLIAM DAVIS STEVENS.

12. WILLIAM STEVENS, son of William (4) Stevens, m. Ann Collings, dau. of John Collings.

The 1723, 1724, 1725 and 1736 tax lists of SO Co., Pocomoke Hundred, show Ellenor Stevens as head of household. Living in the household were William Stevens (1723 and 1724). William Stevens was living in Pocomoke Hundred in household of Samuel Dorman in 1730, as head of household in 1733 through 1740. Living in his household are: Edward Stevens (1734, 1735), Samuel Clark (1738), slave Mokey (1739), slave Harry (1740). William Stevens is cited as head of household in Bogerternorton, 1731-1739 and head of household in Baltimore Hundred in 1740.

John Collings, Sr., WO Co., d. leaving a will dated 26 Sep 1759, proved 1 Aug 1760. To wife, estate real and personal; at her decease, to son William Collings, all land that I hold on the west side of the branch, whereon my houses, called *Freeman's Contentment*; 1 s. To son Belletha Collings, all land that I hold on the east side of the same branch, being part of same tract, to him, and 10 pounds money to be paid out in learning. To Solomon Collings, 150 a. called *Collings' Lott*, on the head of Sandy Branch. To son Elisha Collings, 50 a. of cypress swamp called *Collings' Wentour*. To grandson William Collings, son of Elizabeth, he to be under care of Joseph Smith and Solomon Collings, 1 s. To dau. Mary Monford, 1 s., to be her part of estate. To dau. Elizabeth Bescon (or Besca), 1 s. To dau. Ann Stevens, 1 s. After wife's decease, all personal estate to be equally divided between my 6 children: Solloman, Beletha, Elisha and Roady Collings, Sarah Collins and Jerusha Collins. Wife, extx. 8 Aug 1760: Sarah Collins, widow, stands by the will. {MWB 31:1127}

On 17 Dec 1763 William Stevens and his wife Ann (William being the son of William) conveyed to Jehu Mumford the tract called *Chance* which is back in the woods and begins at a white oak standing on a ridge on the w. side of the county road that leads from Snow Hill to Pennsylvania and near an old bridge and containing 50 a. {WOD F:68}

On 6 March 1765 Nathaniel Enniss Jr. and his wife Elizabeth conveyed to William Stevens, son of William, a tract near St. Martins taken up by John Murphen and containing 36 a. called *Kilkaney*. {WOD F:304}

13. EDWARD STEVENS, prob. son of William (4) Stevens.

The 1723, 1724, 1725 and 1736 tax lists of SO Co., Pocomoke Hundred, show Ellenor Stevens as head of household. Living in the household were Edwain (Edward) Stevens (1725 and 1736). Edward Stevens was living in the household of John Fleming in 1730 and 1733; in the household of Samuell Dorman in 1731; in the household of William Stevens in 1734 and 1735; and head of his own household, 1738-1740, and 1753. {SOTL}

Edward Stephens was serving in a militia company of Capt. John Waters, SO Co., c1748. {COES:80}

14. JOHN STEVENS, son of John (5) Stevens.

The tax lists of SO Co., Pocomoke Hundred, show John Stevens living in the household of James Noble, 1730-1731, and head of his own household, 1733-1740. {SOTL}

Fourth Generation

15. WILLIAM STEVENS, son of William (10) Stevens.

On 9 March 1795 William Stevens granted to Joseph Bousee ½ a., part of a tract joining the warehouse land on the Pocomoke River beginning at the 2nd bounder of the Pits Creek warehouse and running to the s. corner of Thomas Furniss's lot. This is ½ a. of an acre devised "to the good of the publick for the use of a meeting house by Edward Stevens grandfather of the above named William Stevens." This part now conveyed is 1/4 a. {WOD Q:134}

William Stevens d. leaving a will dated 16 Jan 1798, proved 23 July 1799. To nephew John Stevens, exec., all estate "in lieu of his estate that I am guardian to him for being subject to the payment of all my just debts." To sister Betty Stevens, a home on testator's dwelling plantation house, garden ground, potato ground and flax ground. Negro woman Naomi to be free and have a home in testator's kitchen, and other privileges. Mentioned nephews Robert and Levin King and Niece Polly King. Witnessed by John Hayward, James Davis, Handcock Lawes. {EB17:729}

16. EPHRAIM STEVENS, b. 16 Jan 1747/8, son of William (10) and Mary Stevens, m. 18 April 1773, Milcah Dashiell (b. 20 Jan 1746/7, d. 22 Dec 1788), dau. of Louther and Anna Dashiell. {Dashiel records by Oliver Louis Dashiell}

Louther Dashiell, SO Co., d. leaving a will dated 26 Nov 1764, proved 3 April 1765. Mentioned children: Jane, Milca, Louther, Jr., Arthur, Matthias and Wm. Dashiell. Wife: Ann. Tracts: on Wiccomico Creek, *Dashiell's Lot* and *Chance*. {MWB 33:156}

Anna Dashiell, SO Co., Stepney Parish, d. leaving a will dated 21 March 1773, proved 15 April 1773. Mentioned children: Mathias, Arthur, William, Jane, Milcah. {MWB 39:520}

On 24 June 1763 John Jenner sold to Ephraim Stevens (to put up as bond for bail money) the tract *Jenners Good Luck* (50 a.). On 7 April 1778 Josiah Polk, exec. sold to Ephraim Stevens 50 a. that John Jenner sold to John Caldwell who willed it to be sold by exec. Josiah Polk. In 1785 Ephraim Stevens of WO Co. sold 50 a. to son William Augustus Dashiell Stevens. {WILR:225}

On 4 April 1767 Littleton Dennis sold to Ephraim Stevens, son of William Stevens, 150 a. of *Piney Point*, situated on the Pocomoke. {WOD G:101}

On 6 May 1799 William Stevens sold 150 a. to John Stevens. On 4 June 1799 John Stevens sold 4 1/2 a. to James Burnett. On 2 June 1800 John Stevens sold to James Burnett 104 a. of *Piney Point* and *Wooten Underedge*. {WOLR:478}

Ann Dashiell, WO Co., d. by 10 May 1773 when the inventory of her estate was filed by James Robertson. Signed as next of kin: Ephraim Stevens, Matthais Dashiell. {MINV 113:329}

Ephraim Stevens served as 1st lieutenant in the Somerset Militia, Salisbury Battn., Capt. Josiah Dashiell's Wicomico Creek Company, 22 Sep 1777 to 24 July 1780 or later. He was appointed as one of three purchasers of cattle in SO Co. for the use of the Continental Army on 7 Jan 1778. {RPWS:281}

In his will dated 9 Dec 1780, proved 14 Dec 1780, William Augustus Dashiell of BA Co., Surgeon in the Continental Army, left to Arthur Stevens and John Stevens, sons of bro. in law Ephraim Stevens, £250, to be paid to them by their father when they come of age. {SOW EB1:146}

Ephraim Stevens of WO Co. (proved in SO Co.) d. leaving a will dated 16 Oct 1786, proved 18 Feb 1787. To son Arthur Dashiell Stevens, a black mare and saddle. To son John Stevens a mare and saddle. To son William Augustus Dashiell Stevens, plantation (50 a.) called *Jonnasses Good Luck* (?), a bond from testator's bro. William Stevens for tract called *Piney Point* which testator's father left testator for the sum of £205.11.8 with interest, a mare and saddle. To bro. William Stevens the tract for which he has a bond, called *Piney Point*, 250 a. To wife Milcah, extx., 1/3 of remainder of estate. To dau. Anne Stevens and dau. Milcah Stevens, remaining 1/3 of personal estate at age 16 or day of marriage. Robert Jenkins King and son William Stevens to act as guardians for the education of sons Arthur and John. Witnessed by John Woolford, Samuel Sloan, Jonathan Hudson. {SOW EB1:256}

Milcah Stevens d. leaving a will dated 29 Sep 1788, proved 5 Feb 1789. To daus. Anne Stevens and Milcah Stevens, tract now in the possession of William Done and formerly the property of Joseph Piper, son of John - when the tract is recovered it is to be divided equally between them. To youngest son William Augustus Dashiell Stevens the above tract should both daus. die without issue. Mentions son Arthur Dashiell Stevens and son John Stevens. Henrietta Dashiell friend and relation to have care of eldest dau. Anne. Niece Jenny Stewart to have care and upbringing of younger dau. Milcah. Robert Jenkins King, exec. Witnessed by Nancy Anno, Elizabeth Anno, Catherine Maddux. {SOW EB17:43}

Ephraim was father of ARTHUR DASHIELL, b. 1 Nov 1777; JOHN DASHIELL, b. c1765; WILLIAM AUGUSTUS DASHIELL, b. 14 April 1781; ANNE, b. 22 June 1779; MILCAH, b. 17 Feb 1783, d. 20 Dec 1788. {Dashiel records by Oliver Louis Dashiell}

17. WILLIAM DAVIS STEVENS, prob. son of Samuel (11) Stevens, m. Sophia Farwell (Farrell), dau. of Thomas Farwell (Farrell).

Thomas Farwell, planter, WO Co., d. leaving a will dated 26 April 1774, proved 27 Feb 1776. To wife Mary Farwell, extx., my dwelling house and all housings and 1/3 part of whole estate both real and personal and what money I now have for her. To grandson Thomas Farwell, son of John Farwell the rest of my lands to be possessed at age 22 years. To son John Farwell, all wearing apparel, 1 s. To dau. Comfort Hamlen, 10 pounds of moveable estate. To dau. Leviner Tubbs, 1 s. To daus. Comfort Hamblen and Sophia Stevens, residue equally. Joseph Hamblen, exec {MWB 41:74}

On 28 Jan 1786 posted a bond for £240 on the plantation called *Addition to Venture* for a term of 7 years providing John pay to Sophia the sum of £170 on 1 Jan 1792. [In a loose paper found on the same page: "Mr. James R. Morris please to Deliver the motigage [mortgage] Bond or instrument of Writing from John Steven to his mother Sofier Steven to Littleton Robins & you." {WOD L:465}

Williams Luck was surveyed on 13 March 1765 for William Davis Stevens and patented 2 Dec 1766. {WORR}

Stevens's Chance was surveyed for William Davis Stevens on 15 March 1768 for 30 a. beginning at a marked iron white oak standing on a flat piece of ground on the s. side of the St. Martin's River and to the westward of Thomas Farrell's plantation; patented 5 Nov 1768. {WORR}

On 12 Aug 1769 Zeno Evans, planter (and acknowledged by his wife Agnes), conveyed to William Davis Stevens 70 a. of a tract called *Endeavor*. {WODH:84} On 5 July 1788 Joshua Stevens conveyed to Comfort Walter part of the tract *Endeavour*, it being the land sold by Zeno Evans unto William Davis Stevens and given by William Davis Stevens by his last will to his son Joshua Stevens and containing 70 a. {WOD M:396}

William Davis Stevens d. leaving a will dated 25 March 1777, proved 25 Oct 1777. To son John Stevens the tract called *Addition to Venture*. To son Joshua Stevens 70 a. called *Indevers* purchased of Zeno Evans. To dau. Comfort 30 a. called *Stevens Chance* lying about 2 miles from St. Martins Creek. To wife Suffia her thirds and Negroes Peter, woman Febe, boy Isaac. Execs. Wife and eldest son John. {WOW JW4 Part II:357} On 5 Nov 1777, an inventory was filed on his estate, by Sophia Stevens. Signed as next of kin: John Farwell, Benjamin McCormick. {WOI:JW#12}

John Stevens, WO Co., d. leaving a will dated 27 Jan 1784, proved 11 Feb 1786. Legatees: mother Sophia, brother Joshua. Executor: brother Joshua.

{WOW:JW#13:103} On 11 Feb 1786, an inventory was filed on his estate by Sophia Stevens and Joshua Stevens. Signed as next of kin: John Farewell, Joseph (?). {WOI:JW#12}

Sophia Stevens, WO Co., d. leaving a will dated 17 April 1788, proved on 1 Sep 1789. Legatees: dau. Comfort, extx. {WOW:JW#13:238}

On 6 June 1795 John Jones and wife Comfort sold to Joseph Watson 30 a. of the tract *Stevens's Chance* surveyed for William Davis Stevens in 1768 for 30 a. {WOD Q:295}

William was father of JOHN, d. 1786; JOSHUA; COMFORT, m. John Jones.

Fifth Generation

18. WILLIAM AUGUSTUS DASHIELL STEVENS, son of Ephraim (16) Stevens.

On 6 March 1799 William Stevens, SO Co., of Ephraim Stevens, dec'd., conveyed to John Stevens of SO Co. the tract *Port Royal*, 150 a. on e. side of Pocomoke River being all the part which was purchased by the said William Stevens of Ephraim Stevens dec'd.; 52 a. of part of the tract called *Wooten Under Edge*; part of the tract *Cowly* containing 150 a. which adjoins the land of James Townsend. {WOD T:160}

19. JOSHUA STEVENS, son of William Davis (17) Stevens, m. Susanna (N).

Joshua Stevens served as private in the Worcester Militia, Sinepuxent Battn., Capt. John Rackliff's Company, 1779/1780. {RPWS:281}

On 25 April 1789 Joshua Stevens for £22 sold to Samuel Holland, Negro boy Ben. {WOD M:534}

On 9 Nov 1793 Joshua Stevens and his wife Susanna conveyed all the tracts that John Stevens, bro. of Joshua Stevens, was seized of before his decease called *Venture* and *Addition to Venture*. {WOD P:339}

On 6 June 1795 John Jones and his wife Comfort conveyed *Stevens's Chance*, surveyed for William Davis Stevens in 1768, to Joseph Watson. {WOD Q:295}

THE JOHN STEVENS FAMILY of Ledbourn, England & Wicomico Hundred

1. JOHN STEVENS of Ledbourn, England.
John was father of WILLIAM; RICHARD.

Second Generation

2. RICHARD STEPHENS, b. c1641, d. 1713, son of John (1) Stevens, m. 1st Frances (N) and m. 2nd Abigail (Horsey) Kibble, dau. of Stephen Horsey and

widow of John Kibble. {See The Horsey Family, vol. 8 of this series.}

Richard Stevens, bro. of William Stevens of SO Co., MD, was youngest son of John Stevens of Llebourn [Ledbourn] in Mealemore Parish of county of Buckingham in England; d. at the house of his bro. William afsd. on 22 April 1667 and bur. at his plantation called *Rehoboth* 25 April 1667. {IKL}

On 20 May 1666 Edward Hasard (Hazzard) sold a cow to Richard Stevens of Wiccocomico. {ARMD LIV:624} Richard Stevens of Wiccomocmico first recorded his cattle mark in SO Co. in 1666. {ARMD LIV: 748}

On 6 Aug 1667 *Hilliards Choice* was surveyed for Richard Stevens lying on the n. side of the Pocomoke River in Dividing Creek in Nascoato Neck and on the e. side of the creek. Assigned to William Stevens. {SORR}

On 11 Nov 1674 Richard Stevens, aged 33 or thereabouts stated

"I being at the house of mr Winder soone after I came out of England And he Shewed me A letter which he said Came from Edward Dickeson And he told me that Edward Dickeson did write to him to provide for his Chilld But said he I will have the whore whipt Soe farr I say & further Saith not. "

On 9 Sep 1683 (OS) a tract called *Goddard's Folly* on n. side of Wicomico Creek, 800 a., was granted to Richard Stevens (surveyed 10 Dec 1677) (OS). On 9 May 1685 (OS) Richard Stevens and his wife Abigail sold to Peter Parsons 200 a. out of 800 a. called *Goddard's Folly*, lying on n. side of Wicomico Creek. {SOD EI:150}

John Truman, SO Co., d. leaving a will dated 8 Aug 1685, proved 6 July 1686. To brother John Makbride and cousin Robert Truman, personalty. To 3 daus., viz., Dorothy, Elizabeth and Catherine, at age, residue of estate, real and personal. Richard Stevens to have care of dau. Dorothy; John Booth to have care of dau. Elizabeth, and James Dashields to have care of dau. Catherine. Richard Stevens, Jno. Booth, Jas. Breden, execs. {MWB 4:215}

Richard Stevens later recorded cattle marks in SO Co. in 1687 and 1696. {COES:38, 40}

Richard Stephens (Stevens), SO CO, d. leaving a will proved 3 Nov 1713. To son Richard, part of *Gotherd's Folley*, beginning at mouth of Back Creek and running down to Wickocomaco Creek. To wife Abigail, residue of *Gotherd's Folley* during life, to pass at her decease to son Isaack. To dau. Sarah Bounds, 300 a., *Cowes Six*. At her decease to pass to her son Jonathan Bounds; he dying without issue, to next male heir of his mother, and lacking such to his sister Sarah Bounds, and if she die without issue, to 3 daus., Ann Stephens, Abygale Stephens and Hanna Stephens. To son Isaack afsd., at 18 yrs., 80-100 a., *Stephen's Conquest*, and jointly with grandson Jonathan Bounds afsd., the great marsh belonging to 300 a. afsd. To son John, part of *Fairfields*, also land, the old plantation adjoining same. To son Richard, residue of 900 a., *Fairfields*. Should any dispute arise among sons named regarding their land, such disputes to be settled at meeting of Quakers. To sons and dau. Hannah afsd., and to dau. Elizabeth Emmit, personalty. To wife Abagail, extx., dower rights and personal estate during widowhood. Overseers: Richard Waters, Benjamin Cotman, William Cibble. {MWB 13:686} On 1713? the inventory of his estate was filed. Signed as next of kin: Richard Stevens, John Stevens. {INAC 35A:254} On 30 June 1716 the admin. account of the estate of Richard Stevens was submitted by Abigall Stevens, extx. {INAC 36C:272}

The tax lists of 1723, 1724, and 1725 show Abigal Stevens as head of household in Wicomico Hundred. Living in the household were slaves Jack (1723) and Bess (1723 and 1725). .

Abigall Stevens, SO Co., d. by 17 May 1727 when the inventory of her estate was filed by Richard Stevens. Signed as next of kin: William Kibble, Hannah Stevens. {MINV 13:346} 1 June 1731 the admin. account of her estate was submitted by Richard Stevens, admin. Payments included Hannah Stevens (for legacy from her father (unnamed). {MDAD 11:92}

Richard and Frances were parents of ELIZABETH, b. at Wickocomoco 17 Nov 1667, m. (N) Emmit; FRANCEAS, b. at Wicomocomoco 20 Jan 1669.

Richard was also father of RICHARD; ISAACK; SARAH, m. 1st James Bounds, 2nd John Gunby; ANN; ABYGALE; HANNA; JOHN.

Third Generation

3. RICHARD STEVENS, son of Richard (2) Stevens, m. 25 Dec 1730, Rachael Hacker. Rachel m. 2nd Matthew Kemp.

Richard Stevens age 47, deposed on 29 July 1736 regarding the tracts *Bears Quarter* and *Good Luck*. {Miller:36}

The tax lists of SO Co. show Richard Stevens as head of household in Wicomico Hundred, 1723, 1724, 1727, 1730-1739. Living in the household was Robert Miller (1723), Robert Malone (1724) and slaves Pompey/Pumbow (1723, 1730-1739), Ceasar (1730-1731), Sue (1730-1733), Alse (1731-1739), Tobie (1735), Scipio/Sib (1738-1739).

John Booth, SO Co., d. by 25 June 1726 when the inventory of his estate was filed by Judith Booth. Signed as next of kin: Elizabeth Sarmon, Richard Stevens. {MINV 11:858}

William Kible, SO Co., d. by 29 April 1734 when the inventory of his estate was filed by Ursley Kible. Signed as next of kin: Richard Stevens, John Stevens. {MINV 18:405}

Richard Stevens, SO Co., d. by 6 June 1739 when the inventory of his estate was filed by Rachael Cemp, wife of Matthew Cemp. Signed as next of kin: Jonathon Bounds, William Kibble. {MINV 25:148} On 3 July 1743 the admin. account of his estate was submitted by Rachel Kemp, admx., wife of Mathew Kemp. Payments included widow (unnamed, 1/3). Residue to children: Ellinor, Mary, Stephen. {MDAD 19:460}

Stevens Lott was patented in 1737 for 73 a. {MPL EI2:689; EI3:509} On 19 Oct 1756 Stephen Stevens, heir of Richard, sold to Joseph Morris 73 a. of *Stevens's Lott* lying on s. side of the Wicomico River adj. land of George Dashiell, dec'd., called *Dashiell's Meadow*, which said parcel became the right of the grantor at the death of Richard Stevens as heir. {SOD 1753-1759:143}

On 21 June 1750 a second admin. account of the estate of Richard Stevens of SO Co. was submitted by Rachel Kemp, admx., wife of Mathew Kemp. Payments included widow (unnamed, 1/3). Residue to children (unnamed). {MDAD 28:155}

Richard and Rachel were parents of NELLEY (Ellinor), b. 28 Oct 1731, m. James Raey on 11 June 1761 {SOST} ; MARY HACKER, b. 28 Dec 1733, m. Richard Stevens Bounds; STEVAN (Steven, Stephen), b. 5 Aug 1735.

3. ISAAC STEVENS, son of Richard (2) Stevens, m. 26 Oct 1723, Ann Roe. {SOSP}

The tax lists of SO Co. show Isack Stephen was head of household in Wicomico Hundred in 1724 and 1725. In 1730 Ann Stevens is shown as head of household in Wicomico Hundred. Living in the household was slave Jack.

Isaac Stevens, SO Co., d. by 11 Nov 1727 when the inventory of his estate was filed by Anne Stevens. {MINV 13:274}

On 4 March 1728 the admin. account of his estate was submitted by Ann Stevens, admx. {MDAD 9:391}

In 1713 Richard Stevens willed to son Isaac Stevens at age 18, 100 a. of *Stevens Conquest*. On 13 July 1792 Thomas Collins Sr. and wife Rebecca sold to Thomas Collins Jr. a part of the tract. {WOLR:390}

The 1730 tax list of Wicomico Hundred shows Ann Stevens as head of household. Living in the household was slave Jack. {SOTL} Living in the household in 1727 was Ambrose Riggen.

Isaac and Ann were parents of REBECAH, b. 7 Aug 1727. {SOSP} Rebecca m. Thomas Collins.

4. JOHN STEVENS, son of Richard (2) Stevens, m. Anne Horsey, dau. of Stephen and Hannah Horsey.

John Stevens (Stephens) was living in Wicomico Hundred, 1723-1735, as shown by the tax lists of SO Co. Living in the household were John George Terry (1730); John Roatch (1734); slaves: Bess (1730-1735), Jack (1731-1733), Isaack (1734).

Stephen Horsey, Sr., Monnocan Parish, shipwright, d. leaving a will dated 10 Jan 1721, proved 3 Oct 1722. To son John, *Horsey Downs*, adj. land of Anthony Nanny, and dwelling plantation 640 a. *Hannah's Delight*. Should he die without issue, sd. plantation to 3 daus. Sarah Wheatly, Ann Stevens and Elizabeth. To son Stephen, *Watkin's Point*. To son and dau. John and Elizabeth and in trust to them for dau. Abigail, personalty. To 6 children afsd., personalty at decease of wife. Wife Hannah extx. with sons John and Stephen. {MWB 17:308}

Hannah Horsey, widow, SO Co., d. leaving a will dated 8 Nov 1733, proved 20 July 1734. To son John, residue of *Hannah's Delight* (except that part already given to dau. Elizabeth Outerbridge) during his life, at his decease to son Stephen for life, and after his decease to his son Stephen. To son John and daus. Anne Stevens and Sarah Roach, personalty. To grandson William Outerbridge, 200 a. as laid out and alienated to dau. Elizabeth; also certain personalty at age of 18; sd. grandson dying without issue sd. personalty to other 2 grandchildren Stephen and Mary Outerbridge. To nephew William son of Randall Revall, 170 a. on Rackcoon Point, Mannocan River, by virtue of testatrix' right from Anne Tought. To 2 daus. Sarah Roach and Anne Stevens, land lying between *Hannah's Delight* and the afsd. land bequeathed to William Revell during their lives, after their decease to be equally divided between William Wheatly and Hannah Stevens. To children, viz.: John and Stephen Horsey, Sarah Roach and Anne Stevens, all the upper part of this neck above *Hannah's Delight* as granted by Lord Baltimore to predecessors of testatrix. Testatrix states that there is a law suit pending for recovery of land claimed by virtue of Anne Tought, and directs that any beneficiary of sd. claim refusing to bear their part of sd. suit shall be excluded from all benefits of same. Child. charged to take special care of dau. Abigall and also to do what they can for Betty's children. Should dau. Sarah Roach possess that part given her of Anne Tought's Right of Testatrix, then bond given to her void only to assist her brother John in his needs. Sons John and Stephen, execs. Codicil: 5 May 1734. Bequest of personalty to dau. Sarah Roach revoked, sd. dau. being deceased, sd. personalty to be delivered to William Wheatly, Sarah Wheatly and Stephen Roach, children of deceased dau., when of age; should either of afsd. grandchildren die before they all come of age, survivors to inherit portion of deceased. Devise of land above *Hannah's Delight* to Sarah Roach declared void. {MWB 21:171}

On 31 March 1761 William Roach swore that Hannah Horsey sent for him to come and look over some of the papers and accounts and that among the papers he saw some receipts from and under the hand of John Horsey, Michael Roach, Stephen Horsey, John Stevens, Elizabeth Horsey and Abigail Horsey in full for their part of Stephen Horsey's estate, the husband of the late Hannah Horsey. {SOD C:81}

Mr. John Stevens, SO Co., d. by 14 May 1736 when the inventory of his estate was filed by William Kibble. Signed as next of kin: Jonathon Bound, Richard Stevens. {MINV 21:533} On 17 May 1739 the admin. account of his estate was submitted by William Kibble, admin. {MDAD 17:134}

John and Anne were the parents of: HANNAH, b. 25 Feb 1721 (OS) {Stepney Parish}, m. William Kibble on 20 April 1736 {Stepney Parish}; MARY, b. 24 December 1719, d. 1743/1746, m. Joseph Morris on 20 Nov 1739.

5. STEPHEN STEPHENS, son of Richard (2) Stevens, m. (N)[26]

On 24 Aug 1748 (OS) Clement Dashiell and Louther Dashiell appointed to valuate the land that did belong to Richard Stevens now under the care of Samuel Ackworth as guardian appointed by the court to Stephen Stevens, found an old dwelling house with 2 brick chimneys 35 feet long and 15 feet wide very much out of repair, an old 20 foot barn, old milk house 5 foot square, 179 apple trees, old peach orchard with 100 indifferent trees, 700 sound logs. The value of sd. land is not more than the quit rent. {SOD X:316}

The 1753 tax list of SO Co., Wicomico Hundred, shows Stephen Stephens as living in the household of Jonathon Bounds, Sr. {SOTL}

On 25 March 1757 Joseph Tulley, planter, sold to Stephen Stevens a moiety of land which Joseph purchased from Charles Acworth and his wife Elizabeth called *Acworth's Delight* on e. side of the Nanticoke River and on the s. side of Barren Creek, containing 92 a. {SOD 1753-1759:170} Stephen Stephens, planter, conveyed the land to Stephen Parrimore on 12 Oct 1758. {SOD 1753-1759:222}

On 15 Sep 1767 Stephen Stephens conveyed to Isaac Coston a Negro man Will. {SOD D:124}

Stephen Stephens, SO Co., d. leaving a will dated 24 Feb 1793, proved 13 May 1793. To son Richard Stephens Negro man Samson and Negro boy Levin. To grandson Henry Jackson and granddau. Patience Jackson, Negro woman Binah and Negro boy Abram. To dau. Temperance Jackson use of Negroes left to grandchildren until they arrive at age. To son Clement Stephens Negro man David, Negro boy Joshua, furniture. Remainder of estate to be divided between children, Richard, Temperance and Clement. Exec. son Clement. Negro woman Nel to have her freedom. Witnessed by Matthew Kemp, John McCallister. {SOW EB17:244}

Stephen was father of RICHARD, b. 26 Feb 1762; TEMPERANCE, b. 19 Nov 1769, m. (N) Jackson; JOHN, b. 7 Oct 1771; SAMUEL, b. 28 April 1774; CLEMENT. {SOSP}

Fourth Generation

6. HANNA STEVENS, dau. of John (4) Stevens, m. 20 April 1736, William Kibble.

William Kibble, SO Co., d. by 17 June 1771 when an inventory was made on his estate. Administrator: George Kibble. Signed as next of kin: William Kibble, George Parsons. {MINV:106:265}

They were parents of WILLIAM KIBBLE, b. 21 Sep 1740, d. 1773, m.

---

26. She is probably Betty, the daughter of Jonathon Bayley and his wife (daughter of Samuel Jackson).

Elizabeth Stewart on 24 July 1763; GEORGE KIBBLE, b. 17 Jan 1744, d. 1775, m. Mary (N); ANN STEVENS KIBBLE, b. 1 Jan 1746/7; SARAH KIBBLE, b. 18 Sep 1748; JOHN, b. 6 April 1763. {SOSP}

THE JOHN STEVENS FAMILY (2) of Wicomico Hundred

1. JOHN STEVENS m. Margrett Cox, dau. of Thomas Cox: Margrett Cox Stevens later m. John Disharoon.

John Stevens, SO Co., d. by 10 May 1704 when the inventory of his estate was made. {MWB:3:326} On 11 June 1705 the admin. account of his estate was submitted by Margrett Disharoons, wife of John Disharoons. {INAC 25:284}

Cox's Fork was patented on 16 Dec 1681 by Thomas Cox at the head of the Rokiawalkin River for 300 a. The rent rolls, 1666-1723, show the tract possessed by John Holder (150 al) and John Disharoon (150 a.). In 1716/7 John Holder willed to sons John and Joseph Holder. On 10 April 1726 John Disharoon and wife Margaret Disharoon and John Stevens of Sussex Co., DE, with wife Frances, sold to William Oliphant 150 a. that Thomas Cox and wife Rebecca sold to John Stephens. The land descended to his son John Stevens.

Thomas Cox, Sr., SO Co., d. leaving a will dated 20 Nov 1724, proved 13 Jan 1724. To son Thomas, parts of *Allder bury* and *Wilton* (for desc. see will), 1/3 of debts due from Ebenezer Handy; also to son afsd. and grandsons Hill and Thomas, 60 a. of *Plumtum Saltash*. To grandchildren Archibald and Sarah Ann Smith, 200 a. *Plumtum's Saltash*, on main branch of Rocawalkin. To dau. Liddia, 178 a. of *Alderman Bury*; residue of *Wilton* not sold to Ebenezer Handy, and personalty. To grandson John Stevens, 117 a. in Broad Creek Neck. To James Lawley, 100 a. __ should he produce bond for same. To John Davis, Rachel Wallton and her 2 children _, personalty. To daus. Sarah Turpen, Jane Disharoune and Margratte and son John Davis, 1s. each. To William Hearn, privilege of spoon moulds during life. Dau. Liddia (wife of Jeremiah Wright) extx. and residuary legatee. {MWB 18:371}

Living in the household of John Disherune of Wicomico Hundred in 1725 and 1730 was William Stephens. {SOTL}

John was father of: JOHN; WILLIAM, b. before 1709; THOMAS.

Second Generation

2. JOHN STEVENS, son of John (1) Stevens, m. Frances Crew, dau. John and Annabella Crew (Sussex Co).

Cox's Fork was patented on 16 Dec 1681 by Thomas Cox at the head of the Rokiawalkin River for 300 a. The rent rolls, 1666-1723, show the tract possessed by John Holder (150 al) and John Disharoon (150 a.). In 1716/7 John Holder willed to sons John and Joseph Holder. On 10 April 1726 John Disharoon

and wife Margaret Disharoon and John Stevens of Sussex Co., DE, with wife
Frances, sold to William Oliphant 150 a. that Thomas Cox and wife Rebecca sold
to John Stephens. The land descended to his son John Stevens.

On 20 Dec 1715, Thomas Cox patented *Coxes Folly* for 117 a. on Broad
Creek. {WOLR:150}

Thomas Cox, Sr., SO Co., d. leaving a will dated 20 Nov 1724, proved
13 Jan 1724. To grandson John Stevens, inter alia, he left 117 a. in Broad Creek
Neck. {MWB 18:371}

John Stevens was living in the household of step-father John Disharoon
in 1725 in Wicomico Hundred. In 1725 he was living in the household of Capt.
Edward North in Wicomico Hundred. {SOTL}

On 2 Feb 1727, Richard Bracy and his wife Annabella deeded a release
to her children Anne Stockly, Honor Tindal, and Francis Stevens (daus. of John
Crew) *West Chester* 900 a. {SUDELR:F:270}

On 7 May 1728, John Stevens and his wife Frances deeded to John
Harmanson, their interest in *West Chester*. {SUDELR:F:288}

On 11 Nov 1729, John Stevens (SO Co.) and his wife Frances deeded to
John Adams (SU Co, DE), ⅓ of 2 lots in Lewes. {SUDELR:F:336}

John Stevens had the following tract patented in SO Co.: 35 a. on 4 Oct
1725 called *Security*. {MPL PL6:127; PL7:454} *Security* was surveyed on 19 Sep 1722
for John Stevens, lying on the easternmost side of a creek issuing from the
Wicomico River called Wicomico Creek and between two tracts of land being
Dear Fields and *Stephens Conquest*. {SORR}

John Stevens, WO Co., d. leaving a will dated 28 Aug (no year), proved
on 22 Oct 1762. Legatees: son Thomas, *Coxes Folly* 117 a. and *Security* 50 a.;
son Avery 125 a. entered with Mr. Shankland under Pennsylvania Rights; son
William, 90½ a. which William Beavens is to convey to him; dau. Margaret.
Balance: children and son Michael Stevens. Executor: son Avery. {MWB:31:751}
On 11 Oct 1762 an admin bond was posted by Avery Stevens. Sureties: Joseph
Collins, Jonathon Bell. {WED} On 25 March 1763, an inventory was filed on his
estate, by Avery Stevens. Signed as next of kin: William Stevens, Thomas
Stevens. {MINV:80:92} On 2 Sep 1763 the admin. account of his estate was
submitted by Avery Stevens. Distribution to widow (unnamed), children
(unnamed). {MDAD 49:413}

John is the father of: THOMAS; AVERY; WILLIAM; MARGARET; MICHAEL.

3. WILLIAM STEVENS, b. c1701, son of John (1) Stevens, m. Margaret Pollett, dau. of Thomas Pollett. [Following the death of Thomas Pollett his widow Sarah m. (N) Dowdle.]

The tax lists of SO Co. show William Stevens living in Wicomico Hundred in household of John Disharoon in 1723 & 1724, and in household of John Disharoon in 1730. He is cited as head of household, Wicomico Hundred 1733-1740. Living in William's household in 1738 was Richard Rogers. {SOTL}

On 8 Jan 1734, Isaac Handy deeded to William Stevens, *Whittington's Choice*. {WILR:434}

Thomas Pollet, SO Co., d. leaving a will dated 23 Nov 1743, proved 26 Jan 1743. To son Thomas, plantation where he now dwells being part of *Trouble and Deutery*. To son William, personalty. To wife Sarah, extx., dwelling plantation this being part of *Smithfield Lomaroons Ridge* and *Come by Chance* with residue of personal estate during widowhood. To son George, plantation afsd., at death or remarriage of his mother. To sons Jonathan and John and daus. Mary Disheroon, Margaret Stevens, Elizabeth, Sarah and Priscilla, personal estate at death or remarriage of mother. {MWB 23:350}

William Stevens owned 150 a. of *Whittington's Choice* in 1759. {Debt Book}

William Stevens, age 62, deposed on 20 June 1763 regarding the bounds of *Askills Choice* (aka *Ascue's Choice*). {Miller:36}

On 25 April 1764 William Stevens and wife Margaret sold 150 a. of the tract *Whittington's Chance*, on n. side of the Wicomico River, whereon Stevens now lives, to George Handy. {SOD C:87}

William Stephens, SO Co., d. leaving a will dated 18 Dec 1769, proved 21 March 1770. To wife Margaret, Negro Rose, use of plantation and Negro boy Jerey for life. To Hester Mills (eldest dau.), Negro girl Case. To next eldest dau. Betty, Negro girl Dilly; To next eldest dau. Sarah, Negro girl Leah. To son Benjamin Stephens, Negro girl Dinner and coopers tools. To son George Stephens, £20. To son William Stephens, a gun. To son Levi, dwelling house, plantation and orchards and all land belonging to it. Witnessed by Joseph Hitch Jr., Joshua Hitch, Risdon Nicholson. {MWB 37:517; SOW EB5:154} On 8 May 1770 the inventory of his estate was filed by Margaret Stevens. Signed as next of kin: James Nien, Obadiah Disharoon, George Disharoon. {MINV 104:290} The admin. account was submitted by Margaret Stevens on 17 July 1771. {MDAD 63:418}

Sarah Dowdel, being older but of perfect memory, SO Co., d. leaving a will dated 10 Dec 1771, proved 24 Dec 1771. Children: Jonathan Pollet, John Pollet, Mary Disheron, Margaret Stevens, Elizabeth Finch. {MWB 38:613}

William was father of HESTER, m. (N) Mills; BETTY; SARAH; BENJAMIN, b. c1751, d. 14 Feb 1820; GEORGE; WILLIAM; LEVI, b. 1757, d. 16 Dec 1834.

4. THOMAS STEVENS, son of John (1) Stevens.

The tax lists for Somerset County cite Thomas Stevens as living in Wicomico Hundred in the household of John Disharoon in 1723, 1724, and 1727. He was living in the household of Capt. Edward North of Wicomico Hundred in 1725. In 1730-1734 he was head of household in Wicomico Hundred and Nanticoke Hundred in 1735. {SOTL}

Thomas Stevens, patented 100 a. in SO Co. on 5 July 1732 called *Forest Chance*. {MPL PL8:561; AM1:99} On 1 Aug 1767 James Vance and his wife Ann of SO Co. by a devise from Thomas Stevens to the afsd. Ann, conveyed the afsd. tract, situate on the s. side of the main branch of Broad Creek, to Isaac Jones. {WOD G:139}

Thomas was father of ANN who m. James Vance.

Third Generation

5. BENJAMIN STEVENS, c1751, d. 14 Feb 1820, son of William (3) Stevens, m. c1797, Priscilla (N).

Benjamin served as private in the Somerset Militia, Salisbury Battn., Capt. James Bennett's Salisbury Company, 1778/1780. he served as private in the Maryland Line, applying for a pension in SO Co. in April 1818, age 67, stating he had enlisted at Salisbury. Benjamin d. 14 Feb 1820 leaving a widow Priscilla whom he m. c1797. She d. 7 April 1821 leaving a son James, b. 17 July 1799. Son James lived in SO Co. in 1857. {RPWS:280}

Benjamin was father of JAMES.

6. GEORGE STEVENS, son of William (3) Stevens.

George Stevens served as private, Somerset Militia, Salisbury Battn., Capt. James Bennett's Salisbury Company, 1778/1780.

7. LEVI STEVENS, b. 1757, d. 16 Dec 1834, son of William (3) Stevens, m. Aug 1791, Mary Furniss, dau. of William and Sarah (Boston) Furniss. {The Boston Family:392; RPWS:281}

Levi Stevens served as private in the Somerset Militia, Salisbury Battn., Capt. James Bennett's Salisbury Company, 1778/1780. He served as private in the Maryland Line, applying for a pension in July 1833, living in WO Co. {RPWS:281}

Levi and Mary were parents of JOHN, b. 23 Dec 1791, d. a minor; SALLY, b. 12 Aug 1794; ANNA, b. July 1796; WILLIAM, b. 21 Nov 1797; DAVID, b. 6 Nov 1799; BETSY, b. 3 Oct 1802; SUSEY, b. 20 Nov 1803; JOSIAH, b. 20 Dec 1805; JULY, b. 10 Nov 1808; HENRY, b. 6 Dec 1812.

140

{RPWS:281}

THE THOMAS STEVENS FAMILY of Nanticoke Hundred

1. THOMAS STEVENS, m. Elizabeth (N).

Ephraim Polke, admin. of Thos. Walter, DO Co., vs. Thomas Stevens, planter, Monocan Hundred, complained of a debt for 5000 lbs. of tobacco. {SOJR 1715-17:45}

Bartholomew Warren, SO Co., d. by 23 May 1713 when the inventory of his estate was filed. Signed as next of kin: Sarah Warren, Thomas Stevens. {INAC 34:58}

Thomas Stevens, SO Co., d. by 7 Nov 1718 when the inventory of his estate was filed. {MINV 1:485} On 16 May 1721 the admin. account of his estate was submitted by Elizabeth Stevens, admx. {MDAD 3:396}

Elizabeth Stevens was head of household in Nanticoke Hundred in 1724 and 1725. Living in the household in 1724 was Thomas Stephens. She is cited as the widow Stevens in 1727; living in her household is William Stevens. {SOTL}

Thomas and Elizabeth are probably the parents of: THOMAS; WILLIAM; JOHN.

Second Generation

2. WILLIAM STEVENS, prob. son of Thomas (1) Stevens, m. Mary (N).

In 1724 Robert Collier conveyed to William Stevens, planter, 120 a. of the tract *Shadwell* on s. side of the Nanticoke River and 120 a. of *Stevens Inheritance* adjoining. {SOD 1722-1725:169}

On 13 Dec 1763 Thomas Stevens sells to Benjamin Mezick one moiety of 50 a., being part of the tract *Shadwell* which William Stevens purchased from Robert Collier lying on the e. side of the Nanticoke River, the moiety having been alienated to William Stevens, father of Thomas. {SOD C:197}

William and Mary were parents of THOMAS, b. 28 Aug 1724; WILLIAM, b. 28 Feb 1726/7. {SOSP}

3. JOHN STEVENS, prob. son of Thomas (1) Stevens.

The tax lists of SO Co. show John Stephens (Stevens) as head of household in Nanticoke Hundred, 1730-1740.

Third Generation

4. THOMAS STEPHENS, son of William (2) Stevens, m. Mary (N).

The tax lists for Somerset Co. show Thomas Stevens in Nanticoke Hundred: in the household of John Anderson in 1744, as head of household in 1748, 1750, 1753, 1754, 1757, and 1759. Living in his household in 1750 is John

Ange.

On 3 Dec 1750, Joseph Husk deeded to Thomas Stevens *Late Discovery* 50 a., and pt. *Dudley* 20 a. {SORR}

In 1759, Thomas Stevens was paying tax on: pt. *Dudley* 20 a., *Late Discovery* 50 a., and *Shadwell* 50 a. {Debt Books}

On 13 Dec 1763, Thomas Stevens deeded to Benjamin Mezick *Shadwell* 50 a. {WILR:373}

The 1783 Assessment for Somerset Co., Nanticoke District, shows Thomas Stevens as paying tax on *Dudley* 20 a., *Late Discovery* 50 a. There is 1 male and 3 females in his household.

Thomas Stephens, SO Co., d. leaving a will dated 6 Jan 1795, proved 10 Jun 1800. To son William Stephens all rights to land. To granddau. Sarah Stephens, all lands after William's decease. Witnessed by Philip Covington, George Dashiell Walter, Samuel Townsend. {SOW EB23:17}

Mary Stevens, SO Co., d. leaving a will dated 18 June 1788, proved 9 Feb 1806. To dau. Betty Stevens, extx., all estate. Witnessed by James Cooper, John Peden. Then came William Stevens, Esq., son of Mary Stevens, and believed the signatures on the will to be those of the subscribers James Cooper and John Peden. {SOW EB17:483}

Thomas was father of WILLIAM; BETTY.

Unplaced

(N) STEVENS m. Elizabeth Taylor, dau. of Samuel Taylor.

Samuel Taylor, Sr., planter, WO Co., d. leaving a will dated 6 Dec 1756, proved 4 Feb 1757. Children: Samuel Jr., Mary Buttler, Elizabeth Stevens, Esther Thakley. Grandchildren: Betty Buttler, dau. of Ezekiel; Solomon Taylor, son of Samuel; Joseph Gray Taylor, son of George; Shadrack Buttler, son of son-in-law Ezekiel Buttler and his wife Mary Buttler. Tracts: *Sam's Folly, Nodd* on southern side of branch clearing, *Golden Purchase*. Samuel Taylor, exec {MWB 30:258}

(N) STEVENS m. Eleanor Townsend, dau. of William Barkly and Jemima Townsend. {See The Jeremiah Townsend Family, vol. 9 of this series.}

On 2 July 1790 articles of agreement were made between Barkley Townsend, Ellenor Stevens and Levi Townsend. Whereas William Barkley Townsend, dec'd., in his last will did devise parts of his river swamp land *Philadelphia, New York* and *Chance* to be equally divided among the above named children. Now this agreement is that Levi is to take *New York* for his 1/3 part containing 54 a. and lying on the e. side of the Pocomoke River. {O:144}

ARCHIBALD STEVENS served as private, Somerset Militia, Salisbury Battn., Capt. William Turpin's Rewastico Company, 1778/1780. {RPWS:280}

142

BETTY STEVEN. (See Stephen Stevens above.)
Samuel Jaxson, SO Co., d. leaving a will dated 11 Feb 1753, proved 9 April 1754. To wife Sarah Jackson, dwelling plantation, with moveable estate, during her widowhood. To grand-son Samuel Jaxson Baley, plantation with all rights and property of that tract called *Jaxson's Lott* with a large iron-bound chest. But if he die without issue, I give to grand-son Benjamin Baley, above-named land called *Jaxson's Lott*. To grand-son Benjamin Baley, furniture. Balance of estate to grand-children: Samuel Jaxson Baley, Betty Stevens, Benjamin, Jonathan, Sarah, George, Mary and Elener Baley. Wife and grand-son Samuel Jaxson Baley, execs. {MWB 29:138}

DANIEL STEVENS served as private, Worcester Militia, Wicomico Battn., Capt. John Parramore's company, 15 July 1780. {RPWS:280}

ELENOR STEVENS is mentioned as dau. in the will of Sarah Tull, dated 30 Sep 1796, proved 8 Nov 1796 in which she devised to dau. Elenor Stevens Negro woman Sue, Negro boys Coffee and Able. {SOW EB17:565}

ELEANOR STEVENS
Eleanor Stevens stored corn in WO Co. for the use of the military on 10 Oct 1780 and rented her house to the military on 15 Oct 1780. {RPWS:280}

ISAAC STEVENS
Isaac Stevens was living in the household of Richard Wallace in Wicomico Hundred, 1731, in the household of Geo. Godert, Wicomico Hundred in 1733, in the household of Marsillas Hobbs, Monie Hundred, 1734-1736, in the household of William Langsten, Nanticoke Hundred in 1737, in the household of Absolom Hobbs, Wicomico Hundred in 1738, in the household of Thomas Hobbs, Monie Hundred in 1739, in the household of Joy Hobbs, Monie Hundred in 1740. {Russo}

JOHN STEVENS (This land is actually located in Worcester Co.)
John Stevens had the following tracts patented in SO Co.: *Chance* (32 a.) on 28 Sep 1728, *Security Resurveyed* (213 a.) on 11 July 1734; and *Cabbin Neck* (100 a.) on 18 March 1727/28. {MPL ILA:629; EI3:410; EI4:292; EI3:503; EI6:26; Debt Book, 1734-1759}

JOHN STEVENS was serving under Capt. Joshua Sturges, in the SO Co. militia, c1748. {COES:80}

LITTLETON STEVENS (African American)

Circa 1796. "Whereas I have purchased my dau. Nelli Stevens and her girl named Anna of John Watson for the consideration of in full he has given me a receipt wherefore I do hereby manumit her my said dau. and her child. Nelli being about 21 years and the child age 4 years. Signed by Littleton Stevens. {WOD R:249}

ROBERT STEVENS

The SO Co. tax lists for Nanticoke Hundred in 1725 shows Robert Stephens as head of household. Living in the household was Mathew Skillet. {SOTL}

THOMAS STEVENS m. Rebecca (N).

JOHN, son of Thomas and Rebecca Stevens, b. 28 June 1684. {IKL}

WILLIAM STEVENS m. Ann Nolton.

William Stevens formerly called Robert Lewin m. Ann Nolton 17 Aug 1668 by Henry Boston, Justice of the Peace. {IKL}

John, son of William and Ann Stevens, b. 23 April at Wickocomoco 1669. {IKL}

William, son of William Stevens and his wife Ann, b. 5 Nov 1672 at Wickocomoco. {IKL}

James Stevens, son of William Stevens, planter, and his wife Ann, b. at Wickocomoco 17 Oct 1676. {IKL}

William Stevens, son of William Stevens, planter, and his wife Anne, b. 27 Sep 1680. {IKL}

William and Ann were parents of JOHN, b. 23 April 1669; WILLIAM, b. 5 Nov 1672; JAMES, b. 17 Oct 1676; WILLIAM, b. 27 Sep 1680.

WILLIAM STEVENS m. Mary (N).

JANE, dau. of William and Mary Stevens, b. at Manny 27 Sep 1680. {IKL}

WILLIAM STEVENS

The tax lists for SO Co. in 1725 show a William Stevens living in the household of William Wroath, Pocomoke Hundred and a William Stephens living in the household of John Gibson in Matapany Hundred. {SOTL} In 1723 & 1724, William Stevens was living in Mattapony Hundred in household of John Pope.

WILLIAM STEVENS

The tax list for SO Co., in 1753 shows a William Stevens living in the household of James Mourn in Pocomoke Hundred and a William Stephens as head of household in Wicomico Hundred. Living with the latter were James Pope

144

and slave Ross. {SOTL}

WILLIAM STEVENS

Francis Joyce, SO Co., d. leaving a will dated 25 Feb 1714-15. To Richard, son of George Bizard (Blizard), dec'd., 100 a. of *Nothing Worth*, next to Girdletree Mill. To wife Ann, extx., residue of estate, real and personal, absolutely; shd. she not dispose of same, William Stevens (a boy in care of testator) to inherit real estate, personal estate to orphan child under wife's care at her decease. {MWB 17:27}

WILLIAM STEVENS served as 1st lieutenant, Somerset Militia, Salisbury Battn, Capt. William Turpin's Rewastico Company, 1778/1780. {RPWS:282}

WILLIAM STEVENS served as private in the Somerset Militia, Salisbury Battn., Capt. John Span Conway's Nanticoke Point Company, 1778/1780.

THE WILLIAM STEVENSON FAMILY of Worcester County

1. WILLIAM STEVENSON, b. c1660, m. Isabel (N).

William Stevenson was one of the persons of Mattapany Hundred appointed to divided the county into parishes in 1692/3. {OSES:153}

On 15 Jan 1715 (OS) William Stevenson and Isabell conveyed to Christopher Glass and his wife Elizabeth a tract called *Exon*, which Stevenson purchased from Richard Odewe and his wife Rebecca in 1694. {SOD 1735-1737:130} This tract lay about 2 miles from Bogernorton [*sic*] Landing. {SORR}

At Nov Court 1718, there was a suit of Mary Stockley vs. William Stevenson (All Hallows Parish, carpenter) and Samuel Bratten (blacksmith), alias dictus William Stevenson, Sr. Witness: Hugh Stevenson. Date: 7 March 1711/12. {SOJR:1717-1718:135}

William Stevenson, age 66, deposed on 11 June 1726 regarding the bounds of the tracts *Green Herd* and *Denyall*. {Miller:36}

In 1723, 1724, 1725, and 1727, William Stevenson was living in Baltimore Hundred, owning 3 slaves. {SOTL}

William Stevenson, Sr., carpenter, SO Co., d. leaving a will dated 14 June 1725 & 29 Jan 1727-8, proved 5 July 1728. To wife _____, Moses Goodin and Rebecka O'Brian for the remainder of their time; he by indenture and she by judgement of Court at Dividing Creeke, Ju., 1721, judged to be 6 yrs. old; and personalty. To son William and John, dau. Margaret, Samuel Brain, granddau. Mary Stevenson, grandson William Hall, Moses Goodan and Rebecka O'Brian, grandchildren Margaret Braban and Hugh Braban, personalty. To dau. Elizabeth, 1s. To wife _____, son William and dau. Margaret, residue of estate. Wife _____ and son William, execs. {MWB 19:468} On 18 Jun 1729 an inventory was filed on his estate by Isabel Stevenson as surviving extx. Signed as next of kin: John Stevenson, Samuel Bratten. {MINV:14:144} On 20 Aug 1729 the admin. account of the estate of William Stevenson, SO Co., was submitted by Isabell Stevenson, extx. Legatees: Margaret Bratten, Hugh Bratten, Elizabeth Stevenson. {MDAD 10:47} On 21 Dec 1730 a second admin. account of his estate was submitted by Isabell Stevenson, extx. Legatees: extx., Margaret Stevenson, William Stevenson, John Stevenson, Elizabeth Hall. {MDAD 11:83}

William was father of WILLIAM; JOHN; MARGARET; ELIZABETH, m. (N) Hall; MARY, m. Samuel Bratten.

Second Generation

2. WILLIAM STEPHENSON, son of William (1) Stevenson, m. Hannah (N). Hannah m. 2nd 25 April c1730/40?, John Deal Jr. {St. Martin's Parish Register}

The 1723 tax list of Bogerternorton Hundred, SO Co., shows William Stevenson living in the household of Samuell Broton, Senr. Also living in the household was John Truitt. In 1724, William Stevenson is cited in the household of James Truitt in Bogerternorton Hundred. In 1725 William Stephenson was head of household in Bogerternorton Hundred. In 1727, William Stevenson, Jr. is cited in the household of Samuel Bratten, Jr. in Bogerternorton Hundred. {SOTL}

William Stephenson, SO Co., d. by 8 Jan 1731 when an admin bond was filed on his estate by John Dale, Jr. Sureties: Samuel Bratten, Sr., Samuel Bratten, Jr. {TP:29:167} On 8 Jan 1731 the inventory of his estate was filed by John Deal, Jr. Signed as next of kin: Margaret Stephenson, Mary Bratton. {MINV 16:505} On 4 Sep 1733 the admin. account of his estate was submitted by John Deall, admin. Mentions: Child: William. {MDAD 12:103} On 18 June 1735 a second admin. account of his estate was submitted by John Deal, admin. Payments included widow (unnamed, 1/3). {MDAD 13:167}

William and Hannah were the parents of: WILLIAM.

3. JOHN STEVENSON, son of William (1) Stevenson.

The tax lists of SO Co. show John Stevenson as head of household in Baltimore Hundred, 1724, 1725, 1727, 1730-1740. Living in the household were Robert Stevenson (1724, 1725, 1727); Joseph Stevenson (1730); William Stevenson (1731-1734); slave Harry (1740).

John was prob. father of ROBERT, b. c1709; JOSEPH, b. 1711/1714; WILLIAM, b. c1715.

4. MARGARET STEVENSON, dau. of William (1) Stevenson.

William Stephenson, SO Co., d. by 8 Jan 1731 when an admin bond was filed on his estate by John Dale, Jr. Sureties: Samuel Bratten, Sr., Samuel Bratten, Jr. {TP:29:167} On 8 Jan 1731 the inventory of his estate was filed by John Deal, Jr.

Signed as next of kin: Margaret Stephenson, Mary Bratton. {MINV 16:505} On 4 Sep 1733 the admin. account of his estate was submitted by John Deall, admin. Mentions: Child: William. {MDAD 12:103} On 18 June 1735 a second admin. account of his estate was submitted by John Deal, admin. Payments included widow (unnamed, 1/3). {MDAD 13:167}

William Stevenson, SO Co., d. by 23 June 1737 when the inventory of his estate was filed by John Deal (deceased is underage). Signed as next of kin: Samuel Bratten, John Bratten. {MINV 22:340} On 24 March 1737 the admin. account of his estate was submitted by John Dale, admin. {MDAD 16:114}

5. ELIZABETH STEVENSON, dau. of William (1) Stevenson, m. (N) Hall.
    Elizabeth was mother of WILLIAM HALL.

6. MARY STEVENSON, dau. of William (1) Stevenson, m. Samuel Bratten.
    William Stephenson, SO Co., d. by 8 Jan 1731 when an admin bond was filed on his estate by John Dale, Jr. Sureties: Samuel Bratten, Sr., Samuel Bratten, Jr. {TP:29:167} On 8 Jan 1731 the inventory of his estate was filed by John Deal, Jr. Signed as next of kin: Margaret Stephenson, Mary Bratton. {MINV 16:505} On 4 Sep 1733 the admin. account of his estate was submitted by John Deall, admin. Mentions: Child: William. {MDAD 12:103} On 18 June 1735 a second admin. account of his estate was submitted by John Deal, admin. Payments included widow (unnamed, 1/3). {MDAD 13:167}

William Stevenson, SO Co., d. By 23 June 1737 when the inventory of his estate was filed by John Deal (deceased is underage). Signed as next of kin: Samuel Bratten, John Bratten. {MINV 22:340} On 24 March 1737 the admin. account of his estate was submitted by John Dale, admin. {MDAD 16:114}

Samuel and Mary Bratten were the parents of: MARGARET BRATTEN; HUGH BRATTEN.

Third Generation
7. WILLIAM STEVENSON, son of William (2)Stephenson.
    William Stevenson, SO Co., d. By 23 June 1737 when the inventory of his estate was filed by John Deal (dec'd. is underage). Signed as next of kin: Samuel Bratten, John Bratten. {MINV 22:340} On 24 March 1737 the admin. account of his estate was submitted by John Dale, admin. {MDAD 16:114}

8. ROBERT STEVENSON, son of John (3) Stevenson, b. c1709, m. Hannah Mills, dau. of John Mills. {See The Mills Family, vol. 10 of this series.}
    The tax lists of SO Co. show Robert Stevenson living in the household of John Stevenson in Baltimore Hundred in 1724, 1725, and 1727. Robert Stevenson was living in the household of Samuell Mills in Pocomoke Hundred in 1731 and as head of household in Pocomoke Hundred, 1738-1740.

On 10 April 1735 (OS) William Bozman conveyed 220 a. of *Leverton* to Robert Stevenson. {SORR}

In 1735, Robert Stevenson paid tax on *Leverton*. {Debt Books, Somerset Co.}

In 1756, 1757, 1759, and 1760, Robert Stevenson paid tax on *Leverton*. {Debt Books, Worcester Co.}

Robert Stevenson, wheelwright, WO Co., (?) d. leaving a will dated 29 Oct 1760, proved June 1761. To wife Hannah Stevenson, plantation I now dwell on, during widowhood: at her decease, to be divided between sons Samuel and James, equally. To son Robert Stevenson and to dau. Polly, slaves. Wife and son Robert, execs. {MWB 31:328}

Robert was father of ROBERT (eldest son); SAMUEL; JAMES; POLLY.

9. JOSEPH STEVENSON, son of John (3) Stevenson, m. 1st Rebeccah Gillet, dau. of John Gillet and m. 2nd Rachel (N). {See The Gillett Family, vol. 10 of this series.}

The tax lists of SO Co., show Joseph Stevenson living in the household of John Stevenson in Baltimore Hundred in 1730 and as head of household in Pocomoke Hundred., 1731-1740 except for 1733 when Joseph Stephenson was living in the household of John Gillet, Junr. in Pocomoke Hundred. Living in the household were William Stephenson (1736-1740); slaves: Harry (1730-1733) and Nanne (Nancy) (1730-1733).

John Gillet (Gillett), SO Co., d. leaving a will dated 25 March 1737, proved 22 Nov (1738?). To son Samuel, 350 a. ____, where he now lives; and personalty. To German Gillet, son of son Samuel, personalty. To son John, 200 a. *Newmaker*; and personalty and to his son Airs, personalty. To wife ____, certain personalty and to divide residue of personal estate with dau. Rebekah Stevenson, except a legacy to John Stevenson. Sons Samuel and John, execs. {MWB 22:7}

John Gillet, SO Co., d. by 14 Feb 1738 when the inventory of his estate was filed by Samuel Gillett. Signed as next of kin: Joseph Stevenson, John Gilbert. {MINV 24:12}

In 1733 Thomas Paremore, gent., of Accomack, VA, and his wife Joanna Custes, wife of Thomas Paremore and dau. of William Hope, dec'd., conveyed to Joseph Stephenson, blacksmith, 250 a. of *Fooke's Choyce*. One of the witnesses was Robert Stevenson. On 6 May 1743 (OS) Joseph Stevenson and others conveyed 150 a. of *Fook's Choice* to William Stevenson. {SOD EI:40; SORR}

On 22 Aug 1739 Isaac Piper and wife Temperance sold 63 a. of *Fooks Choice* to Joseph Stephenson. On 18 Aug 1742 they sold 187 a. to Joseph Stevenson. On 6 March 1743 Joseph Stevenson, blacksmith, and wife Rachel sold 150 a. to William Stevenson. On 7 June 1756 William Stevenson sold to Joseph Stevenson, blacksmith, 150 a. In 1781 Joseph Stevenson willed lands unnamed to sons George Stevenson (105 a.), Benjamin Stevenson (180 a.), and Joseph

Stevenson (200 a.). {WOLR:231}

On 6 March 1743 Joseph Stevenson, blacksmith, and his wife Rachel conveyed to William Stevenson the tract granted to William Anderson (now dec'd.) called *Fookes Choice* on s. side of Pocomoke River about 4 miles back in the woods and containing 500 a. By sundry means the tract became the right of Joseph and Rachel. Now Joseph and Rachel for £80 convey 150 a. {WOD A:146}

James Stevenson, son of Joseph and Rachel Stevenson b. 11 July 1745. {SOCO}

Joseph Stevenson was serving as private in the militia company of Lt. Moses Mills c1749. {COES:78}

In 1757, 1759, 1760, 1762, 1768, 1768, 1771, 1773, and 1774, Joseph Stevenson paid tax on *Addition, Foolk's Chance, Goshen,* and *Timber Swamp/Grove.* {Debt Books, Worcester Co.}

Goshen was re-surveyed for Joseph Stephenson on 28 Sep 1752. It was composed of *Fouke's Choice* (500 a.) and *Tiber Swamp* (100 a.) in WO Co. {WORR{ On 16 Oct 1754 Joseph Stevenson patented *Goshen* (663 a.). {MPL BC6:256; BC9:89}

The tract *Addition* was patented on 17 Jan 1762 by Joseph Stevenson for 52 a. {MPL BC20:113; BC21:138} On 26 March 1787 Benjamin Stevenson sold the land to John Harris. {WOLR:9}

Joseph Stevenson, Sr., blacksmith, WO Co., d. leaving a will dated 3 April 1781, proved 6 June 1781. To son George Stevenson after death of wife Rachell, dwelling plantation containing 200 a. and the right to timber on the land of Joseph and Benjamin Stevenson called *Goshen*; also still and worm, blacksmith tools. To son James, Negro man Daniel. To son Joseph 200 a. of *Goshen.* To son Benjamin 181 a. To son Jonathan 200 a. of land bounded on the line of tract *Salem.* To dau. Rebecka after death of wife, negro woman Rose, fellow Bosen, woman Dinah and furniture. To dau. Jemiah Negro woman Phillis, girl Suse. To dau. Rachel Negro woman Nan, girl Nice. To wife Rachel lands for life. Execs. sons George and James. Witnessed by James Tull, Ayres Gillett, Samuel Mills. {WOW JW4 II:476}

James Stevenson and George Stevenson were witnesses to the will of Hugh Mills, dated 13 April 1781. On 15 March 1793 when the will was proved came Jonathan Stevenson, bro. of James Stevenson and George Stevenson who states that the names signed are his bros. and they have since moved out of the state. {WOD JW18 Part I:114}

Joseph was father of GEORGE; JAMES, b. 11 July 1745; JOSEPH; BENJAMIN; JONATHAN; REBECKA; JEMIAH; RACHEL; JOHN.

10. WILLIAM STEVENSON, son of John (3) Stevenson, m. Tabitha (N) who later m. (N) Smith.

William Stevenson was serving as private under Capt. Moses Mills c1749. {COES:78}

The tract *Friendship* was patented on 17 March 1764 by William Stevenson and John Postley for 56 a. On 3 Jan 1798 Tabitha Stevenson, widow of William Stevenson, conveyed to her children Elizabeth Derrickson, Isaac Evans Morris, James Morris, John Stevenson, Molly Stevenson, Sally Stevenson, Edward Stevenson, all her goods, chattels, plate, Negroes, leases and personal estate. {MPL 23:529; BC24:328; WOD S:145}}

In 1768, 1769, 1773, and 1774, William Stevenson, et.al., paid tax on *Friendship*. {Debt Books, Worcester Co.}

William Stevenson, WO Co., d. leaving a will dated 12 April 1769, proved 2 Feb 1770. To wife: Tabitha, Negro woman Leah, Negro boy Simon, furniture, remainder of estate. Mentioned: Riley Wilborn, son of Daniel Wilborn; William Stevenson, son of Jonathan Stevenson. Cousin: James Stevenson, son of Robert Stevenson. Wife Tabitha, and James Stevenson, son of Robert, execs. {MWB 37:535; WOW JW4 Part I:33}

The inventory was filed on 14 Feb 1770 by John Stevenson and Tabitha Smith. Signed as next of kin: Joseph Stevenson, Jonathon Stevenson. {MINV 108:234}

Fourth Generation

11. ROBERT STEVENSON, son of Robert (8) Stevenson.

In 1762, 1768, 1769, and 1771, Robert Stevenson paid tax on *Leaverton* and *James' Choice*. {Debt Books, Worcester Co.}

On 24 March 1764 Robert Stevenson, son of Robert gave to his bro. Samuel Stevenson, 200 a. of *Kingsland* purchased by John Mills, grandfather of sd. Robert, from Homy Bayly and his wife Elizabeth and Whittington Bayly and Lisha his wife, being part of a tract called *Highland* containing 500 a. on s. side of Pocomoke River about 4 miles from the said river near the divisional line between MD and VA. This land now conveyed begins at the first bounder of the tract *Kings Land* and now laid out for 200 a. Robert also conveys to Samuel one Negro man named Peter. {WOD F:100}

On 20 March 1764 Robert Stevenson and Samuel Stevenson, planters, conveyed to Benjamin Scott for 5 shillings, the right to three Negroes: Dinah, Nancy and Pleasant. {WOD F:102}

12. JAMES STEVENSON, son of Robert (8) Stevenson.

On 24 March 1764 Samuel Stevenson sold 220 a. of *Leverton* to Robert Stevenson in Forked Neck near the division line of MD and VA. {WOD F:101}

On 13 Jan 1773 James Stevenson, son of Robert Stevenson, sold to James Patterson land devised him. {WOLR:360}

13. SAMUEL STEVENSON, son of Robert (8) Stevenson.

On 24 Sep 1766 Samuel Stevenson sold to John Mills a Negro man

Ceasor. {WOD F:544} On the next day Samuel Stevenson, son of Rob., sold to Alexander Mills all his corn and fodder on the plantation whereon Samuel's father lived; also two feather beds and 20 lbs. of pewter. {WOD F:545}

This is probably the same Samuel Stevenson who served as private in the Worcester Militia, Wicomico Battn., Capt. Benjamin Dennis' Company, 15 July 1780. {RPWS:283}

14. GEORGE STEVENSON, son of Joseph (9) Stevenson, m. Sarah (N).

George Stevenson served as private in the Worcester Militia, Wicomico Battn., Capt. James Patterson's Company, 15 July 1780. {RPWS:282}

On 1 April 1789 George Stevenson and wife Sarah sold to John Rackliffe 144 a. of *Goshen* and *Mayfields*. {WOLR:270}

15. JAMES STEVENSON, b. 11 July 1745, son of Joseph (9) and Rachel Stevenson.

James Stevenson, son of Joseph Stevenson re-urveyed 5 a. called *Stevensons Lot* on 1 Sep 1766. {MPL BC33:376; BC34:416} This was a resurvey of *Henrys Lot*, located on n. side of Pitt's Creek, also the 1st bounder of a tract called *Cherry Stones* now belonging to John Mills. Patented 29 July 1768. {RORR}

In 1769, 1773, and 1774, James Stevenson (of Joseph) paid tax on *Stevens' Lott* on *Henry's Lott*. {Debt Books, Worcester Co.}

James Stevenson of Joseph took the Oath of Allegiance in WO Co. in 1778. {RPWS:283}

16. JOSEPH STEVENSON, son of Joseph (9) Stevenson.

Joseph Stevenson served as sergeant, Worcester Militia, Wicomico Battn., Capt. James Patterson's Company, 15 July 1780. {RPWS:283}

17. BENJAMIN STEVENSON, b. 23 July 1746 or 1749, d. Woodford Co., KY, 27 Oct 1832, son of Joseph (9) Stevenson, m. Mary (Polly) Cox (b. 19 Nov 1750, d. Woodford Co., KY, 8 May 1815), dau. of John and Hannah (Whittington) Cox. {Except for Benjamin's militia service, this entire entry is based on *The Littleton Heritage:17-18*, citing Margaretta Stevenson, *Stevenson Family History from the Eastern Shore of Maryland to Woodford County, Kentucky* (NY, 1966)}

Benjamin Stevenson served as ensign, Worcester Militia, Wicomico Battn., Capt. James Patterson's Company, 15 July 1780. He was recommended for promotion to 2nd lieutenant on 4 Aug 1780. {RPWS:282}

Benjamin Stevenson had 8 3/4 a. surveyed in WO Co. On 7 Sep 1773 called *Pease and Plenty*, patented 16 May 1785. {WORR}

Benjamin and his family migrated to Woodford Co., cMarch 1789.

Benjamin and Mary were parents of (1st seven born in WO Co.)
ALEXANDER CAMPBELL, b. 3 Jan 1775, d. 22 Sep 1818, m. Mary (N);

JAMES, b. 26 Dec 1771, d. Putnam Co., IN, 27 Jan 1828, m. 29 Nov 1801, Margaret Campbell (b. 1782, d. 5 Sep 1834); SAMUEL, b. 5 Oct 1778, m. Jane (N); DAUGHTER, b. 5 Oct 1780, d. 9 Oct 1780; SON, b. 5 Sep 1781, d. 9 Sep 1781; MARY WHITTINGTON, b. 4 Aug 1782, m. John Long, bro. of Lucy who m. his cousin, William Whittington; BENJAMIN, b. 3 Oct 1785, d. Woodford Co., KY, 3 Sep 1835, m. Elizabeth Dunlap(?); WILLIAM, b. 13 March 1789, d. 15 March 1879, HENRY, b. Woodford Co., KY, 29 March 1791, d. 17 Feb 1879; SALLIE, b. Woodford Co., 31 Oct 1794, m. Robert Elliott, moved to MO; JOHN, b. 4 Jan 1799, unm.

18. JONATHAN STEVENSON, son of Joseph (9) Stevenson, m. 1st (N) and m. 2nd Nancy (N).

Jonathan Stevenson served as ensign, Worcester Militia, Wicomico Battn., Capt. James Patterson's Company, 28 June 1777 and 2nd lt. 15 July 1780. {RPWS:283}

On 7 March 1773 Jonathan Stevenson surveyed 33 a. in WO Co. called *Luck*, patented 16 May 1785. {WORR}

Jonathan Stevenson, blacksmith, WO Co., d. leaving a will dated 10 March 1796, proved 22 July 1796. To son Joseph Stevenson, dwelling plantation with the lines of *Goshen Renewed* being all the land w. of bro. Joseph's land. Blacksmith tools to son Robert when he comes of age. To wife Nancy half of dwelling plantation for widowhood which at her death to be divided among her two sons and two daus; also Negro Vinah. To son William Stevenson part of *Goshen Renewed* beginning at the line of *Addition to Salem* and running s. with Thomas Harris's line and then e. to the line of *Gillett Choice*. To son Jonathan Stevenson remainder of *Goshen Renewed*. Mentioned son Thomas, son Robert, son Elijah; daus. Sarah and Polly to whom he left Negro woman Nice. To dau. Sarah, chest that was her mother's. To children Thomas, Robert, Hugh, Mills, James, Sarah, Polly, Nancy, Rebekah, remainder of estate. Exec. sons William and Joseph. Witnessed by Hugh Nilson, Joseph Stevenson, Edward Stevenson. {WOW JW18 Part II:258}

Jonathan was father of JOSEPH; ROBERT; WILLIAM; JONATHAN; THOMAS; ELIJAH; SARAH; POLLY (Mary); HUGH; MILLS; JAMES; NANCY; REBEKAH. [Perhaps four of these children were in fact his step-children.]

19. JOHN STEVENSON, son of Joseph (9) Stevenson, m. Sarah (N). She m. 2nd Joshua Riggen.

In 1760, 1762, 1768, 1769, and 1774, John Stevenson (of Joseph) paid tax on *Tanner's Hall* and *Bratten's Chance*. {Debt Books, Worcester Co.}

On 5 June 1765 Marshall Skinner in Accomack Co., VA, and his wife Leah, conveyed to John Stevenson and his wife Sarah, 150 a. called *Tanners Hall*

152

situated on the seaboard side of the county on the w. side of Swansagut Creek ...
running to the divisional line drawn between VA and MD. {WOD F:385}

Jarman Gillett, WO Co., d. by 20 Nov 1772 when the inventory of his
estate was filed by Ayres Gillett. Signed as next of kin: Margaret Warrington,
Sarah Stevenson. {MINV 111:258}

Sarah Stephenson, relict of John Stephenson m. 4 Dec 1777, Joshua
Riggen. {SOCO}

Fifth Generation

20. JONATHAN STEVENSON, son of Jonathan (18) Stevenson, m. Lydia Mills.
{WO Co. marr. lic. dated 27 May 1795}

Lydia was dau. of Hugh and Comfort Mills. {See The Mills Family, vol. 10 of
this series.}

21. ELIJAH STEVENSON, son of Jonathan (18) Stevenson.
A bond was issued on 24 Sep 1803 to William Stevenson, admin. of
Elijah Stevenson who d. intestate. {WO Co. Wills and Admin. Bonds, 1802-1807 JBR6:83}

THE HUGH STEVENSON FAMILY (1)

1. Rev. HUGH STEVENSON, m. Comfort Fassitt, dau. of William and Elizabeth
Fassitt. Comfort m. 2nd Charles Rackliff.

Hugh Stevenson was a Presbyterian minister, arriving in America from
Ireland in 1726. He resided at New Castle DE. 1727-1728, Lewes DE, and
Nottingham, PA. He was ordained at Snow Hill MD before June 1729 and lived
there, 1729-1733. He was at Potomac Church, Northumberland Co. VA in 1733.
A teacher at Philadelphia, 1739-1744, he died there in May 1744. {Colonial Clergy of
MD, DE, and GA:p. 64, 84}

The tax lists of SO Co. show Hugh Stevenson as head of household in
Bogerternorton Hundred, 1730-1738. He is cited as Hugh Stevenson in 1730,
1736, and 1738. He is cited as Mr. Hugh Stevenson in 1733 and 1735. He is cited
as Rev. Hugh Stevenson in 1734. (The first name for the entry in 1737 is
illegible.) Living in the household were Christopher Mullin (1730), Richard
Travis/Travers (1733-1736); Samuell Stevenson (1736).

Adam Spence, SO Co., d. leaving a will dated 13 Feb 1732, proved 14
Jan 1734-5. To son Adam, exec, 150 a. *Middlesex*, 190 a. *Middlemore*, lot No. 5
Snow Hill Town; residue of estate not otherwise bequeathed. To sons-in-law
James Stevenson, Robert Hall and Rev. Hugh Stevenson, personalty. {MWB
21:266}

On 21 Jan 1733, Samuel Davis deeded to Hugh Stevenson, *Groves*
(surveyed in 1680 as *Mulberry Grove*) 167 a.{SORR:WOLR:418}

William Fassitt, SO Co., d. leaving a will dated 22 Jan 1734/5, proved 30 May 1735. Legatees: son William, plantation, *Carmel, Fishing Harbor*; son John, old plantation in Sinepuxin, *Fishing Harbor*; dau. Rhoda Bowin; dau. Katherine Round, *Gosen*; dau. Elizabeth; dau. Mary Whittington; son Rouse, *Maryfields;* son Lambert; dau. Rachel; dau. Sarah, *Burley*; dau. Comfort, *Burley*; wife Mary. {MWB:21:385} On 21 May 1736, an inventory of his estate was filed by William Fassett. {MINV:21:374} On 21 May 1736, admin accounts were filed on his estate. Payments to (their portions): Rouse Fassitt, Rhoda Bowen, Charles Rackliffe for his wife, James Round for his wife, Hugh Stevenson, John Miller who married Sarah Miller, Southy Whittington, John Fassitt, Lambert Fassitt, William Fassitt, widow (⅓). {MDAD:15:17}

Mary Fassitt, widow of William, All Hallows Parish, WO Co., d. leaving a will dated 30 June 1743, proved 23 May 1744. To children John Fassitt, Rachel Rackliffe, Comfort Stevenson, Mary Whittington, Sarah Miller, Rowse, Lambert, and William Fassitt, personal estate. To Mary, dau. of Comfort Stevenson, afsd. personalty. To son William Harrison, personalty. He not to lay claim to any estate of testator. Husband William. Testator wills that should her son William lay claim to more of the estate by reason of testator living on plantation, he to be cut off in her will with 1 s. Son Rowse, exec. {MWB 23:521} On 26 May 1744 the inventory of the estate of Mary Fassitt, WO Co., was filed by Rouse Fassitt. Signed as next of kin: William Hanson [prob. William Harrison], Comfort Stevenson. {MINV 29:360}

Mr. Hugh Stevenson, WO Co., d. by 28 March 1744, when an admin bond was posted on his estate by Comfort Stevenson. Sureties; Rous Fassitt, Lambert Fassitt. {TP:31:461} On 13 June 1744 the inventory of his estate was filed by Comfort Stevenson. Signed as next of kin: Rous Fassitt, Lambart Fassitt. {MINV 29:355} On 27 Sep 1747 the admin. account of his estate was submitted by Comfort Rackliff, admx., wife of Charles Rackliff. {MDAD 24:158}

In 1756, 1757, 1759, 1762, and 1771, the heirs of Hugh Stevenson paid tax on *Burley, Castle Quarter* alias *Enlargement*, and *Mulberry Grove*. {Debt Books, Worcester Co.}

Charles Rackliffe, WO Co., d. leaving a will dated 30 March 1787, proved on 7 April 1787. Legatees: granddau.-in-law Comfort Selby; granddau.-in-law Zipporah Pennewell; stepson William Stevenson, executor. {WOW:JW#13:142}

Hugh and Comfort were the parents of: MARY; WILLIAM; poss. others.

Second Generation

2. WILLIAM STEVENSON, son of Rev. Hugh (1) Stevenson.

In 1768, 1769, 1773, and 1774, William Stevenson paid tax on *Burley, Castle Quarter* alias *Enlargement, Mulberry, Mulberry Grove*, and *Poor Lot*. {Debt Books, Worcester Co.}

154

On 22 Aug 1777, William Stevenson sold to Isaac Coulbourn, *Burley* 100 a. {WOLR:86}

Charles Rackliffe, WO Co., d. leaving a will dated 30 March 1787, proved on 7 April 1787. Legatees: granddau.-in-law Comfort Selby; granddau.-in-law Zipporah Pennewell; stepson William Stevenson, executor. {WOW:JW#13:142}

THE HUGH STEVENSON FAMILY (2)

1. HUGH STEVENSON, m. 1st Janet (N), m. 2nd Elizabeth (N)[27].

Elizabeth Killock, SO Co., d. by Oct 1701, when her administrator Hugh Stevenson was summoned to render accounts on her estate. {TP:18B:95}

On 12 May 1708 John Godden sold 140 a. of *Rochester* in Bogertemorton Hundred to Hugh Stevenson. On 15 May 1714 Hugh Stevenson and wife Janet sold 140 a. to John Dryden. {WOLR:527}

On 12 July 1708 (OS) John Godden conveyed 140 a. of *Castle Fine* to Hugh Stevenson. Hugh Stevenson and others conveyed (acreage not given) to John Dredon on 15 July 1714. {SORR}

Alexander Kellock, SO Co., d. by 16 April 1710 when the admin. account of his estate was submitted by Hugh Stevenson, admin. {INAC 31:247}

At Nov Court 1718, suit of Mary Stockley vs. William Stevenson (All Hallows Parish, carpenter) and Samuel Bratten (blacksmith), alias dictus William Stevenson, Sr. Witness: Hugh Stevenson. Date: 7 March 1711/12. {SOJR:1717-1718:135}

Hugh Stevenson, SO Co., d. by 18 Sep 1716, when an admin bond was posted on his estate by Elizabeth Stevenson. Sureties: John Bratten, James Bratten, Jr. {TP:23:109} In 1717 the inventory of his estate was filed by Elizabeth Stevenson. Signed as next of kin: Hugh Nelson, Samuel Bratton. {INAC 38A:143} On 19 Feb 1721 the admin. account of his estate was submitted by Elizabeth Stevenson, admx. {MDAD 4:122}

THE JAMES STEVENSON FAMILY

1. JAMES STEVENSON, b. c1680, m. Sarah Spence, dau. of Adam Spence.

James Stevenson, aged 50, deposed on 28 Sep 1730 regarding the bounds of the tract *Mt. Ephraim* and on 2 June 1733, aged 57, regarding the bounds of *Salem*. {Miller:36}

The SO tax lists show James Stevenson as head of household in

---

[27] She is most probably the daughter of James Bratten (d. 1720).

Bogerternorton Hundred, 1723, 1724, 1725, 1727, and 1730-1740. Living in the household were John Penniwell, 1725; Adam Stevenson (1736-1740), Samuell Stevenson (1737-1740).

London Derry was patented on 5 Nov 1687 by Adam Spence for 200 a. lying in the n.e. side of the Pocomoke River. On 15 Feb 1721 (OS) Adam Spence conveyed the tract to James Stevenson. {SORR}

In 1733, 1734, 1735, and 1748, James Stevenson paid tax on *Londonderry*. {Debt Books, Somerset Co.} In 1756, 1757, and 1759, James Stevenson paid tax on *Londonderry*. {Debt Books, Worcester Co.}

Adam Spence patented 200 a. in Bogertgernorton Hundred called London Derry. On 15 Dec 1720 Adam Spence Jr. and wife Margaret sold to James Stevenson and wife Sarah Stevenson. On 25 July 1735 James Stevenson and wife Sarah sold to Thomas Inglish and wife Margaret Inglish 100 a. known also as *Free Guift*. On 14 March 1766 James Stevenson and wife Nanny sold to Benjamin Bishop 100 a. On 7 Jan 1788 Adam Stevenson sold to Anna Robins 100 a. {WOLR:372}

Adam Spence, SO Co., d. leaving a will dated 13 Feb 1732, proved 14 Jan 1734-5. To son Adam, exec, 150 a. *Middlesex*, 190 a. *Middlemore*, lot No. 5 Snow Hill Town; residue of estate not otherwise bequeathed. To sons-in-law James Stevenson, Robert Hall, and William Hall, personalty. To Rev. Hugh Stevenson, personalty. {MWB 21:266}

James Stevenson, WO Co., wheelwright, d. leaving a will dated 3 Nov 1757, proved 6 July 1759. To son James dwelling plantation. Witnessed by John Dryden, Joyce Dryden, Martha Dryden. {MWB 30:720; WOW JW3:11} The inventory was filed by James Stevenson on 7 Nov 1759. Signed as next of kin: Samuel Stevenson, Adam Stevenson. {MINV 68:156} The admin. account was submitted by James Stevenson. Distribution to children: Margret, Sarah, Betty, Hannah, Adam, Samuel, Hugh, Catherine, accountant. {MDAD 47:130} Distribution of the estate was made on 3 Oct 1761 by James Stevenson to Margaret, Sarah, Betty, Hannah, Adam, Samuel, Katherine, Hugh, the accountant James. {BFD 3:93}

James was father of MARGRET; SARAH; BETTY; HANNAH; ADAM, b. c1720; SAMUEL, b. c1721; HUGH; CATHERINE; JAMES.

Second Generation

2. ADAM STEVENSON, b. c1720, son of James (1) Stevenson.

In 1756, 1757, 1759, 1760, 1762, 1768, 1771, 1773, and 1774, Adam Stevenson paid tax on *Free Gift* alias *Londonderry*. {Debt Books, Worcester Co.}

Adam Stevenson took the Oath of Allegience in WO Co. in 1778. {RPWS:282}

In 1783, Adam Stevenson of Boquerternorton Hundred paid tax on *Londonderry* 90 a. In his household are 1 male & 3 females. {1783 Assessment}

On 7 Jan 1788, Adam Stevenson deeded to Anna Robins, *Londonderry*

100 a. {WOLR:372}

On 12 June 1794 Adam Stevenson, age 74, said that he remembered that about 64 years ago the mill called Calkers Mill Creek Mill, now in Capt. George Spence's possession, was built and that about 30 years ago this deponent kept said mill and that he never heard any complaints in the neighborhood concerning the waters injuring the lands upon which the said mill drowned in the previous years. He was about 10 years old at the time there was a grist mill erected and after that a saw mill. The deponent saith that he lived for about one year at the mill (about 30 years ago) and has not lived in the neighborhood since. {WOD P:469}

3. S'AMUEL STEVENSON, b. c1721, son of James (1) Stevenson, m. Mary (N).

The tax lists of SO Co. show Samuel Stevenson living in the household of Hugh Stevenson in 1736 and head of his own household in Bogerternorton, 1738-1740.

Samuel Stevenson, son of James Stevenson, was serving as private in the in the militia under Capt. Joseph Mitchell c1748. Samuel Stevenson was serving as private in Capt. Joseph Mitchell's Company of militia c1749. {COES:79}

On 2 Aug 1749 Samuel Stevenson (acknowledged by his wife Mary) conveyed to Robert Nilson 34 a. of a tract called *Conveniency* on the river swamp between Samuel Stevenson's house and the place called the *Indian Landing*. On the same day Robert Nilson and his wife Elizabeth conveyed the land back to Samuel Stevenson. {WOD B:190, 191} On 27 March 1752 Robert Nilson and his wife Elizabeth conveyed 100 a. of the tract *Convenience*. {WOD B:442}

On 5 Nov 1767 Samuel Stevenson and wife Mary sold 112 a. of the tract *Conveniency* to Moses Nelson. In 1770 Samuel Stevenson willed to son James Stevenson land bought of Robert Nelson, unnamed. On 25 Dec 1772 Hugh Stevenson, son of Samuel Stevenson, with wife Margaret, sold to James Stevenson, 13 a. On 8 Jan 1773 Littleton Dennis sold to Hugh Stevenson, son of Samuel Stevenson, 21 a. On the same day Littleton Dennis sold to James Stevenson, son of Samuel, 21 a. On 7 Sep 1773 James Stevenson, son of Samuel, merchant, with wife Mary, sold to Nehemiah Davis, 154 a. On 23 June 1775 William Teague sold to James Stevenson, 100 a. On the same day he sold another 30 a. to James Stevenson. On 22 March 1776 James Stevenson, merchant, sold to Hannah Teague, widow of William Teague, part purchased of William Teague. The 1783 tax list shows that James Stevenson owned 250 a. of the tract. On 14 Feb 1792 James Stevenson and wife Mary sold to Walter Smith 136 1/4 a. On 8 July 1795 Moses Nelson sold to James Stevenson 6 3/8 a. On 11 Jan 1806 Edward Stevenson, son of James and his wife Nancy sold to Josiah Nelson 96 a. {WOLR:137}

In 1756, 1757, 1759, 1760, 1762, 1768, 1769, and 1771, Samuel Stevenson paid tax on *Conveniency* and a lot in Snow Hill. {Debt Books, Worcester Co.}

Samuel Stevenson, WO Co., d. leaving a will dated 18 April 1770, proved 20 Sep 1770. To wife Mary, plantation and Negro woman Tamer and mulatto boy Jesse. To son James Stevenson, land and plantation after wife's death and also land where he now lives bought of Robert Nilson; Negro girl Hannah and £110. To dau. Betty Stevenson, Negro girl Hannah and £110. To dau. Hannah £110. To all grand children alive at the time of my death. To grandson Samuel Stevenson, son of John Stevenson, storehouse in Snow Hill Town and house and lot purchased of the Outtens. Wife Mary and son James, execs. {MWB 38:61; WOW JW 4 Part I:32} The inventory was filed on 29 Sep 1770 by James Stevenson. Signed as next of kin: Moses Nilson, Hugh Stevenson. {MINV 108:245} The admin. account was submitted on 23 May 1772 by James Stevenson. {MDAD 67:344}

Samuel was father of JAMES; BETTY; HANNAH; JOHN; HUGH (not mentioned in his father's will but see below).

4. HUGH STEVENSON, son of James (1) Stevenson.

Hugh Stevenson, son of James, patented *Contented Bachelor* in WO Co. (50 a.) on 28 Dec 1763. {MPL BC24:532; BC26:313} In 1768, Hugh Stevenson paid tax on *Contented Bachelor*. {Debt Books, Worcester Co.} On 23 March 1770, Hugh Stevenson (Dobbs Co. NC) appointed Joshua Townsend to confirm a deed to Jacob Sturgis for *Contented Bachelor*. {WOLR:133}

5. JAMES STEVENSON, son of James (1) Stevenson, m. Nanny Jarman, dau. of William Jarman of Bogerternorton Hundred. {See The William Jarman (German) Family, vol. 10 of this series.}

On 29 Sep 1764 James Stevenson patented 70 a. called *Peru* in WO Co. {MPL BC24:475; BC26:301} On 6 July 1770 James Stevenson, son of James, and wife Nanny, sold to Margaret Spence 70 a. {WOLR:470}

On 14 March 1766, James Stevenson and his wife Nancy deeded to Benjamin Bishop, *Londonderry* 100 a. {WOLR:372}

On 3 June 1767 Emanuel Roberts of Northampton Co., VA, and wife Rachel, sold to James Stevenson of WO Co., part of the tract *Flattland*. On 26 May 1769 James Stevenson and wife Nanney sold to Henry Johnson 100 a. {WOLR 226}

In 1760, 1762, and 1771, James Stevenson paid tax on *Londonderry*. In 1768 and 1769, James Stevenson (of James) paid tax on *Flatland* and *Peru*. {Debt Books, Worcester Co.}

Third Generation

6. JAMES STEVENSON, son of Samuel (3) Stevenson, m. Mary (N).

In 1773 and 1774, James Stevenson (of Samuel) paid tax on *Conveniency* and lot in Snow Hill. {Debt Books, Worcester Co.}

James Stevenson, son of Samuel Sr., took the Oath of Allegiance in WO

158

Co. in 1778. {RPWS:282}

In 1783, James Stevenson paid tax on *Conveniency* 250 a., in Mattapony Hundred. Living in his household were 5 males and 8 females. {1783 Assessment}

James Stevenson[28], WO Co., d. leaving a will dated 3 Nov 1797, proved 1 Feb 1799. Legatees: wife Mary; daus. Catherine, Mary, Betty, Ede, Priscilla, Gatty; grandson Henry Stevenson son of William; granddau. Elizabeth Stevenson dau. of William; son Edward, land. Exec. son Edward. {WOW:JW#18:415}

James was father of CATHERINE; MARY; BETTY; EDE; PRISCILLA; GATTY; WILLIAM; EDWARD.

7. JOHN STEVENSON, son of Samuel (3) Stevenson, m. 1st Rachel (N) and m. 2nd Rhoda (N)[29].

On 7 July 1768 John Stevenson, son of Samuel Stevenson, patented 390 a. called *Johns Industry* in WO Co. {MPL 34:444; BC35:265} This was a resurvey of *Brattens Choice*. On 6 March 1771 John Stevenson, son of Samuel Stevenson, with wife Rachel, sold 187 a. to Thomas Martin. (mortgage) On 3 March 1773 John Stevenson and wife Rhoda sold 18 a. to Nathaniel Bratten. On 15 March 1776 John Stevenson, son of Samuel Stevenson, sold to Thomas Johnson 41 a. In 1776 John Stevenson re-surveyed it to 390 a. {WOLR:333}

In 1768 and 1771, John Stevenson (of Samuel) paid tax on *Bratten's Choice.* {Debt Books, Worcester Co.} In 1769, 1773, and 1774, John Stevenson (of Samuel, merchant) paid tax on *John's Industry* and lots in Snow Hill. {Debt Books, Worcester Co.}

Joshua Bratten, WO Co., d. by 20 April 1774 when the inventory of his estate was filed by Hugh Wilson. Signed as next of kin: Lese Bratten, Rhoda Stevenson. {MINV 123:128}

On 5 March 1783 Samuel Stevenson, son of John , sold to Joshua Townsend 500 sq. feet [in Snow Hill] bought from John Martin, John Ross, William Allen and Thomas Dashiell on 3 Dec 1762. {WOLR:583}

In 1783, John Stevenson paid tax on *Bratten's Choice,* 112 a. and *John's Industry,* 50 a., in Boquerternorton Hundred. Living in his household were 4 males and 4 females. {1783 Assessment}

John was father of SAMUEL. {See the will of his grandfather, Samuel Stevenson.}

8. HUGH STEVENSON, son of Samuel (3) Stevenson, m. Margaret (N). On 5 March 1742 William Dukes and wife Mary sold to Samuel

---

28. In the Worcester Co. Estate Docket, he is cited as James Stevenson of Samuel.

29. She is most probably a daughter of Quinton Bratten (d. 1731). His admin accounts cite a son Joshua and a daughter Rhoda, among others.

Stevenson, Sr., 100 a. of the tract *Conveniency*. On 2 Aug 1749 Samuel Stevenson and Robert Nelson with wife Elizabeth Nelson settled their boundary lines. {WOLR:137}

On 2 Oct 1749 (OS) Robert Nilson conveyed 34 a. of *Conveniency* to Samuel Stevenson. {SORR}

On 8 Aug 1766 Hugh Nilson conveyed to Hugh Stevenson, son of Samuel, 100 a. of *Conveniency* and 92 a. of *Castle Hill*. {WOD F:529}

In 1768, 1769, 1773, and 1774, Hugh Stevenson (of Samuel) paid tax on *Castle Hill* and *Conveniency*. {Debt Books, Worcester Co.}

On 5 Nov 1767 Samuel Stevenson and wife Mary sold 112 a. of the tract *Conveniency* to Moses Nelson. In 1770 Samuel Stevenson willed to son James Stevenson land bought of Robert Nelson, unnamed. On 25 Dec 1772 Hugh Stevenson, son of Samuel Stevenson, with wife Margaret, sold to James Stevenson, 13 a. On 8 Jan 1773 Littleton Dennis sold to Hugh Stevenson, son of Samuel Stevenson, 21 a. On the same day Littleton Dennis sold to James Stevenson, son of Samuel, 21 a. On 7 Sep 1773 James Stevenson, son of Samuel, merchant, with wife Mary, sold to Nehemiah Davis, 154 a. On 23 June 1775 William Teague sold to James Stevenson, 100 a. On the same day he sold another 30 a. to James Stevenson. On 22 March 1776 James Stevenson, merchant, sold to Hannah Teague, widow of William Teague, part purchased of William Teague. The 1783 tax list shows that James Stevenson owned 250 a. of the tract. On 14 Feb 1792 James Stevenson and wife Mary sold to Walter Smith 136 1/4 a. On 8 July 1795 Moses Nelson sold to James Stevenson 6 3/8 a. On 11 Jan 1806 Edward Stevenson, son of James and his wife Nancy sold to Josiah Nelson 96 a. {WOLR:137}

Hugh Stevenson served as private, Worcester Militia, Wicomico Battn., Capt. William Handy's Company, 15 July 1780. {RPWS:282}

In 1783, Hugh Stevenson paid tax on pt. *Conveniency* 120 a. and *Castle Hill* 92 a., in Mattapony Hundred. Living in his household are 3 males and 2 females. {1783 Assessment}

On 19 May 1797 Joseph Stevenson of Hugh Stevenson with wife Sarah sold to John Kellum Truitt 19 1/4 a. of *Scotland*. On 26 Feb 1803 John K. Truitt with wife Mary sold to Littleton Purnell. As John Teague owned *Scottland* and *Spaulding*, he willed to son William Teague who d. intestate leaving 2 daus. Sally Stevenson, wife of Joseph Stevenson, and Mary Truitt afsd. {WOLR:547}

On 19 Dec 1798 Jesse Riggin and wife Sarah conveyed to Joseph Stevenson Jr. a tract called *Convenience* that Hugh Stevenson in his will dated 19 Jan 1793 bequeathed to his dau. Sarah. This tract begins by the side of the county road that leads from Snow Hill to Cokers Creek. {WOD T:65}

On 15 April 1795 Hugh Stevenson and wife Margaret sold to Joel Nelson 8 3/10 a. of *Castle Hill*. {WOLR:98}

Hugh was father of SARAH, m. Jesse Riggin; JOSEPH, m. Sarah

Teague, dau. of William Teague, b. before 1772.

Unplaced

CHRISTOPHER STEVENSON

The tract *Stevenson* in SO Co. (150 a.) was surveyed on 16 Nov 1664 for Christopher Stevenson and patented to William Smith, on s. side of the Pocomoke River. "Know not the Land nor who was possd." {SORR}

EDWARD STEVENSON, son of John Stevenson.

On 21 Sep 1742 John Stevenson being seized of a moiety of a parcel of land called *Inch* being that part of the land that lies in a neck between a small creek and St. Martin's River and on the s.w. side of the said river containing 200 a. which was alienated to Stevenson by William Fassitt and his wife Elizabeth in exchange for 60 a. of *Winter Quarter* and 40 a. of *Powell's Lott* and 25 a. of *The Slipe*. On 25 Aug 1759 Edward Stevenson conveyed to John Gibbons 60 a. of *Winter Quarter*. On 25 Aug 1759 Edward Stevenson conveyed 40 a. of *Powell's Lott* to John Gibbons. {SOD X:9, 10; SORR}

Edward Stevenson patented *School House Ridge* (35 a.) in WO Co. on 15 Nov 1754. Edward Stevenson conveyed it to John Gibbons on 25 Aug 1759. {MPL GS2:388; BC4:184; WORR}

On 4 Nov 1756 Edward Stevenson of Sussex Co., DE, traded 150 a. with William Perkins for part of *Powells Lott* and *Winter Quarter*. {WOLR:322}

On 25 Sep 1742 William Perkins traded 25 a. of *Slipe* with John Stevenson for a tract called *Inch*. On 25 Aug 1759 Edward Stevenson of Sussex Co., DE, son of John, sold to John Gibbons, blacksmith, 25 a. {WOLR:569}

On 25 Sep 1742 William Perkins sold 50 a. of *Winter Quarter* to John Stevenson. On 4 Nov 1756 Edward Stevenson, heir of John of Sussex Co., DE, sold to William Perkins of WO Co. {WOLR:680}

In 1756, 1757, 1759, and 1760, Edward Stevenson paid tax on *Powell's Lott, Slipe, School House Ridge*, and *Winter Quarter*. {Debt Books, Worcester Co.}

On 1 April 1760, Isaac Brittingham, Sr. (WO) deeded to Edward Stephenson (SU), *Collings Folly* 300 a. {SUDELR:I:310}

On 1 May 1760, Andrew Fullerton (SU) deeded to Edward Stephenson (WO), 215 a. {SUDELR:I:248}

On 7 May 1778 Edward Stephenson (SU) and his wife Margaret deeded to Nehemiah Reed, *Collins Folly* 300 a. {SUDELR:M:195}

On 27 Aug 1779, Edward Stephenson (SU) and his wife Margaret deeded to Robinson Savage, 236 a. {SUDELR:M:299}

HENRY STEVENSON m. Ann Henry, dau. of Robert Jenkins Henry. She was the widow of Capt. Edward Round.

In 1764 Robert Jenkins Henry gave to dau. Ann Henry 400 a. of *Providence* at Dividing Creek. On 17 June 1786 Henry Stevenson and wife Ann sold to Samuel Sloan a resurvey by Robert Jenkins Henry, 343 2/4 a. of *Providence*. {SOLR:346}

Edward Round, WO Co., d. by 10 May 1773 when the inventory of his estate was filed by Ann, wife of Henry Stevenson. Signed as next of kin: William Morris, John Round. {MINV 118:281}

HUGH STEVENSON, m. Margaret (N).

James Stephenson, Sussex Co., DE, d. leaving a will dated 30 Dec 1762, proved on 24 Jan 1763. Legatees: wife Jennet; daus. Elizabeth Stephenson, Jane Stephenson, Martha McNeal. Executrix: wife Jennet. Witnesses: John Clowes, Jr., Hugh Stephenson, Mary Stephenson. {SUW:B:261}

On 3 Aug 1769, Joseph Atkens and his wife Mary deeded to Hugh Stephenson, 85 a. {SUDELR:L:403}

On 8 May 1772, Hugh Stephenson deeded to Abel Nottingham, pt. 21 a. granted to said Stephenson in 1740. {SUDELR:M:446}

On 30 Jan 1773, Hugh Stevenson is cited as a debtor to estate of James Stephenson, extx. is Jennet Stephenson. {SOOC:A:116}

On 8 May 1778, Hugh Stephenson deeded to Nehemiah Coffin, 85 a. {SUDELR:M:194}

On 26 April 1779, Charles Coulter deeded to Hugh Stephenson, 175 a. in Broadkiln Hundred. {SUDELR:M:271}

On 10 Nov 1782, John Stephenson (son of Hugh) and his wife Rhoda (dau. of Absolam Hudson), Ann widow of John Hill, and Walter Hudson deeded to Nathaniel Waples, *Rock Hole*. {SUDELR:M:426}

On 30 May 1789 Hugh Stephenson and his wife Peggy of Sussex Co., DE, conveyed to Robert Hood of sd. co., 161 1/4 a, in Broadkiln Hundred on n.w. side of Mill Creek, conveyed to Hugh Stephenson by Charles Coulter in 1779. {SUDELR O14:79}

JAMES STEVENSON served as private in the Worcester Militia, Wicomico Battn., Capt. William Handy's Company, 15 July 1780.

JAMES STEVENSON served as 2nd lieutenant, Worcester Militia, Wicomico Battn., Capt. James Patterson's Company 28 June 1777 and 1st lieutenant, 15 July 1780. {RPWS:282}

JAMES STEVENSON Jr., served as private in the Worcester Militia, Sinepuxent Battn., Capt. Elisha Purnell's Company, 1779/1780. {RPWS:283}

JAMES STEVENSON Sr. served as private in the Worcester Militia, Sinepuxent

Battn., Capt. Elisha Purnell's Company, 1779/1780. {RPWS:283}

JAMES STEVENSON m. Mary Jarman, dau. of John Jarman and widow of (N) Houston. {See The William Jarman Family, vol. 10 of this series.}
On 2 June 1779 James Stevenson Jr. and wife Mary sold rights to *Boshworth* to William Jarman. {WOLR:64}
John Jarman d. intestate and left to daus. Mary Jarman, Sarah Jarman and Zeporah Jarman the tract *Discovery*. On 2 June 1779 William Jarman sold to Mary Stevenson 33 a. of *Discovery*. The 1783 tax list shows James Stevenson owned 66 a. of the tract. On 6 March 1787 James Stevenson and wife Mary sold 40 a. to Littleton Robins. On 28 Sep 1793 James Stevenson and wife Mary sold to William Jarman Houston, son of afsd. Mary, 30 a., part of a tract in Queponco called *Discovery* lying on the n. side of the tract Deep Swamp. {WOD P:121}

JAMES STEVENSON, m. Nanny Jarman, dau. of William Jarman of Boquerternorton Hundred. {See the William Jarman Family, vol. 10 of this series.}

JAMES STEVENSON
On 15 Aug 1756 James Stevenson patented *Stevenson's Design* (40 a.) in WO Co. It began 4 poles n. from a cart road leading from Cypress Swamp to Blackfoot Town. {MPL BC8:720; BC11:156; WORR}
In 1761, James Stevenson paid tax on *Stevenson's Design*[30]. {Debt Books, Worcester Co.}

LUCY/LESEY STEVENSON
The SO Co. tax list of 1730 shows Lesey Stevenson, widow, as head of household in Bogerternorton Hundred. Living in the household was James Richardson.

ROBERT STEVENSON
Nov Court 1718, Robert Stevenson vs. John Caldwell, Jr. {SOJR:1717-1718:135}
Richard Stevenson, SO Co., d. by 16 July 1727 when the inventory of his estate was filed by Robert Givan. Signed as next of kin: Richard Water, Marion Walaw. {MINV 14:163} On 5 Sep 1727, the admin bond on his estate was posted by Robert Givan. Sureties: Samuel Alexander, Ephraim Wilson. {TP:28:94} On 19 Aug 1730, admin accounts were filed by Robert Givan. {MDAD:10:460}

---

31. This land is now located in Sussex Co. DE. {Card index of Patents at the Maryland State Archives}

ROBERT STEVENSON m. Ann Dale, dau. of John Dale Junr.

Kendall Stevenson, son of Robert and Ann Stevenson, Buckingham, was baptised on 10 Oct 1773. {Lewes & Cool Spring Presbyterian Church, DE}

Nancy Stevenson, dau. of Robert (carpenter) and Ann Stevenson, C.S., was baptised on 17 Nov 1776. {Lewes & Cool Spring Presbyterian Church, DE}

John Dale Junr. d. leaving a will dated 24 Jan 1775, proved 14 March 1778. Mentioned: sons James, John, and Thomas Dale; daus. Martha Whaley, Sarah Evans, Rhoda Hatfield, Ann Stevenson (to whom he left a Negro girl Lydia); grandchildren: Elizabeth, dau. of John, Hannah, dau. of dau. Martha, Mary Stevenson. {WOW JW4 Part II:368}

On 1 June 1785, Robert Stevenson witnessed a deed. {SUDELR:N:157}

Robert Stevenson, Sussex Co., DE, d. leaving a will dated 4 March 1786, proved 12 April 1790. Legatees: sons Kendall & Robert Wilson Stevenson; daus. Mary, Sally, Nancy, Betty McKnight Stevenson. Executors: Thomas Deal, James Vent. {SUW:D:293}

Robert and Ann were the parents of: KENDALL, b. 10 Oct 1773; NANCY, b. 17 Nov 1776; MARY; SALLY; NANCY, b.c. 1783; BETTY McKNIGHT; ROBERT WILSON.

SAMUEL STEVENSON

Caleb Williams conveyed 100 a. of *Rome* to Samuel Stevenson and William Nelson on 26 Jan 1747/48 (OS). {SORR; WOLR:530}

On 8 June 1749, Caleb Williams, Samuel Stevenson, and William Nelson deeded to John Crawford (VA), *Rome* 100 a. {WOLR:530}

WILLIAM STEVENSON served as 1st lieutenant, Worcester Militia, Sinepuxent Battn., Capt. Samuel H. Round's Company, 9 Aug 1780. {RPWS:283}

WILLIAM STEVENSON served private, Worcester Militia, Sinepuxent Battn., Capt. John Rackliff's Company, 1779/1780. {RPWS:283}

WILLIAM STEVENSON.

On 22 Aug 1739 Isaac Piper and wife Temperance sold 63 a. of *Fooks Choice* to Joseph Stephenson. On 18 Aug 1742 they sold 187 a. to Joseph Stevenson. On 6 March 1743 Joseph Stevenson, blacksmith, and wife Rachel sold 150 a. to William Stevenson. On 7 June 1756 William Stevenson sold to Joseph Stevenson, blacksmith, 150 a. In 1781 Joseph Stevenson willed lands unnamed to sons George Stevenson (105 a.), Benjamin Stevenson (180 a.), and Joseph Stevenson (200 a.). {WOLR:231}

On 6 March 1743 Joseph Stevenson, blacksmith, and his wife Rachel conveyed to William Stevenson the tract granted to William Anderson (now dec'd.) called *Fookes Choice* on s. side of Pocomoke River about 4 miles back in the woods and containing 500 a. By sundry conveyances and mutations the tract became the right of Joseph and Rachel. Now Joseph and Rachel for £80 convey 150 a. {WOD A:146}

In 1756, 1757, 1759, 1760, and 1762, he paid tax on *Foolk's Choice* and *Timber Swamp*. {Debt Books, Worcester Co.}

WILLIAM STEVENSON, m. Tabitha (N). She m. 2nd Isaac Collins. {WO Co. marr. lic. dated 3 Jan 1798}

THE SUMMERS (Summer, Somers, Sumner) FAMILY of Somerset County

1. BENJAMIN SUMMER, m. 1st 1666/7 Isabel Wale, m. 2nd Deborah (N), m. 3rd Mary (N).

Ben: Sumner was one of the persons transported into Virginia as indicated by a certificate granted to Stephen Horsey, cooper, on 7 May 1655 in payment for head rights on 5 persons. {Northampton Co., VA, Record Book:133}

This is probably the same Benjamin Summer who was transported into the Province by 1661. {M)PL 4:580}

Benjamin Summer was in Annemessex by 1662. {OSES}

Benjamin Sumner recorded his cattle mark in SO Co. on 10 Feb 1665. {ARMD LIV:743}

William Sumner, son of Benjamin and Isabel Sumner b. at Annamessex 8 Aug 1671. {IKL}

Thomas Sumner, son of Benjamin Sumner and his wife, b. at Annamessex 23 Sep 1680. {IKL}

Mrs. Isabell Summer d. and bur. at her husband's plantation in Annemessex, Dec 1675. {OSES}

Marriage banns for Benjamin Summers and Agnes Wooldridge were published 18 April 1676. {OSES}

Deborah Sumners, wife of Benjamin Sumners, d. 29 Oct 1685. {IKL}

Benjamin Sumner Junr. d. and was bur. at Annamessex last day of Feb 1687. {IKL}

The tract *Emmessex* was patented on 10 Feb 1663 for 300 a. by Benjamin Summers in now Crisfield Election District. It was re-surveyed in 1676 and found to be only 250 a. In 1709 Benjamin Summers devised to sons William Summers, Thomas Summers, and John Summers. On 4 May 1723 William Summers, sailor, and wife Martha, appointed William Coulburn, atty., to make over to Southy Whittington the tract *Emmessex* according to our grandfather Benjamin Summers. On 29 June 1725 Joseph Summers only surviving son of William Summers, dec'd., who was one of the sons of Benjamin Summers, sold to

Southy Whittington, 1/3 part of 250 a., 84 a.. William Summers at death left to
sons Benjamin Summers, William and Joseph Summers. Benjamin Summers and
William Summers d. intestate without issue so 1/3 fell to Joseph Summers with
Littleworth. On 27 Aug 1732 Thomas Summers gave to sons Jonathan Summers
and George Summers, *Emmessex*. On 24 Jan 1782 Jonathan Summers and
Thomas Summers sold 35 a. to Dukes Riggin. On 16 Feb 1785 Jonathan Summers
sold to Thomas Summers, son of Jonathan Summers and Jonathan Summers and
Thomas Summers, son of Thomas, his rights. {SOLR:148}

 Musketa Hummock was patented on 23 Sep 1683 by Benjamin Summers
for 200 a. in now Crisfield Election District. In 1709 Benjamin Summers devised
200 a. to sons William Summers, Thomas Summers and John Summers.
{SOLR:303}

 On 7 March 1702 Benjamin Summers patented *Little Worth* (100 a.) in
SO Co. {MPL DSF:405; DD5:67}

 Benjamin Sommers, SO Co., d. leaving a will dated February 1709,
proved 22 Dec 1715. To: sons William, Thomas, John, 250 a. *Emessex* and 200 a.
Muskato Hamock; granddaughter Mary Giddens cattle with mark of Thomas
Giddens; Elizabeth wife of Thomas Giddens; daughter Ann Scott; wife Mary.
{MWB:14:132} On 22 Dec 1715, an admin bond by filed by Mary Summers and
John Summers. Sureties: Cornelius Ward, Michael Roch. {TP:23:13} The inventory
of the estate of Benjamin Summers was filed on 25 Feb 1715. Approvers:
Benjamin Sumers, John Sumers, Thomas Summers. {INAC:37A:81} In 1718, admin
accounts were filed. {TP:23:217}

 On 11 December 1716, an administration bond was filed on estate of
Mary Sumers by Thomas Sumers & John Sumers her administrators, with
sureties: William Wheatly, Benjamin Sumers. {TP:23:110} Mary Sumner, SO Co.,
d. by 1716 when the inventory for her estate was filed. Approvers: William Scott,
Joseph Summer. {INAC:38A:140}

 On 29 June 1725 Joseph Summers, only surviving son of William
Summers, dec'd., who was one of the sons of Benjamin Summers, planter, dec'd.,
conveyed to Southy Whittington, gent., 1/3 of a tract called *Emessex* containing
250 a., 85 a., which said 85 a. was part of the tract granted on 17 Nov 1677 to
above named Benjamin Summers, dec'd. who by his last will dated 2 Feb 1709,
did give to his son William Summers, dec'd. and to his bros. Thomas and John
Summers, the afsd. tract which said William Summers at the time of his death left
issue to three sons: Benjamin, William and the above named Joseph, party to
these presents and d. intesate as also the said Benjamin, William, the bros. of said
Joseph are both of them dec'd. intestate without issue by now in whereof the sole
right of the said third part of the said 550 a. is wholly vested in Joseph and also
one other tract called *Little Worth* in Annamessex containing 100 a. {SOD 1722-
25:258}

 Benjamin and Isabel were parents of BENJAMIN, 1668-87/8;

WILLIAM, 8 Aug 1671. {OSES}

Benjamin and Deborah were parents of THOMAS, 1680; JOHN. {OSES}

Benjamin is the father of ANN, m. (N) Scott; probably ELIZABETH, m. Thomas Giddens.

Second Generation

2. WILLIAM SUMMERS, b. 8 Aug 1671, son of Benjamin (1) and Isabel Summers, m. Margarett Butler.

William Sumner and Margarett Butler m. 18 Sep 1691. {IKL}

William Summers d. by 22 December 1715 when an administration bond was filed by Margrett Sumers, with surety: Thomas Ward. {TP:23:13} On 27 Dec 1715 the inventory of his estate was filed. Approvers: John Summers, Benjamin Summers. {INAC 36C:195} Admin accounts were filed on 2 June 1718 by Margrett Summers. {MDAD:1:150; TP:23:217}

The tax list of 1723 and 1724 for SO Co., Annemessex Hundred, shows Marget Somurs, widow as head of household with Isac Somurs and Thomas Sumurs living in the same household. {SOTL}

On 4 May 1723 William Summers, sailor, and his wife Martha, appointed William Coulbourn as atty. to make over to Southy Whittington land according to our grandfather Benjamin Summers. On 29 June 1725 Joseph Summers, the only surviving son of William Summers, dec'd., son of Benjamin Summers, sold his 1/3 part of *Littleworth* to Southy Whittington, that his father William left to sons Benjamin Summers, William Summers and Joseph Summers. Benjamin Summers and William d .intestate without issue so it fell to Joseph Summers afsd. {SOLR:260}

William was father of BENJAMIN, d.s.p. by 1725; WILLIAM, d.s.p. by 1725, m. Martha (N); JOSEPH; prob. ISAAC, d.s.p. by 1725; prob. THOMAS, d.s.p. by 1725.

3. THOMAS SUMMERS, b. c1680, son of Benjamin (1) and Deborah Summers, m. Sarah (N).

On 11 December 1716, an administration bond was filed on estate of Mary Sumers by Thomas Sumers & John Sumers her administrators, with sureties: William Wheatly, Benjamin Sumers. {TP:23:110}

Cornelius Ward, SO Co., d. By 24 Feb 1722, when an admin bond was posted on his estate by his executors Margaret Ward and Samuel Ward. Sureties: Thomas Summers, John Riggen. {TP:26:138}

On 27 Aug 1732 Thomas Summers gave to sons Jonathan Summers and George Summers, *Emmessex* and in Annamessex. {SOLR:148}

On 15 June 1736 Thomas Summers and his wife Sarah conveyed land to William Mister. Whereas Henry Smith, dec'd., late of the co., had due to him 1000 a. being part of an island now called *Smith's Island* as the patent will more fully make appear. At the decease of said Henry his grandson John Smith of Sussex Co., DE, became heir and possessed of said land and he conveyed part of said land to Arthur Parks and Thomas Summers. Thomas Summers and his wife Sarah sell to William Mister all their part of said 150 a. [Bounds described] {SOD EI:69}

Thomas Summers patented the following tracts in SO Co.: *Hard Fortune* (50 a.) on 17 Nov 1738. {MPL EI5:321; EI6:86}

The Debt Books for SO Co. for 1733 show Thomas Summers, et.al., as paying tax on *Pitchcroft.*

Thomas Somers, aged 61,deposed on 7 April 1740, regarding the bounds of *Pitch Croft.* On 12 April 1746 Thomas Sumers, aged 66, deposed regarding *Hills Folly.* On 14 June 1746, aged 66, he deposed on the bounds of *Bear Point* and *Chesnut Ridge.* He mentioned he was the son of Benjamin Sumers. {Miller:37}

The tax lists of SO Co., Annemessex Hundred, show Thomas Summers as head of household, 1723-1725, 1727, 1730-1740. Living in the same household was Jonathan Summers (1723-1725, 1727, 1730-1733); George Summers (1724, 1725, 1727, 1730-1740); Thomas Summers (1730-1739); John Dukes (1731); John Redding (1733); Sollomon Benson (1737); Samuel Summers (1738-1740). Thomas Sumers, Sr. is cited as head of household in 1744 and 1748; as Thomas Sumers as head of household in 1750; as Thomas Sumners as head of household in 1753 & 1754. He disappears from the tax lists by 1757. Cited in his household in 1744 is John Summers.

The tax lists of SO Co., Annemessex Hundred, show Sarah Summers as head of household in 1757, with Parks Summers in her household. Parks Summers is cited in the household of Solomon Bird in 1759.

Thomas was father of JONATHAN, b. c1708; GEORGE; THOMAS; SAMUEL; JOHN.

4. JOHN SUMMERS, b. c1682, son of Benjamin (1) and Deborah Summers, m. Joannah (N).

On 11 December 1716, an administration bond was filed on estate of Mary Sumers by Thomas Sumers & John Sumers her administrators, with sureties: William Wheatly, Benjamin Sumers. {TP:23:110}

The tax lists of SO Co., Annemessex Hundred show John Summers (Sumners) as head of household, 1723-1725, 1730-1740, 1744, 1748, 1750, 1753, 1754, 1757, 1759. Living in the household were Jonathan Williams (1723-1725); David Summers (1730-1736, 1738, 1744); Benjamin Summers (1736-1740, 1744); Richard Summers (1739-1740, 1744, 1748, 1750, 1753, 1754, 1757, 1759); Arthur Parks (1737); Thomas Montgomery (1739); Lazarus Summers (1744, 1748, 1750); Isaac Summers (1750, 1753, 1754, 1757, 1759); slave Locus/Lopes (1725, 1730-1731).

John Summers, aged 64, deposed on 14 June 1746 regarding the bounds of *Chesnut Ridge* and *Bear Point*. On 7 May 1757 at age 74 he deposed regarding the bounds of *Prices Vineyard*. {Miller:36}

The Debt Books for SO Co. for 1734, 1735, 1745, 1755, 1759, 1761, 1764, 1768, 1769, and 1774 show John Summers as paying tax on *Emmessix* and *Musketo Creek.*[31]

John Summers, SO Co., d. leaving a will dated 13 Aug 1758, proved Nov 1760. To eldest son David Summers, tract *Marsh Pasture*. To children Mary Ward, Benjamin and Lazarus, 1 shilling. To grandson Isaac Summers, cattle. To dau. Deborah Sterling, furniture. To granddau. Grace Sterling, same. To son Richard Summers, stock and remainder of land. To wife Joannah Summers, chattles; at her decease to be divided between Richard, Isaac and Betty Summers, sons and dau. Execs. Richard and Isaac Summers. Witnessed by Cornelius Ward, George Summers, Jonathan Martin; also another evidence, Jonathan Martine. {MWB 31:1} On 26 Jan 1761 an inventory of his estate was filed by Richard Summers, exec. Signed as next of kin: Jonathon Summers, George Summers. {MINV:76:144}

John was father of DAVID; BENJAMIN, b. c1720; RICHARD, b. c1723; MARY, m. (N) Ward; LAZARUS; DEBORAH, m. (N) Sterling; ISAAC; BETTY.

Third Generation

5. BENJAMIN SUMMERS, son of William (2) Summers.

Benjamin Summers and William Wheatly were sureties on the administration bond filed on 11 Dec 1716 on the estate of Mary Summers by Thomas Sumers and John Summers, her admins. {TP:23:110} Mary Sumner, SO Co., d. by 1716 when the inventory was filed. Approvers: William Scott, Joseph Summer. {INAC:38A:140}

Benjamin Summers, SO Co., d. by 20 March 1722, when an admin bond was posted on his estate by William Summers. Surety: William Colebourne. {TP:26:138} In 1724, at July Court 1725, and at July Court 1726, William Summers was summoned to produce inventory and accounts on said estate. {TP:27:84, 87, 315} At July Court 1726, it was exhibited that William Summers, administrator of Benjamin Summers, was dead. {TP:27:317}

6. WILLIAM SUMMERS, d. by July 1726, son of William (2) Summers, m. Martha (N).

On 20 March 1722 William Summers posted an administration bond on the estate of Benjamin Summers. Surety: William Colebourne. {TP:26:138} In 1724, at July Court 1725, and at July Court 1726, William Summers was summoned to

---

32. For the period, 1761 through 1774, the tax is no doubt being paid by the heirs of John Summers.

produce inventory and accounts. {TP:27:84, 87, 315} In July 1726, it was reported that William Summers, admin. of Benjamin Summers, was dead. {TP:27:317}

On 4 May 1723 William Summers, sailor, and his wife Martha, appointed William Coulbourn as atty. to make over to Southy Whittington land according to our grandfather Benjamin Summers. On 29 June 1725 Joseph Summers, the only surviving son of William Summers, dec'd., son of Benjamin Summers, sold his 1/3 part of *Littleworth* to Southy Whittington, that his father William left to sons Benjamin Summers, William Summers and Joseph Summers. Benjamin Summers and William d .intestate without issue so it fell to Joseph Summers afsd. {SOLR:260}

On 3 Jan 1723, William Summers received payment from estate of Samuel Morris. {MDAD:5:326}

7. JOSEPH SUMMERS, son of William (2) Summers.

On 4 May 1723 William Summers, sailor, and his wife Martha, appointed William Coulbourn as atty. to make over to Southy Whittington land according to our grandfather Benjamin Summers. On 29 June 1725 Joseph Summers, the only surviving son of William Summers, dec'd., son of Benjamin Summers, sold his 1/3 part of *Littleworth* to Southy Whittington, that his father William left to sons Benjamin Summers, William Summers and Joseph Summers. Benjamin Summers and William d .intestate without issue so it fell to Joseph Summers afsd. {SOLR:260}

On 3 Jan 1723, Joseph Summers received payment from estate of Samuel Morris. {MDAD:5:326}

On 11 Dec 1716, an administration bond was filed on estate of Mary Sumers by Thomas Sumers and John Sumers her administrators, with sureties: William Wheatly, Benjamin Sumers. {TP:23:110} Mary Sumner, SO Co., d. by 1716 when the inventory for her estate was filed. Approvers: William Scott, Joseph Summer. {INAC:38A:140}

On 29 June 1725 Joseph Summers, only surviving son of William Summers, dec'd., who was one of the sons of Benjamin Summers, planter, dec'd., conveyed to Southy Whittington, gent., 1/3 of a tract called *Emessex* containing 250 a., 85 a., which said 85 a. was part of the tract granted on 17 Nov 1677 to above named Benjamin Summers, dec'd. who by his last will dated 2 Feb 1709, did give to his son William Summers, dec'd. and to his bros. Thomas and John Summers, the afsd. tract which said William Summers at the time of his death left issue to three sons: Benjamin, William and the above named Joseph, party to these presents and d. intesate as also the said Benjamin, William, the bros. of said Joseph are both of them dec'd. intestate without issue by now in whereof the sole right of the said third part of the said 550 a. is wholly vested in Joseph and also one other tract called *Little Worth* in Annamessex containing 100 a. {SOD 1722-25:258}

8. JONATHAN SUMMERS, b. c1708, son of Thomas (3) Summers, m. Anne (N).

The tax lists of SO Co., Annemessex Hundred, show Jonathan Summers living in the household of Thomas Summers, 1723, 1724, 1730-1733, and as head of household in Annamessex Hundred, 1734-1740, 1744, 1748, 1750, 1753, 1754, 1757, 1759. Living in the household of Jonathan Summers in 1740 was Thomas Summers. Living in the household of Jonathon Summers in 1759 was Thomas Summers, Jr.

On 27 Aug 1732 Thomas Summers gave to sons Jonathan Summers and George Summers *Emmessex* and in Annamessex. {SOLR:148}

Jonathan Summers, aged 41 deposed on 28 Oct 1745 regarding the bounds of *Horeworth, Horseys Down, Bells Purchase, None Such, Littleworth* and *Gilford*. On 7 May 1757, aged 51, he deposed regarding the bounds of *Prices Vineyard*. On 1 May 1758, aged 50, he deposed regarding the bounds of *Scotland* and on 30 Dec 1760, aged 50, he deposed regarding the bounds of *Cork*. {Miller:36}

The Debt Books for SO Co. for 1745, 1755, 1759, 1761, 1764, 1768, 1769, and 1774 show Jonathon Summers as paying tax on *Emessix, Littleworth, Jonathon's Addition, Summers' Hard Fortune*.

On 16 Feb 1785 Jonathan Summers sold to Thomas Summers, son of Jonathan Summers and Jonathan Summers and Thomas Summers, son of Thomas, his rights to *Emessix*. {SOLR:148}

Jonathan and Anne were parents of THOMAS, b.c. 1743; OBED, b. 21 March 1748/49. {SOCO}

9. GEORGE SUMMERS, b.c. 1711, son of Thomas (3) Summers.

The tax lists of SO Co., Annamessex Hundred, show Thomas Summers as head of household, 1723, 1727, 1730-1740. Living in the same household George Summers (1727, 1730-1740). George Summers is cited as head of household in 1744, 1748, 1750, 1753, 1754, 1757, and 1759.

On 27 Aug 1732 Thomas Summers gave to sons Jonathan Summers and George Summers *Emmessex* and in Annamessex. {SOLR:148}

The Debt Books for SO Co. for 1734, 1735, 1745, 1755, 1759, 1761, 1764, 1768, 1769, and 1774 show George Summers as paying tax on *Tower Hill, Emmessix, Littleworth*, and *Summers' Hard Fortune*.

10. SAMUEL SUMMERS, b.c. 1722, son of Thomas (3) Summers, m. Elizabeth (N).

The tax lists of SO Co., Annemessex Hundred, show Thomas Summers as head of household, 1723, 1727, 1730-1740. Living in the same household was Samuel Summers (1738-1740). Samuel Summers is cited as head of household in 1748, 1750, 1753, 1754.

Samuell and Elizabeth Summers were parents of GEORGE, b. 23 Oct 1746; SAMUEL, b. 14 May 1749; ELIAS, b. 29 April 1752. {SOCO}

11. THOMAS SUMMERS, b.c. 1714, son of Thomas (3) Summers, m. 4 Feb 1762, Ann (N). {SOCO} She is the widow of Esau Boston, Jr. {MDAD:48:37}
The tax lists of SO Co., Annemessex Hundred, show Thomas Summers as head of household, 1723, 1727, 1730-1740. Living in the same household was Thomas Summers (1730-1739). Thomas Summers, Jr. is cited as head of household in 1744, 1748, 1750, 1753, 1754. He is cited as head of household in 1757 and 1759. {SOTL}
Esau Boston, SO Co., d. by 10 April 1762 when distribution of his estate was made by Ann Summers, admx. Distribution to (equally): Jesse Boston, Jacob Boston, Mary, Martha, Ephraim, David. {BFD:3:132}
Thomas and Ann were parents of THOMAS, b. 11 Dec 1762; JONATHAN , b. 29 June 1767; ANN, b. 8 March 1770. {SOCO}

12. DAVID SUMMERS (Sommors), b.c. 1711/1714, son of John (4) Summers, m. 14 Dec 1749, Mary Jurdin (Jordan). {SOCO} Mary was prob. the sister of John Jordan.
The tax lists of SO Co., Annemessex Hundred show John Summers (Sumners) as head of household, 1723-1725, 1730-1740, 1744, 1748, 1750, 1753, 1754, 1757, 1759. Living in the household were David Summers (1730-1736, 1738, 1744). David Summers is cited as head of household in 1748, 1750, 1753, 1754, 1757. He is probably the David Summers cited in the household of Solomon Bird in 1759.
John Jordan, in his will dated 12 Jan 1777, prove 13 May 1777 he mentioned cousin Betty Summers. {SOW EB5:97}
David Summers served as private in the Somerset Militia, Salisbury Battn., Capt. Sampson Wheatly's Company, 1780. {RPWS:288}
In 1783, David Summers was living in Little Annamessex Hundred, with *Emmessix* 90 a., with 2 males & 4 females in his household. {1783 Assessment}
David Sommers, planter, SO Co., d. leaving a will dated 15 Jan 1791, proved 14 Dec 1792. To wife Mary, possession of the dwelling house and 5 a. To son Stephen Sommers that part of my land beginning at a marked pine thence ... To son David land left to son Stephen should Stephen die without heirs. To son John Sommers equal division of *Muskeeto Hummock*. Witnessed by Richard Sommers, Sarah Kimpe, John Kimpe. Execs. wife and son Stephen. {SOW EB17:233}
David and Mary were parents of JOHN, b. 25 April 1750; BETTY, b. 18 May 1752; STEPHEN, b 7 March 1755; JEMIMA, b. 13 Oct 1757; MARTHA, b. 7 April 1760; DAVID. {Births from SOCO except for David who is mentioned in father's will.}

13. BENJAMIN SUMMERS, b.c. 1720, son of John (4) Summers.
      The tax lists of SO Co., Annemessex Hundred show John Summers (Sumners) as head of household, 1723-1725, 1730-1740, 1744, 1748, 1750, 1753, 1754, 1757, 1759. Living in the household were Benjamin Summers (1736-1740, 1744). Benjamin Summers is cited as head of household in 1750, 1753, 1754, 1757, 1759. {SOTL}

14. RICHARD SUMMERS, b.c. 1723, son of John (4) Summers.
      The tax lists of SO Co., Annemessex Hundred show John Summers (Sumners) as head of household, 1723-1725, 1730-1740, 1744, 1748, 1750, 1753, 1754, 1757, 1759. Living in the household were Richard Summers (1739-1740, 1744, 1748, 1750, 1753, 1754, 1757, 1759).
      In 1783, Richard Summers was living in Little Annamessex Hundred, with *Emmessix* 90 a., with 1 male & 1 female in his household. {1783 Assessment}

15. LAZARUS SUMMORS, b.c. 1728, son of John (4) Summers, m. 2 Feb 1755, Catheron Pettet. {SOCO}
      The tax lists of SO Co., Annemessex Hundred show John Summers (Sumners) as head of household, 1723-1725, 1730-1740, 1744, 1748, 1750, 1753, 1754, 1757, 1759. Living in the household were Lazarus Summers (1744, 1748, 1750). Lazarus Summers is cited as head of household in 1753, 1754, 1757, 1759.
      Lazarus Summers served as private, Somerset Militia, Salisbury Battn., Capt. Sampson Wheatly's Company, 1780, 1780. {RPWS:289}
      In 1783, Lazarus Summers was living in Little Annamessex, with no land. There were 4 males & 4 females in his household. {1783 Assessment}
      Lazarus and Catheron were parents of ISAAC, b. 16 Feb 1756; STEPHEN, b. 1 June 1758. {SOCO}

16. ISAAC SUMMERS, b.c. 1732/4, son of John (4) Summers.
      The tax lists of SO Co., Annemessex Hundred show John Summers (Sumners) as head of household, 1723-1725, 1730-1740, 1744, 1748, 1750, 1753, 1754, 1757, 1759. Living in the household were Isaac Summers (1750, 1753, 1754, 1757, 1759).

Fourth Generation

17. THOMAS SUMMERS, son of Jonathon (8) Summers.
      Thomas Summers served as corporal, Somerset Militia, Princess Anne Battn., Capt. Henry Miles's Little Annemessex Company, 1780. {RPWS:290}
      On 16 Feb 1785 Jonathan Summers sold to Thomas Summers, son of Jonathan Summers and Jonathan Summers and Thomas Summers, son of Thomas, his rights to *Emessix*. {SOLR:148}

18. OBED SUMMERS, son of Jonathon (8) Summers.
Obadiah Summers served as private, SO Co., Capt. John Gunby's 2nd Independent Maryland Company, present on 26 June 1776; mustered 21 Aug 1776. {RPWS:289}

19. GEORGE SUMMERS, son of Samuel (10) and Elizabeth Summers.
George Summers served as private in the Somerset Militia, Princess Anne Battn., Watkins Point Company under Capt. John Williams. 1780. {RPWS:288}

20. ELIAS SUMMERS, b. 29 April 1752, son of Samuel (10) and Elizabeth Summers.
Elias Summers served as private in the Somerset Militia, Princess Anne Battn., St. Asaph's Company, 1780. {RPWS:288}
In 1783, Elias Summers was living in Great Annamessex Hundred, with no land. There were 4 males & 2 females in his household. {1783 Assessment}

21. THOMAS SUMMERS, b. 11 Dec 1762, son of Thomas (11) and Ann (Boston) Summers.
Thomas Summers served as private in the Somerset Militia, Salisbury Battn., Capt. Sampsons Wheatley's Company, 1780. {RPWS:290}
On 24 Jan 1782, Jonathon Summers and Thomas Summers deeded to Dukes Riggen, pt. *Emessex* 35 a. {SOD:G:290}
In 1783,Thomas Summers was living in Little Annamessex Hundred, with *Emmessix* 60½ a. There are 3 males & 5 females in his household. {1783 Assessment}
On 16 Feb 1785 Jonathan Summers sold to Thomas Summers, son of Jonathan Summers and Jonathan Summers and Thomas Summers, son of Thomas, his rights to *Emessix*. {SOLR:148}

22. JONATHON SUMMERS, b. 29 June 1767, son of Thomas (11) and Ann (Boston) Summers.
Jonathon Summers served as private, in the Somerset Militia, Salisbury Battn., Capt. Sampson Wheatly's Company, 1780. {RPWS:289}
On 24 Jan 1782, Jonathon Summers and Thomas Summers deeded to Dukes Riggen, pt. *Emessex* 35 a. {SOD:G:290}
In 1783, Jonathon Summers was living in Little Annamessex Hundred, with *Emmessix* 60½ a. There are 3 males & 2 females in his household. {1783 Assessment}

23. JOHN SUMMERS, b. 25 April 1750, son of David (12) and Mary Summers, prob. m. Jemima Cullen.

John Summers m. 10 Sep 1775, Jemima Cullen. {SOCO}

John Summers served as sergeant in the Somerset Militia, Princess Anne Battn., Capt. Henry Miles' Little Annemessex Company, 1780 and in the Select Militia, SO Co., as of 15 Aug 1781. {RPWS:289}

24. STEPHEN SUMMERS, b 7 March 1755, son of David (12) and Mary Summers.

This may be the same Stephen Summers who served as private in the Somerset Militia, Princess Anne Battn., Capt. Henry Miles' Little Annemessex Company, 1780. {RWPS:290}

Unplaced

BETTY SUMMERS

In 1783, Betty Summers was living in Little Annamessex Hundred, with no land, with 2 males & 2 females in his household. {1783 Assessment}

GEORGE SUMMERS served as private in the Somerset Militia, Salisbury Battn., Capt. Sampson Wheatly's Company, 1780. {RPWS:280}

In 1783,George Summers was living in Little Annamessex Hundred, with no land. There are 4 males & 4 females in his household. {1783 Assessment}

HORSEY SUMMERS, b. 1762, d. 25 Feb 1852, m. Nancy Rew.

Horsey Summers served as private in the Maryland Line. He applied for a pension in Accomack Co., VA, on 12 Sep 1851, agge 89, stating he was b. in SO Co., and lived there at the time of his enlistment. Shortly after the war he moved to Accomack Co. where he m. Nancy (N). {For more details see RPWS:288 which cites Stratton Nottingham's *Soldiers and Sailors of the Eastern Shore of Virginia in the Revolutionary War*:74}

JACOB SUMMERS served as private in the Somerset Militia, Princess anne Battn., Capt. Henry Miles' Little Annemessex Company, 1780. {RPWS:289}

JAMES SUMMERS served as private in the Somerset Militia, Princess Anne Battn., Capt. Henry Miles' Little annemessex Company, 1780. {RPWS:289}

In 1783, James Summers was living in Little Annamessex Hundred, with no land. There are 2 males & 4 females in his household. {1783 Assessment}

MARGET SOMMORS m. 6 July 1761, Matthews/Matthias Boston. {SOCO}

They were the parents of: MARTHA, b. 26 March 1762; JAMES, b. 1

Nov 1763, d.p. June 1768. {SOCO}

   Margaret Boston was the mother of an illegitimate child by Dennis Montgomery, b. cMay 1767. Thomas Summers stood security for Margaret Boston. {Boston Family, p. 356}

   Margaret Boston was the mother of an illegitimate child by Samuel Smiley, b. cFeb 1770. {Boston Family, p. 356}

   Margaret Boston was the mother of an illegitimate child by an unidentified father, b. cJune 1774. {Boston Family, p. 356}

MARTHA SOMMORS, m. 28 Jan 1761, Dukes Riggen. {SOCO}

   Dukes Riggin served as private in the Somerset Militia, Princess Anne Battn., Capt. Little Annemessex Company, 1780. {RPWS:250}

   On 24 Jan 1782, Jonathon Summers and Thomas Summers deeded to Dukes Riggen, pt. *Emessex* 35 a. {SOD:G:290}

   Dukes and Martha were the parents of: NANCY RIGGIN, b. 27 Jan 1762; SOPHIA RIGGIN, b. 1 Nov 1763; MARTHA RIGGIN, b. 3 Aug 1765; ELISHA RIGGIN, b. 20 April 1770. {SOCO}

MOSES SUMMERS m. 29 May 1765, Prissilla Lawson. {SOCO}

   They were parents of SAMUEL, b. 27 March 1772; JESSE, b. 25 March 1770; AMELIA, b. 22 April 1767. {SOCO}

   In 1783, Moses Summers was living in Little Annamessex Hundred, with no land, with 5 males & 3 females in his household. {1783 Assessment}

RICHARD SUMMERS, b. 1759, d. 1850, m. Elizabeth (N).

   Richard Summers served as private in the Somerset Militia, Salisbury Battn., Capt. Sampson Wheatly's Company, 1780. His widow Elizabeth, m. 1st on 21 Nov 1822, George Lewis, a Revolutionary soldiers and he d. 9 May 1834. She m. 2nd Richard Summers in 1836 in Accomack co., VA; he d. there 7 July 1850. Richard had enlisted in SO Co., MD, and shortly after the war he moved to Accomack Co.,VA. His bro. Horsey Summers served with him and also lived in Accomack Co. {RPWS citing Stratton Nottingham's *Soldiers and Sailors of the Eastern Shore of Virginia in the Revolutionary War*:64}

SARAH SUMMERS In 1783, Sarah Summers was living in Great Annamessex Hundred, with no land, with 0 males & 7 females in his household. {1783 Assessment}

WILLIAM SUMMERS

   William Summers served as private in the Somerset Militia, Princess Anne Battn., Capt. George Waters' Pocomoke Company, 1780. {RPWS:290}

   In 1783, William Summers was living in Dividing Creek Hundred, with no land, with 2 males & 1 females in his household. {1783 Assessment}

THE THOMAS SUMMERS FAMILY of Dorchester County

1. THOMAS SUMERS, m. 22 April 1656 Mary Soane at Parish Church of St. James' Dukes Place, London. She was the dau. of Francis Soane. He was living in Shadwell, London in 1666. {DOLR:2:97}

      On 14 June 1677, he patented *Addition to Clark's Neck.* {DORR}

      On 30 June 1677, he patented *Meekins Folly*, for 56 a. {DORR}

      On 14 Aug 1678, he patented *Tewksbury* 50 a. {MPL:24:156; 29:190}

      On 3 Feb 1679, Thomas Sumers and his wife Mary sold to John Merridith, *Tewksbury* 50 a. {DOLR:4:86}

      On 20 Sep 1684, he patented *Little Britain* 50 a. {MPL:25:206; 32:447}

      On 17 Nov 1721, Edward Billiter and his wife Anne in their right and as attorney for John Sumers to William Trippe, *Guinney Plantation,* 100 a. Power of attorney from John Sumers (son of Thomas Sumers (of London, dec'd.)) and Mary his wife (dec'd.) who was the dau. of Francis Soane (dec'd.) and niece of Joseph Soane (dec'd.) to Edward Billiter and Anne his wife, brother and sister of said John Sumers. Mary dau. of Francis Soane was baptized on 3 Jan 1632 at St. Mary Newington, Surrey. {DOLR:2:97}

      Thomas and Mary were the parents of: THOMAS; JOHN; ANNE, m. Edward Billiter; prob. MARY, m. (N) Molhorne.

Second Generation

2. THOMAS SUMERS, son of Thomas (1) Sumers, m. Elizabeth (N). She is probably the daughter of John Flower (d. 1726).

      On 21 July 1717, Thomas Summers was one of appraisers of estate of William Bennett. {MINV:1:236}

      On 27 March 1721, Thomas Sumers (DO Co.) and his wife Elizabeth deeded to Henry Dean *Little Britain*. {DOLR:8:22}

      Pettigrew Salsbury, DO Co., d. leaving a will dated 25 Sep 1719, proved 10 Mar 1719. Legatees: son Andrew, *Andrew's Charge*, dau. Sarah, Rachel Stanford, Thomas Sumers 16 a., wife Mary. {MWB:16:32}

      John Flowers, DO Co., d. leaving a will dated 3 Sep 1726, proved 8 Nov 1726. Legatees: grandsons John Somers, Andrew Salsbury, granddau Mary Somers, son-in-law Richard Pritchard, son Lambrock Flowers estate in MD and VA, grandson William Pritchard, *Manlove's Grove*, wife Elizabeth. {MWB:18:546} On 22 Dec 1726, an inventory was filed on estate of John Flowers. Signed as next of kin: L. Flowers, Thomas Somers. {MINV:11:829} On 11 Dec 1728, admin accounts were filed. {MDAD:9:274}

Thomas was the father of: JOHN; MARY.

3. JOHN SUMERS, b. 5 June 1666, son of Thomas (1) Summers, m. (N).

On 13 Sep (1709), Thomas Taylor (son & heir of John Taylor) sold to his aunt Jane Teate, *Gotham* 150 a. & *Guinney Plantation* 100 a. {DOLR:6:136}

On 17 Nov 1721, Edward Billiter and his wife Anne in their right & as attorney for John Sumers to William Trippe, *Guinney Plantation* 100 a. Power of attorney from John Sumers (son of Thomas Sumers (of London, dec'd.)) and Mary his wife (dec'd.) who was the dau. of Francis Soane (dec'd.) and niece of Joseph Soane (dec'd.) to Edward Billiter and Anne his wife, brother & sister of said John Sumers. Mary dau. of Francis Soane was baptized on 3 Jan 1632 at St. Mary Newington, Surrey. {DOLR:2:97}

On 12 Nov 1723, John Summers received payment from estate of John Macgovery (DO Co.). {MDAD:5:282}

On 29 Aug 1726, John Sumers witnessed will of Hugh Handley (DO Co.). {MWB:19:697}

On 2 Jan 1726, John Sumers witnessed will of Mathew Gadd (DO Co.). {MWB:20:668}

On 1 Aug 1727, John Sumers witnessed will of Capt. Richard Smart (DO Co.). {MWB:19:714}

4. ANNE SUMERS, dau. of Thomas (1) Summers, m. Edward Billiter.

Mary Molehorne, DO Co., d. leaving a will dated 1 Aug 1721, proved 21 Oct 1721. Executor: Abraham Griffith. Witnesses: George Andrews, Eleanor Andrews, Anne Billiter. {MWB:17:46}

On 17 Nov 1721, Edward Billiter and his wife Anne in their right & as attorney for John Sumers to William Trippe, *Guinney Plantation,* 100 a. Power of attorney from John Sumers (son of Thomas Sumers (of London, dec'd.)) and Mary his wife (dec'd.) who was the dau. of Francis Soane (dec'd.) and niece of Joseph Soane (dec'd.) to Edward Billiter and Anne his wife, brother & sister of said John Sumers. Mary dau. of Francis Soane was baptized on 3 Jan 1632 at St. Mary Newington, Surrey. {DOLR:2:97}

THE JOHN SUMMERS FAMILY of Dorchester County

1. JOHN SUMMERS

On 6 Jul 1738, John Summers is cited as surety to Elizabeth Green, admx./extx. of William Green. John Summers also received payment from said Green's estate. {MDAD:16:239}

John Summers, DO Co., d. by 9 March 1740 when an admin. bond was filed by John Nicholls. Sureties: Edward Hargarton, Moses Nicolls. {TP:31:192} On

9 March 1740, Thomas Summers as nearest of kin assigned administration to John Nichols, Jr. {TP:31:192} On 10 Jul 1741 an inventory of his estate was filed by John Nicols, Jr. Signed as next of kin: Thomas Summers, Isbell Summers. {MINV:26:191; TP:31:220} On 28 Jul 1742 admin accounts were filed on his estate by John Nicols, Jr. {MDAD:19:165}

At Aug 1744 Court, John Nicols, Jr., John Harris, and Edward Leadenham were bound to children of John Summers (dec'd.): Isaac, William, Mary Ann, John, Joseph. {DOJR:1743-1745:133}

John was the father of: ISAAC; WILLIAM; MARY ANN; JOHN; JOSEPH.

2. THOMAS SUMMERS, prob. brother of John (1) Summers.

On 13 Jan 1728, Thomas Summers witnessed a deed. {DOLR:8:258}

In Aug 1733 Court, Thomas Summers was cited in suit by Daniel Sullivan. {DOJR:1733-1734:76}

In Aug 1733 Court, Thomas Summers of Great Choptank Parish was fined for assaulting Thomas Corson. Isabell Sumers was in attendance. {DOJR:1733-1734:94}

Thomas Summers, DO Co., d. by 31 Jan 1742 when Mary Summers and Isabell Summers renounced administration on the estate of their brother. {TP:31:381} On 18 Feb 1742 an admin bond was filed on his estate by Col. Henry Hooper. {TP:31:381} On 18 Feb 1742 an inventory was filed on his estate by Col. Henry Hooper. Signed as next of kin: John Summers, Isabella Summers. {MINV:28:114} On 30 Apr 1744 admin accounts were filed on his estate by Col. Henry Hooper. {MDAD:20:202}

3. MARY SUMMERS, sister of Thomas (2) Summers and prob. sister of John (1) Summers.

Joseph Kennedy, DO Co., d. by 16 July 1757 when an inventory was filed on his estate by Priscilla Kennedy. Signed as next of kin: Mary Summers, Isabell Hubbard. {MINV:63:533} On 18 May 1758, admin accounts were filed on his estate. Mentions: Ann (child). {MDAD:42:275}

4. ISABELL SUMMER, sister of Mary (3) Summers and Thomas (2) Summers and prob. sister of John (1) Summers, m. Titus Hubbert.

Joseph Kennedy, DO Co., d. by 16 July 1757 when an inventory was filed on his estate by Priscilla Kennedy. Signed as next of kin: Mary Summers, Isabell Hubbard. {MINV:63:533} On 18 May 1758 admin accounts were filed on his estate. Mentions: Ann (child). {MDAD:42:275}

William Summers, DO Co., d. leaving a will dated 20 Jan 1763, proved 14 June 1764. Legatees: sister Mary Ann Summers. {MWB:33:14} On 12 June 1765 an inventory of his estate was filed by Mary Ann Summers. Signed as next of kin:

John Summers, Isbell Hubbert. {MINV:86:342} On 24 Oct 1765 admin accounts were filed on his estate by Mary Ann Summers. Sureties: Titus Hubbert, Nehemiah Hubbert. {MDAD:53:199} On 11 June 1766 additional admin accounts were filed by Mary Ann Summers. {MDAD:54:162}

On 12 Aug 1747, Titus Hubbert and his wife Isabell deeded to Samuel Hubbert and Thomas Cook, *Brooks Outhold* 100 a., *Indian Quarter* 50 a., and *Taylor's Hap* 50 a. {DOLR:14:154}

Second Generation

5. ISAAC SOMMERS, son of John (1) Summers, m. Mary Roach, dau. of John Roach.

On 3 Oct 1763, John Rumbly, Jr. (DO Co.) & his wife Elizabeth sold to Isaac Sumers (DO Co.), *Parris* 275 a. & pt. *Williams' Prevention* 12 a. {DOLR:19:79}

On 17 Nov 1767, Isaac Sumers (SO) & his wife Mary sold to James Safford (DO Co.), *Paris* 160 a. & pt. *Williams' Prevention* 12 a. {DOLR:22:131}

On 22 Aug 1767, John Roach deeded to Isaac Summers (shoemaker), pt. *Longtown* 59 a. {SOLR:268}

John Roach, Coventry Parish, SO Co., d. leaving a will dated 3 April 1769, proved 21 Nov 1770. Wife Rebecca, Extx. Children: Nancy, Betty, Alice, Horsey wife of Absolum Rue, Jonathan, Mary wife of Isaac Summers, to whom he left Negro Peter, Rebecca wife of Hugh Vestary. Grandson Planer Roach. Witnessed by Ann Starling, John Starling, William Roach. {MWB 38:186}

The Debt Books for SO Co. for 1774 show Isaac Summers as paying tax on *Longtown*.

In 1783, Isaac Summers is cited as living in Little Annamessix, paying tax on *Longtown* 80 a., with 3 males and 4 females in his household. {1783 Assessment}

They were parents of MARY ROACH, b. 14 Oct 1763 {DODO}; ISAAC, b. 29 Aug 1768; JEMEY, b. 19? July 1770 {SOCO}

6. WILLIAM SUMMERS, son of John (1) Summers.

William Summers, DO Co., d. leaving a will dated 20 Jan 1763, proved 14 June 1764. Legatees: sister Mary Ann Summers. {MWB:33:14} On 12 June 1765 an inventory of his estate was filed by Mary Ann Summers. Signed as next of kin: John Summers, Isbell Hubbert. {MINV:86:342} On 24 Oct 1765 admin accounts were filed on his estate by Mary Ann Summers. Sureties: Titus Hubbert, Nehemiah Hubbert. {MDAD:53:199} On 11 June 1766 additional admin accounts were filed by Mary Ann Summers. {MDAD:54:162}

Unplaced

FELIX SUMMER

On 21 Jan 1747, Benjamin Nicolls & Dorcas his wife to Felix Summers (pedlar, DO) pt. *Richardson's Choice* 100 a. {DOLR:14:211}

On 21 Jan 1747, William Edmondson & his wife Mary Ann to Felix Summers (pedlar, DO Co.), pt. *Eldridge* now called *Perry's Purchase* 95 a. {DOLR:14:214}

On 5 Sep 1750, Rice Leveanus leased to Felix Summers (DO Co.), pt. *Richardson's Choice* 100 a. {DOLR:14:473}

On 9 Nov 1751, Felix Summers leased to Henry Carey, pt. *Richardson's Choice*. {DOLR:14:556}

On 13 Nov 1754, Guy Cook conveyed to Felix Summers, chattel. {DOLR:15:164}

On 1 Mar 1755, Guy Cook conveyed to Felix Summers, chattel. {DOLR:15:206}

On 28 Mar 1768, Felix Summers (QA Co.) and his wife Elizabeth sold to Charles Goldsborough, pt. *Richardson's Choice* 100 a., pt. *Perry's Purchase* 95 a., and leased *Richardson's Choice* and *Skipton*. {DOLR:17:286}

JOHN SUMNER

On 15 Jan 1673, John Sumner witnessed a power of attorney. {DOLR:3:78}

JOHN SUMMERS, m. Susannah (N) who later m. Hugh Handly.

John Summers, DO Co., d. leaving a will dated 28 Dec 1732, proved 27 Jan 1732. Legatees: wife Susannah, daus. Anne, Sarah. {MWB:20:537} In 1733, an inventory was filed of his estate by Susannah Summers & Owen Ward. Signed as next of kin: Thomas Summers, Gudy Fran[k]lin. {MINV:17:131} On 9 May 1734 admin accounts were filed on his estate by Susannah wife of Hugh Handly. {MDAD:12:303} On 8 Aug 1737 additional admin accounts were filed on his estate by Susannah wife of Hugh Handly. Distribution to: Susannah (widow), Anne (dau), Sarah (dau, now dec'd.). {MDAD:14:307}

John and Susannah were the parents of: ANNE; SARAH, d. 1734/1737.

JOHN SUMMERS

John Summers, DO Co., d. by 2 Sep 1737 when an inventory of his estate was filed by Mary Summers. {MINV:22:396} On 9 Aug 1738 admin accounts were filed by Mary Summers. Cited: Luke Summers (son). {MDAD:16:246}

John was the father of: LUKE.

On 22 Jan 1742/3, James Pattison deposed in the presence of Luke Summers, et.al. {DOLR:14:44}

On 14 Nov 1749, Luke Summers witnessed a deed. {DOLR:14:397}

In 1749, Luke Summers was cited as a debtor to estate of Maj. Thomas Nevett (DO Co.). {MINV:42:145}

JOHN SUMMERS

In Mar 1729, John Carter (DO Co.) & his wife Mary deeded to John Sumers (DO Co.) pt. *Brit's Hope* 250 a. {DOLR:8:315} [Jeremiah Carter resurveyed in 1770. 1783: *Brits Hope*: James Carter 177½ a., John Carter 177½ a.]

On 10 Mar 1729, John Sumers witnessed deed on 10 March 1728, 6 Aug 1730 and 13 March 1733. {DOLR:8:326; 369, 395; 9:148, 152}

ROGER SUMMERS

On 10 Sep 1716, Roger Summers patented *Sommers Adventure*. {MPL:FF#7:5;PL#4:102}

On 5 March 1746, Roger Summers and his wife Mary sold to Robert Davis (Kent County on Delaware Bay) *Summers Adventure* 50 a. {DOLR:14:117}

THOMAS SUMMERS

On 10 June 1712, William Smith (DO Co.) deeded to Thomas Summers (DO Co.) pt. *Fisher's Choice* 315 a. & *Cable and Ankor* 52 a. {DOLR:6:189}

On 28 Feb 1742, Thomas Sumers, Kent Co., PA (DE) deeded to Joseph Ennalls pt. *Fisher's Choice* 38 a. {DOLR:10:389}

THE JOHN WALLACE FAMILY

1. JOHN WALLIS m. Jane (N).

John Wallis, Sr., of Ireland and Manokin Rivers, SO Co., d. leaving a will dated 3 July 1685. To wife Jane, half of estate (personal). To nephew John Wallis, Jr., William Stevenson, Matthew and James Wallis, residue of estate. Exec. not named. {MWB 4:169}

On 13 June 1688, Henry Smith and his wife Anne deeded to Samuell Johnston and Jeane Wallace, *Smith's Resolution* 350 a. on the Manokin River. {SOD:MA:917}

Jane Wallis, SO Co., d. by 15 Sep 1693 when an inventory of her estate was filed. {INAC:12:23}

THE WILLIAM WALLACE FAMILY

1. WILLIAM WALLACE.

Rum Ridge was patented on 1 April 1680 for William Stevens for 300 a.

in Wicomico Hundred, and assigned it to Thomas Cox. The land belongs to Matthew Wallace who is now removed to Cecil County or thereabouts. {SORR} On 10 Nov 1696, William Wallace deeded to James Watts, *Rum Ridge* 300 a. {SOD:L:384}

 Great Neck was patented on 17 April 1695 by William Wallace for 100 a. {MPL:37:48}

 Golden Quarter was patented on 1 Jun 1695 by William Wallace for 100 a. {MPL:37:225}

 William Wallase[32], Sr., d. leaving a will dated 18 May 1698, proved on 15 June 1698. Legatees: brother James; brother Robert; cousin John Bound; cousin John son of Richard Wallace; cousin William Wallace & his brother Thomas Wallace & their sister Mary Wallace; cousin William Wallace, Jr. (under age 16); cousin Jane Macknitt. Executors: brother James, brother Robert. Witnesses: William Wallace, John Macknitt. {MWB:6:149} At August Court 1698, an admin bond was posted on his estate by James Wallace. Surety: John Macknitt. {TP:17:187} On 25 July 1698 the inventory of the estate of William Wallase, Sr. was filed. {INAC 16:218}

2. JAMES WALLACE, brother of William (1) Wallase.

 John Wallis, Sr., of Ireland and Monokin Rivers, SO Co., d. leaving a will dated 3 July 1685. To wife Jane, half of estate (personal). To nephew John Wallis, Jr., William Stevenson, Matthew and James Wallis, residue of estate. Exec. not named. {MWB 4:169}

 On 5 Aug 1695, James Wallace patented *Wallace's Adventure* for 200 a. In Nanticoke Hundred. {MPL:37:66}

 Alexander Kilock/Kellock, SO Co., d. by 19 March 1700 when an admin bond was posted on his estate by Hugh Stevenson. Surety: James Wallis. {TP:18B:70}

 On 6 April 1704, James Wallace deeded to George Smith, *Wallace's Adventure* 200 a. {SOD:CD:441}

3. ROBERT WALLACE, brother of William (1) Wallace and James (2) Wallace.

 Camp was patented on 10 April 1680 by Col. William Stevens for 300 a. {SORR}

 On 25 Nov 1695, George Layfield and his wife Elizabeth (extx. of Col. William Stevens) deeded to Robert Wallis, *Camp* 300 a. {SOD:L:311}

 The rent rolls, 1666-1723, show the tract *Camp* possessed by Richard Wallace (150 a.) and James Smith (150 a.). On 1 June 1718 John Holder, atty. of James Wallace, sold to James Smith. In 1718 James Smith willed all to sons

---

33. Misread or mis-recorded as Wallare in Baldwin's, *Calendar of Maryland Wills*.

David Smith and James Smith. On 23 Oct 1723 James Wallace of Cecil Co., MD, made over to Richard Wallace of SO Co. (bond). On 3 March 1741 James Smith gave to son Moses Smith 100 a. at the s. end being 1 moiety bought of Robert Wallace and made over by James Wallace his son. On 7 Sep 1744 Richard Wallace made over to son Thomas Wallace the right to bond of James Wallace. In 1754 Thomas Wallace willed 100 a. near *Golden Quarter* to daus. Agnes Wallace, Janet Donelson and Katherine Wallace, lands where I live (unnamed). On 14 Sep 1789 Elizabeth Wallace of DO Co. sold to Moses Claywell Smith of WO Co., 150 a. {WILR:53}

4. MATTHEW WALLACE, possible brother of William (1) Wallace, James (2) Wallace, and Robert (3) Wallace.

Rum Ridge was patented on 1 April 1680 for William Stevens for 300 a. in Wicomico Hundred, and assigned it to Thomas Cox. The land belongs to Matthew Wallace who is now removed to Cecil County or thereabouts. {SORR} On 10 Nov 1696, William Wallace deeded to James Watts, *Rum Ridge* 300 a. {SOD:L:384}

John Wallis, Sr., of Ireland and Monokin Rivers, SO Co., d. leaving a will dated 3 July 1685. To wife Jane, half of estate (personal). To nephew John Wallis, Jr., William Stevenson, Matthew and James Wallis, residue of estate. Exec. not named. {MWB 4:169}

On 31 Oct 1687, Phenix Hall and his wife Elizabeth conveyed to Matthew Wallace, *Friend's Denyall*. {SOD:MA:796}

Kirkmister was patented on 29 May 1689 by Matthew Wallace for 200 a. in Wicomico Hundred. Matthew Wallace deserted the country. He lives in the woods at the head of Delaware Bay. Land is not possessed. {SORR}

On 1 Dec 1707, Mathew Wallis (New Castle, DE) gave a power of attorney to his kinsman William Alexander, Jr. {SOD:CD:90}

On 10 March 1707, Mathew Wallis (New Castle, DE) conveyed to John Polke, *Friend's Denyall*. {SOD:CD:91}

In 1692 Matthew Wallis of Wiccocomoco was appointed as one of the persons to assist in the laying out of parishes in the county. {OSES:153}

John Wallis, son of Matthew and Elizabeth Wallis, b. 24 June 1687. {IKL}

At October Court 1700, an admin bond was posted on estate of William Carlyle by his administrator Alexander Carlyle. Sureties: George Hutchins, Mathew Wallice. {TP:18B:10}

On 6 Sep 1704 Mathew Wallis gives 20 head of cattle to son David Wallis and Richard Wallis, youngest son of Mathew Wallis. {ESVR 1:160}

Matthew was father of JOHN, b. 24 June 1687; DAVID; RICHARD.

THE RICHARD WALLACE FAMILY of Monie Hundred

1. RICHARD WALLACE[33], m. 1st (N), m. 2nd Grace White, dau. of John White.

William Wallase, Sr., d. leaving a will dated 18 May 1698, proved on 15 June 1698. Legatees: brother James; brother Robert; cousin John Bound; cousin John son of Richard Wallace; cousin William Wallace & his brother Thomas Wallace & their sister Mary Wallace; cousin William Wallace, Jr. (under age 16); cousin Jane Macknitt. Executors: brother James, brother Robert. Witnesses: William Wallace, John Macknitt. {MWB:6:149} At August Court 1698, an admin bond was posted on his estate by James Wallace. Surety: John Macknitt. {TP:17:187} On 25 July 1698 the inventory of his estate was filed. {INAC 16:218}

Father and Sons Desire was patented on 18 Nov 1699 by John White and Richard Wallace for 85 a. in Dames Quarter, in Annamessex Hundred. {SORR}

Friends Acceptance was patented on 13 Aug 1701 by Richard Wallace for 95 a. in now Dames Quarter Election District. On 13 July 1779 David Wallace gave to Richard Wallace 95 a. of *Friends Acceptance* with *Meadow, Dam Quarter, Father and Sons Desire*. In 1783 Mary Wallace and Margaret Wallace owned 25 a. On 29 July 1788 Richard Wallace and wife Rebecca sold to William Roberts all his rights. {SOLR:167}

John White, SO Co., d. leaving a will dated 5 July 1718, proved 20 Jan 1722-3. To son John, dwelling plantation _____ with land between Ball and Crab Creek and part of land bought with son-in-law Richard Wallace of Col. William Whittingham. To son Francis, plantation bought of James Watts and 100 a. *Instill*, at hd. of Dame Quarter Creek. To dau. Grace Wallace, 40 a. *Dame Quarter*, where she and her husband now live, between Williamson's and Crab Creeks, conditionally. To 5 daus., viz. Grace Wallace, Susannah Saser, Mary Urnser, Elizabeth Miller and Rebecca Urnser, 1 s. each. To grand-dau. Margaret Miller, personalty. To dau. Margart, residue of estate. {MWB 18:5}

Meadow was patented on 3 June 1721 by Richard Wallace for 50 a., bounding a tract belonging to said Wallace called *Friends Acceptance*. {SORR}

Owen Oday, SO Co., d. by 18 June 1731 when the inventory of his estate was filed by Richard Mitchell. Signed as next of kin: Richard Wallace, John Oday. {MINV 21:245}

The tax lists of SO Co. show Richard Wallace as head of household in Monie Hundred, 1723, 1724, 1727, 1730-1740, 1744. Living in the same household were Matthew Wallace (1723, 1724), Thomas Wallace (1723, 1724, 1727, 1730-1737); James Wallace (1727, 1730-1740); David Wallace (1730-

---

34. Richard Wallace is no doubt related to William Wallace (d. 1698). However, the exact relationship has not been determined.

1733); Charles Stewart (1739); slaves: Ceaser (1730-1740), Bess (1730-1737). {SOTL}

On 8 Oct 1738 Richard Wallace, Sr., assigned over to his son Thomas a bond from James Wallace on ½ of a tract called *Camp* lying at the head of the Rockwalkin River about 3 miles back in the woods from the creek of the said river where it makes into 2 branches. {SOD X:125}

In the will of Thomas Walker (dated and proved in 1744) he refers to Richard Wallas, of Dame's Quarter and land he has paid me for. {MWB 23:674-677}

Richard Wallace, SO Co., d. leaving a will dated 15 Feb 1744, proved 14 Oct 1745. To wife Grace Wallace, land lying between Crab Creek and Dam Quarter's Creek, during life. To daus. Mary Wallace and Margaret Wallace. To son James Wallace, pay to his bro. Richard Wallace, 10 pounds sterl. To son Thomas Wallace, 150 a. which lyeth in the forrest of Wikcomoco River, Somerset Co. To son Matthew Wallace, my land on S. W. side Crabb Creek. Children: John Wallace, Richard Wallace, Thomas Wallace, Elizabeth Lynn, James Wallace, David Wallace. To grand-son John Wallace, son of Oliver Wallace, 1 s. sterl. {MWB 24:225} On 26 March 1746 the inventory of his estate was filed by Matthew Wallace. Signed as next of kin: Mary Wallace, Margaret Wallace. {MINV 33:261} On 31 July 1747 the admin. account of his estate was submitted by Matthew Wallace, exec (acting). Payments to (1/3 each): Grace, Mary Wallace, Margarett Wallace. {MDAD 24:46}

The tax lists of SO Co. show Grace Wallace as head of household in Monie Hundred, 1748, 1750, 1753, 1754, 1757, 1759. Living in the same household were Samuel Wallace (1759). {SOTL}

In 1759, Grace Wallace paid tax on *Friend's Acceptance* 95 a., *Father & Sons* 51½ a., and *Dam Quarter* 40 a. {Debt Books}

Richard was father of MARY, b c1691; MARGARET; RICHARD; MATTHEW, b. c1700; THOMAS; JAMES, b. c1713; JOHN; ELIZABETH, m. (N) Lynn; DAVID.

Second Generation

2. MARY WALLACE, b. c1691, dau. of Richard (1) Wallace.

David Wallace (planter), SO Co., d. by 14 Aug 1745 when the inventory of his estate was filed by Teague Dickson. Signed as next of kin: Richard Wallace, Mary Wallace. {MINV 31:234}

3. RICHARD WALLACE, son of Richard (1) Wallace, m. Martha Samuels, dau. of Richard and Ann Samuels.

The tax lists of SO Co. show Richard Wallace as head of household in Monie Hundred, 1723, 1724. In 1724, he is cited as Richard Wallace, Jr. In 1727, he is cited as head of household in Manokin Hundred. In 1730-1740, 1744, 1748, he is cited as head of household in Nanticoke Hundred. {SOTL}

David Wallace (planter), SO Co., d. by 14 Aug 1745 when the inventory of his estate was filed by Teague Dickson. Signed as next of kin: Richard Wallace, Mary Wallace. {MINV 31:234}

The tract *Ware* was patented on 13 June 1674 by William Woodgate who assigned it to Richard Samuels, 300 a. In 1709 Richard Samuels willed land to son Richard and wife Isabell and son Peter Samuels. On 10 Nov 1729 Richard Samuels and wife Ann gave 16 a. to dau. Ann Phipps, wife of John Phipps, *New England*, out of tract *Ware*. On 15 Aug 1730 Peter Samuels and wife Hanna sold 140 a. to John Hopkins, now called *Hopkins Gift*. In 1732 Richard Samuels willed plantation to dau. Martha Samuels. On 18 Oct 1757 Martha Wallace, widow, and Richard Samuels Wallace, sold 145 a. to John Gupton, mariner, part that Richard Samuels gave to dau. Martha Samuels. {WILR:419}

Ann Samuels, Stepney Parish in Maryland, SO Co., d. leaving a will dated 18 April 1748, proved 10 May 1748. To grand-dau. Sarah Sammons, the dau. of Peter Samons, my son, furniture. To dau. Elizabeth Hopkins, 20 s. To dau. Sarah Watter (or Walter), 20 s. To dau. Martha Wallis, and her son Samuel Wallis, and her dau. Grace Wallis, equally, to be divided between the 3. {MWB 25:361}

The tax lists of SO Co. show Martha Wallace as head of household in Nanticoke Hundred, 1753, 1754, 1757. Living in her household was Richard Samuels Wallace (1753-1757).

Richard and Martha Wallace were the parents of: RICHARD SAMUELS, b. c1734/7; GRACE.

4. MATHEW WALLACE, b. c1700, son of Richard (1) Wallace, m 1st (N), m. 2nd Mary Jones, sister of George Jones. Mary m. 2nd 1 Aug 1762, Rencher Roberts, son of John Grandee and Elizabeth (Rencher) Roberts. His first wife was Mary Hopkins, dau. of John Hopkins. {ASOS:222}

The tax lists of SO Co. show Richard Wallace as head of household in Monie Hundred, 1723, 1724, 1727, 1730-1740, 1744. Living in the same household were Matthew Wallace (1723, 1724). The tax lists of SO Co., Monie Hundred, show Mathew Wallace as head of household, 1727, 1730-1740, 1744, 1748, 1750, 1753, 1754, 1757, 1759. Living in the same household were Samuell Rose (1735); William Waller (1738); David Haylor (1739); slaves: Sibb/Sibilla (1730-1740), Tom (1731-1740), Richard Wallace (1744). {SOTL}

John Waller, SO Co., d. by 16 Aug 1749, when an admin bond was posted by his admx. Mary Waller. Sureties: Mathew Wallace, John Wallace. {TP:33.1:44}

Mathew Wallace, aged 52, deposed on 14 Jan 1754 regarding the bounds of *James Delight*. Reference was made to his father Richard Wallace. Mathew Wallace, aged 59, deposed on 2 Sep 1756 regarding the bounds of *Davids Destiny*. {Miller:40}

In 1759, Matthew Wallace paid tax on *Contention* 36 a., *Gunner's Range* 64 a., *Golden Quarter* 53 a., *Long Delay* 53 a., *Meadow* 25 a., *Friend's Content* 67½ a. {Debt Books}

Matthew Wallace, SO Co., d. leaving a will dated 19 June 1761, proved 25 May 1762. To wife Mary Wallace, dwelling plantation and liberty of land in Rock Creek during her widowhood; the day of her marriage or death, to son Joseph Wallace; if he die without issue, to son David Wallace. To dau. Bridgett Reavell, son Richard Wallace, grand-son George Travis, son Matthew Wallace, son William Wallace, everyone of my children, 1 s. in silver. To dau. Mary Roe, 10 pounds. To dau. Elizabeth Travis, 10 pounds. To dau. Leah Wallace, a slave. To Ann Windsor, dau. of my wife, Mary Wallace, slaves. 4 children: Joseph, David, James and Mary Wallace. Wife, extx. {MWB 31:625}

At September Court 1761, William Wallace brought suit against Mary Wallace extx. of Matthew Wallace. He maintained that the will exhibited was not a valid will. Mary Wallace (spinster), age 70 deposed; Leah Wallace, age 18, deposed; Jabez Travers (husband of Elizabeth Wallace), age 26, deposed. {TP:38:205} At May Court 1762, the suit mentions: William Wallace as son of Matthew, Mary Wallace as widow of Matthew and mother-in-law of said William, Mary's son Joseph Wallace, Mary's daughter Leah Wallace, Leah's sister Betty Traverse, *Golden Quarter*, *Long Delay*, Mary Wallace as sister of George Jones. Said Mary said to said William Wallace: "Billy Wallace, you may go back to Dorchester Co." George Jones, age 54 deposed. Ruling: will found to be valid. {TP:38:356}

On 28 June 1762 the inventory of his estate was filed by Mary Wallace. Signed as next of kin: James Wallace, Margaret Wallace. {MINV 79:460} On 4 July 1763 a second inventory of his estate was filed. {MINV 81:164} The admin. account was submitted by Mary Roberts, wife of Rencher Roberts. Legatees: Jabus Travers, William Wallace, Nicholas Rowe, Leah Wallace, Bridget Revill. {MDAD 49:476}

Matthew was father of WILLIAM; RICHARD; JOSEPH; DAVID; BRIDGETT, m. (N) Revell; MATTHEW; MARY, m. (N) Roe; ELIZABETH, m. Jabez Travis; LEAH, b. c1743.

4. THOMAS WALLACE, son of Richard (1) Wallace.

The tax lists of SO Co. show Richard Wallace as head of household in Monie Hundred, 1723, 1724, 1727, 1730-1740, 1744. Living in the same household was Thomas Wallace (1723, 1724, 1727, 1730-1737). The tax lists of SO Co. show Thomas Wallace as head of his own household in Monie Hundred, 1738, 1739. Living in the household is slave Jean (1738), slave Bess (1739). {SOTL}

5. JAMES WALLACE, b. 1713, son of Richard (1) Wallace.

The tax lists of SO Co. show Richard Wallace as head of household in Monie Hundred, 1723, 1724, 1727, 1730-1740, 1744. Living in the same household were James Wallace (1727, 1730-1740). James Wallace is cited as head of household in Monie Hundred in 1744, 1748, 1750, 1753, 1754, 1757, 1759. {SOTL}

In 1759, James Wallace paid tax on *Meadow* 25 a., *Friend's Content* 67½ a. {Debt Books}

James Wallace, aged 53, deposed on 26 April 1766 regarding the bounds of *Wooledge*. {Miller:40}

Robert Hatton, age 43, c1767 swore that he heard James Wallise say that he gave a Negro girl named Fender and her increase to his dau. Sarah Wallace instead of a Negro boy named Bobb and Sarah agreed to take the Negro girl. {SOD D:82}

On 29 July 1788 Richard Wallace and wife Rebecca sold to William Roberts his rights to *Meadow* that descended to David Wallace, heir of James Wallace, dec'd., and willed by Richard Wallace to sons Matthew Wallace and James Wallace, father of David Wallace and conveyed by David to Richard Wallace. {SOLR:284}

James was father of DAVID; SARAH.

6. DAVID WALLACE, son of Richard (1) Wallace.

The SO Co. tax lists show David Wallace (Wallis) living in the household of Richard Wallace in Monie Hundred, 1730-1733, and as head of household, 1734-1740, 1744 in Nanticoke Hundred. {Russo}.

David Wallace (planter), SO Co., d. by 14 Aug 1745 when the inventory of his estate was filed by Teague Dickson. Signed as next of kin: Richard Wallace, Mary Wallace. {MINV 31:234} On 9 Aug 1746 the admin. account of his estate was submitted by Teague Dickeson, admin. Payments included widow (unnamed), 2 children (unnamed). {MDAD 22:356}

Third Generation

7. JOSEPH WALLACE, son of Matthew (3) Wallace.

Persons appointed to view the estate of the orphan, Joseph Wallace, son of Mathew Wallace - guardian is George Jones. They found the following: 1 dwelling house, 20 x 16, framed and covered with oak clapboards and weather boarded with oak clapboards - in middling good repair with the exception of the chimney which is a wood chimney that has been much damaged by fire, part of the loft covered with pine slabs; 421 panels of fence in middling good repair. Allowed the guardian to clear 5 a. of land to the easternmost side of the lands called *Golden Quarter* and *Long Delay* - the land being at Crab Creek now belonging to Joseph Wallace, 1 kitchen with 1 brick chimney covered with chestnut shingles and weather boraded with pine plank - the kitchen being 20 x 15 and much out of repair; 1 framed house 20 x 16 covered with pine plank and weather boarded with pine plank in middling good repari; 1 old milk house 14 x 9 covered and weather boarded with oak clapboards - very rotten and out of repair; 21 apple trees; 1 pear tree - the chief of them to be sorry old trees; 111 panels of middling good fence; 163 panels of very sorry rotten fence. The rent estimated at £2.10.0 exclusive of quit rents. {SOD D:103}

On 2 Sep 1742 Absalom Hobbs sold to Matthew Wallace for 5 shillings 106 a. of *Golden Quarter* and *Long Delay* now called *Hobbs His Choice*. On 8 Sep 1774 Joseph Wallace sold to Charles Hall 106 a. of the same. {SOLR:265}

On 8 Sep 1774 John White and wife Rebecca sold to Joseph Wallace 22 a. of *Friends Content*. {SOLR:169}

8. DAVID WALLACE, prob. son of Matthew (3) Wallace.

Mr. Nehemiah Bozman, SO Co., d. by 9 Jan 1772 when the inventory of his estate was filed by Nelly Bozman. Signed as next of kin: Thomas Bozman, David Wallace. {MINV 108:394}

David Wallace served as private in the Somerset Militia, Princess Anne Battn., Capt. Thomas Irving's Monie Company, 1780. {RPWS:117}

9. RICHARD WALLACE, prob. son of Matthew (3) Wallace, served as private in the Somerset Militia, Princess Anne Battn., Capt. Thomas Irving's Monie Company, 1780. {RPWS:317}

THE WILLIAM WALLACE FAMILY of Monie Hundred

1. WILLIAM WALLACE[34], m. Ellinor Laws, sister of Robert Laws.

William Wallase, Sr., d. leaving a will dated 18 May 1698, proved on 15 June 1698. Legatees: brother James; brother Robert; cousin John Bound; cousin John son of Richard Wallace; cousin William Wallace & his brother Thomas Wallace & their sister Mary Wallace; cousin William Wallace, Jr. (under age 16); cousin Jane Macknitt. Executors: brother James, brother Robert. Witnesses: William Wallace, John Macknitt. {MWB:6:149} At August Court 1698, an admin bond was posted on his estate by James Wallace. Surety: John Macknitt. {TP:17:187} On 25 July 1698 the inventory of his estate was filed. {INAC 16:218}

On 3 Jul 1698, William Wallace was one of the appraisers of the estate

35. William Wallace is no doubt related to William Wallace (d. 1698). However, the exact relationship has not been determined.

of Amos Persons[35]. {INAC:6:100}

On 17 April 1703, William Wallace and his wife Ellinor deeded to John Hall, *Golden Quarter* 100 a. {SOD:GI:48}

Peter Elzey, SO Co., d. by 26 Sep 1716, when an admin bond was posted on his estate by his executrices Frances Elzey and Elizabeth Elzey. Sureties: William Stoughton, William Wallace. {TP:23:110}

On 12 Aug 1721, Thomas Willson (KE Co., PA) and his sister Mary Manliffe deeded to William Wallace, *Middlesex* and *Tarrkill Hammock*. {SOD:IK:168}

On 18 Jan 1721, William Wallace deeded to William Stoughton, *Chance*. {SOD:IK:195}

The tax lists for Somerset County cite William Wallace as head of household in Nanticoke Hundred, 1724, 1727. {SOTL}

On 6 Oct 1729, William Wallace deeded to John Shockley, *Great Neck*. {SOD:SH:186}

William Wallace, SO Co., d. by 15 Nov 1727 when an admin bond was posted on his estate by Robert Laws and Thomas Laws administrators. Sureties: John Laws, George Bosman. {TP:28:127} On 30 Dec 1727 the inventory of his estate was filed by Robert Laws, Thomas Laws. Signed as next of kin: William Alexander, Catherine Alexander. {MINV 13:50} On 20 Sep 1732 the admin. account of his estate was submitted by Robert Laws, Thomas Laws, admin. Representatives: John, William, Robert, Thomas, George Wallace. {MDAD 11:546}

William was father of JOHN; WILLIAM; ROBERT; THOMAS; GEORGE, b. c1721.

Second Generation

2. JOHN WALLACE, son of William (1) Wallace, m. Eleanor Laws, dau. of Robert Laws.

The tax lists for Somerset County cite John Wallace as living in the household of Thomas Laws in Monie Hundred, 1730, 1731. John Wallace is cited as head of household in Monie Hundred, 1733-1739. John Wallace is cited as head of household in Nanticoke Hundred, 1740, 1744, 1748, 1750, 1753, 1754. Living in his household was Thomas Wallace (1736-1738). {SOTL}

Robert Laws, SO Co., d. leaving a will dated 6 April 1745, proved 21 March 1750. To son William, 200 a., a tract called *Taylor's Hill* in DO Co. To John Wallace, 1 shilling, in full of his dec'd. wife Eleanor's part of my estate. To sons Panter, exec., and William, personal estate. Witnessed by Robert Jones, Thomas Jones and Benjamin Jones. {MWB 27:525; SOW EB4:3}

John Waller, SO Co., d. by 16 Aug 1749, when an admin bond was

---

36. John Macknitt is the administrator of this estate.

posted by his admx. Mary Waller. Sureties: Mathew Wallace, John Wallace. {TP:33.1:44}

Wallaces Venture was patented in 1761 by John Wallace for 705 a. On 7 Sep 1764 William Walker and wife Ann sold to Hugh Porter and wife Elizabeth (settlement of boundaries) as Ann and Elizabeth are co-heirs of John Wallace. In 1788 Hugh Porter willed to wife Sarah Ann Porter and after death to grandson Francis Porter. On 15 May 1792 William Walker and wife Ann gave to son William Walker Jr. all interest and if no issue then to heirs of Winder Walker. In 1783 Hugh Porter owned 454 a. of the tract. On 16 March 1810 Francis Porter and wife Ann sold 8 a. to John Donoho. {WILR}

John was prob. father of ANN, m. William Walker; ELIZABETH, m. Hugh Porter.

3. WILLIAM WALLACE, son of William (1) Wallace.

The tax lists for Somerset County cite William Wallace in the household of John Laws in Monie Hundred, 1730, 1731. {SOTL}

4. ROBERT WALLACE, son of William (1) Wallace.

Robert Wallace was living in the household of James Martin, Pocomoke Hundred, 1733-1734, in the household of Robert Downs, Monie Hundred, 1735-1736, in the household of Robert Laws, Monie Hundred, 1737-1738. Also living in the household of Robert Laws was George Wallace, 1737-1738. Robert Wallace was head of household in Monie Hundred, 1739-1740, 1744. Living with him were George Wallace, 1739-1740 and Thomas Wallace in 1740.

Nelson Waller, WO Co., d. by 5 April 1755 when the inventory of his estate was filed by Ann Waller. Signed as next of kin: George Waller, Robert Wallace. {MINV 61:82}

5. THOMAS WALLACE, b. c1718, son of William (1) Wallace.

The tax lists of SO Co. show Thomas Wallace as living in the household of John Wallace in Monie Hundred, 1736-1739, and in the household of Robert Wallace in Monie Hundred, 1740. He is cited as head of his own household in Monie Hundred, 1740, 1744, 1748, 1753, 1757, 1759. In 1754, he is cited in the household of Samuel Jones. Living in the household is George Wallace (1744, 1748). {SOTL}

Thomas Wallace, aged 38, deposed on 24 July 1756 regarding the bounds of Something Worth and Sassers Folly and Roude. Note that George Wallice, aged 36 on 24 July 1756 also made statements re the bounds of Rowde, Something Worth and Sassers Folly. {Miller:40} [These are probably the same George and Thomas Wallis who appear in the tax lists in Nanticoke Hundred.]

6. GEORGE WALLACE, b. c1720, son of William (1) Wallace.

The tax lists of SOCo. show George Wallace living in the household of Robert Laws in Monie Hundred, 1737, 1738. George Wallace was living in the household of Robert Wallace in Monie Hundred, 1739, 1740. George Wallace was living in the household of Thomas Wallace in Monie Hundred, 1744, 1748. George Wallace is cited as head of household in Monie Hundred, 1750, 1753, 1754.

George Wallace of DO Co., whose uncle was Robt. Lawes, deposed at age 36 in 1756 re the bounds of *Something Worth, Sassers Folly* and *Rowde.*

THE THOMAS WALLACE FAMILY of Baltimore Hundred

1. THOMAS WALLACE, brother of William (1) Wallace of Monie Hundred, m. Jennet Campbell, widow of Peter Campbell. {INAC 16:218}

The tax lists of SO Co. show John Wallace & Thomas Wallace & John Stinson as head of household in Baltimore Hundred in 1723. Thomas Wallace is cited as head of household in 1724, 1727, 1730-1740. Living in the same household were Thomas Wallas (1735), Nathanill Juitt (1735), Urias Bowls (1735), Thomas Nugen (1738); slave Hector (1730-1734)

Peter Campbell, SO Co., d. leaving a will dated 10 Feb 1708/9, proved 18 March 1708/9. Legatees: son John, *Ripley*; his 4 sisters; wife Jennet. Executrix: wife Jennet. Overseer: brother-in-law William Pattin. {MWB:2-12:245} On 23 June 1709, an inventory was filed. {INAC:30:413} On 4 Nov 1710, Thomas Wallis who married the extx. of Peter Cambell was summoned. {TP:21:297} On 20 Aug 1726 the admin. account of his estate was submitted by Thomas Wallis, admin. {MDAD 8:34}

Robert Nicholas, SO Co., d. by 4 Aug 1714 when an admin bond was posted by William Mackcoye. Sureties: Thomas Wallace, John Whealler. {TP:22:378}

On 17 June 1719, Armwell Robert Vigerous and his wife Naomi deeded to Thomas Wallis, *Golden Quarter*. {SOD:IK:91}

Nathaniel Wale, SO Co., d. by 5 July 1728 when an admin bond was posted on his estate by William Wale executor. Sureties: Edward Franklyn, Thomas Wallace. {TP:28:243}

Robert Mills, SO Co., d. by 20 Aug 1729 when an admin bond was posted on his estate by Mary Mills. Sureties: Thomas Wallace, Samuel Adams. {TP:28:433}

In 1738 Thomas Wallace re-patented *Golden Quarter* for 100 a. On 4 Dec 1741 John Campbell and wife Mary traded to Thomas Wallace *Johnsons Folly*, part of *Golden Quarter* bequeathed him by Peter Campbell, for *Wallaces Chance, Golden Quarter* and *Ripple*. On 22 Aug 1755 Matthew Wallace of Kent

Co., DE, and wife Agnes Wallace, a dau. of Thomas Wallace, sold 100 a. to John Campbell. In 1754 Thomas Wallace willed to dau. Agnes Wallace the plantation I live on and to daus. Katherine Wallace and Janet Donelson, all other lands. On 28 March 1755 William Dunlap and wife Katherine Dunlap (formerly Katherine Wallace) sold to Samuel Donelson, Ripple and *Golden Quarter*. On 26 Nov 1756 Samuel Donelson and wife Janet sold to William Selby 350 a. of *Ripple, Golden Quarter*, and *Johnsons Folly*. {WOLR:260}

Thomas Wallace, WO Co., d. leaving a will dated 27 May 1754, proved 7 Dec 1754. To dau. Catherine Wallace, furniture. To grand-dau. Elizabeth Wallace, furniture. To 3 daus. Agnes, Jannet Donelson and Catherine Wallace. To Agnes Wallace, tract on sea board side head of a neck called *Golden Quarter* Neck of 100 a. To 2 daus. Jannet and Catherine, plantation. Dau. Catherine Wallace, extx. {MWB 29:253}

Thomas was father of CATHERINE, m. William Dunlap; AGNES, m. Matthew Wallace; JANNET, m. Samuel Donelson.

THE CATHERINE WALLACE FAMILY

1. CATHERINE WALLACE, prob. sister to William (1) Wallace of Monie Hundred, m. William Alexander, Jr.

Daintry was patented by John Parsons on 19 Jul 1677 for 150 a. It was possessed by John Parsons, but lately by William Alexander, Jr. who re-patented it in 1728 for 300 a. On 24 June 1736, Moses Alexander (clocksmith) son of William sold to Listian Alexander his interest in land of William Alexander. On 2 Nov 1738, Moses Alexander sold to Agnes Alexander 150 a. of *Daintry*, with part of *Trouble*. On 9 April 1745, Moses Alexander and his eldest son John Alexander (blacksmith) sold to Alexander Adams 230 a. of *Daintry* and *Trouble*. On 24 May 1749, John Laws and his wife Agnes sold to Thomas Pollitt 170 a. part of *Daintry* and *Trouble*, that Moses Alexander deeded to Agnes Alexander now Agnes Laws. {SOLR:113}

Hog Quarter was patented by William Alexander on 25 April 1689 for 100 a. It was possessed by William Alexander, Sr. On 2 May 1749, Moses Alexander sold to John Alexander 100 a. In 1749, John Alexander patented *Addition to Hog Quarter* for 446 a. On 6 Aug 1751, John Alexander and his wife Mary sold to William Jones, *Addition to Hog Quarter*, 446 a. {SOLR:215}

On 5 Nov 1687, Cornelius Anderson sold to William Alexander, *Hunting Quarter* 100 a. On 2 May 1749, Moses Alexander gave to his son Samuel Alexander, *Hunting Quarter*. On 21 March 1751, Samuel Alexander (wheelwright) sold to John Dorman, *Hunting Quarter*. {SOLR:227}

On 1 Dec 1707, Mathew Wallis (New Castle, DE) gave a power of attorney to his kinsman William Alexander, Jr. {SOD:CD:90}

The tax lists for Somerset County cite William Alexander as head of household in Wicomico Hundred, 1724, 1727, 1730, 1731, 1733, 1734. Living in his household are: James Alexander (1727, 1730, 1731, 1733), Listian Alexander (1731, 1733, 1734).

Catherine Alexander and William Alexander signed as next of kin the inventory of the estate of William Wallace which was filed on 3 Dec 1727 by Robert Laws. {MDAD 11:546}

William Alexander, SO Co., d. leaving a will dated 7 March 1732, proved 18 June 1735. Legatees: wife Catherine, extx., plantation; son Samuel, executor; son Moses, land; son James, land, son Listian, *Trouble*; daughter Agnes. Mentions: father William. {SOW:EB#9:174} William Alexander made a second will dated 21 March 1734, proved 19 July 1735. Legatees: son James, *Dantry*; son Moses, *Hogg Quarter*; dau. Agnes; Mary dau. Moses Alexander, her sister Elizabeth; dau. Mary Mills. {SOW:EB#9:177} On 10 Nov 1735, an inventory was made of his estate. Signed as next of kin: Moses Alexander, Agnes Alexander. Executor: Listian Alexander. {MINV:21:223} On 29 Jul 1737, admin accounts were filed. Payments to (in equal amounts): Moses Alexander, Agnes Alexander, Listian Alexander (accountant), James Alexander (now dec'd.'). Legatees: Mary Alexander, Mary Mills, Agnes Alexander, Elizabeth Alexander. Executor (surviving): Listian Alexander. {MDAD:14:350}

9 April 1745. As William Alexander was m. to Catharine Wallace and has several children and all his sons d. childless except his second son Moses Alexander. {SOLR:113}

William and Catherine were the parents of: SAMUEL ALEXANDER; MOSES ALEXANDER; JAMES ALEXANDER; LISTIAN ALEXANDER; AGNES ALEXANDER; MARY ALEXANDER, m. (N) Mills.

Second Generation

2. SAMUEL ALEXANDER, son of Catherine (1) Wallace and William Alexander.

The tax lists for Somerset County cite Samuel Alexander as head of household in Wicomico Hundred, 1724, 1727, 1730, 1731.

3. MOSES ALEXANDER, son of Catherine (1) Wallace and William Alexander, m. 1st (N), m. 2nd Elizabeth widow of James Weatherly.

Daintry was patented by John Parsons on 19 Jul 1677 for 150 a. It was possessed by John Parsons, but lately by William Alexander, Jr. who re-patented it in 1728 for 300 a. On 24 June 1736, Moses Alexander (clocksmith) son of William sold to Listian Alexander his interest in land of William Alexander. On 2 Nov 1738, Moses Alexander sold to Agnes Alexander 150 a. of *Daintry*, with part of *Trouble*. On 9 April 1745, Moses Alexander and his eldest son John Alexander (blacksmith) sold to Alexander Adams 230 a. of *Daintry* and *Trouble*. On 24 May

1749, John Laws and his wife Agnes sold to Thomas Pollitt 170 a. part of Daintry and Trouble, that Moses Alexander deeded to Agnes Alexander now Agnes Laws. {SOLR:113}

The tax lists for Somerset County cite Moses Alexander as head of household in Wicomico Hundred, 1724, 1727, 1730-1731, 1734-1740, 1744, 1748, 1750. Moses Alexander is cited as head of household in Nanticoke Hundred in 1733. Living in his household are: James Weatherly (1733), John Hodge (1736), John Polke (1739), John Alexander (1740, 1744), Samuel Alexander (1744, 1748), John Jurden (1750), slave Tom (1734-1740).

Listian Alexander, SO Co., d. leaving a will dated 20 March 1737, proved 23 Jul 1738. Legatees: William (under age 21) son of Moses Alexander, *Trouble, Daintry*; cousin Alexander Mills; sister Agnes, extx. {MWB:EB#9:203}

On 17 Jul 1741, Moses Alexander and his wife Elizabeth, extx. of James Weatherly, filed additional admin accounts on estate of said Weatherly. {MDAD:18:241}

Moses is the father of: JOHN ALEXANDER, m. Mary (N); SAMUEL ALEXANDER; MARY ALEXANDER; ELIZABETH ALEXANDER.

4. JAMES ALEXANDER, son of Catherine (1) Wallace and William Alexander.

The tax lists for Somerset County cite William Alexander as head of household in Wicomico Hundred, 1724, 1727, 1730, 1731, 1733, 1734. Living in his household are: James Alexander (1727, 1730, 1731, 1733). James Alexander is cited as head of household in 1734. Living in his household is: John Hodge (1734).

James Alexander, SO Co., d. leaving a will dated 30 March 1735, proved 18 June 1735. Legatees: brother Listian, land, executor: sister Agnes, executrix; brother Moses; sisters Mary Mills, Agnes. Mentions: Samuel son of brother Moses. {MWB:21:392}

5. LISTIAN ALEXANDER, son of Catherine (1) Wallace and William Alexander.

The tax lists for Somerset County cite William Alexander as head of household in Wicomico Hundred, 1724, 1727, 1730, 1731, 1733, 1734. Living in his household were: Listian Alexander (1731, 1733, 1734). Listian Alexander is cited as head of household in 1735-1737. Living in his household was John Hodge (1735).

Listian Alexander, SO Co., d. leaving a will dated 20 March 1737, proved 23 Jul 1738. Legatees: William (under age 21) son of Moses Alexander, *Trouble, Daintry*; cousin Alexander Mills; sister Agnes, extx. {SOW EB#9:203}

6. AGNES ALEXANDER, dau. of Catherine (1) Wallace and William Alexander, m. John Laws.

On 2 Nov 1738, Moses Alexander sold to Agnes Alexander 150 a. of *Daintry*, with part of *Trouble*. On 9 April 1745, Moses Alexander and his eldest son John Alexander (blacksmith) sold to Alexander Adams 230 a. of *Daintry* and *Trouble*. On 24 May 1749, John Laws and his wife Agnes sold to Thomas Pollitt 170 a. part of *Daintry* and *Trouble*, that Moses Alexander deeded to Agnes Alexander now Agnes Laws. {SOLR:113}

The tax lists for Somerset County cite Agnes Alexander as head of household in Wicomico Hundred, 1738. Living in his household was Jonathon Carey (1738).

7. MARY ALEXANDER, dau. of Catherine (1) Wallace and William Alexander, m. Robert Mills.

The tax lists for Somerset Co. cite Robert Mills as head of household in Pocomoke Hundred in 1724 and 1727. {SOTL}

Robert Mills, SO Co., d. by 13 March 1729 when an inventory was made of his estate. Signed as next of kin: John Mills, William Mills. Admx.: Mary Mills. {MINV:15:414} On 18 Aug 1731, admin accounts were filed by Mary Mills. {MDAD:11:188}

The tax lists for Somerset Co. cite Mary Mills (widow) as head of household in Pocomoke Hundred in 1730, 1731, 1733-1735. Living in her household were: Moses Mills (1731, 1733, 1735), Smith Mills (1733-1735), Roger Taylor (1733-1735), slave Hector (1730, 1731), slave Simon (1734-1735). {SOTL}

The tax lists for Somerset Co. cite Moses Mills as head of household in Pocomoke Hundred in 1736-1740. Living in his household were: Alexander Mills (1740). {SOTL}

In his will dated 20 March 1737, proved 23 July 1738, Listian Alexander named his sister Agnes as extx. {MWB:EB#9:203}

Robert and Mary were the parents of: MOSES MILLS; SMITH MILLS, d. 1757, m. Mary (N); ALEXANDER MILLS, d. 1761, m. Elizabeth (N); ROBERT MILLS.

THE JANE WALLIS FAMILY

1. JANE WALLIS[36], m. John Macknitt.

Jane Wallis m. 28 March 1693, John McKnitt by Mr. Burnett. {IKL}

James Smith, SO Co., d. by 18 Sep 1695, when admin accounts were filed on his estate. Payments to: John MacKnitt, et.al. Administratrix: Meriam Smith. {INAC:10:391}

William Wallase, Sr., d. leaving a will dated 18 May 1698, proved on 15 June 1698. Legatees: brother James; brother Robert; cousin John Bound; cousin John son of Richard Wallace; cousin William Wallace & his brother Thomas Wallace & their sister Mary Wallace; cousin William Wallace, Jr. (under age 16); cousin Jane Macknitt. Executors: brother James, brother Robert. Witnesses: William Wallace, John Macknitt. {MWB:6:149} At August Court 1698, an admin bond was posted on his estate by James Wallace. Surety: John Macknitt. {TP:17:187} On 25 July 1698 the inventory of his estate was filed. {INAC 16:218}

Amos Parsons, SO Co., d. by 29 Oct 1698, when admin accounts were filed on his estate. Administrator: John MacKnitt. {INAC:17:131}

Edward Bennett, SO Co., d. by 22 Nov 1707, when admin accounts were filed on his estate. Payments to: John Macknett, et.al. {INAC:28:8}

Alexander Kellock, SO Co., d. by 16 Apr 1710, when admin accounts were filed on his estate. Payments to: John McNitt, et.al. Administrator: Hugh Stevenson. {INAC:31:247}

William Russell, SO Co., d. by 29 Aug 1711, when an inventory was made of his estate. Debtor: John Macknett, et.al. {INAC:34:185}

Capt. John King, SO Co., d. by 2 Nov 1711, when admin accounts were filed on his estate. Payments to: John Macknett, et.al. {INAC:32C:172}

James Gray, SO Co., d. by 3 Jul 1712, when admin accounts were filed on his estate. Payments to: John Macknett, et.al. {INAC:33B:180}

John Crapper, SO Co., d. by 29 Jan 1723, when admin accounts were filed on his estate. Payments to: John Macknett, et.al. {MDAD:5:370}

---

37. Jane Wallace is no doubt related to William Wallace (d. 1698). However, the exact relationship has not been determined.

198

Unplaced

CHARLES WALLISS
 The tax lists of SO Co. show Charles Walliss as head of household in 1738 in Nanticoke Hundred. {SOTL}

GEORGE WALLACE.
 Daniel Kelly, WO Co., d. leaving a will dated 4 Jan 1769, proved 4 Feb 1769. Wife: Elizabeth. To Joseph Kelley Volx son of Year Volx, George Kelly, John Kelly, Daniel, son of John Kelly, William Kelly, Barsheba Williams, Warrenton Volx. Tracts: *Draw Forward* and *Convenancy*. Wife Elizabeth and George Wallace, execs. {MWB 37:106} George Wallace refused administration. {WOW:JW#3:192}

HUGH WALLACE m. Mary Selby, widow of Philip Selby.
 Moses Petitt, WO Co., d. by 4 Oct 1765, when an admin bond was posted for his estate. Administrators: John Mitchel, Esmey Bailey, Hugh Wallace. Sureties: Isaac Morris, James Round. {TP:41:245}
 Michael Leonard, WO Co., d. by 21 April 1767, when an admin bond was posted on his estate. Administrator: James Houston. Sureties: Esmy Bayly, Hugh Wallis. {TP:42:105}
 Philip Selby, WO Co., d. by 14 Oct 1768 when the distribution of his estate was made by Mary Wallace, wife of Hugh Wallace, extx., residue to (equally): Mary (widow), Daniel (son), Philip (son). {BFD 5:173}
 Andrew Smyly, WO Co., d. by 3 Dec 1768, when an admin bond was posted on his estate. Administrator: Samuel Smyly. Sureties: Nathaniel Ramsey, Hugh Wallace. {TP:43:8}
 Gideon Jones, WO Co., d. by 28 May 1773, when an admin bond was posted on his estate. Administrator: Fisher Walton. Sureties: Hugh Wallace, John Purnell Robins. {TP:45:178}
 Elijah Mitchell, WO Co., d. by 10 March 1775, when an admin bond was posted on his estate. Administrator: James Houston. Sureties: John Done, Hugh Wallace. {TP:46:217}
 James Buchanan, WO Co., d. by 23 Feb 1776, when an admin bond was posted on his estate. Administrators: Mary Buchanan, John Mitchel. Sureties: Hugh Wallace, Samuel Smyly. {TP:47:33}
 Hugh Wallace d. leaving a will dated 23 April 1777, proved 16 Aug 1777. To wife Negroes Abraham, Dinah, Hannah, Guy, upon wife paying to my sister Ann Scott the appraised value of the Negroes. To sister Ann Scott, rest of estate. Execs. Capt. Thomas Martin, Moses Scott and wife Mary. Witnessed by John Milbourne, Levin Hill, Lemuel Johnson. {WOW JW4 Part II:360}

JAMES WALLACE served as private in the Somerset Militia, Princess Anne Batth., Capt. Thomas Irving's Monie Company, 1780. {RPWS:317}

JAMES WALLACE.
The tax lists for Somerset County cite James Wallace in the household of James Caldwell in Nanticoke Hundred, 1724. {SOTL}

JOHN WALLACE, m. Mary Givan, dau. of Robert Givan. Mary m. 2nd John Johnson and m. 3rd Henry Ackworth.{See The Givans Family, vol. 15 of this series and The Ackworth Family, vol. 8.}
Mr. John Wallace, SO Co., d. by 1 March 1734/5 when an admin bond was posted on his estate (as John Wallas) by Mary Wallas. Surety: John Gray. {TP:30:20} On 30 July 1735 the inventory of his estate was filed by Mary Wallace. Signed as next of kin: Richard Wallace, Richard Wallace, Jr. {MINV 21:115}
Robert Givan, Stepney Parish, SO Co., d. leaving a will dated 29 May 1735, proved 4 Oct 1735. To son Robert, exec, dwelling plantation with tracts belonging to it, viz.: 150 a. *White Marsh's Delight* (divided from James Givan's by a ditch), 100 a. *Addition*, 7 a. of William Farrington's tract *Beginning*, 6 a. *Addition* being part of *Lyon's Lott*, 100 a. *Den Pasture* on Nanticoke River; and personalty. To son Thomas, 181 a. *Inclosed*, 72 a. *Cypress Swamp*; and personalty. To son George, part of *Cypress Swamp*, part of 100 a. adjacent thereto; and personalty. To son Day, the plantation lying below the small branch, part of *Cypress Swamp*; and personalty. To daus. Jean wife of Robert Smith, Marion wife of Adam Bell, and Katherine, personalty. To dau. Mary Wallace, personalty and 21 pounds due from estate of John Wallace. Should sons George or Day die during minority, survivor to inherit portion of deceased. To children Robert, Thomas, George, Day, Mary Wallace and Katherine, residue of estate. 100 a. White Oak Swamp to be sold for benefit of estate. {MWB 21:451}
William Givan (gentleman), SO Co., d. by 15 Dec 1735 when the inventory of his estate was filed by Robert Givan. Signed as next of kin: Thomas Givan, Mary Wallis. {MINV 21:220}

OLIVER WALLACE.
Oliver was father of JOHN. {John is cited in will of Richard Wallace (d. 1745) as his grandson, son of Oliver.}

RICHARD WALLIS m. Esther (N) who later m. John Fletcher.
The tax lists of Somerset County show Richard Wallis as head of household in Wicomico Hundred in 1730, 1731, 1733. He is head of household in Nanticoke Hundred in 1734-1739, 1748, 1750, 1753, 1754. Living in his household is: Isaac Stevens (1731), Henry Oday (1735, 1738).
On 19 Dec 1733 Andrew Scott sold to Richard Wallace a part of the

tract *Caldwells Lott*. In 1763 Richard Wallace (wife Esther) willed to Hudson Lowe 100 a. he purchased of me on the s. side of *Caldwells Lott*. On 13 July 1768 John Fletcher and wife Esther sold to Hudson Lowe 100 a. (as Richard Wallace willed to Esther Wallace, his then wife, extx. with power to make over to Hudson Lowe). {WILR:51}

In 1759, Richard Wallis paid tax on *Caldwell's Lott* 200 a. {Debt Books}

Richard Wallis, SO Co., d. leaving a will dated 20 Jan 1763, proved 19 June 1764. To wife Esther Wallis, 35 pounds money to make over to Hudson Lowe, 1,000 a. of my lands which he and I have bargained for already, adj. lands lying on the south end of a tract called *Caldwell's Lott*. Easter Wallis made her election. {MWB 32:283}

ROBERT WALLACE.

The tax lists for Somerset County cite Robert Wallace as living in the household of James Martin in Pocomoke Hundred, 1733, 1734. {SOTL}

SAMUEL WALLACE m. Priscilla who later m. Peter Highway.

On 5 Sep 1752 Powell Patey, yeoman, and wife Rachel sold 200 a. of *Pateys Folly* to Samuel Wallace. In 1750 *Pateys Folly Rectified* was patented by Samuel Wallace for 326 a. In 1756 it was re-surveyed to *Masseys Chance*. On 11 March 1763 Samuel Holloway and wife Jerusha (formerly Jerusha Wallace, dau. of Samuel) sold to Joshua Holloway 100 a. of *Pateys Folly*. On 1 June 1765 Joshua Holloway and Jerusha Holloway, dau. of Samuel, sold to Joshua Rogers 100 a. that Samuel Wallace left to two daus. On 20 Feb 1770 Cornelius Evans and wife Desire sold 100 a. to Richard Tull. On 12 May 1770 John Evans and wife Sarah sold to Solomon Rogers. {WOLR:466}

Mr. Samuel Wallis (also Samuel Wallace), WO Co., d. by 12 April 1753 when the inventory of his estate was filed by Priscilla Hinary [Hiway] (late Priscilla Wallace). {MINV 55:154} Samuel Wallace, WO Co., d. by 8 Nov 1754 when the admin. account of his estate was submitted by Priscilla Highway, admx., wife of Peter Highway. Payments included widow (acct. 1/3), residue to children: Jernsha Wallace, Desire Wallace. {MDAD 36:509}

Samuel was father of JERUSHA, m. Samuel Holloway; DESIRE, m. Cornelius Evans.

THE JAMES WILLIS FAMILY

1. JAMES WILLIS, m. 13 March 1679 Rebecca Barnaby, dau. of James Barnaby. They were married by David Richardson, clerk. {IKL}

James Willis recorded his cattle mark in SO Co. on 30 July 1680. {ARMD LIV:775}

Barnabys Lott was patented on 12 March 1663 by James Barnaby for 200 a. In 1667 he willed it to son James. Mary Barnaby, widow, m. Edward Jones. The rent rolls of 1666-1723 show *Barnabys Lott* owned by John Henderson who m. Elizabeth Barnaby, 146 a.; and James Willis who m. Rebecca Barnaby, 54 a. On 26 Aug 1727 Barnaby Willis and Collebrah Willis his wife sold to William Turpin, 32 a. taken out of *Barnabys Lott* and *Willises Choice*. On 14 Sep 1736 John Henderson Sr. and wife Elizabeth gave to Barnaby Willis 200 a. On 7 Jan 1772 Jabez Willis (eldest son of William Willis) sold to James Willis part of *Barnabys Lott* and *Envy*. On 6 March 1772 James Willis sold to Thomas Seon 8 a. of *Barnabys Lott* and part of *Envy*. In 1783 James Willis owned 30 ½ a. of *Barnabys Lott*. {SOLR:27}

James Willis, son of James and Rebecca Willis, b. at Manokin, 25 May 1680. {IKL}

Sarah Willis, dau. of James and Rebecca Willis, b. at Back Creek 24 May 1689. {IKL}

Rebecca Willis, dau. of James and Rebecca Willis, b. at Back Creek 30 Jan 1691. {IKL}

Mary Willis, dau. of James and Rebecca Willis, b. at Back Creek 15 July 1694. {IKL}

Barnaby Willis, son of James and Eleanor Willis, b. 1 March 1696. {SOSO}

James and Rebecca were parents of JAMES, b. 25 May 1680; SARAH, b. 24 May 1689; REBECCA, b. 30 Jan 1691; MARY, b. 15 July 1694.

James and Eleanor were the parents of BARNABY, b. 1 March 1696. {SOSO}

Second Generation

2. JAMES WILLIS, son of James (1) Willis.

On 18 Jan 1716, James Willis witnessed the will of Lazarus Maddox. {SOW:EB#9:62}

The tax lists for SO Co. cite him as head of household in Manokin Hundred for 1723. After that, he disappears from the records.

3. BARNABY WILLIS, son of James (1) Willis, m. Collebrah (N).

Barnaby Willis is shown as head of household in the tax lists of SO Co., Manokin Hundred, 1723, 1724, and 1725, 1727, 1730-40, 1744, 1748, 1750, 1753, 1757, 1759. Living in the same household were Joseph Walston (1736), Wilson Dorman (1736-1740), William Willis (1744, 1748), James Willis (1753, 1757, 1759), Barnaby Hammon (1757, 1759). In 1754, Barnaby Willis is cited in the household of William Willis.

John Dorman, SO Co., d. by 4 April 1724 when the inventory of his estate was filed by Barnaby Willis. Signed as next of kin: Samuel Dorman, Robert

Melvin. {MINV 10:56} On 2 April 1735? the admin. account of his estate was submitted by Barnaby Willis, admin. {MDAD 6:340}

Barnaby Willis patented *Good Luck* (50 a.) in SO Co. in 30 June 1741. {MPL EI5:563; EI6:458}

On 27 Feb 1745, Barnaby Willis witnessed the will of William Miles. {SOW:EB#9:265}

On 28 March 1757 Thomas Seon and wife Jane sold to James Willis 9 ½ a. of *Invey* (*Envy*) that Barnaby Willis, father of James, gave to Thomas Seon. On 7 Jan 1772 Jabez Willis, eldest son of William Willis, sold to James Willis, all of *Banarbys Lott* and *Envy*. On 6 March 1772 James Willis sold to Thomas Seon 2 a. {SOLR:233}

Barnaby Willis paid tax in 1759 on pt. *Barnaby's Lott* (40¼ a.), *Good Luck* (15 a.), and *Littleworth* (6 a.).

Barnaby was father of WILLIAM; JAMES.

Third Generation

4. WILLIAM WILLIS, son of Barnaby (3) Willis, m. Tabitha (N).

William Willis is shown in the household of Barnaby Willis in Manokin Hundred in 1744, 1748. William Willis is cited as head of household in Manokin Hundred in 1750, 1753, 1754, 1757, 1759. Living in the same household in 1754 is Barnaby Willis and James Willis.

Mr. William Willis (also William Williss), SO Co., d. by 17 Oct 1769 when the inventory of his estate was filed by Tabitha Williss. Signed as next of kin: James Willis, Willson Dormond. {MINV 102:202}

The admin. account was submitted by Tabitha Willis, widow. Distribution to accountant (1/3) with residue to Jabus, William, James, Sarah, Tabitha, Elijah, Grace Willis.

On 9 Oct 1770 distribution of his estate was made by Mrs. Tabitha Willis, admx., to widow (unnamed, 1/3), residue to children (equally): Jabus, William, James, Sarah, Tabitha, Elijah, Grace. {BFD 5:377}

William was father of JABUS; WILLIAM; JAMES; SARAH; TABITHA, m. William Tilghman; ELIJAH; GRACE.

5. JAMES WILLIS, son of Barnaby (3) Willis.

James Willis is shown in the household of Barnaby Willis in the tax lists of SO Co., Manokin Hundred, 1753, 1757, 1759. In 1754, James Willis is cited in the household of William Willis.

On 28 March 1757 Thomas Seon and wife Jane sold to James Willis 9 ½ a. of *Invey* (*Envy*) that Barnaby Willis, father of James, gave to Thomas Seon. On 7 Jan 1772 Jabez Willis, eldest son of William Willis, sold to James Willis, all of *Banarbys Lott* and *Envy*. On 6 March 1772 James Willis sold to Thomas Seon 2 a. {SOLR:233}

James Willis paid tax in 1759 on *Good Luck* (53 a.) and pt. *Envy* (9½ a.).

James Willis served as private, Somerset Militia, Princess Anne Battn., Capt. Isaac Handy's Great Annemessix Company, 1780. He was drafted from SO Co. to serve in the Continental Army but was subsequently excused. {RPWS:337}

On the 1783 Assessment for SO Co., James Willis is cited in Manokin Hundred, with no land, with 2 male and 2 female inhabitants in his household.

Fourth Generation

6. JABEZ (Jabus) WILLIS, son of William (4) Willis, m. 23 Feb 1774, Elizabeth Fleming.{SOCO}

On 14 March 1772 Thomas Barns and wife Rebecca sold to Jabez Willis, 35 a. of *Donohoes Choice*. On 14 April 1790 Jabez Willis and wife Elizabeth sold part of the tract to Robert White. On the same day they sold part of the tract to Thomas Dryden. {WOLR:184}

Amarithy Willis, dau. of Jabez and Elizabeth Willis, b. 25 May 1775. {SOCO}

Charlotte Willess, dau. of Jabez and Elizabeth Willes, b. 4 Oct 1777. {SOCO}

Salley Willess, dau. of Jabez and Elizabeth Willess, b. 23 April 1780. {SOCO}

Joshua Willess, son of Jabez and Elizabeth Willess, b. 26 Feb 1783. {SOCO}

Jabez Willis served as private, Worcester Militia, Wicomico Battn., Capt. Philip Quinton's Company, 15 July 1780. {RPWS:3337}

On the 1783 Assessment for WO Co., Jabez Willis is cited in Pocomoke Hundred, paying tax on pt. *Donahoes Choice* (150 a.), *Johns Luck* (37 a.), pt. *Donahoes Choice* (10 a.), with 4 male & 5 female inhabitants in his household.

Jabez and Elizabeth were parents of AMARITHY, b. 25 May 1775; CHARLOTTE, b. 4 Oct 1777; SALLEY, b. 23 April 1780; JOSHUA, b. 26 Feb 1783.

7. WILLIAM WILLIS, son of William (4) Willis.

William Willis served as private, Worcester Militia, Wicomico Battn., Capt. Philip Quinton's Company, 15 July 1780.

8. TABITHA WILLIS, dau. of William (4) Willis, m. 13 Sep 1774, William Tilghman. {SOCO}

THE NATHANIEL WILLIS FAMILY

1. NATHANIEL WILLIS

Nathaniel Willis was head of household in Wicomico Hundred, 1734-1740. Living in the same household were William Savage (1739) and Edmund Willis (1740).

On 6 Dec 1742 Henry Toadvine and wife Alice sold to Nathaniel Willis 75 a. of *Arabia* on e. side of the main branch of the Wicomico River. On 7 May 1768 Benjamin Willis sold to Elijah Shockley. On 4 March 1771 John Willis and wife Betty and Benjamin Willis, sons of Nathaniel Willis sold to Joseph Dashiell 75 a. {WILR:18}

Nathaniel Willis patented the following tracts in WO Co.: *Hobson's Choice* (50 a.) on 10 May 1758; *Tit for Tat* (50 a.) on 11 Sep 1759. {MPL BC8:505; BC10:630: BC11:127; BC12:169}

Nathaniel Willis, planter, WO Co., d. leaving a will dated 10 Jan 1761, proved 3 March 1761. To son John Willis, 50 a. where he now lives, called *Prosperity*. To son Nathaniel Willis, 50 a. called *Hobson's Choice*. To son James Willis, 100 a. called *Lost*. To son Ovel [Abel] Willis, stock. To son Elijah Willis, 50 a. called *Tettfortat*. To son Benjamin Willis, dwelling plantation, 75 a. To dau. Ann Mary Willis, cattle. Mentions my 7 children: John, Nathaniel, James, Able, Elijah, Benjamin and Ann Mary Willis. Wife Mary Willis, extx. {MWB 31:231}

On 21 March 1761 the inventory of his estate was filed by Nathaniel Willis. Signed as next of kin: John Willis, James Willis. {MINV 73:236} On 6 July 1763 the second inventory was filed by Nathaniel Willis. {MINV 81:151}

The admin. account was submitted by Nathaniel Willis on 6 July 1763. Mentions widow (unnamed), now dead. Legatees (children): John Willis, Abel, Ann Mary. Distribution to (in equal parts) son John Willis, accountant, James Willis, Abell Willis, Elijah Willis, Ann Mary Willis, son (unnamed, infant). {MDAD 49:467}

Nathaniel was father of JOHN; NATHANIEL; JAMES; ABLE; ELIJAH; BENJAMIN; ANN MARY; poss. EDMUND, b. c1723.

Second Generation

2. JOHN WILLIS, son of Nathaniel (1) Willis, m. Betty (N).

On 6 Dec 1742 Henry Toadvine and wife Alice sold to Nathaniel Willis 75 a. of *Arabia* on e. side of the main branch of the Wicomico River. On 7 May 1768 Benjamin Willis sold to Elijah Shockley. On 4 March 1771 John Willis and wife Betty and Benjamin Willis, sons of Nathaniel Willis sold to Joseph Dashiell 75 a. {WILR:18}

John Willis patented the following tracts in WO Co.: *Prosperity* (50 a.) On 18 May 1758. {MPL BC8:447; BC11:120}

John Willis served as private, Worcester Militia, Sinepuxent Battn.,

Capt. Thomas Purnell's Company, 1779/1780. {RPWS:337}

3. NATHANIEL WILLIS, son of Nathaniel (1) Willis, prob. m. Mary (N).

Nathaniel Willis patented the following tracts in WO Co.: *Tull's Knavery* (95 a.) on 23 Aug 1773. {MPL BC8:505; BC10:630: BC11:127; BC12:169; BC44:213; BC45:232}

Nathaniel Willis made purchases at Nelms' store in Salisbury in 1765. Mary Willis maintained an account at the store, 1775-1787. {Nelms:86}

Nathaniel Willis, WO Co., d. by 10 Aug 1774 when the inventory of his estate was filed by Mary Willis. Signed as next of kin: Abel Willis, Benjamin Willis. {MINV 123:158}

4. JAMES WILLIS, son of Nathaniel (1) Willis.

James Willis maintained an account at Nelms' store in Salisbury, 8 Jan 1767 - 9 Nov 1768. He received credit for 3 mos. and 20 ½ days work for Nelms at 20 shillings per month and made 14 weavers slays for Nelms for credit of £5.1.8. He did work for Hieron Reddish and Nathan Culver and paid on account of Nathaniel Willis. {Nelms:86}

5. ABEL WILLIS, son of Nathaniel (1) Willis.

Abel Willis maintained an account at Nelms's store in Salisbury, 7 Jan 1767 - 6 July 1787. In 1786 he was charged 12 shillings, 6 pence for renting Nelms' horse for 5 weeks. He gave a note for 17 shillings, 5 pence in 1787. Nelms:85}

Abel Willis served as private, Worcester Militia, Wicomico Battn., Capt. Elijah Shockley's Company, 15 July 1780. {RPWS:336}

6. BENJAMIN WILLIS, son of Nathaniel (1) Willis, m. Betty Benson.

Benjamin Willis maintained an account at Nelms' store in Salisbury, 1765 - 11 Aug 1787. In 1786 he was charged £2 for rent of Nelms' plantation for the year. He purchased sundry items such as shoemakers punchers, all blades, shoe knife, a lame and trace ropes. {Nelms:85}

William Benson, WO Co., d. leaving a will dated 10 Oct 1774, proved 18 Nov 1774. To son William Wright Benson, tract *Teach*, 119 a., furniture. To grandson Lihue Benson, 40 a. of tract *Long Creek*. To son-in-law Benjamin Willis, tract *Long Crook*. To grandson William Hugens, remaining part of tract *Long Crook*. Daniel Melson, Jr., exec {MWB 40:13} On 18 Jan 1775 the inventory of his estate was filed by Daniel Melson. Signed as next of kin: John Benston, Betty Willis. {MINV 120:137}

Benjamin Willis served as private, Worcester Militia, Snow Hill Battn., Capt. Ebenezer Handy's Company, 9 April 1776 and private in the Wicomico Battn., Capt. Elijah Shockley's Company, 15 July 1780. {RPWS:336}

Unplaced

DAVID WILLIS served as private, Worcester Militia, Sinepuxent Battn., Capt. Thomas Purnell's Company, 1779/1780. {RPWS:337}

EDMOND WILLIS was living in the household of Richard Niblett in 1739 in Wicomico Hundred, SO Co.

THOMAS WILLIS, m. Elizabeth (N).
      Thomas Willis patented *Bashan* (200 a.) on 30 Nov 1681. {MPL 24:382} *Amity* was patented in 1683 by Thomas Willis for 150 a. {MPL 29:430}
      Thomas Willis, planter, SO Co., d. leaving a will dated 11 Aug 1715, proved 21 March 1716-17. To John Coleburne, exec, (planter of Somerset Co.), 150 a., *Amity*. To wife Elizabeth and John Coleburne afsd., residue of estate, equally. {MWB 14:280}
      On 7 June 1717 the inventory of his estate was filed. Signed as next of kin: Eli. Willis, Elizabeth Colburn. {INAC 38A:145}

INDEX

ABBOT, Mason, 80
ABERGAVENY, 42
ACWORTH (Ackworth), Betty, 56;
  Charles, 135; Elizabeth, 35, 135;
  Henry, 50, 51, 199; John, 56;
  Louder, 56; Mary, 50, 51, 199;
  Samuel, 135; Thomas, 36, 56
ACWORTH'S DELIGHT, 135
ACWORTH'S FOLLY, 36
ADAMS, Alexander, 3, 105, 194,
  196; Jacob, 12; John, 137;
  Samuel, 192; Sarah, 13; William,
  99
ADDITION, The 6, 11, 44, 148, 199
ADDITION TO CLARK'S NECK,
  176
ADDITION TO HAMMER, 11
ADDITION TO HOG QUARTER,
  193
ADDITION TO SALEM, 151
ADDITION TO MONMOUTH, 6
ADDITION TO VENTURE, 129,
  130
ADKINS. See Atkins.
ADVENTURE, 72, 73, 75, 76, 77,
  115
AGNEW & LARGEE, 36
AGREEMENT, 84
AIREY (Airy), Jane, 85, 86; Jean, 86;
  Margaret, 86; Rachel, 86;
  Thomas, 63; William, 85, 86
AIRS, Jacob, 74
AKALOW, 54
ALDERMAN BURY, 136
ALEXANDER, Agnes, 193, 194,
  195, 196; Catherine, 190, 194,
  195, 196; Elizabeth, 194, 195;
  James, 194, 195; John, 193, 194,
  195, 196; Listian, 193, 194, 195,
  196; Mary, 193, 194, 195, 196;

  Moses, 193, 194, 195, 196;
  Samuel, 162, 194, 195; William,
  114, 183, 190, 193, 194, 195
ALFORD, John, 78
ALLDER BURY, 136
ALLEN, George, 78; Mary, 78;
  William, 158
ALLEN'S DISAPPOINTMENT, 116
AMITY, 206
ANDERSON, Cornelius, 193; Isaac,
  45; James, 45; John, 45, 107,
  140; Joseph, 45; Joshua, 45;
  Sarah, 45; Thomas, 62; William,
  148, 163
ANDRAS, Rebecca, 13; Robertson,
  13
ANDREW, Eleanor, 176; George,
  176
ANDREWS, Comfort, 79; Eleanor,
  177; Elizabeth, 79, 80; George,
  177; Isaac, 79; Nathaniel, 79, 80;
  William, 79
ANDREW'S CHARGE, 176
ANNO, Elizabeth, 128; Nancy, 128
ANYTHING, 109
AQUINTICA, 92
ARABIA, 204
ARACCO, 95
ARRACOCO, 96
ASCUE, Lydia, 41, 104; Phillip, 41,
  42, 104; Phillips, 42
ASCUE'S CHOICE, 138
ASKILLS CHOICE, 138
ASTIN. See Auston,
ATKINS (Adkins, Atkens, Atkinson),
  Joseph, 161; Mary, 20, 21, 161;
  William, 20, 21
ATKINSON (Atkisson, Atkerson),
  Betty, 8, 9; Elizabeth, 21; George
  D., 9; Isaac, 8, 9; James, 9, 72,

77; John, 9; Joshua, 8, 9, 20, 21,
28; Mary, 21; Nancy, 9; Patience,
72; William, 8, 21
AUSTON (Astin, Austen), Edward,
106
James, 105
AYEDLOTT, William, 89
BACKER, James, 14
BACON, John, 16, 18
BADLY, Richard, 65
BAILEY (Baily, Baley, Bayley,
Bayly), Benjamin, 142; Betty,
135; Edmund, 82; Elener, 142;
Elisha, 118; Elizabeth, 118, 149;
Esme, 110; Esmey, 198; Esmy,
198; George, 142; Henry, 118,
119; Homy, 149; Jonathan, 135,
142; Lisha, 149; Mary, 142;
Richard, 119; Samuel Jaxson,
142; Sarah, 142; Whittington,
118, 119, 149
BAILEYS CHANCE, 53
BAKER, James, 82; John, 24
BALEY. See Bailey.
BALLARD, Charles, 14, 81, 100,
114; Elizabeth, 114; John, 116;
Levin, 81; Mary, 116; Robert, 81
BANKS, Christopher, 74
BANSTER, Charles, 54
BARNABY, Elizabeth, 201; James,
200, 201; Mary, 201; Rebecca,
200, 201
BARNABYS LOTT, 201, 202
BARNS, Rebecca, 203; Thomas, 203
BARREN POINT, 62, 63
BARRON POINT, 62
BARTH, Dorothy, 45; John, 43, 45;
Sarah, 43, 45
BARTHELMY, Jeremiah, 85
BASHAN, 206
BASHAW, Andrew, 1, 2, 3, 4; Ann,
2, 3, 4; Elener, 2, 4; Ellener, 3;

Giles, 1, 2, 3, 4; Jarrett, 2, 3, 4;
Mary, 1, 3; Sarah, 3, 4; Thomas,
1, 2, 3, 4
BATCHELLORS LOTT, 53
BATCHELORS CHOICE, 56
BAYLEY. See Bailey.
BAYNARD, Elizabeth, 61
BEAR POINT, 167, 168
BEARD, Ann Hack, 80, 82; Ann
Hack Pitt, 80, 82; Catherine, 82;
Charles, 82; James, 7; Mary, 4;
Matthew, 80, 82; Sarah, 2, 4, 7,
105, 106, 116; Thomas, 2, 4, 7,
105, 106
BEARS QUARTER, 132
BEAVENS, William, 137
BECKMAN, 36
BECKNAM, 33
BEDFORD, 31
BEGINNING, 199
BELL, Adam, 199; Jonathan, 137;
Marion, 199
BELLIN, Thomas, 120
BELLS PURCHASE, 170
BENJAMIN'S GOOD SUCCESS, 32,
34
BENNESTON. See Benson.
BENNETT (Bennet, Bennit), Ann,
49; Bescaner, 67, 70; Betty, 59;
Charity, 59; Edward, 47, 48, 49,
59, 197; Elizabeth, 49, 58, 59;
George, 48, 49, 59; James, 73;
Jean, 59; Joanne, 59; John, 49;
Micajah, 73; Nancy, 73; Richard,
59; Scarborough, 30; William, 49
BENNETTS PURCHASE, 73
BENSON (Benston, Benneston,
Benstone), Ann, 76; Ezekiel, 73,
75; Grace, 75; Hannah, 73, 75;
James, 75; John, 75, 205;
Levinah, 73, 75; Lihue, 205;
Mary, 24, 25, 31, 32, 75;

Elizabeth, 126; Ganer, 104;
Isaac, 164; Jane, 104; Jerusha,
126; John, 103, 104, 113, 126;
Joseph, 137; Mary, 126;
Rebecca, 133; Roady, 126;
Sarah, 126; Solomon, 126;
Tabitha, 164; Thomas, 133;
William, 126
COME BY CHANCE, 97, 98, 138
CONNER (Connor), Betty, 89;
Elizabeth, 88, 89, 90, 91;
Frederick, 90; James, 12; John,
88, 89, 90, 91; Richard, 89, 90;
Sophia, 90
CONTENTED BACHELOR, 157
CONTENTION, 103, 186
CONVENANCY, 198
CONVENIENCE, 10, 156, 159
CONVENIENCY, 11, 12, 13, 156,
157, 158, 159
CONWAY, John Span, 115, 116
COOK, Guy, 180; Thomas, 179;
William, 65, 66
COOPER, Ann, 35; Eunice, 40; Isaac,
101; James, 141; John Rock, 93;
Mary, 35, 40; Thomas, 40, 99
COOPER'S CHOICE, 32, 34
COPEDGE, John, 61
CORBELL, Willis, 70
CORBIN, Covington, 37
CORDERY, David, 35
CORK, 170
CORNISH, Wine, 2, 3, 4
CORSON, Thomas, 178
COSTIN (Costen, Coston), Ezekiel,
87, 88; Henry R. K., 14; Isaac,
135; Priscilla, 14
COTMAN, Benjamin, 132
COTTINGHAM, Charles, 22; Daniel,
22; Elisha, 22; John, 39;
Jonathan, 21, 22; Leah, 39;
Margaret, 22; Mary, 21, 22;

Sarah, 22; Thomas, 22; William,
22, 39
COULBOURN, Isaac, 154; William,
166, 169
COULBOURNE, William, 83
COULBURN, William, 164
COULTER, Charles, 161
COVENTRE, 13
COVINGTON, Elizabeth, 17, 47;
James, 49; Nehemiah, 17; Philip,
141; Phillip, 32; Priscilla, 32;
Samuell, 47; Thomas, 47
COVINGTONS FOLLY, 47
COVINGTONS VINEYARD, 47
COWLEY, 125
COWLY, 130
COX, Jane, 136; John Davis, 136;
Liddia, 136; Margaret, 136;
Margratte, 136; Mary, 150;
Polly, 150; Rebecca, 136; Sarah,
136; Thomas, 136, 137, 182, 183
COXES FOLLY, 137
COX'S FORK, 136
CRAMBROOK, 102
CRAPPER. See Cropper.
CRAWFORD, Henry, 14; John, 163
CREW, Annabella, 136; Frances,
136; John, 136, 137
CROCKETT (Crocket), Ann, 25;
Anne, 25; Bridget, 25; Bridgett,
25; Elizabeth, 25, 114; John, 24,
25, 114; Levin, 25; Mary, 25;
Nehemiah, 25
CROOKED ISLAND, 81
CROPPER, John, 93, 197.
CROUCH, Elizabeth, 42, 43, 44;
Robert, 43, 44
CULLEN, Jemima, 174; John, 84
CULVER, Nathan, 205
CURREY, Philip, 35
CUSTIS, Hancock, 80; John, 82;
Thomas, 82

GOTHERD'S FOLLEY, 131
GOULDING, William, 67
GRACE, Samuel, 186
GRAHAM, Ann, 32; Henry, 12;
    William, 32
GRAMMELL, Richard, 78
GRAY (Grey), Allen, 10, 11, 12;
    Benjamin Dingly, 67, 68, 69, 70;
    Dingley, 69; Dingly, 67, 70;
    Jacob Johnson, 69; James, 16,
    197; Jamima, 69; Jemima, 69;
    John, 11, 124, 199; Johnson
    Violata Louise, 69; Joseph, 16;
    Mary, 10, 11, 12, 69, 124;
    William, 10, 12
GREAT NECK, 182, 190
GREEN, Alice, 67; Elizabeth, 177;
    George, 68; James, 18; John, 23,
    27, 28, 67; Polly, 23, 27, 28;
    Sarah, 113, 114; William, 177
GREEN HERD, 144
GREENLAND, 16, 21
GRIFFITH, Abraham, 177
GRIMES, Thomas, 116
GROVES, 152
GUINNEY PLANTATION, 176, 177
GULLET (Gillet, Gullett, Gyllot),
    Abraham, 57; Airs, 147; Ayres,
    148, 152; George, 57; German,
    147; Jarman, 152; John, 57, 147;
    Mary, 57; Rebeccah, 147;
    Rebekah, 147; Samuel, 147;
    William, 41, 56, 57
GUNBY, Charity, 59; Francis, 71;
    John, 132; Kirk, 101; Sarah, 132
GUNNER'S RANGE, 186
GUPTON, John, 186
GURLLING, William, 18
GUTHREY, Angelica, 12; Joshua,
    12; Patrick, 12; Phillip, 9
GYNEATH, 81
HAB-NAB, 113

HACK, Ann, 80; George Nicholas,
    66; Matilda, 80
HACKER, Rachael, 132
HAGAN, William, 62
HALL, Abigail, 13; Ann Hack Pitt,
    82; Charles, 189; Dixon, 82;
    Elizabeth, 145, 183; Henry H.,
    82; John, 190; Phenix, 183;
    Robert, 152, 155; Stephen, 44,
    50; William, 81, 144, 155
HAMBLEN, Joseph, 129
HAMBLETON'S PARK, 66
HAMLEN, Comfort, 129
HAMMER, The, 11
HAMMOND (Hammon), Barnaby,
    201; Edward, 17; Elizabeth, 16,
    17; John, 16, 17
HANDLY (Handley), Hugh, 177;
    Susannah, 180
HANDY, Ann, 33; Betty, 33; Charles,
    19; Ebenezer, 136; Henry, 97;
    Isaac, 8, 33, 138; John, 33, 58,
    97, 98, 114, 115; Mary, 30, 33
HANNAH'S DELIGHT, 133, 134
HAPHAZARD, 42, 44, 72
HARDFORTUNE, 167
HARDSHIP, 12
HARDY, Ann, 59; George, 102;
    James, 34, 35, 117; Phillis, 19;
    Robert, 4; Sarah, 2, 3, 4;
    Susanna, 34, 35; Susannah, 35,
    36
HARGARTON, Edward, 177
HARGIS, Mary, 11, 12, 13
HARPER, Edward, 123; Mary, 123;
    William, 13
HARRELL, William, 61
HARRIS, Alse, 37; Elinor, 117;
    Elizabeth, 99; Jane, 106; John,
    37, 178; Solomon, 6, 7, 37;
    Thomas, 151; William, 37, 51,
    106

MEARES, Robert, 15
MEEKINS FOLLY, 176
MELALEY, Patrick, 56; Thomas, 56
MELSON, Daniel, 205; David, 54;
    Samuel, 56
MELTON, John, 116
MELVILLE, Avid, 62
MELVIN, Florence, 122; Robert,
    121, 122, 125, 202; William, 120
MERCHMENT, Samuel, 71, 72
MEREDITH (Merridith), Eleanor,
    20; John, 176
MERRILL (Merril), Comfort, 90;
    Elizabeth, 73; Jemima, 90; John,
    73, 75; Levin, 75; Thomas, 80;
    William, 75, 96
MEZICK (Mesick, Messick), Aaron,
    32, 33; Aron, 6; Benjamin, 17,
    25, 140, 141; Covington, 6;
    Dinah, 6; Elihu, 6; Elizabeth, 6;
    Isaac, 17, 25; Jacob, 6, 17, 25;
    James, 6; John, 17, 25, 46;
    Joseph, 17, 25; Joshua, 6, 17, 25;
    Julin, 17, 25; Mary, 17, 25, 32,
    33; Nehemiah, 17, 25; Priscilla,
    17, 25; Rachell, 6; Sarah, 17, 25;
    Susanna, 7
MICKLE MEADOW, 84
MIDDLEMORE, 152, 155
MIDDLESEX, 152, 155, 190
MIDDLETON, Ann, 58
MIDFIELD, 106
MIGHT HAVE HAD MORE, 115
MILBOURNE (Milbourn), Deborah,
    14; Elijah, 14; Grace, 14; John,
    13, 198; Lodowick, 81; Mary,
    13, 14; Ralph, 96; Saloma, 14;
    Tabitha, 14; Thomas, 13, 14
MILBOURNE'S MISTAKE, 81
MILBURN, Elizabeth, 12
MILBY, John, 68
MILES, William, 202

MILL LOT, 58
MILL WRIGHT'S GOOD INTENT,
    101
MILLER, Elizabeth, 184; John, 153;
    Margaret, 184; Robert, 132;
    Sarah, 153; Thomas, 92
MILLS, Alexander, 150, 195, 196;
    Ann, 54; Comfort, 152;
    Elizabeth, 196; Hannah, 146;
    Hester, 138; Hugh, 148, 152;
    John, 118, 149, 150, 196; Lydia,
    152; Mary, 192, 194, 195, 196;
    Moses, 196; Patty, 54; Robert,
    71, 72, 192, 196; Samuel, 146,
    148; Sarah, 11, 12, 13; Smith,
    196; William, 196; William
    Washington, 54
MISTER, William, 166, 167
MITCHELL (Mitchel), Elijah, 198;
    John, 198; Joshua, 110; Patrick,
    84; Richard, 184
MOLHORNE (Molehorne), Mary,
    176, 177
MONFORD, Mary, 126
MONKEY, John, 78
MONMOUTH, 6, 7
MONTGOMERY, Dennis, 175;
    Thomas, 167
MOORE (More), Amelia, 34; Ann,
    106; Betty, 89; Charity, 106;
    Elizabeth, 89, 106, 107, 110,
    111; Isabella, 59; James, 6, 7,
    107; John, 106, 107, 110; Joshua,
    35; Levin, 107; Martin, 93;
    Mary, 106; Rachel, 104, 105,
    107; Rachell, 107; Ralph, 107;
    Sarah, 106, 111; Thomas, 107,
    110; William, 105, 107
MOORS VENTUR, 107
MORGAN, Ann, 78
MORRIS (Morriss), Ann, 79; Bevins,
    77; Dennis, 79; Elizabeth, 79, 80;

226

Parthena, 40; Peggy, 25, 31, 34;
Phillis, 19, 28; Polly, 23;
Priscilla, 25, 32; Rachel, 15, 16,
19; Richard, 15, 16, 18, 19, 26,
35, 36, 38, 40, 100; Risdon, 138;
Roger, 15, 16, 17, 18, 23, 24, 25,
26, 32, 33, 34, 35, 36, 37;
Samuel, 15, 17, 18, 23, 27, 28,
29, 30, 31; Sarah, 15, 16, 17, 18,
20, 21, 31, 37; Susanna, 20, 34,
36; Susannah, 20, 35, 36;
Tabitha, 23, 31; Thomas, 26, 28,
33; Violet, 39; William, 37, 38,
39, 67
NICHOLSON'S LOTT, 15, 18, 19,
26, 27
NICK'S BRANCH, 63
NIEN, James, 138
NOBLE, James, 127; John, 78;
Robert, 66; William, 123
NOBLE QUARTER, 8, 115
NODD, 141
NOLTON, Ann, 143
NONE SUCH, 170
NORSWORTHY, Elizabeth, 77;
George, 70, 78; Martha, 78;
Sarah, 78; Tristram, 78
NORTH, Edward, 137, 139
NORTHFIELD, 92
NORWOOD, Henry, 91
NOTHNIG WORTH, 144
NOTTINGHAM, Abel, 161
NUGEN, Thomas, 192
NUTTER, Christopher, 5, 112, 113;
John, 85; Matthew, 112, 113
O'BRIAN, Rebecka, 144
ODAY, Henry, 199; John, 184;
Owen, 184
ODEWE, Rebecca, 144; Richard, 144
O'DONELLE, Daniel, 101
O'DULLOVAN, Daniel, 101

OGLE, Andrew, 63; John, 63; Mary,
63
OLIPHANT, William, 136, 137
OUTERBRIDGE, Elizabeth, 134;
Mary, 134; Stephen, 134;
William, 134
OUTTEN, Abraham, 10, 21; Levi,
27, 28, 29; Obed, 57; Rhoda, 13
OUTTENS SECURITY, 10
OWENS (Owin), Elizabeth, 32;
Jonathan, 94, 95; William, 32
OXBURY, 42, 43
OXHEAD, 84
PAINE (Pain), Isaac, 90; William,
123
PARAMOUR'S DOUBLE
PURCHASE, 39
PARIS, 74
PARISH, 74
PARKER, Andrew, 62; George, 31,
101; Henry, 61; Jacob, 101;
John, 23, 31, 101; Sarah, 101;
Tabitha, 20, 23
PARKER'S FRESHES, 61
PARKS, Arthur, 167; Job, 59; Mary,
59
PARRAMORE (Parremore,
Parrimore, Perremore),
Elizabeth, 108; Isaac, 45; Joanna
Custes, 147; Joseph, 109;
Matthew, 36; Stephen, 135;
Thomas, 108, 109, 147
PARRIS, 179, George, 26
PARSONS, Amos, 197; Frances, 24;
George, 135; Jane, 66; John, 193,
194; Peter, 131; Thomas, 66
PARTNERS CHOICE, 10
PARTNERSHIP, 60
PASSONS, Sarah, 16
PATEY, Powell, 200; Rachel, 200
PATEYS FOLLY, 200
PATEYS FOLLY RECTIFIED, 200

232

SECURITY, 14, 58, 137
SECURITY RESURVEYED, 142
SELBY, Comfort, 153, 154; Daniel,
198; John, 89; Mary, 198; Philip,
198; William, 27, 28, 29, 30, 82,
193
SEON, Jane, 202; Thomas, 201, 202
SERLE, Susanna, 78
SHADWELL, 140
SHANKLAND, Mr., 137
SHAW, Jean, 59
SHEILD. See Shiles.
SHERDAN, William, 23
SHERMAN, Sarah, 45; Thomas, 45;
William, 45
SHERWOOD, Elizabeth, 61, 62;
John, 61, 62
SHIELDS. See Shiles.
SHIELDS HIS CHOICE, 112, 113
SHIEL'S MEADOWS, 113
SHILES (Sheals, Sheild, Shields),
Alce, 111, 112, 113; Alice, 5, 76,
112, 113; Ann, 114, 115, 116,
117; Bridget, 113, 114, 115;
Edmond, 117; Elinor, 117;
Elizabeth, 112, 113, 114, 117;
John, 5, 76, 112, 113, 114, 115,
116; Kendal, 117; Margaret, 117;
Naomi, 113; Naomy, 112;
Neomi, 114; Patrick, 117;
Rachel, 66; Rhoda, 66; Rindal,
117; Rindal Hog, 116; Sarah,
113, 115, 117; Thomas, 14, 111,
112, 113, 114, 115, 116, 117;
William, 66
SHILLES FOLLEY, 33
SHIRMAN (Shearman, Shurman,
Serman, Sirman, Surman,
Surnam), Betty, 45; Charles, 4,
106; Edward, 45; Esther, 45;
Isaac, 45; Joseph, 45; Margaret,
45; Peter, 45, 104; Richard, 45;

Sarah, 45; Susanna, 3; Susannah,
4, 105; Thomas, 45; William, 45
SHOCKLEY, John, 190
SHOHANNIS, Mary, 20
SIDNEY, 115
SILLIVEN (Silivan), Bridget, 57;
William, 57
SIRMAN. See Shirman.
SKILLET, Mathew, 142
SKINNER, Leah, 151; Marshall, 151
SKIPTON, 180
SLIPE, The, 160
SLOAN, Samuel, 128, 161
SLOVIUM, Ruth, 39
SMALL, Mary, 72
SMART, Richard, 177
SMILEY (Smyley), Andrew, 198;
Samuel, 175, 198
SMITH, Ann, 40, 41, 120; Anne, 120,
181; Archibald, 136; Arthur, 78;
Betty, 33; Charlton, 58; David,
183; Eve, 97, 98; George, 83,
182; Henry, 40, 41, 53, 120, 166,
167, 181; Isaac, 67, 68, 70; Jame,
97; James, 76, 77, 97, 98, 99,
182, 183, 197; Jean, 199; John,
58, 67, 68, 69, 70, 95, 167;
Joseph, 126; Martha; 83;
Meriam, 197; Moses, 183; Moses
Claywell, 183; Rebekkah, 69;
Robert, 78, 199; Sarah, 78; Sarah
Ann, 136; Steven, 100; Tabitha,
149; Walter, 156, 159; William,
85, 160, 181
SMITHFIELD, 42, 43
SMITHFIELD LOMAROONS
RIDGE, 138
SMITHS HOPE, 40, 41
SMITH'S ISLAND, 83, 166
SMITH'S RESOLUTION, 181
SMITTY'S INVENTION, 31

Heritage Books by Vernon L. Skinner, Jr.:

Abstracts of the Administration Accounts of the Prerogative Court of Maryland,
1718–1724, Libers 1–5

Abstracts of the Administration Accounts of the Prerogative Court of Maryland,
1724–1731: Libers 6–10

Abstracts of the Administration Accounts of the Prerogative Court of Maryland,
1731–1737: Libers 11–15

Abstracts of the Administration Accounts of the Prerogative Court of Maryland,
1737–1744: Libers 16–20

Abstracts of the Administration Accounts of the Prerogative Court of Maryland,
1744–1750: Libers 21–28

Abstracts of the Administration Accounts of the Prerogative Court of Maryland,
1750–1754: Libers 29–36

Abstracts of the Administration Accounts of the Prerogative Court of Maryland,
1754–1760: Libers 37–45

Abstracts of the Administration Accounts of the Prerogative Court of Maryland,
1760–1764, Libers 46–51

Abstracts of the Administration Accounts of the Prerogative Court of Maryland,
1764–1768, Libers 52–58

Abstracts of the Administration Accounts of the Prerogative Court of Maryland,
1768–1771, Libers 59–66

Abstracts of the Administration Accounts of the Prerogative Court of Maryland,
1771–1777, Libers 67–74

Abstracts of the Balance Books of the Prerogative Court of Maryland:
Libers 2 and 3, 1755–1763

Abstracts of the Balance Books of the Prerogative Court of Maryland:
Libers 4 and 5, 1763–1770

Abstracts of the Balance Books of the Prerogative Court of Maryland:
Libers 6 and 7, 1770–1777

Abstracts of the Inventories and Accounts of the Prerogative Court of Maryland,
1674–1678, 1699–1703

Abstracts of the Inventories and Accounts of the Prerogative Court of Maryland,
1679–1686

Abstracts of the Inventories and Accounts of the Prerogative Court of Maryland,
1685–1701

Abstracts of the Inventories and Accounts of the Prerogative Court of Maryland,
1688–1698

Abstracts of the Inventories and Accounts of the Prerogative Court of Maryland,
1697–1700: Libers 16, 17, 18, 19, 19½A, 19½B

Abstracts of the Inventories and Accounts of the Prerogative Court of Maryland,
1699–1704: Libers 20–24

Abstracts of the Inventories and Accounts of the Prerogative Court of Maryland,
1708–1711: Libers 29, 30, 31, 32A, 32B

Abstracts of the Inventories and Accounts of the Prerogative Court of Maryland,
1711–1713: Libers 32C, 33A, 33B, 34

Abstracts of the Inventories and Accounts of the Prerogative Court of Maryland,
1712–1716: Libers 35A, 35B, 36A, 36B, 36C

Abstracts of the Inventories and Accounts of the Prerogative Court of Maryland,
1715–1718: Libers 37A, 37B, 37C, 38A, 38B, 39A, 39B, 39C

Abstracts of the Inventories and Accounts of the Prerogative Court of Maryland,
1699–1708: Libers 25–28

Abstracts of the Inventories of the Prerogative Court of Maryland, 1718–1720

Abstracts of the Inventories of the Prerogative Court of Maryland, 1720–1724

Abstracts of the Inventories of the Prerogative Court of Maryland, 1724–1727

Abstracts of the Inventories of the Prerogative Court of Maryland, 1726–1729

Abstracts of the Inventories of the Prerogative Court of Maryland, 1728–1734

Abstracts of the Inventories of the Prerogative Court of Maryland, 1733–1738

Abstracts of the Inventories of the Prerogative Court of Maryland, 1738–1744

Abstracts of the Inventories of the Prerogative Court of Maryland, 1744–1748

Abstracts of the Inventories of the Prerogative Court of Maryland, 1748–1751

Abstracts of the Inventories of the Prerogative Court of Maryland, 1751–1756

Abstracts of the Inventories of the Prerogative Court of Maryland, 1755–1760

Abstracts of the Inventories of the Prerogative Court of Maryland, 1760–1763

Abstracts of the Inventories of the Prerogative Court of Maryland, 1763–1766

Abstracts of the Inventories of the Prerogative Court of Maryland, 1766–1769

Abstracts of the Inventories of the Prerogative Court of Maryland, 1769–1772

Abstracts of the Inventories of the Prerogative Court of Maryland, 1772–1774

Abstracts of the Inventories of the Prerogative Court of Maryland, 1774–1777

Abstracts of the Proceedings of the Orphans' Court of Sussex County, Delaware:
Libers 1, 2, 3, 4, A (1708–1709, 1728–1777)

Abstracts of the Proprietary Records of the
Provincial Court of Maryland, 1637–1658

Abstracts, Worcester County, Maryland Estate Docket, 1742–1820

Colonial Families of the Eastern Shore of Maryland:
Volumes: 10, 18, 20 and 22
Vernon L. Skinner, Jr. and F. Edward Wright

Other Wills in the Prerogative Court for Somerset and Worcester Counties, 1664–1775

Provincial Families of Maryland, Volume 1

Somerset County Will Books, 1750–1772

Somerset County Wills, 1667–1748: Liber EB9

Somerset County Wills, 1770–1777 and 1675–1710: Liber EB5

Supplement Abstracts Inventories and Accounts, Prerogative Court, 1691–1706

Worcester County Inventories and Accounts, 1694–1742: Inventory Book JW15

Worcester County Wills: Will Book MH3, 1666–1742

Heritage Books by F. Edward Wright:

*18th Century Records of the German Lutheran Church at Philadelphia, Pennsylvania
(St. Michael's and Zion): Volume 1, Baptisms, 1745–1769*
Robert L. Hess and F. Edward Wright

*18th Century Records of the German Lutheran Church at Philadelphia, Pennsylvania
(St. Michael's and Zion): Volume 2, Baptisms, 1770–1786*
Translated by Robert L. Hess, Ph.D. Edited by F. Edward Wright

*18th Century Records of the German Lutheran Church of Philadelphia, Pennsylvania
(St. Michael's and Zion): Volume 3, Baptisms, 1787–1800*
Translated by Robert L. Hess, Ph.D. Edited by F. Edward Wright

*18th Century Records of the German Lutheran Church at Philadelphia, Pennsylvania
(St. Michael's and Zion): Volume 4, Marriages and Confirmations*
Robert L. Hess and F. Edward Wright

*18th Century Records of the German Lutheran Church at Philadelphia, Pennsylvania
(St. Michael's and Zion): Volume 5, Burials*
Robert L. Hess and F. Edward Wright

Abstracts of Bucks County, Pennsylvania, Wills, 1685–1785

Abstracts of Cumberland County, Pennsylvania, Wills, 1750–1785

Abstracts of Cumberland County, Pennsylvania, Wills, 1785–1825

*Abstracts of Philadelphia County, Pennsylvania, Wills:
Volumes: 1682–1726; 1726–1747; 1748–1763; 1763–1784; 1777–1790;
1790–1802; 1802–1809; 1810–1815; 1815–1819; and 1820–1825*

Abstracts of South Central Pennsylvania, Newspapers, Volume 1, 1785–1790

Abstracts of South Central Pennsylvania, Newspapers, Volume 3, 1796–1800

Abstracts of the Newspapers of Georgetown and the Federal City, 1789–99

Abstracts of York County, Pennsylvania, Wills, 1749–1819

Adams County [Pennsylvania] Church Records of the 18th Century

Baltimore Directory of 1807

Berks County, Pennsylvania, Church Records of the 18th Century, Volumes 1–4

Bible Records of Washington County, Maryland

*Bucks County, Pennsylvania, Church Records of the 17th and 18th Centuries,
Volume 1: German Church Records*

*Bucks County, Pennsylvania, Church Records of the 17th and 18th Centuries,
Volume 2: Quaker Records: Falls and Middletown Monthly Meetings*
Anna Miller Watring and F. Edward Wright

*Bucks County, Pennsylvania, Church Records of the 17th and 18th Centuries,
Volume 4*

Caroline County, Maryland, Marriages, Births and Deaths, 1850–1880

Citizens of the Eastern Shore of Maryland, 1659–1750

Colonial Families of Cape May County, New Jersey, Revised 2nd Edition

*Colonial Families of Delaware:
Volumes: Volume 1; Volume 2: Kent and Sussex Counties;
Volume 3 (2nd Edition): Kent and Sussex Counties;
Volume 4: Sussex County; Volume 5: New Castle; Volume 6: Kent*

Colonial Families of New Jersey, Volume 1: Middlesex and Somerset Counties

Colonial Families of Northern Neck, Virginia, Volume 1 and Volume 2
Holly G. Wright and F. Edward Wright

Colonial Families of the Eastern Shore of Maryland: Volumes 1 and 2
Robert W. Barnes and F. Edward Wright

Colonial Families of the Eastern Shore of Maryland: Volume 4
Christos Christou and F. Edward Wright

*Colonial Families of the Eastern Shore of Maryland:
Volumes 5, 6, 7, 8, 9, 11, 12, 13, 14, 16, and 19*
Henry C. Peden, Jr. and F. Edward Wright

Colonial Families of the Eastern Shore of Maryland: Volumes 15 and 17
Ralph A. Riggin and F. Edward Wright

Colonial Families of the Eastern Shore of Maryland: Volumes 10, 18, 20, and 22
Vernon L. Skinner, Jr. and F. Edward Wright

Colonial Families of the United States of America, Volume II
Holly G. Wright and F. Edward Wright

Cumberland County, Pennsylvania, Church Records of the 18th Century

Delaware Newspaper Abstracts, Volume 1: 1786–1795

Early Charles County, Maryland, Settlers, 1658–1745
Marlene Strawser Bates, F. Edward Wright

Early Church Records of Alexandria City and Fairfax County, Virginia
F. Edward Wright and Wesley E. Pippenger

Early Church Records of Bergen County, New Jersey, 1740–1800

Early Church Records of Dauphin County, Pennsylvania

Early Church Records of Lebanon County, Pennsylvania

Early Church Records of New Castle County, Delaware, Volume 1: 1701–1800

Early Church Records of Rockingham County, Virginia

Early Lists of Frederick County, Maryland, 1765–1775

Early Records of the First Reformed Church of Philadelphia, Volume 1, 1748–1780

Early Records of the First Reformed Church of Philadelphia, Volume 2, 1781–1800

Frederick County, Maryland, Militia in the War of 1812
Sallie A. Mallick and F. Edward Wright

Henrico County, Virginia, Marriage References and Family Relationships, 1654–1800

Inhabitants of Baltimore County, Maryland, 1692–1763

Judgment Records of Dorchester, Queen Anne's, and Talbot Counties [Maryland]

Kent County, Delaware, Marriage References and Family Relationships

*King George County, Virginia, Marriage References
and Family Relationships, 1721–1800*
Anne M. Watring and F. Edward Wright

Lancaster County Church Records of the 18th Century, Volumes 1–4

Lancaster County, Pennsylvania, Church Records of the 18th Century, Volume 1
F. Edward Wright and Robert L. Hess

Lancaster County, Pennsylvania, Church Records of the 18th Century, Volume 3

Lancaster County, Pennsylvania, Church Records of the 18th Century, Volume 5

Lancaster County, Pennsylvania, Church Records of the 18th Century: Volume 6
Robert L. Hess and F. Edward Wright

*Lancaster County, Virginia, Marriage References
and Family Relationships, 1650–1800*

Land Records of Sussex County, Delaware, 1769–1782

Land Records of Sussex County, Delaware, 1782–1789: Deed Book N No. 13
Elaine Hastings Mason and F. Edward Wright

Marriage Licenses of Washington, District of Columbia, 1811–1830

*Marriage References and Family Relationships of Charles City,
Prince George, and Dinwiddie Counties, Virginia, 1634–1800*

Marriages and Deaths from Eastern Shore Newspapers, 1790–1835

*Marriages and Deaths from the Newspapers of Allegany
and Washington Counties, Maryland, 1820–1830*

Marriages and Deaths from the York Recorder, *1821–1830*

*Marriages and Deaths in the Newspapers of Frederick
and Montgomery Counties, Maryland, 1820–1830*

*Marriages and Deaths in the Newspapers of
Lancaster County, Pennsylvania, 1821–1830*

*Marriages and Deaths in the Newspapers of
Lancaster County, Pennsylvania, 1831–1840*

Marriages and Deaths of Cumberland County, [Pennsylvania], 1821–1830

Marriages, Births, Deaths and Removals of New Castle County, Delaware

*Maryland Calendar of Wills:
Volume 9: 1744–1749; Volume 10: 1748–1753; Volume 11: 1753–1760;
Volume 12: 1759–1764; Volume 13: 1764–1767; Volume 14: 1767–1772;
Volume 15: 1772–1774; and Volume 16: 1774–1777*

*Maryland Eastern Shore Newspaper Abstracts
Volume 1: 1790–1805; Volume 2: 1806–1812;
Volume 3: 1813–1818; Volume 4: 1819–1824;
Volume 5: Northern Counties, 1825–1829*
F. Edward Wright and Irma Harper;
*Volume 6: Southern Counties, 1825–1829;
Volume 7: Northern Counties, 1830–1834*
Irma Harper and F. Edward Wright;
Volume 8: Southern Counties, 1830–1834

*Maryland Eastern Shore Vital Records:
Book 1: 1648–1725, Second Edition; Book 2: 1726–1750; Book 3: 1751–1775;
Book 4: 1776–1800; and Book 5: 1801–1825*

*Maryland Militia in the War of 1812:
Volume 1: Eastern Shore; Volume 2: Baltimore City and County;
Volume 3: Cecil and Harford Counties; Volume 4: Anne Arundel and Calvert Counties;
Volume 5: St. Mary's and Charles Counties; Volume 6: Prince George's County;
and Volume 7: Montgomery County*

Maryland Militia in the Revolutionary War
S. Eugene Clements and F. Edward Wright

www.ingramcontent.com/pod-product-compliance
Lightning Source LLC
Chambersburg PA
CBHW070757270326
41927CB00010B/2179